STUDENT GUIDE

America's History

VOLUME 1: TO 1877

FOURTH EDITION

STUDENT GUIDE

America's History

VOLUME 1: TO 1877

Timothy R. Mahoney
University of Nebraska–Lincoln

Bedford/St. Martin's
Boston ♦ New York

Copyright © 2000 by Bedford/St. Martin's

All rights reserved. No part of this book may be reproduced, stored in a retrieval system, or transmitted in any form or by any means, electronic, mechanical, photocopying, recording, or otherwise, except as may be expressly permitted by the applicable copyright statutes or in writing by the Publisher.

Manufactured in the United States of America.

4 3 2
f e d c b

For information, write: Bedford/St. Martin's, 75 Arlington Street, Boston, MA 02116   (617-399-4000)

ISBN: 0-312-19408-0

Preface

There are many ways to learn American history in a college level survey course. As a longtime instructor of American history and an enthusiastic user of *America's History*, I make the text an active and essential component of the class. The various ideas, strategies, and experiences I have employed in twenty years of trying to help thousands of students understand American history are incorporated into the features of this thoroughly updated *Student Guide* to accompany *America's History*, Volume 1, Fourth Edition.

The first volume of *America's History*, Fourth Edition is a powerful narrative history that provides a wealth of materials in telling the story of the development of the American people and nation through Reconstruction. The *Student Guide* functions together with this strong narrative and its accompanying features as a tool, paralleling the text chapter by chapter to help students make the most of the information in *America's History*.

Unfortunately, for many students history remains merely a catalog of names, dates and places. The *Student Guide* helps students understand the how and why presented in the text by looking at three levels: its major arguments, its thematic and chronological organization, and the details employed to support the arguments. By highlighting the details students need to know within the context of larger themes, the *Student Guide* helps students master important information so they can sharpen the more advanced skill of putting those details together into a comprehensive understanding of a historical argument. With this goal in mind, the *Student Guide* divides each chapter of the text into nine component parts:

- The **Learning Objectives** introduce a student to the major arguments of each chapter. These consist of four to six broad questions about cause and effect or the relationship among events in the period. If students can reasonably answer these questions, they have succeeded in understanding the main points in the chapter
- The **Chapter Summary** states in more general language the broad outline of each chapter, following the chapter narrative section by section. These brief, general summaries highlight the underlying themes that drive the narrative.
- The **Expanded Timeline,** an annotated version of the timeline that appears at the end of each chapter, reinforces a student's grasp of the cause and effect logic of historical change. These short descriptions of the significance of each major event or development give students the chronological building blocks to tie together material over a series of thematically organized text chapters.

Recognizing that each narrative is an argument based on an interpretation of the available evidence, the next four sections of the *Student Guide* focus on enhancing a student's reading of the evidence.

- The **Glossary** defines both specific names and more general terms employed in *America's History*. Special attention has been given in this edition to expanding the list of basic economic terms to help students grasp principles of trade, currency, and markets. The Glossary also provides new definitions of terms as their meanings change over time—such as the meaning of *Republican* in Jefferson's era, in Lincoln's, and in the twentieth century. Understanding such historically specific definitions allows students to argue broader interpretive

points more effectively and also enhances their sense of how the past differs from today.
- The **Identification** section helps students master the names of the significant individuals, concepts, and places in each chapter. Learning the who, what, where, and when of history enables students to marshal evidence to support the arguments they make in class discussion, in writing assignments, and on tests. The more a student can explain and discuss historical events in the past, as a time and place different from the present, the more effective and nuanced his or her historical writing and thinking will be.
- The **Features Exercises** provide students with tools for evaluating the *American Lives* and *New Technology* essays and the primary documents found in *American Voices* and *Voices from Abroad*. The questions provided in the *Student Guide* help them shape their thinking about these essays and documents, showing them how to incorporate the material from these features into their understanding of the chapter material as a whole.
- The **Maps and Figures Exercises** help students analyze the evidence that has been presented in map or chart form in the text. Making an effort to "read" the visual evidence helps students understand the contribution that geography makes to history and the utility of organizing and interpreting historical information spatially.
- The **Self Test,** which includes **Multiple Choice** and **Short Essay** questions, allows students to determine how well they have mastered the material after working through the chapter. The Multiple Choice questions go beyond who and what to explore issues of how and why. Short Essays ask the main questions that each chapter seeks to answer. Writing a response to one of these questions will give students excellent preparation for writing an essay exam. Each student may check his or her answer with the suggested answer provided at the end of each chapter of the guide.

There is no recommended way to use the *Student Guide*. Each student should tailor use of the guide to his or her own style of studying and learning. However students use the *Guide* in conjunction with the text, their use of the two should develop symbiotically, deepening both their reading skills and their understanding of the historical narrative of the development of the United States. In this way, a successful student will come away with not only more knowledge about the past, but also a better appreciation of the distinctive nature of historical thought. These are the goals of a college-level history course.

ACKNOWLEDGEMENTS

I would like to thank the following individuals at Bedford/St. Martin's for their invaluable advice, support, and editing in producing the *Student Guide:* Gretchen Boger, the development editor, Regan Park, production editor, Erica Appel, managing editor, and Katherine Kurzman, sponsoring editor.

Timothy R. Mahoney

Contents

Preface **v**

What Is History? 1

Why Study History? 3

Part One
The Creation of American Society, 1450–1775   5

    1   *Worlds Collide: Europe and the Americas, 1450–1620*   **7**

    2   *The Invasion and Settlement of North America, 1550–1700*   **21**

    3   *The British Empire in America, 1660–1750*   **36**

    4   *Growth, Diversity, and Crisis: Colonial Society, 1720–1765*   **50**

    5   *Toward Independence: Years of Decision, 1763–1775*   **64**

Part Two
The New Republic, 1775–1820   79

    6   *War and Revolution, 1775–1783*   **81**

    7   *The New Political Order, 1776–1800*   **93**

    8   *Westward Expansion and a New Political Economy, 1790–1820*   **107**

    9   *The Quest for a Republican Society, 1790–1820*   **121**

Part Three
Economic Revolution and Sectional Strife, 1820–1877   133

    10   *The Economic Revolution, 1820–1860*   **135**

    11   *A Democratic Revolution, 1820–1844*   **147**

    12   *The Ferment of Reform, 1820–1860*   **160**

    13   *The Crisis of the Union, 1844–1860*   **171**

    14   *Two Societies at War, 1861–1865*   **183**

    15   *Reconstruction, 1865–1877*   **194**

STUDENT GUIDE

America's History

VOLUME 1: TO 1877

What Is History?

History is the story of the human past. Like all stories, whether told orally or written down, history is full of characters acting their parts within story lines in a wide range of settings. Given the vast diversity and range of human life over thousands of years since people have been recording their experiences, the varieties of history are almost infinite. Generally, however, histories vary according to four characteristics: time frame, setting, subjects, and themes.

The present is considered contemporary time. People record contemporary time by living through it. We mark the passing of time by our physical and mental development and our living each day as part of a story line of experiences. We create a meaningful story line by placing each experience in the context of our memories of past experiences. Historians consider past time from a broader perspective than we have on contemporary time. Some historians do examine the past over very short periods, telling the story of human activity over the course of a few months, days, even hours or minutes. But the pastness of that time fixes it in place, allowing a perspective that no one has on the present. Most historians take advantage of historical perspective to examine events or processes that occurred over longer periods, ranging from years to decades or generations. Still other histories follow patterns of human activity across centuries or millennia. By creating stories that encompass long passages of time, historians place human activity in a new perspective, giving it meaning that couldn't be appreciated as people lived through it.

Historians do more, however, than understand events within the context of the passage of time. They also examine and understand past events within a specific setting. Indeed, understanding events and developments within their specific time and place is what fundamentally defines the study of history. But the scope of the places historians study is as varied as the time frames they tackle. Some histories examine the activities of people in very precise places—a town or city, a village, a section of a town, a neighborhood, a house, or, in the most specific cases, a single room. But most analyze regions, nations, continents, and even the world, placing the events of specific places, including our own, in a broader perspective. Similarly, the number of subjects historians consider can be as diverse as the places they inhabit. Traditionally, historians have studied the people who make up a state, a region, a nation, groups of nations, a civilization, a culture, or even mankind as a whole in the world. But historians also study people as individuals, as well as families, small groups, and large groups based on occupational, social, ethnic, racial, or gender identity.

Thematically, all histories focus on human activity within at least one of the four major themes or aspects of human life: economic, social, political, or cultural activity. Economic activity involves all human actions and behaviors directed toward or motivated by the human impulse to physically survive and maintain oneself. How people have done this, what returns or gains they made from it, and how they have employed those gains to alter their standard of living are all encompassed within economic activity. Social history focuses on the ways in which people have organized themselves in relation to one another in order to facilitate their chances of survival and maintenance. History written from a social perspective tells stories of how individuals, groups, or a mass of people in a past time and place went about the business of living their lives and influencing the lives of others. How people grew up, socially interacted with others, formed families, had and reared children, and assumed adult roles in families are central concerns. How people formed small and large social groups based on family ties, occupational status, level of wealth, cultural values, or ethnic, racial, or gender identity and employed these points of reference to achieve the social goals of survival, protection, socialization, and reproduction are questions at the center of most social history.

Such social agendas usually involve some effort to influence or interact with political activity and government. Thus political history studies the negotiation, competition, and struggle among people of various families, clans, groups, classes, parties or sections, and countries for power and control. Traditionally, political history has examined how leaders, politicians, and government officials acquired power and formulated both domestic and foreign policies. It also studies the various ways in which leaders implemented policy, executed laws, and exerted control through leadership over their own people. From another perspective, political history studies how people interacted with government. Sometimes people were removed from government, had little say in its operations, and did not try to exert any influence over it. At other times, people affected government by gaining a voice in choosing leaders, organizing groups, parties, or institutions to influence or change the nature or focus of government policy, or exerting personal influence to affect government. How people and social groups acted politically to influence or respond to their own government's policies or the policies of another country is a central theme of political history. War is the broadest, most violent activity in the national or international realm of politics.

Finally, cultural histories tell stories of how people in past times and places, as they pursued and acted upon their various economic, social, and political goals, interpreted their activities in oral, artistic, material, spiritual, or intellectual ways to themselves and to others. Stories of people in the past formulating a theory of the cosmos, founding or reinvigorating or reforming a religious theology or practice, expressing themselves in a certain language, celebrating an event or entertaining themselves or others in a particular behavioral or material way, presenting the human body—male or female—in a specific way and clotned in a specific style, producing art or literature in a certain style with certain subjects and themes, or building, designing, or decorating homes, public buildings, and places of work in certain ways are all stories of people acting and behaving culturally. Indeed, the capacity to express culture seems to be what primarily defines people as human beings and distinguishes them from more advanced species of animal life.

History, therefore, is as varied and diverse as the endless range of possible varieties of time frames, settings, themes, and subjects about which one could write in studying people who lived in the past. One of the most powerful aspects of history is trying to discern some of the common patterns and themes in the infinite variety of stories within the human experience. By identifying patterns in history, we fit the many pieces into a comprehensive story or narrative that has relevance to us and thus gives meaning to our own lives. However various and diverse, all these stories are part of the broad canvas, or story of the human past, that is history.

Why Study History?

One can, and many people do, live without any exposure to formal history. The dictum that those who do not understand the past are doomed to repeat it is generally true; but at the same time many people live perfectly satisfying lives without giving much thought to or studying history. Nevertheless, all people, by the act of living in an economy, society, political system and culture in the world, interact with and derive meaning from systems that people in the past helped to establish or construct. All people are, therefore, implicitly historians.

People choose to study history formally, then, because it connects one's life to the lives of other human beings who lived in the past and thus enhances and gives it meaning. History is a fundamental human endeavor that defines one's humanity. In going about everyday activity, every person constructs a story line to plot his or her life. Asking someone who he is is the same as asking him where he has been, what he has done and experienced, where he is going, and what he wants to do. The basic questions we all face, "What do you want to be?" or "What do you do?," are inextricably bound up with "Who are you?" The answers to all of these questions lie in how well we have formulated the narrative of our lives. Happiness in life could be defined as successfully acting as the protagonist of the plot one has written and directed oneself. This general process of personal development is analogous to the practice of history. As individuals pursue their own lives, so, too, on a larger scale across time and space, do families, clans, groups, classes, and nations. While individuals create a meaningful personal narrative through action, experience, behavior, and memory, so, too, does history create for that group or nation a meaningful economic, social, political, and cultural narrative that gives meaning to the members of that group or nation living today.

The study of history has practical value, too. As written by historians, history sharpens one's intellectual and analytic skills. History is a distinctive discipline. It makes use of intellectual methods that are employed across a wide variety of disciplines and uses them in distinctive ways that are shaped by the particular nature of history. By understanding the differences between the methods, assumptions, subjects, and practice of history and those of other disciplines, one sharpens one's intellectual and analytic skills in important, even essential, ways. The subject and methods of history make an understanding of some history, therefore, a foundation for any education, whether its major focus is the liberal arts, the sciences, or professional, technical, or vocational training.

Historians use such rational scientific methods as the study of statistics and data, but their ultimate goal is to tell stories that have a plot. The way they organize the information they gather into that plot is really an interpretation or a theory about how or why something happened the way it did. Many facts seem undisputed—Christopher Columbus landed on El Salvador and discovered America on October 12, 1492; John F. Kennedy was murdered by Lee Harvey Oswald on November 22, 1963—but the significance of those facts, or even the full story of what happened, is less evident than one might think. To understand and explain the past, the historian must develop a thesis, test that thesis, and then defend it, employing the evidence that he or she has gathered.

The type of evidence available to historians is what makes history distinctive. Historians have access only to the evidence that has physically survived over time. Historians of the recent past may have far more evidence than any one person could ever absorb, but even this is not a complete picture. Sometimes new evidence becomes available when it is found by contemporary historians, as when a set of documents, letters, or papers previously believed to have been lost come to light. But in most cases historians find and use new evidence by developing new methods of analysis, asking new questions, or pursuing new story lines that give new relevance to evidence that was previously ignored. Often, historians have evidence, such as diaries, journals, personal letters, or secret documents, to support their thesis that contemporaries living through the events did not have or even know existed. Or they may have no more than fragments of evidence, such as a single statement or a partial list, that do more to obscure than to clarify an understanding of the event in question. Most of the time, historians have an intriguing mix of material that no contemporary would have had, combined with a loss of much material that contemporaries took for granted. Out of this surviving database, historians must develop a theory and try, as best they can, to demonstrate it. Add to these concerns the fact that most historical evidence is circumstantial, rather than the direct testimony of witnesses. Often, historians try to construct a story with little more than a scrap of evidence placing an individual or a group in a time and place but not addressing the specific questions the historian seeks to answer. Historians must be creative in searching the documents they have in ways that will help to answer their questions. Given the uniqueness of the database (which is, in some ways, analogous to memories about events in our past, on which we have broader perspective now but find hard to re-create in total), no historian will ever achieve the finality of the scientist. No historical thesis can be indisputably "proved" because in any human activity there is room for interpretation in telling the story. Many historical theses would fail to convince most trial juries beyond a reasonable doubt. Interpretations of a historical event can vary as widely as the range of views it is possible to have about current events or people living today. History thus uses the scientific method, but within a broader interpretive framework often supported by evidence that is not definitive. Every time one tries to understand the past, therefore, one acquires insight into the uncertainty, biases, and fluidity of any knowledge.

While the fluidity of history sometimes makes it more like a detective story or a fictional novel than an experiment in a laboratory, the practice of history as written adds to that fluidity. Historians generally try to present their theses in the colloquial, nontechnical language in which people speak and read in everyday life. As a rule, they present their stories in narrative form, though often with an analytic thematic framework running beneath the prose. The fact that history tries to fuse an understanding of different areas of activity into a general narrative adds to its intellectual power. History is the art of understanding social, economic, political, and cultural activity, then connecting these elements and trying to explain how they interacted to shape the general course of human events. The ability to articulate complicated ideas in a simple, straightforward way is a powerful skill that we can develop by studying history. Acquiring the skill to rationally examine much of the complex real world around us, develop a thesis about it, and argue the evidence to sustain a thesis is, indeed, one of the primary goals of a college education. History adds to that skill an ability to recognize human complexity within the context of its time and place. While putting a powerful intellectual tool in our hands, history also cultivates and satisfies our deepest human impulses.

Part One

The Creation of American Society, 1450–1775

The Thematic Timeline and Part introduction present, respectively, the most important events and the main interpretive generalizations for each period. The Thematic Timeline for Part 1 organizes the most important developments from 1450 to 1775 topically and chronologically. The topical categories are the economy, society, government, religion, and culture. On page 3, the Part introduction summarizes the generalizations that will be developed in the following chapters. Read the Timeline and the Part introduction together, beginning with the left-hand Timeline column.

First, the principal economic development highlighted in the Timeline is the change "from staple crops to internal growth." The specific entries list the steps in this process: the American economy developed from one dependent on exporting fish, furs, tobacco, and other staples to a mature subsistence economy with a rudimentary manufacturing sector. The third paragraph of the Part introduction explains the significance of this development.

The second column lists the ethnic, racial, and class divisions and conflicts that were so central to colonial society, from chronic warfare between English settlers and Indians and the enslavement of Africans to uprisings by backcountry farmers. The first and fourth paragraphs of the introduction interpret these developments.

Third, the most dramatic change in colonial government was the emergence of a relatively open and free political system that led Americans to abandon monarchy and embrace republican principles. Paragraph five of the Part introduction outlines the reasons for this fundamental change.

Fourth, the religious lives of the colonists evolved "from hierarchy to pluralism," from a general acceptance of clerical authority toward greater toleration and religious diversity. These developments are summarized in paragraph six of the Part introduction.

Fifth, despite their varied backgrounds, people living in the colonies began to create a distinct American identity. Some features of this new identity are discussed in paragraphs seven and eight of the Part introduction.

Now read the Timeline columns across from left to right. This will help you to see which events and developments occurred at approximately the same time, perhaps influencing each other. For the period 1760–1775, for example, many factors are shaking up the old order—from backcountry uprisings to Enlightenment ideas of popular sovereignty.

Part Questions

After you have finished studying the chapters in this Part, you should be able to answer the following questions:

1. Compare the subsistence agricultural societies of medieval Europe and the eastern Woodland Indians of North America, including agricultural technology, social structure, gender roles, and religion.

2. Describe the impact of European conquest and settlement on native Americans from the fall of the Aztecs to 1775.

3. Trace the rise of representative political institutions in the English mainland colonies from 1607 to 1775.

4. When and why was African slavery established in the English mainland colonies? What were the consequences up to 1775?

5. Compare and contrast the economic and social development of New England, the mid-Atlantic region, and the southern colonies. Did most whites achieve their dream of a freeholding society?

6. What was the impact of the Enlightenment and the Great Awakening in America, especially on religious beliefs and practices and political ideology?

Chapter 1

Worlds Collide: Europe and the Americas, 1450–1620

LEARNING OBJECTIVES

The following thematic and conceptual questions will help you to grasp the underlying logic of the historical events explained in this chapter. Your objective is to learn how and why historical events happened the way they did, and what impact those events had on subsequent events. Asking broad questions that explore the logic of historical events enhances your ability to answer essay questions. History is, after all, an extended essay. Historians such as the authors interpret events or argue a thesis about how and why events occurred the way they did by presenting evidence. The more detailed information provided in the text is the evidence upon which their interpretations are based. Specific events, names, and dates simply add detail and depth to the evidence and enhance your more general, conceptual understanding of how and why events took place as they did. No individual can possibly remember all the details. You should, however, try to examine closely sections of the text to see how the authors present detailed evidence to enhance and support their general interpretation.

1. What is a "culture," and how does it develop into a "civilization"?
2. All human cultures and civilizations share certain common features based on how people act and behave in order to survive and live. What are some of these features, and how does the way different groups respond to these needs shape the nature of a culture or a civilization?
3. What characteristics of any culture or civilization affect whether or how it will encounter and interact with other cultures and civilizations?
4. Why, of all the cultures and civilizations in America, Europe, and Africa, were Europeans the first people to move out beyond their traditional boundaries? Among Europeans, why did the Portuguese and then the Spanish lead the way?
5. Which factors determine the ability of a country or a civilization to prevail in a relationship with another culture or civilization? Economy, politics, or culture?
6. What forces—economic, political, social, or cultural—best explain why England emerged as the central European nation in the early development of the Americas in the area that would eventually become the United States?

CHAPTER SUMMARY

In the late fifteenth and early sixteenth centuries, two civilizations that were previously unaware of each other came into contact. On the American continents, approximately 70 million people lived in widely varying societies and cultures, from vast empires to small agricultural villages. On the much smaller European continent, another 70 million people lived in primarily agricultural societies. When some of these Europeans began to navigate in search of increased trade, they encountered the continents of the Western Hemisphere and the societies that inhabited them.

Native American Worlds (pp. 6–12)

In 1500, North and South America were inhabited by as many as 70 million native Americans. Native American economic and social organization ranged from small tribes that supported themselves by hunting and gathering to larger, complex civilizations with elaborate agricultural systems. The latter were as complex and sophisticated as those in European societies.

The First Americans

The origins of American history lie in the encounters between Europeans and the native peoples whose ancestors had by 1500 inhabited Europe and the Americas for thousands of years. Like all humans, native peoples in both the Americas and Europe sustained themselves by producing what they needed to survive and to protect themselves physically. Economically, they hunted and engaged in agriculture as best they could, given the technology they had and the environment in which they lived. They also organized to protect themselves and developed ways of understanding the environment and the cosmos. This helped them to understand themselves and to interpret their role in the world. To do these things, both peoples organized themselves socially into families, clans, social groups, and villages, established political systems, and formulated cultural and religious systems controlled primarily by intellectuals or the clergy. The size, structure, and degree of sophistication of each of these systems built on previous successes in survival that allowed the population to grow and cluster together in increasingly more organized entities. Across the Americas, various groups of native peoples pursued various survival strategies in the thousands of years after their arrival in the hemisphere to lay the groundwork for subsequent population growth and development.

The Maya and the Aztec

In Central and South America, success in agriculture allowed the population to grow and major civilizations to develop. The Mayan, Teotihuacán, and Aztec peoples were the most important of these cultures. As more and more people lived together, elaborate economic, social, political, and cultural systems developed. The Maya developed cities with temples surrounded by extensive agriculture. In Mexico, the Teotihuacán developed similar cities based on agriculture. But these societies gradually declined as a result of changes in the climate and war with neighboring peoples. The Aztec surpassed them both by developing agriculture, constructing large cities, establishing a hierarchical social system, and creating an intricate religion. By 1500, the Aztec ruled by military force and controlled numerous neighboring tribes.

The Indians North of the Rio Grande

In North America, smaller groups were less sedentary and less able to sustain large-scale agriculture. Though they occasionally clustered in larger towns and cities, they were unable to sustain large populations, or succumbed to disease and war and thus remained scattered in smaller tribes and clans that occupied the land extensively. Some of these groups, such as the Adena and the Hopewell peoples, the Mississippian people, and various tribes in the Southwest, developed agricultural systems through plant domestication, irrigation, or planting or farming technology that were sophisticated enough to sustain larger populations. They developed social and political elites who ruled the vast majority of peasants. With the stability this provided, more elaborate cultures were able to develop. In eastern North America, however, various tribes made limited progress in developing agricultural systems. Because they changed residences regularly, the development of large populations organized into social hierarchies and supported by extensive agriculture did not occur. These tribes were therefore unprepared to face European invaders in the sixteenth century.

Traditional European Society, 1450–1550 (pp. 12–18)

In 1450, the lives of most Europeans were shaped by the seasonal cycle of planting and harvesting, and by the traditional religious values that the Catholic Church affixed to that cycle. Technologically and intellectually backward, most Europeans lived according to traditional values and rituals and were satisfied simply to survive from one year to the next.

The Peasantry

In Europe, the social order was arranged in a way that assured that people would physically survive in a harsh world. The majority of the population were peasants who struggled by the exertion of raw muscle to scrape a meager living from subsistence farming in isolated rural villages. Those who were lucky enough to own their own land or to have access to common lands could produce a surplus and improve their station. Many others were eventually forced off the land and into the growing population of roaming poor. Most peasants lived hard, unvarying lives in which planting and harvesting, religion, and even life and death themselves were locked in the annual seasonal cycle.

Hierarchy and Authority

To survive in this harsh world, individuals in families, villages, and societies were compelled to accept the rule of a few powerful people. As fathers ruled peasant families, so, too, noblemen and aristocrats ruled the peasants who lived on their domains, and kings ruled over the noblemen within their states. Having acquired authority by force or historical privilege, they maintained it by providing security and order in an uncertain world.

The Power of Religion

The Roman Catholic Church reinforced and supported those who ruled by investing their authority and power with a moral dimension. Church doctrine and practice interpreted and gave meaning to the annual cycle of the seasons, the cosmos, and life and death, providing spiritual security and comfort. Likewise, the power of the Church allowed it to interpret international events and launch the Crusades to recover the Holy Land. By bringing Europeans into contact with the Arab world, the Crusades broadened Europe's cultural horizons while intensifying its Roman Catholic identity. The Crusades also reoriented Europe in regard to other civilizations and shifted military and political power in ways that had a profound impact on the economic and social foundations of European civilization.

Europe and the World, 1450–1550 (pp. 18–27)

In about 1450, new cultural ideas energized European society and culture. These ideas encouraged merchants to expand their trade, thus initiating contacts between Europeans and the peoples of Africa, Asia, and the Americas.

The Renaissance

Trade with the Middle East and Asia and contact with Arab civilization after 1450 created new wealth and introduced new technology, learning, and culture into Europe. The influx of wealth from foreign trade enabled a new mercantile and manufacturing elite to gain control of city-states in Italy. As this elite amassed political power, they applied the new science and humanism of Arab learning that they had imported into Europe to develop a new political culture of humanism. This culture celebrated the power of individuals to change the world through service to the state and patronage of the sciences and the arts. By fusing wealth, learning, and culture to establish the power of the state, Renaissance city-states became the models that aristocrats and monarchs around Europe would emulate.

Portugal Penetrates Africa and Asia

Geography, political stability, and a Renaissance humanist named Henry the Navigator enabled Portugal to emulate city-states first in pursuit of trade and riches. By trial and error, Portuguese sailors, directed by Henry from his center for exploration, gradually navigated down the African coast during the fifteenth century. Every island they encountered, they put into sugar production, while south of the Sahara they traded European goods with the native peoples for ivory, gold, salt, and wine. To provide labor for their sugar plantations on the islands, they also began to trade in slaves. By the end of the century, the Portuguese had a fully organized colonial system of forts, trading posts, and plantations, interconnected by trading routes to the south and east and generating enormous wealth. The Portuguese success in establishing a colonial trading system became the model for all European states thereafter.

Spain and America

The Spanish followed the Portuguese example by pursuing, at the suggestion of an Italian captain named Christopher Columbus, a westward route to the riches of the East. When Columbus arrived at the Bahama Islands, which he believed were the outer islands of the East Indies off the coast of Asia, he sought gold and trade goods from the native peoples he encountered. He then set up colonial towns and sugar plantations on Hispaniola in which he used first Indian and then African slaves. Though Columbus's efforts earned him neither wealth nor fame during his life, he did establish the framework of a Spanish colonial system. That system would attract, with royal support, waves of Spanish explorers and conquistadors, who would extend Spanish rule across Central and South America in pursuit of wealth and power.

The Conquest

Spanish conquistadors, driven by greed, employed technological superiority, military force, political guile, and cultural hegemony to achieve their goals of dominion over the native peoples of Central and South America. They were also accompanied by a powerful ally—disease. The Spanish explorer Cortés conquered the vastly numerically superior Aztec peoples by forming military alliances with tribes that were enemies of the Aztec. He gained entrance to the Aztec capital by presenting himself as a god. Once there, he used military force to capture the leader, Moctezuma, and wage war against Aztec forces, which had been decimated by an epidemic. He finished the conquest by supporting the uprising of dependent Indian peoples against the Aztec. Francisco Pizarro achieved the same result through similar means against the Incan empire in South America. The Spanish conquest of the Americas had far-reaching demographic, ecological, social, and political consequences in the Americas, Africa, and Europe.

The Protestant Reformation and the Rise of England, 1500–1620
(pp. 27–35)

Both the rising tide of religious fervor and the ideas of the Renaissance contributed to the development of a Protestant challenge to the Catholic Church. As wealth flowed into Spanish coffers, Spain emerged as the predominant Catholic power in Europe. The inflationary economic impact of Spanish wealth on the European economy, as well as the Reformation, converged to elevate England as the major Protestant challenger to Spanish power.

The Protestant Movement

The wealth of its empire in America made Spain a great power in Europe. The rise of Spain and the outbreak of the Protestant Reformation forced England to respond. The Protestant Reformation began when a German monk named Martin Luther protested against the corruption of the Roman Catholic Church. When German princes protected Luther after he was excommunicated, the Protestant movement was born and a reformed Lutheran Church, independent of Rome, was founded. Other groups followed across northern and central Europe, as well as England. Henry VIII of England broke with Rome in the 1530s and established the Anglican Church. The Catholic Church was quickly challenged by other Protestants in England, who wanted more radical changes in its liturgy, clergy, and organization. England under Queen Elizabeth I, as defender of the Reformation, helped the Dutch overthrow Spanish rule and defend themselves against a Spanish invasion. England began to emerge as a significant state.

The Dutch and the English Challenge Spain

England's emergence as a nation-state was based on its rising political power and cultural fervor, supported by economic expansion. As the population increased with a period of good harvests and fewer epidemics, a growing demand for agricultural and manufacturing goods reinforced the general rise in prices caused by the importation of gold and silver from Spanish America. In response, the gentry shifted production from grain to wool and consolidated fields to increase agricultural output. The increase in manufacturing and foreign trade created a new class of merchants and manufacturers, who, along with the gentry, pressed for more political power. As the power of aristocrats declined, the rising gentry threw peasants off the land and, as religious dissenters, challenged the Anglican Church. The economic rise of England created the capital and technology necessary for overseas expansion. It also established the political power of the gentry and the merchants, and undermined the lives of peasants and those from the lesser ranks of the nobility. In doing so, it provided the leadership, the means, and the participants for England's colonization of North America. This would give the encounter between European and native peoples in North America a distinct character and direction.

EXPANDED TIMELINE

30,000–10,000 B.C. **Settlement of eastern North America**
For about twenty thousand years after 30,000 B.C., until the end of the last great Ice Age in about 8000 B.C., thousands of migrants from Asia crossed an ice-free corridor along the coastal mountains from Asia to North America. These immigrants eventually spread across the Americas, from the Arctic to the eastern woodlands, from the Rocky Mountains to the tropics of Mesoamerica, and from the Gulf of Mexico to the tip of South America. For 9,500 years, they lived cut off from the rest of the world. These "first" Americans were the "native" peoples who greeted the white Europeans who arrived in America in 1492.

3000–2000 B.C. **Cultivation of crops begins in Mesoamerica**
The first Americans lived as hunter-gatherers off the land for centuries. As the climate changed, certain species the Indians hunted declined, forcing native Americans to shift to hunting smaller animals and foraging. In Central America, the same incentive led some native peoples to cultivate corn (maize) and other grains and vegetables. Over the centuries, as they learned more about the plants, they bred larger

Expanded Timeline

kinds and a greater variety of vegetables and grains and intensified their farming activity.

100 – 400 B.C.   **Flourishing of Hopewell culture**
As early as 500 B.C., the Adena people in the eastern woodlands of North America began to build villages and large burial grounds. Around A.D. 100 the Hopewell built upon the Adena foundation and developed an even more elaborate culture fed by extensive trade routes across the continent. The Hopewell flourished in the Ohio, Illinois, and Mississippi River valleys for three centuries and then, for unknown reasons, declined around A.D. 500. By that time, the Mississippian culture to the west, infused by the influences of immigrants from Central America, had emerged as a significant culture.

300   **Rise of Mayan civilization**
The first great native civilization to emerge in Mesoamerica was that of the Mayan peoples. The Maya built large religious urban centers with temples, great squares, roads, and elaborate water systems. These cities stood at the center of farms that peasants had hewed from the extensive rain forests of the Yucatan. They also developed a sophisticated system of astronomy, mathematics, and figure writing through which they recorded their history in detail. Internal social friction, and perhaps an extended drought, forced the Maya to abandon some of their larger cities by A.D. 900. While some Maya fled to North America, others were absorbed into nearby peoples, and still others maintained vibrant cities until 1500.

500   **Zenith of Teotihuacán civilization**
To the north, the Teotihuacán people built even larger cities, with more temples, some as large as the Pyramids of ancient Egypt. The capital city, Teotihuacán, contained a hundred temples and thousands of buildings surrounded by a network of artificial lakes interspersed with islands (*chinampas*) on which peasants grew maize, grains, and vegetables to support the city. An extended drought and invasions by various seminomadic peoples from the north led to the decline of Teotihuacán by about A.D. 800.

600   **Emergence of Pueblo cultures**
Even farther north, beyond the deserts of northern Mexico in the present southwestern part of the United States, several tribes, under the influence of other tribes to the south in Mexico, developed somewhat less elaborate cultures. A common feature of the Hohokam, Mogollon, and Anasazi peoples were cities built with adobe that were embedded in the steep cliffs in the mountains of the region for protection. These complexly built *pueblos* (Spanish for "town") had courtyards, temples, apartment houses, and public structures, and were connected by an elaborate road system. But all of these cultures, because of the location of their protected cities above the deserts, supported themselves by a precarious system of food production, under constant threat of invasion. Eventually, later peoples, the Zuni of western New Mexico and the Hopi of northeastern Arizona, built smaller and more dispersed centers amid invasions by nomadic Navajo and Apache peoples.

700–1100   **Spread of Arab Muslim civilization**
After the death of their prophet, Muhammad, in A.D. 632, Muslims—the followers of the Islamic religion—set out to conquer and convert the world. They carried their ideas across North Africa, the Middle East, Turkey, India, and parts of southern Europe, including the Balkans and the Iberian Peninsula (Spain). In each place, they gained converts and established control over an elaborate civilization, while threatening local cultures and religions.

800–1350   **Development of Mississippian culture**
The native peoples of the lower Mississippi Valley, under the influence of emigrants from Central America, developed large cities with temples surrounded by elaborate agricultural systems. Their mixed culture flourished for centuries, until chronic diseases and political instability reduced the size and power of the cities and caused decline. Nevertheless, the first French explorers in the Mississippi River Valley before 1700 encountered vigorous remnants of that culture.

1095–1271   **Crusades link Europe with Arab Muslim learning**
The Roman Catholic Church, to consolidate its power in Europe, urged its followers to launch holy wars against those who had other religious beliefs. For nearly two hundred years Europeans launched attacks against the Muslims to halt their advance into southern Europe and to regain control of the Holy Land in the Middle East, which they held for two centuries. European contacts with the advanced learning of the Islamic world and trade for the riches of Asia, including such spices as cinnamon and pepper, broadened European horizons and set in motion remarkable cultural changes.

1325   **Aztec establish their capital at Tenochtitlán**
The Aztec, a nomadic people from northern Mexico, invaded the central valley of Mexico in the 1300s. In 1325, they built a new capital called Tenochtitlán (now Mexico City) on an island in Lake Texcoco and drew on the techniques and practices of the Teotihuacán peoples. Ruled by a theocratic hierarchy, the Aztec produced great wealth and strong institutions, and ruled by means of a large army. They gradually subjugated most of the other smaller tribes of central

Mexico. By repression and tribute—both financial and human—the Aztec had established a large, powerful empire by 1500.

1400–1550 **Italian Renaissance**
In contrast, Italy was deeply influenced by new trade and cultural influences from Islam. An influx of classical learning, preserved in Islamic libraries, transformed European culture and science. New technologies created a burst of development and innovation. And new resources and luxuries brought wealth and a new demand for humanistic artistic expression. This Renaissance, or rebirth, first occurred in Italian city-states and was led by a new, monied elite. The rise of the merchant elite in other countries provided wealth and power to the monarchy that was at the head of modern nation-states. Only these nation-states would be able to amass the capital necessary to launch Europe into a new age of exploration and discovery.

1440s **Portugal enters trade in African slaves**
In their quest for wealth through trade, Portuguese captains and sailors added humans to the list of cargo that they would carry for trade. Beginning in the 1440s, Portuguese ships began to transport Africans from Senegambia and other points in West Africa, first to Atlantic islands, such as the Azores, and later to Brazil and the West Indies. Portugal was the first European state to enter the slave trade.

1492 **Christopher Columbus's first voyage to America**
After the expulsion of the Muslims from the Iberian Peninsula in the *Reconquista* of 1492, Spain was ready to join Portugal in the race for colonies. An Italian mariner from the city-state of Genoa, Christopher Columbus, won support from King Ferdinand and Queen Isabella to test his plan to reach Asia by sailing westward. Columbus never reached Asia. Instead, he found a New World in the Americas, laying the basis for a Spanish empire stretching across two continents.

1513 **Juan Ponce de León explores Florida**
As Spanish explorers entered the New World and made contact with native peoples, they heard a variety of rumors of great riches that could be found on the American mainland. One of these stories purported to describe a "fountain of youth," whose waters could keep people forever young. Spanish adventurer Juan Ponce de León sought this treasure—along with gold and slaves—in what is now Florida. Ironically, Ponce de León's search for the fountain of youth cost him his life. He was killed by an arrow shot by a Calusa Indian.

1517 **Martin Luther begins Protestant Reformation**
Martin Luther, a German monk, challenged Church authority by condemning the corruption and abuse within the Catholic Church. Luther's broad attack on Catholic doctrine inspired a religious revolution across northern Europe, touching off peasant uprisings and religious wars between Catholic and Protestant sects and among princes across Germany. In time, broader conflicts would sweep across Europe, resulting in religious wars between Spain and Holland, and, finally, between Spain and England.

1519–1521 **Hernando Cortés conquers Aztec empire**
Hernando Cortés, one of many conquistadors who sought their fame and fortune in America, invaded the Aztec empire. With the help of allied tribes that rebelled against the Aztec, Cortés occupied the capital city of Tenochtitlán and gained control of the empire.

1531–1538 **Francisco Pizarro vanquishes Incas in Peru**
By the time Pizarro arrived in the Incan empire in Peru, half the population had died from European diseases brought by Indian traders. Pizarro's forces easily conquered the weakened vestiges of this once-magnificent empire.

1534 **Henry VIII establishes Church of England**
Though Henry VIII initially resisted the spread of Protestantism to England, the pope's denial of his request for a divorce from his first wife, who had not given him a son, persuaded him to break away from Rome and establish the Church of England. Though at first Henry retained most Catholic doctrine and organization, the new church was gradually influenced by the Reformation, touching off religious disputes among the Crown, various Protestant sects, and Catholics for decades. These disputes would eventually encourage some dissenters to leave England for America.

1536 **John Calvin's *Institutes of Christian Religion***
The French theologian John Calvin built upon the challenges to church doctrine introduced by Martin Luther and offered a harsher version of Protestantism. Calvinist theology, specifically the doctrine of predestination, had a profound impact on the Reformation. His doctrines would deeply influence both the Presbyterians and the Puritans in England, sparking religious discord that would lead some to seek freedom from religious persecution in America.

1550–1630 **Price Revolution**
English mercantilism
Enclosure movement
Spain's discovery of gold and silver in America triggered a long period of price increases across Europe after 1550. As Spain spent its money in Europe, other countries, including Holland and England, increased their foreign trade. Rising prices enriched English merchants and gentry farmers, who switched from grain to wool production. To facilitate this change, Parliament passed laws allowing them to throw peas-

ants off the common lands and enclose them for wool production. Thus, by creating a rising merchant class interested in foreign trade, a more aggressive gentry, and an impoverished peasantry, the Price Revolution transformed society in ways that would lead many people in English society to see both profit and opportunity in colonial exploration and settlement.

1556–
1598 **Philip II, king of Spain**
When Philip II ascended the Spanish throne, Spain was the most powerful state in Europe. Philip proposed to expand Spanish power and reestablish the Catholic Church across the Continent. His plans were dashed by England and the Netherlands, which emerged to replace Spain as the dominant political and commercial powers in Europe.

1558–
1603 **Elizabeth I, queen of England**
The age of Elizabeth was one of the brightest periods in English history for literary and artistic development. It was also the time when Protestantism, in the form of the Church of England, was established as the state religion. Elizabeth's resistance to radical religious reforms led to a persecution of dissenters that continued well into the 1600s.

1560s **English Puritan movement begins**
Opposition to continuing Catholic influences in the Church of England and a push to purify the church led to the rise of Puritanism. The marked disagreement of Puritans with Anglican doctrine resulted in persecution of the Puritans and their eventual migration out of England.

1603–
1625 **James I, first Stuart King of England**
James I put aside Elizabeth's long feud with Spain and promoted England as a colonial as well as a commercial and political power. King James saw a variety of benefits in the promotion of colonial settlement in North America. He also, however, intensified persecution of Puritans and Presbyterians and exerted his "divine right" to rule. He thus increased the power of the state through colonization, while pursuing policies that assured that many emigrants would be religious exiles, thereby increasing order at home.

GLOSSARY

culture A coherent set of behaviors, practices, beliefs, rituals, and ideas by which a people understand themselves and explain the world around them to themselves and others. (p. 5)

anthropologist A social scientist who studies the basic characteristics, behaviors, rituals, and practices of men and women, particularly those who are native to a region or *indigenous*. (p. 6)

civilization A highly organized economic, social, and political system that supports an elaborate and sophisticated culture. (pp. 7–8)

elite A small group of people who lead the majority of the people in a society. The status of this group is established by heredity or merit. (p. 7)

chinampas The Teotihuacán people cultivated crops on small artificial islands in natural and man-made lakes. This agricultural plan, called *chinampas*, was adopted by the Aztec, who raised vegetables and flowers on floating islands in Lake Texcoco, the site of their capital city, Tenochtitlán. (p. 8)

seminomadic A group that does not occupy a site permanently but moves around seasonally or annually according to its subsistence and security needs. (p. 8)

clan A group of families defined by a common family name or ancestry. (p. 8)

Mesoamerican Central American. (p. 8)

caste A rigidly defined social group into which one is born and must remain for life. (p. 8)

hierarchical social order A social order characterized by different groups arranged from most to least powerful. Sharp lines of differences defined the groups. (p. 8)

matrilineal A social system in which the name of each individual is defined by his/her mother's name, not his/her father's name (a patrilineal system), as is common in American culture. When this system was tied to inheritance, land and property passed from mother to daughter rather than from father to son. (p. 12)

wampum Shells made into beads that native Americans used as money. Shells and beads were often embroidered into belts or clothing, or strung as necklaces or bracelets. (p. 12)

barter An economic system in which people exchange goods and services for other goods and services instead of money. (p. 13)

peasant A farm laborer who worked the land owned by a landlord. Sometimes peasants owned or leased a small plot in the town and worked collectively with other village peasants on the landlord's land. Sometimes this land, as in England, was arranged in vast, open field settlements unseparated by fences or hedgerows. Often, peasants retained the right to farm some strips within this open-field system. (p. 13)

open fields These are agricultural fields that are not divided by fences or hedges. Instead of being the property and concern of the owner, such fields are tended by all members of the group, each of whom also has a right to use the land according to his needs. (p. 14)

dower A legal right extended to a widow during her lifetime to use one-third of the property of an estate (property owned by a deceased person). (p. 16)

primogeniture The legal practice of transferring most or all of one's wealth to one's first (i.e., *primo*), or oldest, son (i.e., *geniture*—to issue forth from). (p. 16)

patriarch Literally, "the father as ruler." The patriarch was the male leader of a group, family, or clan. He ruled by authority and was responsible for the welfare of his spouse, children, or workers. (p. 16)

infidel A person who is a theological enemy to mainstream views. (p. 18)

public virtue A general ethical set of standards that argued that each and every citizen should participate in and be committed to politics and help shape the nature of governing. (p. 19)

civic humanism A set of political beliefs, attitudes, and ethics that argued that each citizen, though an independent person with a free will who is expected to act in his self-interest, should align that self-interest with public goals and policies and contribute actively to the community through public service. (p. 19)

humanist A thinker, scholar, or public person who believes people—i.e., human beings—have the ingenuity, understanding, and skill to shape the world to their own benefit. (p. 19)

reconquista A campaign undertaken by the Spanish in the late Middle Ages to oust the Moors from the Iberian Peninsula. King Ferdinand and Queen Isabella succeeded in defeating the Moors in 1492. (p. 22)

patron Someone who provides direct economic support for another person's career development. Ferdinand and Isabella were the patrons of Christopher Columbus. (p. 22)

adelantados To encourage Spanish military personnel and adventurers to go to the New World, the Spanish Crown gave them licenses making them "proprietors" or "entrepreneurs." As *adelantados*, they controlled landed estates, and had the right to do whatever was necessary to acquire wealth during a certain time frame or in a certain place. The chance of becoming *adelantados* motivated Spanish adventurers to exploit and subdue the native peoples of the Caribbean. (p. 22)

conquistadors Spanish word for "conquerors." Military leaders such as Hernando Cortés and Francisco Pizarro were conquistadors. (p. 23)

mestizo The Spanish word used to describe someone whose mother and father were of different races. Because most of the Spanish who colonized Central and South America were men, there was considerable intermarriage between Spanish men and Indian women. These couples produced a large mixed-race, or *mestizo*, population that would combine Spanish and Indian values and practices. (p. 27)

assimilation Assimilation is the gradual absorption and incorporation of one culture with or into another. A person from a different culture becomes assimilated when his or her behavior begins to resemble the behavior and practices of people in the dominant culture. (p. 27)

anticlericalism Opposition to the power and privileges of the clergy. In the sixteenth century, abuses by the Roman Catholic clergy created widespread anticlerical feeling among the people of Europe. (p. 27)

indulgences In the theology of the Catholic Church, one's behavior in life would affect how God judged one in the afterlife. If one did good works and acquired grace, one could expect approval. If, on the other hand, one had sinned and had not repented of those sins through penance, one could expect punishment. An indulgence was a certificate that exonerated one from punishment in return for specific good works or outright cash payments to the Church. Martin Luther condemned the sale of indulgences as worthless because they were not achieved by God's grace. (p. 27)

predestination John Calvin argued, in contrast to Catholic theology, that God was all-powerful and man was corrupt and weak and thus unable to know God's eternal design. In particular, Calvin argued that God had chosen certain people for salvation while condemning the rest of mankind to eternal damnation. He emphasized that one could never really know who these people were and therefore one could do nothing to improve one's chances of attaining salvation. (p. 30)

annulment A declaration by the Catholic Church that a marriage is legally invalid. An annulment differs from a divorce in that it invalidates the marriage. The Church therefore does not recognize that the marriage ever took place. When Henry VIII's request to the pope that his marriage to Catherine of Aragon be annulled was refused, he broke with the Roman Catholic Church. (p. 30)

presbyters Laymen who were elected as elders of Presbyterian congregations. Their role was to help the minister run the congregation. Presbyterians sought to reform the church by reorganizing the centralized church into separate congregations. (p. 31)

outwork One of the major costs incurred by manufacturers is the construction of a building in which all the stages of the process of manufacturing are performed. Manufacturers with limited capital often saved money by hiring underemployed people working at their residences to perform various stages in the production process. The manufacturer transported raw materials and picked up finished goods from each of the households and perhaps finished the product at one site. But most of the production took place off-site, in the houses of the employees. The work done off-site was called outwork. The system was called the putting-out system. The English employed this system to produce cloth as early as the sixteenth century. (p. 32)

mercantilism A political economic theory that argued that the power of the state was enhanced by wealth and that state policy, therefore, should be directed toward improving the economy. This was achieved by state policies that aimed at increasing exports and decreasing imports. These policies included subsidizing home manufacturers, funding the development of colonies, and regulating commerce. By prohibiting foreigners from engaging in domestic or colonial trade, limiting direct trade by colonists to and from foreign countries, and requiring that products of the colonies be exported via the mother country, the government maximized economic returns to the state. (p. 33)

Price Revolution The price of goods and services is based on the amount of money that people are willing to pay for them. When increased amounts of gold and silver arrived in Europe from the Spanish empire in America, people had more money and they offered more for goods and services, thus increasing their price. This increase in prices, called inflation, constituted the Price Revolution of sixteenth-century Europe. (p. 33)

gentry Substantial landowners in England who owned efficiently managed estates that they rented or leased to farmers but did not have aristocratic titles or privileges. (pp. 33–34)

yeoman A farmer who owned a moderate-size plot of land. With his family's and occasionally a farm laborer's help, he produced a small crop for sale in the marketplace. As prices increased, yeomen farmers in England enjoyed increased incomes. (p. 34)

enclosure As wool prices increased, many members of the gentry shifted from growing crops to raising sheep for the production of wool. With Parliament's support in the enclosure acts, the gentry pushed peasants off their open fields, took away their traditional rights to farm certain strips of land, and enclosed the fields with fences to allow sheep to graze. Peasants who were thrown off the land were left to fend for themselves as manufacturing workers or were reduced to poverty. (p. 34)

indentured servants A servant who works for someone in a contractual arrangement. The employer promises room and board in return for several years' work. (p. 34)

joint-stock companies In order to pool a larger amount of capital to support overseas expansion, the English formed companies that issued stock according to the amount of one's investment. If the company succeeded, one's share of the profit was determined by the share of company stock one held. If the company lost money or failed, one's loss or obligation was likewise limited. By pooling larger amounts of capital from smaller investors, the joint-stock company considerably increased the amount of capital that became available for overseas expansion and shifted investments in overseas capital from the Crown and the aristocracy to merchants. (p. 34)

dynamic society A traditional society remains the same generation after generation. The economic and material basis of that society remains unchanged and people are born into, live, and die within a particular class or caste social order and culture. Whether large or small, complex or simple, hierarchical or egalitarian, such a society is static. When the economic basis of a society begins to change, however, people who previously lacked power acquire it, and those who once had it often lose it. Shifts in power enable some people to move from one part of the social order to another. This can cause changes in the structure of the social order. A society that is characterized by social change is a dynamic society. (pp. 34–35)

IDENTIFICATION

Identify by filling in the blanks.

1. The Mayan and Aztec civilizations of Mesoamerica drew heavily on the older culture known as _____ which rose around 700 B.C. along the Gulf of Mexico. (p. 7)

2. The people of Teotihuacán built the huge Pyramid of the Sun to honor the sun god in what is now the country of _____. (p. 8)

3. The dietary staple of most native American groups was _____. (p. 10)

4. The greatest city of the Mississippian culture was _____, at the site of present-day East St. Louis. (p. 10)

5. Agricultural "slaves" in western Europe who, until 1450, were legally bound to the land were known as _____. (p. 14)

6. In the mid-fifteenth century, the most dynamic region of Europe was the city-states of _____, which had established themselves as thriving centers of trade. (pp. 18–20)

7. In his political treatise entitled _____ (1513), Niccolò Machiavelli suggested a variety of ways for European monarchs to strengthen their hold on power. (p. 19)

8. The most important spice that traders brought into European markets from the Orient was _____, which was in demand for flavoring and preserving meat. (p. 21)

9. The Muslims, who had invaded Spain around A.D. 700, controlled its southern region until the late 1400s, when they were expelled in the _____. (p. 22)

10. Christopher Columbus won backing for his voyages to the New World from the rulers of Spain, King _____ of Aragon and Queen _____ of Castile. (p. 22)

11. The Spanish adventurer who arrived in Mexico in 1519 and conquered the Aztec was _____. (p. 23)

12. The ruler of the Aztec who was defeated by the Spanish under the leadership of Hernando Cortés was _____. (p. 23)

13. The German monk who complained about indulgences and then sought major reform of the Catholic Church and thus started the Protestant Reformation was _____. (p. 27)

14. John Calvin's most important contribution to the Protestant Reformation was the doctrine of _____, which held that each person's salvation or damnation is determined by God. (p. 30)

15. Queen Elizabeth sought to expand the wealth and power of England by means of government stimulation and control of the economy. This system was known as _____. (p. 33)

16. English investors sought to increase the involvement of small investors in overseas adventures by inventing the _____ company. (p. 34)

FEATURES EXERCISES

New Technology

Indian Women and Agriculture
(pp. 14–15)

Life in premodern times was, given the limited technology, a struggle to survive. People who lived in both North America and Europe focused on the production of food with an intensity that most Americans today, except for farmers, would find hard to understand. The production of food was the source of life. It determined the population size of a group or nation and shaped social relations, political power, and culture. This piece helps to reinforce the underlying theme running through the entire chapter: that wealth, social order, and culture were determined by the ability of the majority of people to produce enough food from the land to survive and that, all things considered, European peasants and native peoples in North America achieved similar degrees of success. As you read this article, ask yourself the following questions:

1. Who was more skillful in planting corn, native American women or Englishmen? Who was more productive? Why?

2. What evidence of the significance of corn in the lives of both the native peoples and English settlers do we have from their cultures?

3. Why did corn become such an important crop for both peoples?

4. How important, in comparison, do you think corn is in the American diet today? Why?

Voices from Abroad

CHRISTOPHER COLUMBUS, First Impressions of Native Americans (p. 23)

Personal observations are based on one's knowledge and assumptions. Christopher Columbus was a well-traveled sea captain who had encountered peoples from across Europe and Africa. Yet when he arrived in the New World or, more specifically, on San Salvador Island in the Bahamas, he was a bit confused about who the people he met were. While reading this account, think about the following questions.

1. How does Columbus's log book reflect his biases?
2. To what extent did Columbus see the people objectively?
3. How would Columbus's attitude toward the native peoples affect the way he interacted with them?
4. Why does Columbus focus so much on the appearance of the native peoples?

American Voices

Aztec Elders Describe the Spanish Conquest (p. 26)

The course of events can usually be explained only by including an understanding of the perceptions and actions of all the people who are involved. In this case, we see the arrival of the Spanish in Mexico from the Aztec point of view. Clearly, Moctezuma and the Aztec were unnerved by the Spanish and devastated by the spread of disease that came with them. As you read this piece, try to answer the following questions:

1. Why did the arrival of the Spanish create such torment in Moctezuma?
2. Why did word that the Spanish had guns add to Moctezuma's fears?
3. Why did Moctezuma seem particularly struck by the fact that the Spanish were white?
4. How does this account, from Moctezuma's perspective, provide us with some insight into how the smaller Spanish forces were able to defeat the Aztec?

American Lives

Cortés and Malinche: The Dynamics of Conquest (pp. 28–29)

Rather than simply overpower the Aztec, Hernando Cortés used a political strategy of negotiation, persuasion, and manipulation of native peoples who paid tribute to the Aztec. In the course of this interaction, real individual diplomatic, social, and even personal relationships between the conquerors and the conquered were established. The story of Cortés and the Painalan woman Malinali, called Malinche by the Spanish, reflects each aspect of this complicated process. As you read the story, think about the following questions:

1. Why did Malinali's parents initially sell her into slavery?
2. How did she become Cortés's slave? What roles did she play, and why?
3. Why did conquest, slavery, and concubinage become intertwined in Mexico?
4. Did Malinche ever acquire her freedom? Why, or why not?
5. Who do you think used whom more in this relationship?

MAPS AND FIGURES

Map 1.1 Native American Peoples, 1492 (p. 9)

1. Among the tribes shown, which were the largest and most powerful? Which do you think were among the smallest and least powerful? Is there any relationship between size and the environment in which the tribes lived?
2. Some contemporary state, city, and local names, as well as the names of rivers and mountains, often originate from native American names and terms. Which of the tribal names shown relate to contemporary names?

Map 1.2 Europeans Seek Control of World Trade, 1460–1560 (p. 21)

Look at this map carefully.

1. How does the angle of the map help you to understand the logistical issues of travel between East and West hundreds of years ago? How does it help you to understand why the Muslims controlled trade? How does it help you to understand why going south around Africa challenged the power of the Muslims in the Eastern trade?
2. One way to get a sense of the routes to the East is to trace the quickest route from its beginning to its end point. What was the quickest route between Calicut (Calcutta) and Venice?
3. How does this map help to explain why Spain and Portugal and England, and not Italy and Turkey and the Holy Roman Empire, were the first to seek other routes to the East?

Map 1.3 *The Spanish Conquest* (p. 24)

1. If read closely, the details of a map can show one the logic of a process or a series of events. How does the arrangement of figures on this map indicate the strategy that the Spanish used to conquer Central and South America?

2. How does the location of silver and gold mines help you to further understand the strategy pursued by the Spanish?

3. How does the sequence of events presented, and the size of the populations the Spanish encountered (as indicated by "empires"), help you to understand the racial and ethnic diversity of Latin America and the Caribbean today?

Figure 1.1 *The Yearly Rhythm of Rural Life* (p. 13)

In earlier times, the annual cycle of nature seems to have affected the annual cycle of human birth and death. Try to follow that cycle in some detail.

1. What is the cycle of nature in the Northern Hemisphere? Why would there be more deaths in late summer and late winter than in midsummer or mid-autumn?

2. What reasons can explain the increase in conceptions in June and December? How does the increase in births in March and September or early October relate to the increase in death rates?

3. Which rate is affecting the other? Is the pattern of conceptions shaping the pattern of deaths? Or is the pattern of deaths shaping the pattern of conceptions and births?

4. Given the implication that births and deaths followed the seasons, what would you expect to be the pattern from month to month in a town or city in the Northern Hemisphere today? How do you explain the difference?

SELF-TEST

Multiple Choice

1. The first people to live in the Western Hemisphere migrated to the Americas beginning about 30,000 B.C. from:
   a. islands in the South Pacific.
   b. Asia.
   c. Africa.
   d. western Europe.

2. The region of the New World known as Mesoamerica was made up of:
   a. the Arctic zone near the Bering Sea.
   b. the area around the Great Lakes.
   c. present-day Mexico and Guatemala.
   d. Peru and Bolivia in South America.

3. The most brutal of the native American civilizations, based in part on the practice of human sacrifice, was that of the:
   a. people of Teotihuacán in the highlands of Mexico.
   b. Maya in the Yucatan peninsula.
   c. Olmec peoples along the Gulf of Mexico.
   d. Aztec in the central Valley of Mexico.

4. The people of Teotihuacán had as a major deity and a prime object of worship the feathered serpent they called:
   a. Tenochtitlán.   c. Toltec.
   b. Quetzalcoatl.   d. Tuscarora.

5. Between A.D. 600 and 1250, *all* of the following native cultures developed in the American Southwest *except:*
   a. Hohokam.   c. Anasazi.
   b. Mogollon. d. Choctaw.

6. In many eastern Woodland tribes, notably the Iroquois, important decisions were made by the senior women, and inheritances—including rights to land and other property—passed from mother to daughter. This kind of society would be described as:
   a. matrilineal.   c. intergenerational.
   b. patriarchal.   d. hierarchical.

7. Martin Luther criticized the Roman Catholic Church for *all* of the following reasons *except:*
   a. the practice of selling indulgences.
   b. salvation by good works.
   c. the pope's refusal to grant the king of England a divorce.
   d. the role of the clergy as mediators between God and people.

8. The most important factor explaining why the Portuguese were the first in Europe to pursue overseas exploration and discovery was:
   a. political stability at home.
   b. a seafaring tradition.
   c. effective leadership.
   d. geographic location.

9. The Portuguese sailor who reached India was:
   a. Prince Henry the Navigator.
   b. Vasco da Gama.
   c. Bartholomeu Dias.
   d. Amerigo Vespucci.

10. Spanish entrepreneurs who were licensed by the Crown to acquire and manage land in the New World in return for promoting Spanish control were known as:
    a. *adelantados.*   c. *chinampas.*
    b. conquistadors.   d. caravels.

11. In the 1520s, Francisco Pizarro began a long trek into the mountains of Peru that resulted in the Spanish conquest of the empire of the:
    a. Incas.   c. Olmecs.
    b. Aztec.   d. Toltecs.

12. The most important factor in Cortés's successful conquest of the Aztec empire was:
    a. Malinche's help.
    b. the rebellion of native peoples.
    c. epidemics.
    d. superior forces and weaponry.

13. *Institutes of the Christian Religion* (1536), a book that depicted God as an awesome sovereign and emphasized the corruption of the human race, was written by:
    a. Martin Luther.
    b. Cardinal Thomas Wolsey.
    c. John Calvin.
    d. St. Thomas Aquinas.

14. Queen Elizabeth of England supported the Dutch in the rebellion against Spain because:
    a. she supported political revolution of all kinds.
    b. she wanted to control Dutch trade.
    c. as a defender of Protestantism she sided with Dutch Protestants against Catholic Spain.
    d. she wanted to conquer Holland.

15. Which of the following groups did not benefit from inflation and the Price Revolution that hit England in the mid-1500s?
    a. the aristocracy.
    b. the landed gentry.
    c. yeomen farmers.
    d. wool merchants.

Short Essays

Answer the following questions in a brief paragraph.

1. How did native Americans first come into the Americas, and where did they settle? (pp. 6–8)

2. What made the life of European peasants so difficult and demanding? (pp. 12–15)

3. What was the status of women in European society during the 1500s and 1600s? (pp. 12–15)

4. Why did the Catholic Church have such a strong hold on the population of Europe after A.D. 1000? (pp. 17–18)

5. What changes occurred in Europe during the Renaissance, from the 1300s into the 1500s, to help prepare European states for the age of exploration and discovery? (pp. 18–20)

6. What enabled the small state of Portugal to seize the lead in the great surge of European expansion? (pp. 20–22)

7. Why did the Spanish find it so easy to conquer the native groups of the Americas in the early 1500s? (pp. 22–27)

8. In what three major areas did Martin Luther's teachings differ from Roman Catholic doctrine? (pp. 27–30)

9. What three great historical changes in England in the 1500s resulted in transatlantic migration and English settlement in North America in the 1600s? (pp. 32–35)

ANSWERS

Identification

1. Olmec
2. Mexico
3. maize
4. Cahokia
5. serfs
6. Italy
7. *The Prince*
8. pepper
9. *reconquista*
10. Ferdinand; Isabella
11. Hernando Cortés
12. Moctezuma
13. Martin Luther
14. predestination

15. mercantilism
16. joint-stock

Self-Test

Multiple Choice

1. b.
2. c.
3. d.
4. b.
5. d.
6. a.
7. c.
8. a.
9. b.
10. a.
11. a.
12. b.
13. c.
14. c.
15. a.

Short Essays

1. Indians migrated across a wide land bridge, over what is now the Bering Strait, that, because of glaciation, was above the level of the ocean about 30,000 to 10,000 years ago. In that period Asian peoples migrated across all the Americas as far as the tip of South America.

2. The primitive means of production meant that yields were minimal. Life was a continual struggle against ever-recurring famine. During these periods, death rates soared, especially during certain times of the year. Life was short, isolated, and brutish.

3. Women lived a constant round of pregnancy and childbirth, and generally died before men did. Though some peasant women worked for aristocrats, most married peasant farmers and surrendered all their property and civil rights. After her husband's death, the only rights a woman had was to a dower. In general, women's lives in Europe were very restricted.

4. In a chaotic and harsh world, the Church brought authority and discipline to society. Catholic theology assured that any individual could achieve salvation by living a sinless life, receiving the sacraments, and accepting the teachings of the Church. Central to those teachings was the idea that God was an active force in the world. Peasants celebrated God's power in a spiritual calendar that followed the seasons. In this way, religion gave meaning to everyday life.

5. The rise of long-distance trade and the development of a merchant class provided a necessary impetus for further discovery and exploration. Across Europe, monarchs formed alliances with these new merchant classes to develop more centralized nation-states. These new nation-states, in search of further riches to strengthen the state, would lead the way in discovery and exploration.

6. Portugal had good location, a seafaring tradition, and a humanist explorer prince. Most important, it had a coherent nation-state that was stable and at peace.

7. With their advanced military technology, the Spanish had a significant military advantage over the native Americans. But this advantage could not alone counterbalance the great population advantage of the Indians. The Spanish were helped by effective organization and leadership, skillfull manipulation and use of disputes among the Indians, luck, and a silent ally, disease, which swept through the Indian populations. With the aid of these, the organized, technologically superior Spanish overwhelmed the divided, confused, and demoralized Indian peoples.

8. Luther condemned the Catholic practice of selling indulgences. He also opposed the Catholic view that one could achieve salvation by good works alone. Finally, he vested far more power in the word of God as presented in the Bible than in the role of the clergy in one's spiritual life.

9. An activist government, supported by merchants, stimulated national wealth through mercantilist policies and was essential in spurring English colonization. That same government, however, actively tried to quash religious dissent. The gentry, meanwhile, experienced a considerable rise in fortunes and gained political strength in government as a result of the Price Revolution, while the peasantry was left impoverished by the Price Revolution and the enclosure of their lands. Merchants, the gentry, peasants, and religious exiles would all play important roles in American colonization.

Chapter 2

The Invasion and Settlement of North America, 1550–1700

LEARNING OBJECTIVES

1. How does any country successfully establish a colony in another part of the world? Drawing on the English, French, Spanish, and Dutch experiences in North America through the 1690s, examine how motivations, goals, organization, strategy, and the conditions settlers encountered affected the outcome of a colonial venture. By 1690, which European country had been most successful at colonization? Why?

2. The European colonization of North America did not occur on a blank slate. The native peoples and the environment that Europeans encountered fundamentally shaped their colonial experiences. How did the native Americans transform English colonization in North America?

3. Different European peoples with different colonial goals and strategies colonized North America. Yet, in the Southwest, the Southeast, and the Northeast, the impact of European colonization on the native peoples, as well as their response, was very similar. How do you explain this paradox?

4. Which social group from England, in which English colony in North America, do you think came closest to achieving their goals in the seventeenth century?

5. The English colonial experience in North America in the seventeenth century established some of the fundamental characteristics of American society, economy, politics, and culture. What are some of these characteristics, and how did they affect subsequent events?

CHAPTER SUMMARY

Following the lead of Spain, which extended its empire into North America in the late sixteenth and early seventeenth century, the French, English, and Dutch sought to establish permanent settlements in North America. The encounter between each group and the native peoples profoundly altered and shaped the character of each colony. As native peoples' lives were transformed by trade, the loss of land, and disease, they responded in increasingly desperate ways. Though each colony developed differently from the way the founders had intended, it nevertheless laid down some of the fundamental characteristics of American society and culture.

Imperial Conflicts and Rival Colonial Models (pp. 40–50)

Each country had its own specific goals and developed distinctive colonizing strategies to meet those goals. The Spanish and French achieved extensive control over Indian tribes by a combination of military and diplomatic strategies and religious conversion. The Dutch established small posts at which they carried on trade with the Indians. The English sought to establish settler colonies as outposts of English society in the New World.

New Spain: Colonization and Conversion

In the 1530s and 1540s, a number of Spanish adventurers and explorers, driven by a quest for gold and wealth, ventured into southern North America. Initially, the Spanish viewed this as a military effort, and the adventurers found themselves fighting the native peoples. The Spanish established military forts on the coast of Florida and the Carolinas. In 1573, the Spanish changed their strategy and sent missionaries instead of military adventurers to pacify, convert, and control the Indians at outpost missions. From these towns and missions, the Spanish demanded tributes and instituted a system of forced labor. The Indians responded with a series of revolts, though they eventually succumbed. The Spanish were so taken aback by the heavy costs of exploration that they decided to wait until the late eighteenth century to colonize California.

New France: Furs and Souls

The French conferred on a settlement company a monopoly over the fur trade and the rights to extensive lands distributed to settlers. In contrast to England, however, peasants in France retained control over their lands and thus had little incentive to resettle on the poorer lands of New France. Few, therefore, joined the enterprise. As a result, a small population of administrators, traders, and Jesuit missionaries established extensive control over native peoples through trade and conversion across a vast extent of North America. Traders pursued trading arrangements with native peoples far to the west and south. Meanwhile, French missionaries, instead of coercing native peoples, achieved conversions by understanding Indian ideas, concerns, and needs and relating Christian doctrine to them. Even so, New France was only a moderate commercial and cultural success.

New Netherland: Commerce

The Dutch developed trading outposts along the coast of North America as extensions of the activities of the Dutch West India Company. They tried to attract settlers and to protect the outposts from Indians and other Europeans by granting extensive tracts of land along the Hudson River to Dutch proprietors. Only one proprietor was able to attract settlers. The policy failed to protect the colony from disputes and wars with the Indians, and from internal dissension among diverse settlers. The weak small colony was easily taken by the English, who renamed it New York in 1664.

The First English Model: Tobacco and Settlers

The Virginia Company launched its first colonial venture to establish an economic outpost in Virginia in 1607. The adventurers and seekers of fortune who established Jamestown had few, if any, survival skills. More interested in looking for gold than in planting crops, the settlers relied on their own meager supplies and on the Indians' help for food. When they alienated the Indians, their food supply was cut off and most of the settlers perished over the winter. The efforts of subsequent leaders to impose discipline enabled the colony to survive from one year to the next, but just barely. Within ten years, the Virginia Company, to draw settlers to the colony, had instituted the headright system, developed tobacco as a cash crop, and established local government. The strategy worked, but as settlers spread farther across the wilderness, Indian resistance increased. An Indian uprising in 1622 inflicted heavy casualties on the colony. Distressed by its poor performance, King James assumed control over Virginia and, by instituting local government under royal control, established the model for royal colonies throughout North America.

The Chesapeake Experience
(pp. 50–56)

The Chesapeake colonies brought wealth to planters and religious freedom to Catholics in Maryland, but European settlement destroyed native American communities and subjected both European indentured servants and African slaves to ruthless exploitation for the sake of profit.

Settling the Tobacco Colonies

The Chesapeake colonies made money, but at a considerable moral and social cost. While Virginia became a royal colony, a royal charter made Lord Baltimore, a Catholic, proprietor of Maryland. Baltimore carefully planned the development of the small colony both as a refuge for Catholics and as a cash-crop colony. The tobacco boom assured its continued economic growth, but friction between Protestants and Catholics persisted. In both colonies, epidemic disease resulted in an extraordinarily high death rate among colonists. The high death rate disrupted families, shifted gender roles, and eroded social institutions.

Servants and Masters

The headright system and a large demand for labor attracted many indentured servants to the Chesapeake colonies. Laborers were bound to a master for several years and compelled to work in often brutal conditions. They were not allowed to marry and were punished harshly for various infractions against a stringent legal code. While half the men died before they were freed, women—being generally in short supply in the Chesapeake—could achieve social mobility by marrying a landlord and sometimes even their master.

The Seeds of Revolt

A collapse in the price of tobacco by 1660 increased social friction throughout the Chesapeake colonies. Lower prices forced many planters deeper into debt even as they grabbed the last available lands in the colonies. Low prices all but eliminated the prospect that a newly freed servant could become a planter. More and more former servants were forced to lease lands from planters as tenant farmers or farm laborers or head west to the frontier in search of cheap land. Government officials exacerbated the tensions by granting more lands to a privileged elite and trying to exclude landless freemen, who by the 1670s constituted half the population, from voting. This effort to translate the widening distance between classes into a political oligarchy sowed the seeds of revolt.

Bacon's Rebellion

As settlers in the western part of the colony, increasingly resentful of the social and political exploitation in the colony, pushed on to the last Indian lands left in Virginia, the pressure boiled over. When westerners led by newcomer Nathaniel Bacon, a member of the governor's council, started a war against the Indians, the governor condemned them, expelled Bacon from the council, and ordered his arrest. Bacon, however, forced the governor to back down and institute reforms. Still not satisfied, Bacon rebelled openly and civil war broke out, only to end when Bacon died suddenly. To prevent further rebellions, the elite, after punishing the rebels, returned voting rights to the lower class, reduced taxes, and instituted an expansionist land policy. They also looked for ways to acquire more control over a labor force that was needed to grow tobacco.

Puritan New England (pp. 56–63)

In contrast to Virginia, New England was settled by dissenters seeking religious freedom. New England Puritans arrived as families and established small villages of yeomen farmers centered around their churches and governed by a strict ethical code.

The Puritan Migration

The first wave of migrants to New England traveled as a joint-stock company and established the Plymouth colony in 1620. Only half survived the first winter, but community discipline thereafter helped the colony to thrive and grow. Named Pilgrims because they had come to America as a holy pilgrimage, the residents of Plymouth nevertheless maintained a separation of church and state authority. As King Charles I increasingly oppressed Puritans in England, a second wave of migrants under John Winthrop left for America to establish a pure, model Christian community. They settled Massachusetts Bay colony, near Plymouth, but, unlike the Puritans, firmly linked the powers of church and state, becoming a religious commonwealth.

Religion and Society, 1630–1670

The Puritans gave the process of settlement and subsequent American history a moral dimension. They sought not only worldly wealth and security but also a place in which they could establish a purified "true" church as a model for the reformation of the Anglican Church. Church membership was limited to those "saints" who were able to demonstrate that they had had a conversion experience and thus might be among the elect. Sometimes members joined together in a collective covenant with God. They were also given influence over secular affairs, transforming Massachusetts Bay into a theocracy. Always a minority of the population, church members ran self-governing congregations. By accepting new membership applications, appointing, screening, and firing ministers, scrutinizing members, and purging heresies and expelling heretics, the elect exerted considerable moral, political, and social power.

The Puritan Imagination and Witchcraft

Like other European peasants imbued with the pagan tradition that still underlay the Christian cosmos, as well as that of the native Americans, the Puritans believed that nature contained spiritual forces. They also believed that both God and evil spirits expressed their will or power through natural signs, miracles, invisible "grace," or negative forces often relayed by wizards or witches. The Puritans' doubts about their original mission and a variety of pressures in the congregations and villages increased their tendency to explain events as the result of evil forces. Not surprisingly, arrests and convictions for witchcraft increased, culminating in a dramatic outbreak of witch-hunting in 1692. In Salem, frustrated farmers resentful of wealthier church members retaliated by accusing scores of their neighbors and friends of witchcraft. Of the 175 people arrested, 20 were executed before proceedings were stopped because of unsubstantiated evidence.

A Yeoman Society, 1670–1700

The Puritans believed that some inequality of wealth was part of the natural order of things. Nevertheless, most townsmen received sufficiently significant tracts in fee simple to establish themselves as yeomen farmers. This relatively equal distribution of land enabled most men to become involved in local politics and gave them unprecedented political power. Even though the dynamics of market competition would further differentiate wealth and push many farmers into tenancy, most settlers in New England achieved a better life than they had had in England.

The Indians' New World
(pp. 63–67)

Native Americans responded to the arrival and expansion of the settlement of European "invaders" by resisting, trying to cope, or immigrating to the West. Whatever their response, however, the Indians found their world fundamentally changed.

Puritans and Pequots

Though one might have expected otherwise, the moralist Puritans, convinced that God was on their side, often treated the Indians as brutally as the Spanish had. When the Indians violently resisted, the Puritans retaliated with brutal attacks. Indians who chose not to resist allowed themselves to be converted in "praying towns." Attempts at conversion provided Puritans with a buffer against further Indian attacks, and Indians with a temporary haven.

Metacom's War

Metacom, the leader of the Wampanoag tribe, believed conversion was not the answer. He forged an alliance of smaller tribes and attacked white settlements across central New England in 1675 and 1676. In retaliation, the Puritans attacked the Indians. They inflicted massive casualties and sold hundreds of captives into slavery. The surviving Indians resigned themselves to losing both their land and their culture.

The Fur Trade and the Inland Peoples

Farther inland, the fur trade transformed Indian life. European traders brought disease, alcohol, and European trade goods. These conditions reduced populations, increased social disorder, and undermined native cultures. The dynamics of the fur trade also intensified intra-tribal warfare, shifted power to younger, more aggressive warriors, and fundamentally transformed the Indians' spiritual relationship with nature. In the end, the Indians, as much as the Europeans, lived in a New World.

EXPANDED TIMELINE

1539–1543 **Coronado and de Soto explore northern lands**
After the conquest of Mexico, the Spanish moved north to explore the southern reaches of North America. In 1539–1543, Hernando de Soto attempted to invade and conquer Florida. In the Southwest, Francisco Vásquez de Coronado launched an expedition in search of the seven cities of Cíbola. When he found only impoverished Zuni towns, he continued on to discover the Grand Canyon, encountered the Pueblo peoples, and even reached southern Kansas.

1565 **Spain establishes St. Augustine, Florida**
Spain established St. Augustine as a fort to secure the coast of Florida and subjugate nearby peoples. St. Augustine provided a foothold that Spain used to control the Florida peninsula for the next two centuries.

1598 **Acoma rebellion in New Mexico**
When a Spanish military leader led an expedition to establish a trading outpost and fort among the Acoma people in New Mexico and brutally seized supplies and murdered and raped those who resisted, the Acoma rose in revolt, killing eleven Spanish soldiers. In retaliation, the Spanish looted the Pueblo and massacred eight hundred men, women, and children. Confronted by a widespread revolt, they then retreated.

1603–1625 **King James I of England**
James put aside Elizabeth's long feud with Spain and promoted England as a colonial as well as a commercial and political power. Seeing a variety of benefits in the establishment of colonies in America, King James encouraged continued settlement in North America. He also, however, intensified persecution of Puritans and Presbyterians and exerted his "divine right" to rule. He thus increased the power of the state through colonization, while pursuing policies that assured that many emigrants would be religious exiles, thereby increasing order at home.

Expanded Timeline

1607 — **English adventurers settle Jamestown, Virginia**
Under a charter from James I, the Virginia Company of London established the first permanent English colony at Jamestown in the spring of 1607. Disorganized and without focus, the colonists sought gold rather than worry about food production. As a result, less than half of them made it through the first winter. In the end, reinforcements, stronger discipline, and better organization enabled the colony to survive.

1608 — **Samuel de Champlain founds Quebec**
The first permanent French colony in North America was established at Quebec by Samuel de Champlain. Isolated and very small, the settlement survived only by establishing an alliance with the Huron to protect it against the Iroquois.

1613 — **Dutch set up fur-trading post on Manhattan Island**
Interested in the New World for commercial rather than spiritual purposes, the Dutch established a trading post on Manhattan Island at the mouth of the river Dutch explorer Henry Hudson had named for himself in 1609. From there, the Dutch government expanded its fur-trading stations throughout the mid-Atlantic region.

1619 — **First Africans arrive in Chesapeake**
The first Africans in the English New World colonies were brought to Virginia as slaves. Chesapeake planters began to import African slaves to replace indentured servants, whom they had to free after a given time and who were therefore less profitable.

Virginia House of Burgesses convened
In the late 1610s, the Virginia Company again tried to make the colony of Virginia work. In 1617, the company established the headright system. It also formed the House of Burgesses, a local legislative body that was given the power to make laws and levy taxes, though both could be vetoed by the governor or nullified by the company. By providing the incentives of land and local self-government, the company attracted a wave of new immigrants through 1622.

1620 — **Pilgrims found Plymouth colony**
"Separatist" Puritans left England to establish their own churches, spread the gospel, and, by example, purify the Anglican Church. First, they went to Holland, but, finding their identity threatened, they decided to make a pilgrimage to America—hence the name Pilgrims. They formed their own government, and, after a harsh initial winter, worked hard to establish an orderly and thriving town on the coast of Massachusetts, south of the current site of Boston.

1620–1660 — **Tobacco boom in Chesapeake colonies**
Growing demand in England for Virginia tobacco caused an escalation of prices and a boom in production. The boom came to an end in the 1660s, when overproduction and oppressive duties imposed by England cut demand and prices dramatically. This decline in the market triggered a social and economic crisis in the Chesapeake colonies.

1621 — **Dutch West India Company chartered**
The Dutch government established its presence in the Atlantic by chartering the Dutch West India Company. The company established a monopoly in the slave trade and plundered the coast of Brazil and Spanish colonies in the Caribbean. It also took over Hudson River trading posts and set up new trading posts along the central coast of North America. The rising power of the Dutch in the Atlantic would eventually force the English to challenge them.

1622 — **Opechancanough's uprising**
The rapid influx of settlers to Virginia between 1617 and 1622 dramatically increased tension on Indian lands. Colonists occupied lands the Indians had cleared and were still using. Alarmed, the Indian leader Opechancanough formed an alliance and launched a surprise attack on the settlers, killing nearly a third of the population. The English waged war against the Indians, killing hundreds and, by destroying their crops and houses, leaving the survivors without food or shelter.

1624 — **Virginia becomes a royal colony**
The massacre of 1622 convinced James I that the Virginia Company was badly managed. As a result, he dissolved the company and took over the colony. James I allowed the House of Burgesses, led by a governor, to remain. He also established the Church of England. Virginia thus became the model for all subsequent royal colonies.

1625–1649 — **King Charles I of England**
King Charles I, a strong supporter of the Anglican Church, was also sympathetic to the Roman Catholic Church and used his influence to push Anglican doctrine back toward Catholic doctrine. Appalled, a vocal Puritan minority in Parliament protested. Charles responded by dissolving Parliament and ruling by "divine right" for ten years. Having thwarted the Puritans in government, he then appointed William Laud archbishop of Canterbury. Laud launched a campaign to oust hundreds of Puritan ministers from their pulpits. Charles's and Archbishop Laud's actions convinced thousands of Puritans that it was time to leave England. The majority who stayed would rise up against him, embroiling England in civil war.

1639 — **Puritans found Massachusetts Bay colony**
Convinced that in order to purify the Anglican Church they would have to leave England, nine hundred Puritans, led by John Winthrop, immigrated to

Massachusetts Bay to create literally a "new" England. Carrying their charter with them, they established their own government. By requiring that those who could vote and hold office be members of a Puritan congregation, the Puritans linked church and state into a religious commonwealth. By 1640, about ten thousand Puritans and as many non-Puritans had followed them to this Puritan "City upon a Hill."

1634 **Maryland settled**
King Charles I favored his friends with extensive land grants in North America. He made Cecilus Calvert, Lord Baltimore, proprietor of Maryland. As proprietor, Baltimore sold lands and encouraged settlement by Catholic refugees fleeing persecution in England as well as Protestants. The colony prospered during the tobacco boom. When religious friction between Catholics and Protestants threatened the peace of the colony, Lord Baltimore pressured the assembly to pass the Toleration Act. In general, though, Maryland would experience economic and social developments that were similar to those of its neighbor Virginia.

1636–1637 **Pequot War**
As Puritans moved into the Connecticut River Valley, they encroached on the lands of the small Pequot tribe. Like other Indians, the Pequots resisted by attacking settlers. The Puritans and their Indian allies retaliated by launching a brutal attack against the main Pequot town. Five hundred were killed, and the survivors were hunted down and sold into slavery.

Roger Williams and Anne Hutchinson banished
Puritan theology upheld the sole authority of the minister to interpret the Bible for the congregation. By such meditation, each individual reaffirmed his or her participation in the covenant between the congregation and God. While Puritan theology, therefore, required the role of the minister, it also left the door open to individual initiative in securing, working for, and discerning one's status in regard to salvation. In 1635, the Puritans banished Roger Williams, who established Rhode Island, for challenging the establishment of the church and its power over members. Similarly, Anne Hutchinson was tried for heresy in 1637 when she argued that she could directly communicate with God through his revelation, thus diminishing the role of the minister. Rhode Island prospered as a democratic-minded enterprise. Anne Hutchinson moved first to Rhode Island, and then to Long Island where she was killed in an Indian raid in 1643.

1640s **Puritan revolution in England**
In response to the arbitrary rule of Charles I and the religious persecution of William Laud, the archbishop of Canterbury, the Puritans rebelled in 1642 and fought a four-year civil war against the king. Oliver Cromwell, the leader of the Puritan forces, established himself as ruler of a republican commonwealth. In 1649, the Puritan Parliament had Charles I executed. When order broke down, Cromwell established himself as a dictator, weakening support for the republican experiment.

Iroquois go to war over fur trade
The Five Nations of the Iroquois of New York launched a long-term war against neighboring tribes to gain control of the fur trade between the Atlantic coast and the Great Lakes. In the course of their efforts, they nearly destroyed several tribes, and the remaining members of several more migrated west. When those refugees regrouped and formed an alliance with the French, they gradually weakened the Iroquois. The Iroquois were eventually forced to give up their plans to monopolize the fur trade and agreed to the Grand Settlement in 1701.

1651 **First Navigation Act**
In the midst of political revolution, Parliament took action to wrest control of trade in the North Atlantic from the Dutch. Drawing on the theory of mercantilism, they excluded Dutch ships from trade within the British system, compelled the colonies to ship "enumerated" goods to London, and raised import duties. English goods, produced in English colonies and traded through the English capital in English ships, provided more money for English people.

1660 **Restoration of English monarchy**
When the dictatorial Oliver Cromwell died, Parliament reinstituted the monarchy, calling Charles II to the throne. The brief period of Puritan rule had ended, and the Church of England was restored.

Poor tobacco market begins
The decline in the price of tobacco in the 1660s set in motion a number of forces that would lead to widespread social and political discord in Virginia. Lower returns on tobacco farming eliminated opportunities for success among all but the largest planters. Freedmen were forced to become tenants or farm laborers, with no prospect of social mobility. As some planters recouped losses with rents from tenants, economic differentiation and social and political tensions increased.

1664 **English conquer New Netherland**
New Netherland, after forty years of existence, remained weak and internally divided. In the Anglo-Dutch war of 1664, residents of New Amsterdam did not resist English forces and accepted English rule. The English renamed New Amsterdam, New York.

1675–1676 **Bacon's rebellion**
In search of more land, disgruntled freedmen, yeomen farmers, servants, and laborers on the Virginia frontier launched an Indian war in 1675. When challenged by

Governor Berkeley, Nathaniel Bacon, the leader of the freedmen, rebelled against the governor and took over the colony. Bacon's sudden death enabled the governor to regain the upper hand. In retaliation, Berkeley defeated the rebel army and had its leaders executed. In response to the rebellion, the elite would dramatically change both the labor system upon which they relied and their style of political leadership. For this reason, Bacon's rebellion was a pivotal event in Virginia's history.

Metacom's uprising

The demand for land by Puritans in New England created pressures in the Indian population on the frontier that were similar to those that existed in Virginia. Though some Indians were drawn into "praying towns," which the Puritans founded to convert them, many others resisted this effort. In 1675, Metacom, the leader of the Wampanoag tribe, formed an alliance of local tribes and launched an attack against Puritan settlements across the New England frontier. After two years of bitter fighting, the Puritans prevailed by nearly destroying the Indian population.

Expansion of African slavery in the Chesapeake region

In response to the disruptions of Bacon's rebellion, and to changes in the international labor market, planters across the Chesapeake gradually switched from white indentured servitude to black slavery as the labor system for cultivating tobacco. Slaves could be held for their entire lives, without any prospect of freedom. This provided the planters with a steady labor supply, while eliminating the demands for freedom made by servants.

1680 ### Popé's rebellion in New Mexico

In the seventeenth century, Spanish settlers and missionaries moved into what is now New Mexico and established a tribute and forced-labor system to control the Indians. The pueblos in which the Indian people lived were severely threatened. In response, an Indian priest named Popé launched a rebellion against the Spanish that the settlers were unable to quell for a decade. Finally, a compromise was reached: The Indian people accepted Spanish rule, and, in return, the Spanish allowed them to practice their own religion, helped them to defend themselves against nomadic invaders, and did away with the forced-labor system.

1692 ### Salem witchcraft trials

As social and political pressures intensified in many New England towns and villages, an increased number of Puritans became convinced that their calling was endangered. More began to see in nature and the behavior of others the influence of evil spirits or spiritual forces. In Salem, in 1692, these pressures boiled over when frustrated townsmen charged more than 200 people in the town with witchcraft. Things quickly got out of hand when local judges, accepting unsubstantiated evidence for indictments, arrested 175 people, put many of them on trial, and convicted and executed 20, 19 of whom were women. This was the last outbreak of alleged witchcraft in New England.

GLOSSARY

pueblos In the sixteenth century, the American Southwest was inhabited by Indians who lived in large, multistory structures called pueblos—named after the people themselves—that were constructed of brick or adobe and built into cliffs, often near rivers or other sources of water. From these elevated positions, the Pueblo could see into the distance and provide early warning of outsiders approaching. (p. 44)

encomenderos The Spanish colonized by giving huge grants, or *encomenderos*, to prominent and well-connected settlers. To promote the settlement process, owners were expected to develop the land. To do this, they were given the right to exact tributes and forced labor from the natives. (p. 44)

bullion Another word for specie, or gold or silver. During the sixteenth century, the Spanish fleet transported the equivalent of millions of dollars of gold and silver bars and coins from Central America to Spain. (p. 44)

repartimiento The forced system of labor employed on the encomienda—the vast farms granted to Spanish *encomenderos*—was the *repartimiento*. (p. 44)

Jesuits The Catholic religious order of priests, the Society of Jesus, are known as Jesuits. Founded by St. Ignatius Loyola, the order sought to convert souls in New France through missionary work. It often did this by showing potential converts how Christian values applied to their concerns. (p. 46)

longhouse The Iroquois towns were organized into a series of large communal buildings in which members of an entire clan lived. When the various Iroquois tribes joined to form a political confederation, the Five Nations, it was called the "longhouse" confederation. (p. 46)

manitou The belief in manitou—strong spirits or supernatural forces—manifests itself in many native religions, especially among the Algonquians. Manitou were generally viewed as representatives of nature, often as animals, although they could take human form. At first, the Algonquians and the Iroquois believed the Jesuit missionaries were manitous because of their various powers, but eventually the inability of the Jesuit god to protect them from disease, famine, and enemy attack convinced them otherwise. (p. 47)

patroon The Dutch sought to encourage settlement of New Netherland by offering privileged Dutch people large estates. The proprietors, or patroons, of these estates were promised title to the land if they brought fifty tenants onto it within four years. The program failed—only one patroon fulfilled the requirements—leaving the Dutch with few permanent settlers in the important region north of New Amsterdam. (p. 48)

corporate colony Exploration and settlement were expensive undertakings that required a wealthy royal patron or creative financing. In the early 1600s, English bankers and merchants introduced the concept of joint-stock companies, which shared the risk and profit of establishing colonies and led to the founding of corporate colonies. This device was used extensively by England; for example, Virginia was a corporate colony under title of the Virginia Company of London. (p. 48)

headright To attract settlers to Virginia and enhance the colony's chances of success, the Virginia Company introduced the headright system in 1617. This program granted to every arriving head of a household 50 acres of land for himself and 50 additional acres for every adult family member or servant he brought with him into the colony. The plan worked by rapidly increasing immigration into Virginia. (p. 49)

royal colony A colony founded by the crown issuing a charter was a royal colony. When James I dissolved the Virginia Company in 1624, he issued a charter for Virginia, making it a royal colony. He maintained a House of Burgesses, appointed a governor and a council, and established the Anglican Church, thus setting a precedent for other royal colonies in North America. (p. 50)

proprietary colony A colony founded by the crown's issuing a charter to a specific individual as proprietor was a proprietary colony. The proprietor had the power to dispose of the land and to organize and run the colony as he wished. Maryland and Pennsylvania, founded by charters issued to Cecilus Calvert and William Penn, respectively, were both proprietary colonies. Because both proprietors organized their colony as they wished, each became a distinctive colony. (p. 51)

indentured servants People who wanted to start life anew in America but could not pay for their passage frequently negotiated with merchants for a labor contract of four or five years of service with room and board in exchange for the price of a ticket. Upon arrival in the Chesapeake, the merchants then signed over the contracted labor to planters who needed laborers to work the tobacco fields. Though many indentured servants came in hopes of finding a better life, the work was brutal and exploitative. Many died before the end of their indenture, and only a few of those who completed their contract managed to escape poverty. (p. 52)

Navigation Acts According to mercantilist theory, colonies existed for the benefit of the mother country. By producing a crop or a product that couldn't be produced or acquired at home, the colony could enhance national wealth by reducing imports as well as by increasing trade. This would happen, however, only if the colony traded solely with the mother country and the trade was carried out by its own merchants. As the English colonies developed, Parliament sought to assure these ends by passing a series of Navigation Acts. The trade laws prohibited foreigners from trading with the English colonies, required colonial goods to be shipped to London, and forbade colonists to trade directly with foreigners. (p. 53)

enumerated The Navigation Acts required that certain goods produced in the colonies be traded only to England. These articles, including tobacco from the Chesapeake, were "enumerated." (p. 53)

social revolution A dramatic or total change in the social hierarchy. In a social revolution, those who were ruled would rise up and take over from those who previously ruled. In this sense, Bacon's rebellion was an attempted social revolution. (p. 55)

Separatists During the Reformation, the Anglican Church was beset by a variety of Protestant groups that wanted to reform, or "purify," it. Some sought to reform the Church from within, either by pressing for reforms at home or by establishing a pure church as a model of reform somewhere else and bringing it back to reform the Church. These groups, including the Massachusetts Bay Puritans, were "non-Separatists." Other Protestants thought reform was pointless and simply separated from the Church and formed their own independent congregations. These groups, such as the Pilgrims, were called Separatists. Because both kinds of Puritans believed in the autonomy of each individual congregation, both were Congregationalists. (p. 59)

predestination Most Puritans followed the teachings of John Calvin (see Chapter 1). John Calvin argued, in contrast to Catholic theology, that God was all-powerful and man was corrupt and weak and thus unable to know God's eternal design. In particular, Calvin argued that God had chosen a few "elect" people for salvation while condemning the rest of mankind to eternal damnation. He emphasized that one could never really know who these people were and, therefore, one could do nothing to improve one's chances of attaining salvation. Though the Puritans believed that no one could effect his or her salvation, they nevertheless sought various ways to deal with the agony of the uncertainty of salvation. (p. 59)

Saints   Only individuals who believed themselves, by various means, to be among the "elect" were allowed to be members of a Puritan church. The Saints set very high standards for themselves and for others, making them a minority of the population. (p. 59)

conversion experience   Some Saints argued that they acquired their status by means of an infusion of their soul with the grace of God. In this experience, they were literally "born again" and could therefore expect—though they had to admit they were still never certain—that salvation was at hand. (p. 59)

covenant   Some Puritans focused on a contract with God in which they recognized God's power and lived according to his laws in exchange for his recognizing them as his "chosen people." Covenants, often contracted by a church of elect Saints, bound church members together and made each member responsible for the soul of the others. (p. 60)

antinomian   Puritans were beset by a range of heresies that questioned the clergy's role in helping members to achieve salvation. Anne Hutchinson argued that if one was on one's own in terms of salvation, there was nothing to stop an individual from receiving a direct revelation from God. This "covenant of grace" directly to the individual from God, not good works or intensive Bible study with ministers of the "word" of God (hence antinomian, "against the word"), was evidence of the bestowal of salvation. Anne Hutchinson was banished for this heresy, which challenged the power of the clergy. (p. 60)

proprietor and **fee simple**   Puritans merged the church and the town to create a new social order based on independent landowners. A group of men who had formed a church were granted, as proprietors, title to a township often up to 6 by 10 miles in size. The proprietors then distributed the land to as many eligible men as applied until it was disposed of. Because they believed in a social hierarchy, they did distribute the land unevenly, based on the wealth of the applicant. All the same, even the smallest plots were more than sufficient to support a family, and were granted in fee simple, giving each grantee and his heirs outright ownership of the land. In addition, each proprietor and grantee had the right to vote and participate in town government. These actions laid the foundations of a society based on the independent yeoman farmer. This method was repeated many times, resulting in the formation of hundreds of towns across New England in the seventeenth century. (p. 62)

town meeting and **selectmen**   Just as they acquired their share of the land, so, too, each settler had a political voice in the town meetings. Voting rights were restricted to adult male householders. Each year, the town meeting would choose selectmen to oversee community affairs; typically, these were men of wealth and property. Although this was not a fully democratic system—women had a voice but no vote, and selectmen were usually gentlemen of means—it gave settlers in New England a greater say in organizing their everyday affairs than colonists in the South or peasants in Europe had. (p. 63)

totem   A totem is a figurative sculpture or object, usually an animal, that symbolically represents the soul or spirit that the animal, like everything in nature, possessed. Each family, tribe, or nation was represented by a totem. To maintain the balance of spirits, Indians venerated each totem and paid their respects by offering prayers and carrying out reverential practices that atoned for the hunt. When the market mentality of the fur trade penetrated Indian life, increased disputes and wars over control of hunting territories, combined with relentless hunting by the Indians, threw the natural spiritual world into upheaval, increasing, in the Indians' view, the displeasure of the spirits of the animal and natural world. (p. 67)

yeoman   A yeoman farmer owned the land he worked outright. Therefore he had complete freedom over the land and could sell, exchange, or deed it to whomever he wished. This ownership of land was the basis of a yeoman farmer's social and political freedom and autonomy. (p. 85)

IDENTIFICATION

Identify by filling in the blanks.

1. The Spanish explorer who sought the seven cities of Cíbola in the Southwest was _____. (p. 40)

2. Spanish voyages of discovery along the Atlantic coast included expeditions into a waterway the Spanish called Bahía de Santa María. To the English, this came to be known as _____. (p. 41)

3. French claims to territory in North America were established in the 1530s, when _____ sailed into the Gulf of St. Lawrence to find a northwest passage. (p. 46)

4. The founder of Quebec in 1608 was _____. (p. 46)

5. When Jesuit missionaries first arrived in New France, the Indians welcomed them as _____, powerful spiritual beings with magical powers. (p. 47)

6. The early governor of Virginia who ran the colony like a dictator and saved it from collapse was _____. (p. 49)

7. Powhatan's brother and successor, who was responsible for the Indian attack on Virginia in 1622, was _____. (p. 50)

8. In 1649, the Maryland assembly passed legislation known as the _____, which granted religious freedom to all Christians. (p. 51)

9. The corrupt governor of Virginia between 1642 and 1652, famous for putting down a second Indian revolt in 1644, and appointed again in 1660, and who then faced an open rebellion led by Nathaniel Bacon was _____. (pp. 54–55)

10. The leader of the Pilgrims at Plymouth colony was _____. (p. 56)

11. The well-educated and highly regarded country squire who led the Puritan exodus from England to Massachusetts Bay in 1630 was _____. (p. 58)

12. Among the more prominent dissenters in Massachusetts, a Puritan wife, mother, and midwife, _____ was accused and convicted of antinomian heresy and banished from the colony. (p. 60)

13. The Puritans, in response to concerns about the failure of the younger generation to gain entrance into the church, made membership hereditary and salvation more predictable in 1662 by passing the _____. (p. 61)

14. The Puritans called Metacom, chief of the Wampanoag tribe, _____. (p. 65)

15. One of the prominent ministers of Puritan New England quoted most often in the text, who expressed strong views on theology, mused on the spiritual meaning of natural forces, and interpreted the fate of the Indians, was _____. (p. 65)

FEATURES EXERCISES

American Lives

Luis de Velasco/Opechancanough/ Massatamohtnock: A Case of Possible Multiple Identities (pp. 42–43)

History is often an account or a story based on scattered pieces of evidence. Often, all we have is information about someone, or some occurrence, at one place or time and another piece of evidence about a person or event from a different place and time that seems to be connected to the first. One must fill in the gap between pieces of evidence with a theory or a story. This account tells the story of one man or perhaps three different men who lived during the century between 1540 and 1640. Whichever it was, the actions of this person or people are incompletely known. Whether one man or three, however, the experience described reflects the nature of the interaction among Europeans and native Americans during the course of European colonization of North America and demonstrates how individuals could indeed shape its course. As you read the intriguing tale of "Multiple Identities," ask yourself:

1. What are the pieces of evidence on which the one-man theory is based? Do you find them convincing?

2. What do the man's motivations seem to have been at various stages of the story? Do similarities or even contradictions in these further support the view that this is the story of a single person?

3. In what ways did this individual shape the interaction between the Pamunkey and the Spanish and between the Powhatan confederacy and the English?

4. Does the characterization of this man convince you? Was he a confident figure who knew what he was doing all the time, or did he sometimes seem confused and unclear as to what action to take?

American Voices

A Franciscan Reflects on Spain's Policies in New Mexico (p. 45)

The Spanish conquest of the southwestern part of North America occurred as an extension of earlier

Spanish activities in Mexico. The Spanish government continued its policy of using conquistadors to explore the frontier, giving the conquistadors returns on whatever they were able to find. This policy seemed to work as long as the conquistadors actually succeeded in subjugating the people they encountered to Spanish rule. When Spanish forces were smaller and the native peoples more spread out, this military policy tended to backfire, setting off a series of Indian wars and rebellions. The Spanish responded by changing their relationship with the native peoples. Instead of conquest, they now sought pacification, to be carried out by missionaries rather than conquistadors. As you read, "A Franciscan Reflects on Spain's Policies in New Mexico," ask yourself:

1. How are the goals of a conquistador and a missionary different?
2. In what ways are the goals of a conquistador and a missionary in agreement?
3. How did the two goals merge together to form a new colonial policy?
4. What would the situation of the native peoples be like as a result of the implementation of this new policy?

Voices from Abroad

RICHARD FRETHORNE, Hard Times in Virginia (p. 54)

This letter describes the condition of an indentured servant in early seventeenth-century Virginia. Hard work, sickness, hunger, isolation, and fear have clearly taken all happiness out of Mr. Frethorne's life. Though no one would be content in such circumstances, the disappointed tone of his letter indicates that Frethorne had expected a much better life in Virginia. As you read "Hard Times in Virginia," ask yourself the following questions:

1. Can you explain how Frethorne came to be in these circumstances? Why is there sickness, hunger, isolation, and fear? What aspects of the settlement process and the environment have contributed to these conditions?
2. What does his letter say about the quality of community life in early Virginia? Why was society like this?
3. If conditions in Virginia were so bad, why do you suppose Frethorne went there? Are there any clues to his former condition in England?

American Voices

MARY ROWLANDSON, Captivity Narrative (p. 66)

The Puritans were both horrified and fascinated by the Indian wartime practice of taking captives, whom they hoped to exchange for Indian prisoners. For Puritans, captives taken by the Indians were deprived of Christian influence and exposed to the sin and degeneracy of Indian life, which was the devil's doing. A captive soul, therefore, was in danger of being lost to the devil, thus bringing into question the nature of the Puritan covenant with God. The Puritans, and Europeans in general, were horrified and dismayed when white captives became acculturated to and sometimes absorbed into Indian life. In return, few if any Indians could accustom themselves to the Christian life of the Puritans in "praying towns." Captivity narratives were, therefore, classic accounts that explored the struggle between good and evil, or God and the devil, or Puritans and Indians, as well as the nature of identity. As you read "A Captivity Narrative," ask yourself:

1. How did Mary Rowlandson react when she was first taken captive by the Indians? How did she change after the first couple of weeks? Do her reactions surprise you?
2. How was Rowlandson able to adjust so quickly to her captors? What was her attitude toward the Indians? What was their attitude toward her?
3. From the Puritan perspective, did Rowlandson succeed or fail to prevail against the Indians in this test of her faith? What evidence can you provide to support your answer?
4. Why did the Indians release her from captivity?

MAPS AND FIGURES

Map 2.1 New Spain Looks North (p. 41)

By the time the English were trying to establish their first North American colony at Jamestown, the Spanish conquistadors and explorers had already traversed a vast extent of the southern part of North America. This map highlights the extent of Spanish expeditions by superimposing them on a map of the United States. As you trace the journeys of different conquistadors, ask yourself the following questions:

1. Do the routes taken by the Spanish explorers indicate any strategy or goals?

2. Why did the Spanish seem to concentrate in the southwest and southeast corners of North America? What does this say about their understanding of the territory and their strategy?

3. Which native peoples did various conquistadors encounter?

4. What factors would cause the dispersal of villages across the colony? What factors explain why towns or villages were not established in certain areas?

5. Why, over time, would some nucleated towns disperse and others not disperse?

Map 2.3 River Plantations in Virginia (p. 52)

The settlement patterns of seventeenth-century Virginia resulted from a combination of factors. The headright system, indentured servitude, tobacco cultivation, the trading system, and geography all played a role. Examine this map closely. Ask yourself the following questions:

1. Geography of the rivers seems to have affected the location of plantations. Even so, large plantations were often 10 or more miles apart. Why?

2. How did the geography of the river affect the shipping of tobacco? Why would this arrangement tend to prevent the development of port towns?

3. How does the arrangement of the plantations in relation to Indian towns suggest social and political issues that Virginians would have to confront?

Map 2.5 Settlement Patterns in New England (p. 64)

The Puritans organized their towns, like the congregational churches to which they were attached, in a way that made them easily replicable, but with certain variations from one place to another. Towns, therefore, spread with churches across the New England landscape soon after the initial settlement of Massachusetts Bay. Examine this map closely, and ask yourself the following questions:

1. Is there any pattern to the arrangements of different types of towns? If so, what is it?

2. Can you relate that pattern to the immigration data presented in Map 2.4, "Puritan Migration to America"? Why might different areas in England have different town arrangements? Why, upon migrating to America, did people from different regions maintain the kinds of towns from which they had come?

3. Based on the general arrangement of the towns, what factors seemed to affect settlers in their decision to locate a town?

SELF-TEST

Multiple Choice

1. Among the English pirates who attacked Spanish ships to steal gold bullions being shipped from the Americas to Spain, the most famous was:
   a. Walter Raleigh.   c. Juan de Oñate.
   b. Francis Drake.   d. William Kieft.

2. In New Spain, the Spanish Crown often allowed privileged settlers to collect tribute from the natives through a system of forced labor called:
   a. *adelantado*.   c. *repartimiento*.
   b. *presidio*.   d. *encomendero*.

3. Most French missionaries in North America came from the religious order known as:
   a. Franciscans.   c. *coureurs de bois*.
   b. Jesuits.   d. Huguenots.

4. In 1609, Henry Hudson, an Englishman, discovered and named the Hudson River while exploring the Atlantic coast under the flag of:
   a. England.   c. the Netherlands.
   b. France.   d. Spain.

5. After founding New Netherland, the Dutch West India Company established trading posts in *all* of the following places *except*:
   a. Connecticut.   c. Pennsylvania.
   b. New Jersey.   d. Virginia.

6. In "Kieft's War" of the 1640s, the Dutch authorities tried to rid New Netherland of potential enemies by sending armed bands against:
   a. the Algonquian tribes.
   b. the Iroquois nations.
   c. patroons in the Hudson River Valley.
   d. English settlers in Massachusetts.

7. After some tensions between Virginia settlers and his native people, in 1609 Powhatan accepted the presence of the English by giving his daughter Pocahontas in marriage to:
   a. Henry Hudson.   c. John Rolfe.
   b. John Smith.   d. Walter Raleigh.

8. The colonial land system that provided 50 acres of land to the head of a household for every family

member or servant brought to America was known as:
a. freehold.   c. fee simple.
b. headright.   d. quitrent.

9. The Act of Trade and Navigation (1651) was intended to cut English colonial trade with non-English states, with the primary impact to be felt by the:
a. Spanish.   c. French.
b. Portuguese.   d. Dutch.

10. The "Manifesto and Declaration of the People" (1676), which advocated the death or eviction of all native Americans from Virginia and proposed an end to rule by the wealthy elite was written by:
a. William Berkeley.
b. Nathaniel Bacon.
c. the Green Spring faction.
d. John Winthrop.

11. In the 1630s, the Puritans of Massachusetts waged "war" and virtually eliminated the native people known as the:
a. Iroquois.   c. Pequot.
b. Huron.   d. Anasazi.

12. Puritan theology in England and America drew mainly on the teachings of:
a. John Calvin.   c. Martin Luther.
b. John Winthrop.   d. Jacobus Arminius.

13. In 1635, Roger Williams was banished from the Puritan colony for his heretical opposition to the authority of the state and ministers. He founded a new colony called:
a. Connecticut.   c. Maine.
b. Long Island.   d. Rhode Island.

14. A year later, Thomas Hooker left the Massachusetts Bay colony to establish another new colony called:
a. Maine.   c. New York.
b. Connecticut.   d. Rhode Island.

15. The fur trade affected Indian life in each of the following ways except:
a. undermined clan unity by intensifying disputes among Indian over rights to exclusive hunting grounds.
b. upset the spiritual balance of nature.
c. increased their standard of living and raised morale.
d. undermined traditional native skills and crafts by importation of European goods.

Short Essays

Answer the following questions in a brief paragraph.

1. How and why did the Spanish extend their colonial empire into the southern tier of North America? (pp. 40–46)

2. What was the French colonial strategy in North America? How did it affect the character of their colonies? (pp. 46–47)

3. Colonization was a learning process. What lessons did the English learn from their early efforts to establish a colony in Virginia? (pp. 48–50)

4. Why, in contrast to New England, did Virginia experience an internal social rebellion in the 1670s? What were the causes of Bacon's rebellion? (pp. 52–56)

5. Why were Puritans so sensitive to and beset by theological challenges or heresies? What impact did these issues have on Puritan life? (pp. 59–62)

6. What factors contributed to an outbreak of witchcraft trials in Salem, Massachusetts, in 1692? (pp. 61–62)

7. How did the Puritans' plan of merging church and town establish the foundations of a yeoman farmer's society? (pp. 62–63)

8. How did the fur trade transform both Europeans and Indians and the relationship between the two groups? (pp. 66–67)

ANSWERS

Identification

1. Francisco de Coronado
2. Chesapeake Bay
3. Jacques Cartier
4. Samuel de Champlain
5. manitou
6. John Smith
7. Opechancanough
8. Toleration Act
9. William Berkeley
10. William Bradford
11. John Winthrop
12. Anne Hutchinson
13. Halfway Covenant
14. King Philip
15. Cotton Mather

Self-Test

Multiple Choice

1. b.	6. b.	11. c.
2. c.	7. b.	12. a.
3. b.	8. b.	13. d.
4. c.	9. d.	14. b.
5. d.	10. b.	15. c.

Short Essays

1. The Spanish moved north in search of wealth, but also to safeguard their settlements farther south as well as the shipment of Spanish treasure to Europe. Initially, they advanced on military expeditions, but in time they switched to missionaries, who imposed a Spanish land and labor system to subjugate the native peoples. In the East, the Spanish established military outposts along the Atlantic coast.

2. The French never established a settler colony. Instead, a small population of merchants and traders established trade relations with the native peoples. Jesuit missionaries helped to pacify native tribes through conversion and influence. They achieved only limited success.

3. The English had tried to establish a trading and military outpost from which to seek gold while depending on the Indians for supplies and food. This was a disastrous strategy. Few people who arrived in Jamestown in 1607 were equipped with basic survival skills. As a result, no serious organization was undertaken to secure a crop, build a palisades, or establish discipline. Not surprisingly, the first winter was devastating. A colony of men and boys, few of whom had survival skills, were dependent on the Indians for survival. This led to violence, which further imperiled their position. The lessons learned were clear: A successful settler colony needed both men and women who possessed basic survival skills. To achieve economic self-sufficiency and independence from the Indians, the colonists needed to protect themselves, sow crops, and find a trade article for production.

4. As death rates declined, more indentured servants achieved their freedom. More freemen pressed for land and political rights against a planter class that had, through the patronage of a corrupt government, controlled most of the land in the East. This forced newly freed men out to the frontier in search of open land. There they faced Indian attack. When they petitioned the government for aid against the Indians and the government refused to respond, western settlers, fed up with the differentiation of social and political power in the colony, launched a rebellion and overthrew the government.

5. Puritan theology was founded on a belief in predestination. God was all-powerful, while man was weak and unable to know the mind of God. No one could be sure who was among the saved. This was a hard theology to live with. In response, Puritans sought various ways to try to discern the mind of God and somehow make their salvation more assured. They created extremely high standards for church membership, they demanded a conversion experience, they prayed intensely, and they formed covenants, or contracts with God, to assure themselves of salvation. In the end, however, even the most sinless saint could not be sure of salvation and faced death in fear of eternal damnation.

6. A highly charged spiritual view of the world, which imagined that God and saints were always under siege by a devil who was actively at work in the world, led many Puritans to interpret everyday events as manifestations of the devil or of God's disfavor. Hence when their faith was under siege, or social tensions ran high, many Puritans attributed the situation to the wrath of God or the work of the devil. In 1692, a combination of social tensions and a sense of theological decline converged to convince some residents of Salem, Massachusetts, that the devil was at work in the world. Once initial charges were made, emotions took over. Before witch hysteria subsided, scores of people had been accused and tried, and twenty had been executed.

7. Towns were established when members of one church petitioned for a grant to form a new town. Each new town had to have a church. The church was open only to those who could demonstrate that they were members of another church, or that they were worthy of admission to the new church. To enter a town, one had to be a church member. On that basis, the elect distributed land according to the social standing of the applicants. Though not equal, the distribution of land was still relatively egalitarian. Moreover, it was given to each member in fee simple. Thus, by binding the church to the town, Puritans assured that each townsman would have the means to establish himself as a yeoman farmer. Though there

were inequities, including people who had no land, these policies allowed most New Englanders to become yeomen farmers.

8. European traders introduced disease and European goods, including liquor, into Indian life. The competition for trade intensified conflict among Indian tribes. At the same time, over-hunting undercut self-sufficient tribal economies and made the Indians more dependent on European trade for survival. The fur trade thus undermined the Indian system of production, created social and spiritual disorder, and decimated the native population.

Chapter 3

The British Empire in America, 1660–1750

LEARNING OBJECTIVES

1. How does a random series or scattering of economic activities evolve into a system of trade? Does a series of events seem to occur on its own or does someone have to coordinate economic activities to make them into a system?

2. Using the example of mercantilism, examine the relationship between economic activity and political power. Why do they seem to develop parallel with each other?

3. How does economic development and growth affect the distribution of wealth and the social order?

4. This chapter explores how states or governments develop economic, social, or political policies that work. Drawing on the evidence of the British experience in establishing the first British Empire, what seems the best way to develop an effective policy? Does one take an ideal of how something is supposed to work and impose it all at once? Or does one start slowly, see how things are going, and then proceed to fine-tune the policy to fit the circumstances? What are the positive and negative aspects of both strategies? Did the British learn any lessons through 1750?

5. Using the evidence from the first British Empire, when, why, and under what circumstances do governments forgo foreign diplomacy to wage war?

CHAPTER SUMMARY

As the pace of English settlement of North America increased, Britain instituted mercantilist policies that gradually resulted in the development of the first British Empire. Though never totally successful, and based on African slave trade, the empire enriched Britain and elevated it to a major European power.

The Politics of Empire, 1660–1713 (pp. 72–80)

In the 1660s through the 1680s, Charles II, after restoring royal authority in England, began the process by which a scattered group of colonies across the North Atlantic, connected by British and European trade, became a trading system, or empire, based on mercantilist theory.

The Restoration Colonies

In an effort to pay off his debts, King Charles II distributed title to vast lands in the colonies of New York, Delaware, Pennsylvania, New Jersey, and North and South Carolina to a few English aristocrats. The character of life in each colony was established by the nature of the population and the power of the proprietor to rule. While small farmers rebelled against proprietary rule in North Carolina, colonists in South Carolina established a poorly governed slave regime. In contrast, Pennsylvania and Delaware were established as Quaker colonies in which farmers held land in fee simple and the people ruled through representative assemblies.

From Mercantilism to Dominion

Recognizing the potential wealth of his colonies, Charles II expanded the concept of mercantilism to encompass the various routes of trade and areas of production that were developing across the English colonies. Through wars against the Dutch and a series of Navigation Acts, Charles banned the Dutch and other foreigners from English trade and required English colonies to trade the goods they produced through England. In doing so, he began the process of transforming a disparate group of colonial economies into an integrated trading system. To administrate this new system, he created a new Board of Trade and imposed customs and duties. When American colonists resisted these initiatives, James II followed up his predecessor's economic policies by tightening the Crown's political and administrative control over the colonies, establishing a vast, centralized colonial administration over the northern colonies called the Dominion of New England.

The Glorious Revolution of 1688

James II's similar imposition of arbitrary power on the English people at home created similar discontent there. When James's Spanish wife, a Catholic, gave birth to a son, the prospect of a Catholic heir's returning to the throne precipitated a bloodless coup known as the Glorious Revolution. In quick order, colonists in Maryland and the Dominion of New England rebelled against the governors appointed by James II. In Maryland and Massachusetts, new royal colonies were established, with appointed governors, colonial assemblies, and the formation of the Anglican Church, or, at least, the right of Anglicans to worship. In New York, Jacob Leisler, who replaced James II's appointed governor, was himself ousted and then executed by members of a faction supported by the wealthy elite, plunging the colony into factional political disputes that continued into the 1710s. In general, the reorganization of royal colonies run by colonial assemblies representing the mercantile class allowed for the further development of a mercantile-based empire.

Imperial Wars and Native Peoples

England's recommitment to Protestantism and to expanding its empire drew it into an on-again, off-again conflict with France and Spain that lasted for most of the eighteenth century. In North America, the British continually resisted or tried to thwart French or Spanish efforts to consolidate or expand their colonial empires. In King William's War (1689–1697) and Queen Anne's War (1702–1713), both the British and the French used Indian alliances to attempt to gain the upper hand. In the South, war raged along the Spanish border of Florida. In the North, forays between Canada and New England were hindered by an Indian alliance that maintained Indian neutrality. While England gained vast Newfoundland and northern Canada, the Spanish fortified their colonies from Florida to Texas. Though the British still sought to create a unified colonial administration, they gradually conceded that ruling haphazardly over a patchwork of rapidly growing and thriving colonies was sufficient.

The Imperial Slave Economy (pp. 80–98)

The engine of wealth driving the development of the British Empire was the South Atlantic system. Using slaves transported from Africa to produce crops on land taken from native Americans, the British produced marketable products that transformed the economies, societies, and political systems of four continents.

The African Background

The diverse social, economic, political, and cultural systems of different African peoples were fundamentally changed by the development of the slave trade. Initially, European trade with Africa had a positive effect on African life, introducing new plants and animals to Africa that allowed African farmers to increase production, and stimulating the African economy. But as Europeans entered the slave trade and expanded it from a localized trade into a vast exportation of human beings from Africa to the Americas, millions of people were taken from the continent in exchange for goods of trade. As the slave trade drained Africa of capital, centralized slave-trading states preyed on smaller egalitarian tribes and nations, social hierarchies became more pronounced, and fundamental social relationships were transformed.

The South Atlantic System

In the West Indies, the use of slaves to produce sugar enriched and empowered a small, wealthy, absentee aristocracy of planters, many of whom spent their wealth in England. Likewise, the cost of furnishing and supplying the West Indies with goods, services, and food enriched manufacturers in Britain as well as merchants and farmers in the American colonies. In the North American colonies, social elites, enriched directly or indirectly by the slave trade, rose to power. In the seaports of the North, a merchant class, many of whom held slaves, rose to social and political power. Beneath them, a vibrant artisan and laboring class also developed. In the South, the planter elite further tightened their social and political control by modeling their behavior on that of the English aristocracy. All this economic development, and the social changes it set in motion, occurred at the expense of Africa. The exportation of millions of people diminished the wealth, uprooted economies, restructured societies, and undermined the cultures of Africa.

Slavery and Society in the Chesapeake

Though initially Africans who arrived as indentured servants in the Chesapeake colonies could gain freedom like any servant, in time Virginia planters, seeking to consolidate social order and responding to the availability of slaves from the developing South Atlantic system, turned to a labor system of African slavery.

The Expansion of Slavery

A combination of better conditions, a more widely dispersed population, and a smaller profit margin, allowed planters in North America to employ less force and violence in disciplining slaves than did planters in the West Indies. Hence slaves in the Chesapeake colonies lived longer than those in the West Indies, and, as a result, they began to form a distinctive slave society.

African American Community and Resistance

In contrast to the West Indies, African slaves in North America established families, developed kin relationships, maintained social and cultural traditions, and, through interaction with other Africans, created a new ethnic "African American" identity and culture. Their impoverished, enslaved status placed severe limits on their creative cultural expression, however. Most slaves resisted oppressive masters in subtle ways and negotiated the nature and conditions of work with their masters in ways unheard of in the West Indies. Only one major slave uprising took place in the eighteenth century, and it was brutally suppressed. For slaves, the cost of resistance was high.

The Northern Maritime Economy

Because sugar production brought such high returns, planters in the West Indies preferred to buy their produce, livestock, and supplies from others than to produce them at home. This provided a ready market for grain, livestock, and supplies produced by farmers or craftsmen in the middle colonies. The need to market these goods to the West Indies in exchange for bills of credit, which colonial merchants then exchanged for manufactured goods from England, triggered the development of several major port towns along the North American coast. At these towns, merchants exchanged goods and services within the empire; manufacturers turned raw materials into finished goods and artisans produced fine goods for local merchants; shipbuilders, suppliers of naval stores, and craftsmen maintained a growing fleet of ships to carry the trade of empire; and laborers and slaves manned the ships, hauled the cargo, and performed menial tasks. Likewise, interior market towns, from which produce from farther inland was shipped to the city, also developed. At all of these places, society was differentiated by wealth, class, and culture. A genteel elite established themselves at the top of seaport society. Beneath, the middle level of society was occupied by a variety of merchants and artisans who had moderate wealth. Poorer artisans, laborers, workers, and seamen formed a lower class, which, during economic downturns, fell into dependence, poverty, and hunger.

The New Politics of Empire, 1714–1750 (pp. 98–103)

To facilitate the growth of trade, British officials decided that when it came to colonial administration, less was more. By allowing the colonists a significant degree of self-government and economic autonomy—in short, by neglecting the need to establish administrative control—they allowed the colonies to continue to grow and develop. This policy of "healthy" or "salutary" neglect, however, would only make it much harder for subsequent ministers to regain control of the system when it was deemed necessary.

The Rise of the Assembly

As the Whigs gained control in England and implemented their policy of "salutary neglect," colonial assemblies acquired more power and control over colonial affairs. Though the assemblies were controlled by members of elite families who sought to rule without referring to the people's wishes, urban mobs, artisans, and yeomen farmers demanded assemblies that were responsive to their needs and independent of British administration.

Salutary Neglect

Sir Robert Walpole, the leader of the Whig party in the House of Commons from 1720 through 1742, created a strong Court party by using an elaborate patronage system. He filled numerous colonial posts with mediocre and corrupt officials and governors who were more interested in self-enrichment than in promoting colonial policy. As a result, American colonial assemblies, dominated by merchant elites who routinely evaded British maritime laws and resisted the rule of corrupt governors, grew accustomed to self-rule and viewed themselves as equals in the empire. Their belief in the assemblies that responded to popular needs, their lack of respect for colonial governors, and their fear of high taxes and standing armies, made Americans, in general, sympathetic to Radical, or Real, Whig criticisms of Walpole's government.

Consolidating the Mercantilist System

Safeguarding British planters and merchants was the main focus of British mercantilist policy during Walpole's ministry. To create a buffer between Spanish Florida and its Carolina colonies, Walpole supported the creation of Georgia and, from 1740 to 1748, fought a sporadic border war with the Spanish to secure it. To channel trade within the mercantile system, British officials also began to crack down on pervasive American violations of the Navigation Acts. In a series of new laws, they limited American manufacturers, prohibited the issuing of currency, and tried to limit the burgeoning trade between the colonies and the French West Indies. In their efforts to control Americans, some British officials began to think that a more rigorous colonial administrative system was needed.

EXPANDED TIMELINE

1651 **First Navigation Act**
The Navigation Acts sought to organize the production of trade among the British colonies according to mercantilist policy. The first trade act, passed in 1651, prohibited the Dutch from trading in the British system. Subsequent Navigation Acts sought to control the system by limiting colonial trade with foreigners, requiring colonial producers to ship their goods to England, and mandating that all trade in the system be carried in British ships with British crews. Though these laws were enforced only haphazardly, allowing many colonists to violate them, enough colonists did follow the laws to make the system work and to enrich Britain.

1660s **Virginia moves toward slave system**
For reasons that are not entirely clear, in about 1660, Virginians began legally to lower the status of African Americans whether they had gained their freedom and become planters or remained servants. After stripping them of many of their rights and prohibiting them from bearing arms, making contracts, receiving baptism, and marrying British subjects, Virginians eventually defined all black residents as slaves and allowed only blacks who were slaves to enter the colony. These laws enabled Virginians to replace white indentured servitude with African slavery.

1663 **Carolina proprietorship granted**
Charles II made a proprietary grant of the colony of Carolina, claimed by Spain, to eight aristocrats. Though the proprietors sought to create a manorial system in which powerful landlords ruled their tenants or serfs (as outlined in the Fundamental Constitutions of 1669), the settlers would have none of it, and, after a rebellion in 1677, forced the proprietors to abandon their claims.

1664 **New Netherland captured; becomes New York**
The British, after a brief war with the Dutch, occupied New Amsterdam and the colony of New Netherland. The Dutch did not resist. Charles II granted the entire colony, as well as lands to the south, to his brother James, the duke of York (later James II), who took control of the colony and renamed it New York. He also gave his rights to the lands south of New York to two proprietors, who named the colony New Jersey.

1681 **William Penn founds Pennsylvania**
In 1681, Charles II paid off a debt to the Penn family by granting the vast lands west of New York to William Penn. Penn instituted a radical form of government in his *Frame of Government* (1681), allowing all settlers fee-simple ownership of the land, a voice in public affairs, and the freedom to worship as they chose. Though he initially desired the colony to be a refuge for Quakers, it became a magnet for other Protestants, from England, Holland, and Germany. Eventually, the colony attracted a mixed racial, ethnic, and religious population that lived in relative peace and prospered under Penn's liberal social and economic policies.

1686–1689 **Dominion of New England**
James II and his supporters, who wanted to enforce royal authority in the colonies, revoked charters in Connecticut, Rhode Island, New York, and New Jersey and established one large colony known as the Dominion of New England. Colonists protested vigorously, and soon joined James's enemies in England to support his overthrow and exile.

1688–1689 **Glorious Revolution in England; William and Mary rule**
Threatened by James II's abuses of power, angry with his tendency to ignore Parliament's advice, and fearful that he would restore Catholicism as the state religion, Protestant leaders in Parliament instigated a bloodless coup against him. Parliament elevated Mary, James II's daughter by his first wife, and her husband, William of

Orange, to the throne to guarantee a Protestant monarchy. In return for being named king and queen, they gave up claims to divine right and agreed to rule as constitutional monarchs, accepting the premise of "mixed government" that divided power among three social orders: the monarchy, represented by the king; the aristocracy, represented by the House of Lords; and the people, represented by the House of Commons. This reduction of royal power would weaken government control over the colonies and allow the power of colonial merchants to increase.

Revolts in Massachusetts, Maryland, and New York
When colonists heard of the Glorious Revolution and James II's ouster from the throne, they rebelled against the oppressive system that he had implemented. In Massachusetts, colonists expelled the governor, dissolved the Dominion of New England, and sought a return to the original charter. In New York, both Dutch residents and English settlers ousted the lieutenant governor of the Dominion and replaced him with Jacob Leisler. Though initially popular among all groups, Leisler quickly lost the support of the wealthy elite, who ousted him and then had him executed. A new governor restored government by representative assembly. But ethnic and class conflicts between English merchants and Dutch residents continued for decades.

1689–1713 **England, France, and Spain at War**
England's rising power and its renewed commitment to Protestantism drew it into a series of wars with France and Spain that would continue intermittently until the late eighteenth century. In North America, the expanding borders of the English colonies, which were pushing up against areas claimed by France and Spain, as well as efforts by both sides to draw the Indians into alliances, dramatically increased tensions that quickly escalated into wars. The first of these was King William's War, fought between the English and the French and their respective Indian allies to clarify the border between New England and New France. In 1702, the English resumed fighting along their colonial borders against the French in the North and the Spanish in the South. In the most active year of the war, 1704, an expedition of English allied with Indians pillaged Spanish missions across northern Florida, burned St. Augustine, and attacked Pensacola, causing the Spanish to attack Charlestown. That same year, a group of Iroquois Indians allied with the French attacked Deerfield, Massachusetts, killing 48 and taking 112 into captivity. In response, the colonists in New England joined the British in an attack against Port Royal in Acadia. Queen Anne's War (known as the War of the Spanish Succession in Europe) ended with the Treaty of Utrecht (Holland). Britain acquired Newfoundland, Nova Scotia, and the region around Hudson Bay from France—giving it access to the western fur trade and Gibraltar, an island at the entrance to the Mediterranean Sea—and trading rights in Central and South America from Spain. The Treaty of Utrecht increased Britain's power in Europe and provided Britain with the opportunity to reform its thriving colonial empire. For political reasons, its leaders would not pursue that opportunity.

1696 **Board of Trade created**
In an effort to establish a uniform system of control over the American colonies, Parliament created the Board of Trade, staffed by officials familiar with colonial affairs. The Board would coordinate previous Navigation Acts and attempt to supervise and enforce the system. Given its recent experience with James II's power grab at home and in the colonies, however, Parliament gave the Board little, if any, coercive power to rule. Hence it had little impact on the administration of the colonial system.

1705 **Full legal slavery enacted in Virginia**
In 1705, the Virginia House of Burgesses completed a legal process that it had been moving toward for thirty years. The statute of that year declared that virtually all Africans brought into Virginia, by reason both of their race and their religion, were slaves. The decision to establish slavery as the labor system of Virginia was complete.

1714–1750 **British policy of "salutary neglect" Rise of American assemblies**
The Treaty of Utrecht and a thriving commercial empire encouraged British officials during the reigns of George I and George II to focus on encouraging trade and maintaining defense of the colonies rather than on supervising them.

1718 **Spanish establish missions and garrisons in Texas**
By the early 1700s, the Spanish had begun to feel threatened by the presence of the French to their north and east in Louisiana. To solidify their hold on the northern stretches of New Spain, the Spanish established permanent settlements—with Franciscan missions and military garrisons—in Texas, the first at San Antonio in 1718.

1720–1742 **Sir Robert Walpole, Chief Minister**
Robert Walpole, a Whig, developed a cooperative relationship between Parliament and the king by creating a strong Court party in Parliament. He did this primarily through patronage. Walpole also extended his patronage system to the American colonies, filling colonial offices with mediocre "placemen" who were more interested in their salary than in developing policy. As a result, he weakened royal bureaucracy in the colonies and fostered a low-key policy of "salutary neglect." The policy brought prosperity, but it also encouraged the rise of colonial assemblies and undermined British authority in America.

1720–1750 **African American community forms**
By the second quarter of the eighteenth century, African slaves in America had begun to fuse their tribal cultures with those of other slaves to create a new African American culture. In South Carolina, this fusion resulted in Gullah, a language that combined African and English words and structures. Elsewhere, the application of African and Muslim religious beliefs to Christianity, or Africans' work skills to production, or even African housing forms or material culture to English ones, provided evidence of this emerging composite culture. This cultural development was supported and reinforced by natural population increase, which led to the development of families and kinship networks. Over time, the number of slaves born in the American colonies steadily increased.

Rice exports from Carolina soar
Rise of planter aristocracy
Expansion of seaport cities
Access to the South Atlantic system began to dramatically affect the pace of economic development and growth in the American colonies after 1720. The planter aristocracy increased its power in the southern colonies on the strength of burgeoning rice and tobacco production. Seaport cities grew rapidly as farmers in the middle colonies and New England responded to an increased demand for grain, livestock, and supplies from the West Indies. In both the North and the South, therefore, the South Atlantic system empowered elite groups, which supported the rise of colonial assemblies and shaped the American response to any efforts by Britain to increase supervision of the empire.

1732 **Georgia chartered**
To provide a buffer to protect the Carolinas and the Chesapeake colonies from attacks by the Spanish or their Indian allies in Florida, King George II accepted James Oglethorpe's petition to form a reform colony south of the Carolinas in the 1730s. The Spanish, outraged by this further British expansion into territory they had claimed for nearly two centuries, tried to oust the British by fomenting a slave rebellion and then war.

Hat Act
One in the set of restrictive Navigation Acts, the Hat Act prohibited the export of colonial hats for intercolonial or British sale.

1733 **Molasses Act**
When American colonists from the middle colonies produced more grain and livestock than the British West Indies needed, they began selling grain and livestock to the French West Indies. In doing so, they helped the French reduce sugar-production costs, allowing the French to cut into the British share of a waning international market for sugar. To protect that market, Parliament allowed supply of the French islands to continue but slapped a high tariff on French molasses imported into the colonies. Though the Americans protested and smuggled French molasses, a resurgence in the sugar market brought back strong profits for both French and British producers, making the issue moot. Consequently, the act was not enforced.

1739 **Stono rebellion**
War with Spain in the Caribbean
Outraged by the founding of Georgia on land claimed by Spain, the Spanish governor of Florida plotted against the nascent English colony by enticing slaves to run away to Florida in return for freedom and land. When the Spanish assaulted a British sailor on a captured ship, war broke out between the two factions. Both sides launched attacks on each other, neither having much effect. While Oglethorpe organized an attack on Florida, seventy-five slaves, responding to the governor of Florida's call, rose in rebellion and marched toward the border. The colonial militia suppressed the rebellion. The war continued for several years, resulting in no territorial gains but establishing the security of Georgia and gaining further British trade access to the Spanish empire.

1740 **Veto of Massachusetts land bank**
To assure an adequate supply of money, colonies often printed their own paper currency. After accepting this practice for some time in different colonies, in 1740 British officials refused to allow Massachusetts to issue currency. This action is considered an early sign of the increasing view of some British officials that more control over the colonies was needed.

1750 **Iron Act**
Following the policy of limiting or discouraging American production of goods that competed with British manufacturers by prohibiting their sale (see Woolen Act of 1699), the Iron Act added plows, axes, skillets, and other iron products being produced in the American colonies to the list. As the American economies matured, artisans and manufacturers increasingly protested these restrictions on economic development.

1751 **Currency Act**
To protect the interest of British creditors, who complained that colonists were trying to pay their debts with worthless currency, the British restricted land banks and prohibited the issue of currency and the use of bills to pay debts.

GLOSSARY

system A set of interdependent units or functions directed toward a common purpose or function among which a change in the size, function, or character of any unit or function within the set alters the size, functions, or character of all the other units or functions within the set. In a system, units or functions are interconnected and affect each other to work toward a common goal. (p. 71)

Restoration The name given to the reign of Charles II, King of England. After four years of civil war, the Puritans, led by Oliver Cromwell, overthrew the English monarchy, executed King Charles I, and established a republican commonwealth. When Cromwell made himself a dictator, Parliamentary support for the republic declined and, after Cromwell died, Parliament reestablished, or "restored," the monarchy by inviting Charles II to ascend the throne. (p. 72)

quitrents In a feudal or proprietary system, farmers and peasants own the land, but they are still required to make small annual payments, called quitrents, to the proprietors or the lord of the manor in exchange for services or in acknowledgment of his ultimate authority. When the proprietors of the Carolinas attempted to impose these quitrents, the settlers rebelled. (p. 73)

inner light George Fox founded a radical protestant sect called the Quakers. Rather than believe that salvation was granted to a few, the Quakers argued that all people could gain salvation because each man and woman was imbued by God with grace or understanding, or "inner light." Quaker meetings focused on individual members of the congregation expressing their inner light without the aid of a minister or a sermon. (p. 73)

fee simple Fee-simple ownership of the land makes one the absolute owner, with no manorial obligations or feudal dues due to any other party, landlord, or proprietor. To own land in fee simple means that one owns the land outright and can maintain, sell, grant, or bequeath it to one's heirs or to whomever one wishes. The Puritans granted townships to town proprietors in fee simple. Townsmen had the right to sell, lease, or rent the land to newcomers, though they were expected to keep it in the family. William Penn made his colony even more attractive to settlers by allowing individuals, not towns, to buy land in fee simple, giving them complete control over their property. (p. 74)

mercantilism A political economic theory that argued that the power of the state was enhanced by wealth and that state policy, therefore, should be directed toward improving the economy. This was achieved by state policies that aimed at increasing exports and decreasing imports. These policies included subsidizing home manufacturers, funding the development of colonies, and regulating commerce. By prohibiting foreigners from engaging in domestic or colonial trade, limiting direct trade by colonists to and from foreign countries, and requiring that products of the colonies be exported via the mother country, the government maximized economic returns to the state. (pp. 74–75)

divine right A theory that argued that the power and legitimacy of the king or queen descended to him or her from God and that the king or queen, therefore, could govern alone through royal edicts or proclamations as he or she wished, without consultation with Parliament or the people. Charles I ruled by divine right after he dissolved Parliament in 1629. This led to his removal and execution in 1642. Charles II, upon his restoration in 1660, articulated the same theory of rule. Upon ascending the throne in 1685, James II did the same, by continuing his brother's effort to expand royal power. When Parliament carried out a bloodless coup against James II and installed Mary and William of Orange as queen and king, they promised to give up the Stuart assertion of divine right and to rule as constitutional monarchs, ending the issue in English history. John Locke, a political philosopher, justified the coup by rejecting the divine right theory. (p. 76)

inalienable rights In his Two Treatises on Government, John Locke argued that government was based on the consent of the governed, who, as individuals, possessed three inalienable rights: life, liberty, and property. This means that these rights are inherent to a person and cannot be taken away (p. 76)

chattel slavery By definition, a chattel is a possession that is movable. In colonial times, this included slaves, who could be moved or sold at will by the owner or master. In time, the word chattel became synonymous with slave. (p. 83)

patriarchy A patriarchy was a family or social order in which men, or fathers, ruled. (p. 85)

middle passage The South Atlantic slave trade was carried out by British traders who acquired slaves along the coast of Africa, herded them into transport ships, and then delivered them to South America, the West Indies, or the American colonies. The sea voyage from Africa to the Americas was called the "middle passage." (p. 86)

genteel A gentleman was "genteel." Gentility was characterized by moral superority, education, and refinement or elegance. In the colonies, many merchants in northern seaboard cities and planters in the South began to imitate this style cultivated by the British upper classes to establish and clarify their social position after 1700. (pp. 86, 97)

bills of exchange When colonial merchants sold grain and produce to the West Indies, they often received a "bill of exchange" as payment. This bill was a credit from a London merchant, which the West Indian planter or merchant had received in exchange for the sale of sugar. By presenting this bill, a colonial merchant could purchase goods from that or another house in London. (p. 96)

competency By the mid-eighteenth century, artisans, entrepreneurs, shopkeepers, and professionals in the colonial seaboard cities earned an income sufficient to support a comfortable and modest lifestyle. They regarded this as gaining a level of "competency." (p. 97)

"mixed government" An English political theory that argued that power, or sovereignty, was not held only or solely by any one of the three social orders—the monarchy, the aristocracy, and the commoners—but was divided equally among them. This theory was not democratic but, rather, granted a share of power to and guaranteed the rights, responsibilities, and privileges of each social order to create a balance, or "mix," of interests and policies within a "constitutional monarchy." (pp. 98–99)

Whigs An English political faction or party that supported the "mixed government" and sought to protect the rights of non-noble commoners. The Whigs were not democrats; they believed that freedom was most broadly assured when a balance among the three social orders was achieved. Robert Walpole was the leader of the Whigs in the House of Commons from 1720 to 1742. His policies as chief minister to the king reflected his Whig political philosophy. (pp. 98, 100)

elitist A social and political elitist is someone who believes that a small group of people who by merit or inheritance have achieved the highest status or power within a group or society should lead and rule that group or society and be deferred to by its members. An elitist is also someone who is aware of being a member of an elite leadership group. (p. 99)

Real, or Radical, Whigs Some Whigs argued that Walpole had corrupted the "mixed" balance at the core of a true constitutional monarchy by creating a strong Court party that supported the king and allowed him to gain more than his legitimate share of power by raising taxes, enlarging the royal bureaucracy, and maintaining a larger standing army than was necessary. "Real" Whigs, they argued, supported a balance and vigilantly resisted any efforts to undermine the power and independence of the House of Commons. Such criticisms struck a responsive chord among American colonists who viewed royal power through the king's representatives, the royal governors. Governors, they argued, possessed arbitrary powers and controlled a bureaucracy that threatened both the independence of colonial assemblies and the individual rights of colonists. The Real, or Radical, Whig view of politics was, therefore, widespread in the American colonies. (p. 100)

placemen The political power of elected officials is often consolidated by appointing people who have been politically loyal to positions in the government. This is called the patronage system. When a person appointed to a public office is neither interested in nor qualified for the position but was appointed only to provide him with a "place" in government, he is considered a "placeman." Robert Walpole established around him a loyal Court party of placemen through the use of the patronage system. In doing so, he undermined the royal bureaucracy and promoted a policy of "salutary neglect." (p. 100)

land bank Within the mercantilist system, most of the gold and silver coin that American merchants received for goods traded to the West Indies was sent to Great Britain as payment to British manufacturers for their goods. Hence there was very little specie (gold and sliver coin) circulating in the colonies. To encourage domestic trade, colonial assemblies established banks that lent paper money to farmers, accepting their land as collateral. These "land banks" thus enabled farmers, artisans, and merchants to carry on everyday trade and commerce. In 1751, Parliament prohibited these banks in order to safeguard the interests of British creditors, who complained that Americans were trying to pay them with "worthless" land-bank currency. (p. 103)

IDENTIFICATION

Identify by filling in the blanks.

1. The British king who returned from exile at the invitation of Parliament in 1660 and restored the Stuart family monarchy was _____. (p. 72)

2. Proprietors in North Carolina tried to continue a feudal practice that required landowners to pay an annual fee known as _____ to continue to hold a deed. (p. 73)

3. The Frame of Government guaranteed political liberty and religious freedom in the colony of _____. (p. 74)

4. In the late 1680s, James II and the Lords of Trade revoked the corporate charters of Connecticut and Rhode Island as a first step toward the creation of a new royal province called the _____. (p. 75)

5. The political tract *Two Treatises on Government* (1690), proposing that legitimacy of government rests on the consent of the governed, was written by _____. (p. 75)

6. The bloodless coup in which Parliament replaced James II, a Catholic, with Queen Mary II and King William III in 1688 was known as the _____. (p. 76)

7. The German immigrant who with the support of the wealthy elite overthrew the governor of New York in 1689 and was himself removed from office and executed was _____. (p. 76)

8. The Mohawk, Oneida, Onondaga, Cayuga, and Seneca tribes of central New York formed the Five _____ nations, a confederation that controlled the region from the Hudson River to the eastern Great Lakes. (p. 78)

9. The Kingdom of Tejas, which gave the state of Texas its name, was a confederacy of the _____ Indians. (p. 79)

10. In West African states, voluntary associations— _____ for men and _____ for women—provided a variety of social needs, including sexual education for children, adult initiations, and enforcement of codes governing conduct and morality. (pp. 81–82)

11. The vast economic system that generated wealth across the British Empire and bound the destinies of four continents—Europe, Africa, and North and South America—together in the eighteenth century was the _____. (pp. 82–83)

12. South Carolina was first settled in the 1680s by land-hungry whites from the sugar island of _____. (p. 90)

13. When the governor of Spanish Florida offered freedom to slaves in Georgia who ran away from their owners, he triggered the _____, the only major slave revolt to occur during the colonial period. (p. 95)

14. The increase in the power of colonial assemblies during the early eighteenth century is referred to, historically, as the _____. (pp. 98–99)

15. During the ministry of Robert Walpole, reliance on patronage brought to political office a number of mediocre appointees known as _____, who held office but did little work. (p. 100)

16. The founder of Georgia, _____, hoped that the new colony would become a colony of small farms where England's poor could find safe haven. (pp. 101–102)

FEATURES EXERCISES

Voices from Abroad

OLAUDAH EQUIANO, The Brutal "Middle Passage" (p. 87)

Africans along the coast of West Africa lived in a world transformed by the South Atlantic system. For generations, the presence of European slave ships along the coast seeking slaves to transport to America had made the capture and transporting of slaves to the coast part of the system. In doing so, it had transformed the political and social makeup of numerous tribes and nations in Africa. Upon reaching the coast, slaves encountered the transport to America, the brutal "Middle Passage." In this selection from his memoirs, Olaudah Equiano gives a remarkable description of his capture, transport to the coast, and shipment to America along the "Middle Passage." As you read "The Brutal 'Middle Passage,'" ask yourself the following questions:

1. How old was Equiano when these things occurred to him? How might that affect the story he tells?

2. His account describes the mechanics of the South Atlantic system in Africa. According to his account of how he got to the coast, how did that system work?

3. What was Equiano's emotional response? How did that make the experience even worse?

4. How could the English participate in such a brutal trade? Why did they treat Africans in this manner?

American Lives

William Byrd II and the Maturation of the Virginia Gentry (pp. 88–89)

The center of England's hierarchical society were the king and queen's court. Beneath them were aristocrats; members of the upper gentry; members of the military;

professionals, merchants, and artisans within an urban middling class; followed by farmers and peasants. Those not born into the aristocracy or upper gentry could rise only by trying to live like the aristocracy and gain royal favor and patronage. Otherwise, the primary ways of moving up socially were through a successful military career, appointment to a government post, or marriage. One way in which many English people in the middling level of society and the lower gentry sought to do this was by going to the colonies to acquire wealth and then returning, or having their children return, to England to pursue an appropriate strategy to achieve social mobility. William Byrd's father adopted this strategy, providing his son William with an English education, schooling in the arts of courtly behavior, and connections to members of London society. Unable to overcome the stigma of a colonial birth, however, William Byrd returned to Virginia to claim his local status but remained unsatisfied and continued to seek improved social status on return trips to England.

As you read "William Byrd II and the Maturation of the Virginia Gentry," answer the following questions:

1. Why was social position so important in seventeenth-century England?
2. What was wrong with Virginia that made it so difficult for William Byrd to be happy there?
3. Why did he not value his achievements in Virginia? What does this say about the character and identity of Virginia culture as late as the early eighteenth century?
4. What lessons did Byrd gradually learn about his desperate desire to gain status in England?
5. In what way was Byrd's experience similar or different from that of other colonists at the time?

New Technology

Rice: Riches and Wretchedness (p. 91)

Like other immigrants, Africans who were brought to America as slaves brought their culture, values, customs, and knowledge with them. They had, therefore, a profound impact on the economy, society, and culture of colonial America. In this case, West African slaves brought to the coast of South Carolina knew how to plant rice, both for their own consumption and for export. Ironically, by employing their knowledge to plant rice, Africans contributed to the wealth of the planters, and their own misery, by encouraging them to develop large plantations along the sea on which thousands of slaves lived hard, short lives.

As you read "Rice: Riches and Wretchedness," ask yourself the following questions:

1. Why were Africans successful in planting and harvesting rice in the colonies where European newcomers had failed?
2. Why did the African slaves provide the English with the knowledge to plant rice?
3. Why was the African method of hulling rice superior to machines?
4. Why was the achievement of African slaves deeply ironic, as the title of this piece suggests?
5. Are there other examples of the English employing the knowledge of the native Americans or African slaves to exploit them to English advantage?

American Voices

PHILIP FITHIAN, Sadism under Slavery (p. 95)

The central dilemma of the slave system was how to make the slaves work. Having no chance to gain freedom and receiving little in return from his or her work, there was no incentive for a slave to do basic work. Planters confronted this problem in a number of ways. Many established incentive systems within the work routine or provided rewards for work well done. But many more planters found that only the use of force worked. Force, however, quickly generated diminishing returns. Some resorted to brutal tortures to make their point or to achieve their ends, as this selection attests. As you read this piece, "Sadism under Slavery," ask yourself the following questions:

1. Why did planters feel that they needed to constantly exert their power?
2. Why did they feel the need to continually increase the force they used? Why did they become frustrated?
3. Do you think there are any other reasons that one becomes cruel and sadistic? What does it say about the planters' comfort with the decision to establish slavery?
4. What evidence of slaves' responses to the planters' cruelty does this piece provide?

GOVERNOR GEORGE CLINTON, The Waning of British Authority (p. 101)

The British policy of "salutary neglect" inspired American opposition to colonial authority and made it difficult to enforce British law in the colonies. Because of Prime Minister Walpole's use of patronage, unqualified men filled many of the leadership roles in the colonies. George Clinton, who received his appointment through family connections, was not a strong governor. He chafed at his inability to control New York.

As you read "The Waning of British Authority," ask yourself the following questions:

1. What was Clinton's relationship with the assembly?
2. What did Clinton believe to be the most important power of the assembly for undercutting British authority? Why? How did the assembly acquire this power?
3. What did Clinton propose as a solution to these problems?
4. What could the British do to stop these usurpations of the king's power by the assembly?

MAPS AND FIGURES

Map 3.2 Britain's American Empire, 1713 (p. 79); Map 3.3 Africa in the Eighteenth Century (p. 81); and Table 3.4 Slave Destinations, 1520–1810 (p. 83)

These two maps and one chart provide the evidence to demonstrate the structure, dynamics, character, and impact of the South Atlantic system. Look at the two maps and chart very closely and try to answer the following questions:

1. Does Map 3.3 confirm the total number of slaves who were taken to America as listed in Table 3.4?
2. How did the geography of the slave trade from Africa change over time?
3. If you could draw lines of destinations to the New World in a thickness proportionate to the Table 3.4 numbers, what would that map look like?
4. Compare the figures of slaves exported in Table 3.4 with the black population of the West Indies and Southern and Northern Mainland listed in Map 3.2. (Assume that about 40 percent of the slaves listed in Table 3.4 had been imported by 1713.) Is there a discrepancy? What does this tell you about slavery?
5. How do the comparative numbers of exports, either calculated annually or per white individual, give you further insight into the character of slavery in various locations?

Map 3.4 The Rise of the American Merchant, circa 1750 (p. 96)

The South Atlantic system was the southern link of the developing trading system that became the first British Empire. The system was organized according to the principles of mercantilism. By 1750, even though the system did not work as well as the British had hoped, it had generated steady increases in the production and trade of colonial goods that spread wealth around the North Atlantic. Though the map presents the system as a unified network, few merchants actually traveled more than one or two trading routes within the system with which they were involved. As you read this map, ask yourself the following questions:

1. Among the various items or products being traded within the system, which were traded in the greatest volume and had the most value?
2. Try to follow the flow of trade of various goods and items around the system. What goods were being traded in exchange for what other goods or returns? How did these exchanges of goods affect the various colonies and England?
3. Having followed the goods, try to find data on or estimate their relative value and determine who was making the most money. Where were the greatest profits going within the system? Was mercantilism working?

Figure 3.2 Wealth Inequality in the Northern Cities (p. 98) and Figure 3.3 Family Connections and Political Power (p. 99)

1. What is the timing of these trends in relation to the development of the mercantilist trading system?
2. How is the rising inequality of wealth related to the pattern of political officeholding in New Jersey by family?
3. According to this evidence, was colonial society becoming more or less egalitarian and democratic by the 1750s? In what ways would this both increase and decrease the political power of the elite?

Table 3.2 Navigation Acts 1651–1751 (p. 74) and Table 3.3 English Wars, 1650–1750 (p. 78)

1. Does the timing of the passage of the Navigation Acts indicate an evolving imperial strategy? How so?

2. How does the nature of the various laws passed indicate the development of leaks, problems, or violations in the system? Why were these problems occurring? Why did the Americans act the way they did, and why did the British respond with legislation?

3. Is there any relationship between the timing of the passage of the Navigation Acts and English wars in North America?

SELF-TEST

Multiple Choice

1. In the seventeenth and eighteenth centuries, England's most valuable overseas colonies were:
   a. the Chesapeake colonies.
   b. the New England colonies.
   c. Pennsylvania and New York.
   d. the West Indian sugar islands.

2. Charles II established by proprietary grants *all* of the following colonies *except*:
   a. New York.   c. Maryland.
   b. New Jersey.   d. North Carolina.

3. William Penn established the colony of Pennsylvania as a refuge for:
   a. Catholics.   c. Anglicans.
   b. Quakers.   d. Puritans.

4. Because of outspoken opposition to the new mercantilism and violations of the Navigation Acts, royal officials in the Dominion of New England aimed their harshest actions against:
   a. Connecticut.   c. Massachusetts.
   b. Rhode Island.   d. New York.

5. The English political philosopher John Locke argued in favor of *all* of the following *except*:
   a. inalienable individual rights.
   b. the divine right of kings.
   c. the Whig theory of "mixed government."
   d. the Glorious Revolution.

6. Jacob Leisler, a German immigrant living in New York, did which of the following things:
   a. led a mob in New York City to close houses of prostitution.
   b. headed a New York militia in defense of Schenectady against the French and Indians in 1690.
   c. overthrew the lieutenant governor of the Dominion of New England in 1689 and became governor of New York.
   d. became governor of New York in the 1730s because his wife was related to Lord Halifax.

7. In the Treaty of Utrecht (1713), the British received *all* of the following French territories in North America *except*:
   a. Newfoundland.
   b. Acadia.
   c. the Hudson Bay region.
   d. Louisiana.

8. In 1713, the administration of the British Empire could be most accurately described as:
   a. an authoritarian system run by the king and administered by the Lords of Trade and Plantations.
   b. a centralized system run by the chief minister of the king, who filled colonial offices with "placemen."
   c. a haphazard system administrating over a patchwork of colonial governments run by a weak Board of Trade.
   d. an integrated system of control and supervision run by a Board of Trade with strong coercive powers.

9. When Europeans opened commercial contacts with West Africa, they often fell victim to tropical diseases that included *all* of the following *except*:
   a. yellow fever.   c. malaria.
   b. cancer.   d. dysentery.

10. The most important foods brought into Africa from the Americas were:
    a. millet and yams.
    b. coconuts and oranges.
    c. maize and manioc.
    d. salt and palm nuts.

11. At the height of the slave trade, between 1700 and 1810, the majority of Africans transported to the Americas were sold to:
    a. tobacco farmers in the Chesapeake region.
    b. cotton planters in the Deep South.
    c. sugar planters in the West Indies.
    d. coffee growers in Brazil.

12. One West African state that steadfastly opposed the slave trade, while other neighboring states were trading and selling their own people, was:

a. Dahomey. c. Barsally.
b. Benin. d. Asante.

13. During the colonial era, rice was grown as the most important cash crop in:
   a. South Carolina. c. Maryland.
   b. Georgia. d. Rhode Island.

14. In West Africa, where many of the American slaves had learned to grow rice, the rice fields were known as:
   a. huskes. c. *lugars*.
   b. guerards. d. paddies.

15. Among the African peoples in America, Gullah was a:
   a. rice dish that was a favored food in Africa.
   b. new dialect that mixed English and African structures and words.
   c. secret slave society that plotted escapes.
   d. planting system organized to plant rice.

16. British leaders supported the founding of the colony of Georgia in the early 1730s because:
   a. Georgia's founders proposed to outlaw slavery.
   b. Georgia's founders wanted to provide refuge for the English poor.
   c. Georgia provided a buffer between the Carolinas and Spanish Florida.
   d. they hoped Georgia would develop into a good source of sugar products.

Short Essays

Answer the following questions in a brief paragraph.

1. What strategies did the king of England undertake in the late seventeenth century to increase his control over the British colonies in North America? (pp. 72–80)
2. Why did the colonists oust the royal governor and lieutenant governor of the Dominion of New England? How does their response indicate developing colonial political views at the time? (p. 75)
3. How did the expansion of the empire and the increase in border disputes with the Spanish and French complicate the political and economic position of the native peoples in eastern North America? (pp. 77–80)
4. What was the South Atlantic system, and how did it affect Africa? (pp. 82–83)
5. Why did Virginia planters decide to switch to an African slave-labor system near the end of the seventeenth century? (pp. 84–85)
6. Why, in general, did American colonists become accustomed to a considerable degree of political self-rule, and what impact did this have on their relationships with British officials? (pp. 98–101)

ANSWERS

Identification

1. Charles II
2. quitrent
3. Pennsylvania
4. Dominion of New England
5. John Locke
6. the Glorious Revolution
7. Jacob Leisler
8. Iroquois
9. Caddo
10. the Poro . . . the Sande
11. South Atlantic system
12. Barbados
13. Stono rebellion
14. "rise of the assembly"
15. placemen
16. James Oglethorpe

Self-Test

Multiple Choice

1. d.   7. d.   13. a.
2. c.   8. c.   14. c.
3. b.   9. b.   15. b.
4. c.   10. c. 16. c.
5. b.   11. d.
6. d.   12. b.

Short Essays

1. Charles II bestowed on friends and people to whom he was in debt vast lands in America, allowing them to establish proprietary colonies. He

Answers

also implemented mercantilist policies, and tried to consolidate colonial administration by creating large royal colonies.

2. New Englanders opposed the revocation of the colony's charter, the banning of self-rule, and the introduction of the Anglican Church. They petitioned the king for redress by claiming their civil rights. After revolting, they ultimately compromised and accepted the allowance of the Anglican Church and the broadening of participation of non-Puritans in government, in return for self-rule. The compromise reflects the colonists' increasing awareness of themselves as citizens of the empire.

3. As the population grew and trade increased, British colonists began to look for room to expand. This inevitably intensified pressures between the colonists and the Indians and French in the interior and to the north as well, as with the Spanish in the South. As Britain and France found themselves increasingly at war with each other, the Indians were caught between the two. Though the Iroquois played the two sides off each other for decades, their doing so would eventually draw them into broader conflicts between the French and the English, forcing them to choose a side and the consequences that went along with that choice.

4. The South Atlantic system was the elaborate trading system that constituted the economic structure of the first British Empire. The cornerstone of the trading system was sugar production. To supply labor for the sugar plantations in the West Indies, British slave traders acquired and shipped millions of slaves to the West Indies as well as to the American colonies. In exchange, the British slavers brought tinware, iron, rum, and cloth to Africa. The value of these imports was only one-tenth to one-third the value of the goods produced by African slaves in the colonies, however. The uprooting of 15 million slaves wreaked havoc on African societies. The slave trade encouraged centralized, militarized states. It also shifted gender relations in Africa, as two-thirds of the slaves taken were male, and initiated a local slave trade, prompting some systems of hereditary slavery in Africa itself.

5. Virginia planters were interested in producing as much tobacco as possible at the lowest cost. Early on, indentured servants and a buoyant market allowed them to do so. When the market declined, the relative cost of indentured servants increased. Meanwhile, freed indentured servants were demanding their own land. This increased social friction, which led to rebellion. The experience convinced many planters that they needed a labor force that was both cheaper and easier to control. When the labor market drove the price of slaves below that of indentured servants, the planters began to switch to slavery. As they did so, they legally lowered the status of all blacks in the Chesapeake region.

6. The American colonists had allowed considerable self-rule from very early in their colonial experience during the period of "salutary neglect." With colonial governments controlled by local assemblies, American colonists in general grew increasingly suspicious of the intentions of Parliament and the king. The regular appointment of "placemen" and often weak and corrupt colonial governors further reduced the colonists' respect for imperial government and reinforced their concerns about any threat to their political rights. Autonomy had convinced many American colonists that they were political equals within the empire, a view the British did not share.

Chapter 4

Growth, Diversity, and Crisis: Colonial Society, 1720–1765

LEARNING OBJECTIVES

1. How did economic development and population growth amid a declining availability of land in colonial America cause both social and cultural change?

2. How did the Enlightenment and the Great Awakening affect social and political development in the American colonies? Given the evidence from eighteenth-century America, what type of influence can major cultural movements have on social and political developments?

3. How did increased immigration and cultural diversity create social and cultural tensions in colonial America?

4. In what ways were the availability or control of land and the prospects for economic opportunity involved, directly or indirectly, in the political tensions between the major European powers, as played out in North America during the eighteenth century?

CHAPTER SUMMARY

The abundance of land in the American colonies enabled most farmers and planters, in contrast to Europe, to own and operate their own farms, take part in the burgeoning Atlantic marketplace, exert considerable control over their families, practice the religion of their choice, and vote and participate as freemen in town and colony politics. Continued migration to the colonies, along with buoyant natural increase, caused a steady growth in population. As society became larger and spread to the West, it faced more challenges and pressures. Increasingly pluralistic and diverse, American colonists confronted the world intellectually and spiritually in more complex and sophisticated ways.

Freehold Society in New England (pp. 108–112)

In New England, population increase gradually outstripped the availability of land. As the freehold ideal came under greater pressure, New Englanders responded in a variety of traditional and creative ways.

Farm Families: Women's Place

Traditional society remained patriarchal. Women, in this world, remained subordinate and had few rights in custom or law. They deferred to men, received less inheritance, had fewer opportunities, and had no role in public life. Their traditional role as mother and helpmate to their man remained intact. The declining size of family farms, however, did compel families to respond by reducing family size and increasing household production. Though control of this production provided women with some basis for exerting more influence, they still remained constricted by law, custom, religion, and culture.

Farm Property: Inheritance

The availability of land remained the distinguishing feature of American life. Though over time it became more difficult to acquire land, especially for indentured servants, the opportunity to own property was still much better in America than in Europe. Land became the universal currency of social and family obligations. Initially, parents had enough land to give each of their children a sufficient plot, and thus maintained some control over their lives. As the amount of land parents were able to give their children declined, however, so too did their control over their children's lives. Marriage, which had often been no more than a legal contractual obligation involving the exchange of lands—the dower right—increasingly became a relationship based on love. As the land became more crowded and family plots grew smaller, parents responded by leaving their lands only to the oldest child, providing for the other children with cash or goods, or making accommodations for them in frontier towns. Either way, most New England towns remained communities of independent landowners.

The Crisis of Freehold Society

By the 1740s, population pressure had divided lands so much that families were increasingly unable to provide for their children in the traditional ways. Consequently, they lost social control over their children. Left without land, many children rejected arranged marriages and migrated west to begin again. Meanwhile, many New England farmers responded to the pressures of a declining standard of living by trying to introduce more currency into the economy, intensifying their farming methods, developing household production, bartering for goods and services with other farmers, or establishing new towns on the frontier.

The Mid-Atlantic: Toward a New Society, 1720–1765 (pp. 112–120)

Because diverse people from across Europe settled in the middle colonies, they lacked the cultural uniformity of New England. Nevertheless, amid diversity, the middle colonies established a social and political order that incorporated freedom and diversity and created a model for the future.

Opportunity and Equality

In the Middle Atlantic colonies, prosperity and immigration failed to assure social equality. Traditional estates in New York left little freehold land available to settlers, forcing many to settle for tenancy. Across the middle colonies, limited technology restrained the progress any individual family could make. The wheat trade and rising land prices differentiated wealth and land ownership even further in the next generation, enabling a class of agricultural capitalists to rise above yeomen farmers and a growing landless class. This landless class was a labor supply that merchants and manufacturers would later tap to create the putting-out system.

Cultural Diversity

These tensions were intensified by a patchwork of social and religious diversity across the middle colonies. Germans, Scots-Irish, Quakers each had their own moral ethics, values, customs, and practices. Rather than try to create a new melting-pot society, each group maintained its own ethnic and cultural identities and contributed to a pluralistic society while living in a British-defined political system.

Religious Identity and Political Conflict

Eventually, however, the separation between church discipline and political power compelled some sects to try to exert social control. When the Quakers translated their self-disciplining strategies into politics, other groups began to oppose them, increasing political and social friction. Nevertheless, the Middle Atlantic colonies were able to develop an open political order that could generally navigate all the various social and political tensions inherent in a pluralistic society.

The Enlightenment and the Great Awakening, 1740–1765 (pp. 120–131)

These pressures, which threatened the freehold ideal, undermined the social order, and thwarted individual action and initiative, made many Americans receptive to two cultural movements from Europe that swept across the colonies before mid-century—the Enlightenment and the Great Awakening.

The Enlightenment in America

Urban merchants, middling people, and some farmers and planters embraced the rationalist ideas of the Enlightenment, which argued that through the scientific method one could analyze, understand, and change both the natural and the human world. Enlightenment thinkers such as Ben Franklin established newspapers, founded institutions of learning, hospitals, and orphanages, and enhanced urban services in order to spread scientific and humanistic knowledge, improve the quality of civic society, and contribute to the progress of humanity. In doing so, they created a secular environment that welcomed rational critiques of society and politics and sought ways to reform both.

Pietism in America

Rural society was more receptive to the Great Awakening, a religious revival that swept the colonies after 1730. Tapping the individualist impulse in American society, the traveling ministers of the Awakening encouraged individuals to become receptive to God's grace by humbling themselves before him, accepting his power, and emotionally committing themselves to lives of faith, piety, prayer, and good works in order to achieve salvation. They preached deeply emotional sermons and led enthusiastic prayer meetings that prompted individual and group conversion experiences. Their influence spread across the colonies, affecting the enthusiastic, the curious, and the skeptical alike in a Great Awakening.

The Awakening in the North

Stirred by highly emotional sermons on the equality of souls, and the power of the individual to effect his or her spiritual fate, "New Light" Presbyterians, Baptists, and Congregationalists, the most powerful forces in the revival, threatened the "Old Light" or Anglican religious establishments across the North. New Light "separatist" churches broke off from Old Light churches. They challenged the traditional clergy, questioned the values of the marketplace, and established new colleges.

Social and Religious Conflict in the South

In the southern colonies, New Light Presbyterians and Baptists challenged the authority of the Anglican Church and the hierarchical social order it supported. Artisans and farmers were empowered by Presbyterianism, while the Baptist Church appealed to poor whites and black slaves, who transformed a religious revival into a challenge to the slave system itself. Both threatened the cultural and political power of the elite and challenged the secular, hierarchical, genteel life of the elite. The Protestant revival became a dominant tradition in American life, empowering yeomen farmers and poor whites, and giving African Americans a new Protestant spiritual identity.

The Midcentury Challenge: War, Trade, and Social Conflict, 1750–1765 (pp. 131–141)

Pietism and the Enlightenment swept across colonies that were being transformed by political pressures arising from continuing prosperity. As the Americans increased their standard of living, they found themselves deeper in debt to British creditors. In addition, the westward push of American settlers increased colonial conflicts between westerners and, more important, led to new disputes with the Indians and the French over rights to western lands. The British decision to wage war to defend the empire ended up redefining it. The war convinced the British that they needed to change their colonial policy and transform their relationship with the American colonies.

The Great War for Empire

The rapid population increase of the American colonies shifted the balance of power among the British, French, and Spanish colonies in North America by increasing British power. It also changed the colonies' relationship with the Indians. When the British sought to draw the Iroquois into an alliance, and a group of American investors organized the Ohio Company to establish land claims along the Ohio River, the French responded by reinforcing their claims militarily. William Pitt, a colonial expansionist, chose to respond to French seizure of an expedition led by George Washington with a full-scale war against the French. For taking Quebec and Montreal, suppressing a widespread Indian revolt, and achieving military success around the world, the British acquired Canada, lands to the east of the Mississippi River, and Spanish Florida, in the Treaty of Paris. Burdened by war debt, and disturbed by the Americans' lack of cooperation and deference during the joint war effort, many British officials became convinced that they had to strengthen British imperial control over the colonies.

British Economic Growth

Britain's power was based on its developing industrial and commercial power. Its best customers were American colonists, who increased their agricultural exports to pay for more and more imports. Their spending outstripped their rising income, however, and as they increased their standard of living they increased debt to British creditors, too. American colonists lived better than ever before, but they were also more dependent on outsiders than ever before.

Land Conflicts and Western Uprisings

The quest for land increased the number of land disputes across the colonies. As more farmers struggled to maintain their status and feared becoming an American tenant peasantry, the ownership of vast lands by proprietors and aristocrats became more unpopular. On the frontier, settlers again found themselves without colonial protection in their confrontation with Indians over land rights. Settlers in western North Carolina felt they had insufficient institutions, were under-represented in the colonial assembly, and were treated unfairly by eastern creditors. Disputes over these issues threatened to erupt into a small civil war a number of times. These social and political tensions, reflecting the rising economic and political power of westerners, presaged a broadening awareness of the potential economic and political power of the colonies.

EXPANDED TIMELINE

1700–1714   **New Hudson River Valley manors created**
English governors granted titles to vast manorial estates along the Hudson River Valley to a few elite families. The control these families developed over the land, forcing small farmers into tenancy, eventually dissuaded new migrants from settling in the area.

1720s   **German and Scots-Irish migration**
Beginning in the 1720s and increasing through the 1750s, thousands of Germans and Scots-Irish arrived in Pennsylvania. Though some came as indentured servants, the majority arrived with enough resources to purchase land and become farmers. Most settled across the western parts of Pennsylvania, Maryland, and Virginia, where they acquired land and maintained their own cultural and social practices within a pluralistic society.

Theodore Jacob Frelinghuysen holds revivals
Frelinghuysen was among the first preachers to lead religious revivals in the colonies. A Dutch minister, he traveled from congregation to congregation among the German inmmigrants of the middle colonies, exhorting them to fervency with his emotional sermons.

1730s   **Enlightenment ideas spread from Europe to America**
In the 1730s, the first influences of the European cultural movement called the Enlightenment reached the American colonies. The Enlightenment was an intellectual movement that advocated the use of reason to analyze, understand, and change the natural and human world. In the colonies, it quickly transformed how well-educated Americans thought about religion, science, and politics.

William and Gilbert Tennett lead Presbyterian revivals among Scots-Irish migrants
Jonathan Edwards preaches in New England
During the same period, a religious revival from Europe that emphasized the need for more emotion and piety to achieve conversion experiences reinvigorated Protestant churches throughout the colonies.

1739   **George Whitefield and the Great Awakening**
Possessing a remarkable presence, and speaking from memory in a highly emotional style, Whitefield drew large crowds and influenced the skeptical and the faithful alike to strive for moral perfection. Itinerant preachers like Whitefield challenged the traditional organization of churches across the colonies.

1740–1748   **War of the Austrian Succession**
Yet another war among Spain and France and England over the succession to the Austrian monarchy was briefly fought in the American colonies as well. In 1745, a force of New England militia captured Louisbourg, a French naval fort at the mouth of the St. Lawrence River. The British were compelled to return it in a peace treaty of 1748.

1740–1760s   **Great Awakening creates conflict between Old Lights and New Lights**
"Old Lights" denounced the impassioned, fervent nature of Great Awakening revival and took steps in some places to suppress it. The "New Lights" rejected the conservatism of Old Light preachers and denounced Old Lights as unconverted sinners.

New colleges founded by religious denominations
Presbyterian, Baptist, Dutch Reformed, and Anglican New Lights also sought to expand educational opportunities in the colonies. But their goal was to train ministers, not scientists or Enlightenment thinkers. One of the first of these new colleges was established in Princeton, New Jersey.

Population pressure on land in New England
Steady population growth in New England forced farmers to divide their lands and give their children smaller plots. By about 1750, many farms were too small to be further broken up, so parents began to deed farms to first sons and provide cash and goods for their other children. Those who received farms were compelled to develop ways to use their land more efficiently. Many introduced new techniques of farming and harvesting to increase yields. Others began to develop and tap the full benefits of household production by making goods in the home and using them for exchange in the local barter economy. Farmers also

demanded more currency. In these ways, farmers who held property tried to maintain their standard of living against a declining supply of land.

Rising grain and tobacco prices assist farmers
Increasing inequality in rural communities
Increasing demand for wheat from Europe transformed the middle colonies into the bread basket of the empire and Europe, while tobacco remained the most important colonial export. This increase of production and trade sustained steady population growth and further economic development. Ironically, as land values rose and competition increased, a class of agricultural capitalists developed above yeomen farmers and more farmers found themselves pushed into tenancy or out of farming altogether.

Falling birth rate increases women's options
In response to smaller farms, married couples began to reduce the size of their families in the middle of the century. As this occurred, women had more time to devote their energies to household production, helping to maintain or enhance their standard of living.

1743 **Benjamin Franklin founds American Philosophical Society**
Enlightenment ideas motivated thinkers such as Benjamin Franklin to print books, magazines, and newspapers, and to found hospitals, libraries, universities, and almshouses to improve society. In Philadelphia, Franklin also forwarded knowledge as an innovator, inventor, and scientist. To promote "useful knowledge," he helped found the American Philosophical Society.

1750s **Industrialization in Britain increases exports to colonies**
Americans export more to pay for British imports
Increased capital from its expanding world trade enabled British inventors to more aggressively replace imports with domestic production. New technology and work regimes enabled British manufacturers to produce better-quality products than craft workers could produce. As production increased, British merchants marketed these goods more aggressively. Offering better credit terms to American merchants, the British stimulated a "consumer revolution" in the colonies that raised the American standard of living. Although the colonists expanded their own production and increased trade to pay for these goods, in general, they increased consumption at an even faster rate, falling deeper into debt.

Ohio Company threatens French land claims in Ohio River Valley
As settlers pushed west in search of land, eastern planters and investors began to recognize the value of western lands. Governor Dinwiddie of Virginia and a group of Virginia planters formed the Ohio Company and obtained a grant to much of the land in the Ohio Valley. Both the Iroquois and the French objected to this claim. To mute the tensions between the Iroquois and the British, the Board of Trade called for an intercolonial meeting in Albany in 1754.

Connecticut's Susquehanna Company seeks land in Pennsylvania
Proprietors assert charter rights to lands
In response to the shortage of land in New England, settlers' companies claimed land in the West and tried to settle it. In Connecticut, the colonial assembly established the Susequehanna Company and laid claim to Pennsylvania lands claimed by the Penn family since 1681. Similar land disputes occurred across the Hudson Valley and eastern New York, as New Englanders, refusing tenancy, purchased titles from land speculators who disputed Dutch titles. In each colony, as well as in New Jersey and Maryland, proprietors reasserted their control of the land against the claims of yeomen farmers.

1754 **French and Indian War begins**
Albany meeting and Plan
To secure the cooperation of the Iroquois against the French in the West, the British Board of Trade called an intercolonial meeting in Albany. Aside from assuring the Iroquois that the British colonists had no designs on their lands, delegate Benjamin Franklin proposed that the colonists form a continental assembly to develop a coordinated policy with the Indians, and to facilitate western trade and defense. Neither the colonists, who wanted their autonomy, nor the British, who feared too much American autonomy, liked the plan.

1756 **Great War for Empire (Seven Years' War) begins**
The French responded to the Albany meeting by constructing Fort Duquesne at the site of Pittsburgh. In response, the governor of Virginia sent George Washington and a small force to warn them off. When the French captured Washington and his troops, the British, led by William Pitt, declared war. Peace between Britain and France had lasted only six years.

1759 **Fall of Quebec**
British forces led by General Wolfe attacked Quebec by way of the St. Lawrence River and defeated the French forces, led by General Montcalm, in front of the city. The following year, the British completed the conquest of Canada by capturing Montreal.

1760s **New York/New England border conflicts**
Settlers continued to challenge the unclear border between Massachusetts and New York, protesting the titles of manorial lords in the Hudson River Valley.

Regulator movements in the Carolinas
Settlers in western South Carolina, tired of the indifference of the colonial leaders to their needs and to

their lack of representation in the colonial assembly, established the Regulators as an extralegal force to establish political control and make demands on the government. Though initially eastern elites resisted and even raised an armed force to discipline them, the two sides compromised and averted conflict in 1769.

Baptist revivals in Virginia

Baptist preachers in the South continued to spread the enthusiasm of the Great Awakening through revivalist meetings. The preachers at these meetings used enthusiasm and emotion to attract a large following among yeomen and tenant farm families in Virginia. By doing so, they challenged the Anglican, aristocratic rule of the elite.

1763 **Pontiac leads Indian uprising**

When the British occupied French forts across the frontier and then stopped the supply of gifts and gunpowder the French supplied to the Indians, Indians across the frontier, led by the Ottawa chief Pontiac, launched a full-scale war against the British. Although the Indians initially succeeded in recapturing most forts, the British gradually wore them down and defeated Pontiac at Detroit.

Treaty of Paris ends Great War of Empire

In return for their military triumphs, the British acquired all of French Canada and all the territory east of the Mississippi River, including Spanish Florida. Spain received Louisiana and Cuba. The French maintained a few sugar islands in the West Indies and two islands off the coast of Newfoundland. Britain's vast acquisitions would transform the geopolitical context in which it administered the colonies of North America.

Paxton Boys in Pennsylvania

Scots-Irish farmers in search of land had been trying to push Indians out of western lands for decades but failed to get colonial support. In 1763, a group of settlers took matters into their own hands and attacked Indians in western Pennsylvania. When the governor tried to arrest the leaders, the Paxton Boys marched on Philadelphia. The revolt was quashed only by the efforts of Benjamin Franklin, who negotiated a fragile compromise. The same issues would reappear ten years later.

GLOSSARY

freeholder One who owns outright the land he lives and works on, without any dues or leases or obligations to any other person. Yeomen farmers were freeholders. (p. 108)

marriage portion When sons and daughters reached an age at which they could get married, their father usually provided them with land, livestock, farm equipment, or money. This marriage gift repaid children for their labors on the family farm as well as ensured that they would remain loyal and support their parents later in life. The practice of giving marriage portions increased as fathers lived longer and sons and daughters were unable or unwilling to wait for an inheritance. (p. 110)

dower right, or **dowry** When a woman in eighteenth-century America married, she surrendered her property to her husband. In compensation, she received the right to use (but not sell) a third of her husband's estate if he died. She received this right only if she remained an unmarried widow. Upon her death, it returned to the family. (p. 110)

land bank In eighteenth-century New England, land was capital. As a result, it was the basis of wealth. In the currency-starved colonies, many colonists thought that one way to solve the problem of cash shortages was to turn the land into cash by offering it as collateral to a bank in return for cash loans from that bank. A bank that would accept land as collateral for loans was called a land bank. Britain vetoed the idea. (p. 111)

household production When New England farmers were faced with diminishing returns, they tried to increase household income in a number of ways. One way was to encourage the women and children of the household to produce goods or develop skills that were in demand by other local farmers. Women and children would often spin yarn or sew; sons might take up work as part-time artisans. They exchanged these products with other farmers for goods and services that they required. This local cashless system of exchange of goods and services among freehold families was called the "household mode of production." (p. 112)

tenancy leases A tenant is someone who works land owned by another. Initially, in the American colonies, all improvements made to the land belonged to the landlord. This dissuaded many individuals from accepting tenancy. As an incentive, landlords began to offer tenancy leases to farmers. In a tenancy lease, the landlord still owned the land, but any improvements the tenant made could be sold to the next tenant. This gave a tenant some incentive to improve and invest in the land. (p. 113)

putting-out system Before they were willing to invest in building factories, many manufacturers sought to produce goods by organizing the production process across a region. They provided the raw materials and organized the production process by hiring underemployed tenants and farmers across the countryside to do various stages of production at their homes. Work, in short, was "put out" from the central production location. (p. 115)

inmates As land in the colonies became more crowded, many colonists fell into tenancy or began to work as farm laborers, earning little. Such individuals, who were called "inmates," joined a growing population of poor people in the colonies. (p. 115)

redemptioners Many immigrants to Pennsylvania came to the colonies under a system that was a type of indentured servitude. Upon arrival in the colony, survivors of the hard journey would be put on the market for purchase as laborers. The purchasers paid for the cost of transit and in return received three to five years of labor from the person they purchased. Sometimes servants acquired the debt for others, such as spouses or children, to ensure that their family remained together. Hence, indentured servants, or redemptioners, would have to work multiple terms to pay off the debt they owed to their owners. (p. 118)

cultural pluralism A culture in which no single group of people dominate. In such a culture a variety of peoples, each with their own specific cultures, coexist in different communities and contribute, through interaction, to a more general culture. (p. 118)

Pietism A spiritual outlook that emphasized devout, or "pious," behavior and an emotional effort to achieve a personal, mystical union with God. Unlike Puritans and most other Protestants, Pietists avoided debates over theological dogma or doctrine and deemphasized the role of intellectual scrutiny of the Bible as the path to God. (pp. 120–21, 123–24)

folk wisdom The lives of peasants and yeomen farmers followed the natural cycle of the seasons. In the daily routines of work and social activity, individuals developed traditional ways of doing things or behaving that, rather than being the result of an empirical process, were continued simply because they had been done in the past. Ideas that passed from generation to generation were folk wisdom. (p. 121)

social compact In the seventeenth century many people believed that political right to rule, or sovereignty, came from God. John Locke, an English political philosopher, argued that rather than coming from God, sovereignty was based on an agreement, or social compact, made among the people and between the people and those who ruled. In that agreement, the rulers vowed to preserve the "natural rights" of the people—i.e., life, liberty, and property. Government was legitimate, therefore, so long as it protected the people's natural rights and the people consented to it. (p. 122)

deist Deists were followers of the Enlightenment who believed that God was a rational being. They believed, therefore, that rather than intervene actively in the world and the affairs of men, God simply created an orderly world that operated according to the laws of nature and then left it alone. For deists, man, as a creation of God, was imbued with a natural reason and moral sense implicit in God himself. Therefore neither belief in the divinity of Jesus Christ nor any other church dogma was necessary to receive God's favor. Both Benjamin Franklin and Thomas Jefferson were deists. (p. 122)

life of the mind An aspiration of intellectuals is to develop and think about ideas for their own sake. The valuation of ideas is necessary to create an active intellectual life in a society. Cultivating thinking to this end is the life of the mind. (p. 123)

conversion experience Ever since John Calvin proclaimed that only a limited number of people would achieve salvation, and that they were powerless to affect God's predetermined choice, Protestants have sought ways to assure themselves of salvation. Puritans and, later, Congregationalists sought reassurance through detailed scrutiny of the Bible's meaning and by living pious lives. Eventually, Congregationalists began to argue that the way to salvation was through a "conversion experience" or second birth that ushered in a life of devotion and piety. Though, initially, preparation for this experience focused on the ministry and the Bible, the Great Awakening emphasized an emotional "enthusiastic" response upon recognizing the power of sin, in which one repented and sought salvation by receiving or accepting God's light and "saving grace." (p. 124)

squatters A squatter is someone who settles on land to which he or she does not have title. Some settlers who squatted were transients simply trying to survive by poaching or stealing. Many settlers, however, would squat in hopes that they could eventually have the first claim to purchase land that had not yet been surveyed and put on the market. (p. 138)

IDENTIFICATION

Identify by filling in the blanks.

1. Colonial farmers who owned their own land outright were known as _____. (p. 108)

2. Women who help prepare expectant mothers for childbirth, were on hand for the delivery, and assisted mother and child after birth were called _____. (p. 108)

3. When sons and daughters of colonial farmers reached a marriageable age, their parents usually gave them an economic head start by providing them with land and livestock. This was called a _____. (p. 110)

4. In response to declining plot sizes, farmers compensated by producing and exchanging goods and services among themselves. This was called a mode of _____. (p. 112)

5. A hand-held agricultural tool that accelerated the harvesting of hay and increased productivity by cutting and then arranging the wheat for easy pickup was _____. (p. 113)

6. The first religious group in the American colonies to advocate the abolition of slavery were the _____. (p. 116)

7. Immigrants to the colonies who were descended from Presbyterians sent to Northern Ireland in the seventeenth century to secure English control of the region were called _____. (p. 116)

8. Because their language resembled that of the Dutch, whom other settlers had encountered in New York, German settlers in Pennsylvania were called the _____. (p. 118)

9. An author, inventor, and scientist living in Philadelphia, _____ was the epitome of the Enlightenment in the American colonies. (p. 122)

10. Ministers of the Great Awakening used revivalist prayer meetings and emotional preaching to cultivate in listeners a higher level of _____ that would lead them toward a conversion experience. (p. 124)

11. A revivalist minister from Connecticut who delivered and then published a famous sermon, "Sinners in the Hands of an Angry God," and sought to reconcile Enlightenment ideas and Pietism was _____. (p. 126)

12. Church members who separated from their congregations to form and support new congregations based on the ideas of the Great Awakening were called _____. (p. 128)

13. As a colonel in the Virginia militia, a young man, _____, was sent into the Ohio River Valley in 1754 to secure British claims in the region. His seizure by the French triggered a course of events that would result in war. (p. 134)

14. The Ottawa Indian chief who organized a rebellion against the British and said, "I am French, and I want to die French," was _____. (p. 135)

15. In the 1760s, vigilante groups that took the law into their own hands in an effort to lower taxes, gain more representation, and prevent foreclosures on western farms by eastern creditors in the Carolina backcountry were called the _____. (p. 139)

FEATURES EXERCISES

Voices from Abroad

GOTTLIEB MITTELBERGER, Perils of Migration (p. 119)

During the eighteenth century, thousands of Germans emigrated from their homeland to the English colonies in America. Most, who could not afford the passage, came as redemptioners, or indentured servants. In this arrangement, immigrants were transported to Pennsylvania and employers in the colonies would then buy the workers for a number of years' labor by paying for their passage. Gottlieb Mittelberger provides an account of the experience of migration and the workings of the redemptioner labor system. As you read this account, ask yourself the following questions:

1. In what ways does the author try to make his point about the immigrants' prospects in America?

2. Compare and contrast this account of immigration with other migration experiences and labor systems in colonial America.

3. What evidence is there that Mittelberger's account may be biased or exaggerated?

American Voices

CHARLES WOODMASON, Social Chaos on the Carolina Frontier (p. 121)

During the Great Awakening, itinerant Presbyterian and Baptist ministers traveled across the frontier and throughout the South spreading the word in a highly emotional preaching style, calling sinners to repent and seek salvation through conversion experiences. In the religious revivals that followed, Presbyterian preachers had a great impact on artisans and farmers, while the Baptists appealed to poor whites and black slaves. In either case, their success drew members away from the Anglican Church and challenged its traditional authority. The Presbyterians and Baptists also threatened the southern colonies' hierarchical social order, which the Anglican Church supported. Charles Woodmason observed these developments as he traveled along the Carolina frontier on behalf of the Anglican Church. As you read this excerpt from Woodmason's journal, ask yourself the following questions:

1. In what ways does Woodmason's account record the progress of the Great Awakening on the Carolina frontier?
2. Though he records considerable social disorder, what evidence of western social order does he provide?
3. Whom does he see as members of the Presbyterian and Baptist churches?
4. What prospects does he see in the region for the Anglican Church?

NATHAN COLE, The Power of a Preacher (p. 125)

George Whitefield and other preachers associated with the Great Awakening in colonial America transformed both the practices and the theology of a number of Protestant churches. Rather than become ministers of a particular church, Whitefield and other preachers traveled from colony to colony and delivered sermons outside on platforms to vast audiences. Like other Great Awakening preachers, Whitefield reasserted the Calvinist belief in the supreme power of God and the humility of man. As listeners contemplated their condition, doubts over their election and fear of eternal damnation triggered an emotional crisis out of which each listener would open up to God's mercy and grace through a conversion experience. Through these methods, Whitefield and other preachers challenged church authority and transformed each listener's relationship with God. As you read this piece, ask yourself the following questions:

1. In what ways did Whitefield's journeying in from out of town increase the expectations of listeners?
2. How did Whitefield get his message across to listeners like Cole?
3. Judging from Cole's response, what did Whitefield apparently preach about?
4. What evidence in Cole's account indicates that he had a conversion experience?

American Lives

Jonathan Edwards: Preacher, Philosopher, Pastor (pp. 126–127)

During the eighteenth century, two cultural movements transformed the culture of the American colonies: the Enlightenment and the Great Awakening, as manifested in Pietism. Often, these movements are viewed as being in opposition to each other. In reality, however, Pietism often drew from the same well as Enlightenment rationalism. It certainly did so in the ideas of Jonathan Edwards, one of the most prominent preachers and thinkers in colonial America. Edwards gained a wide audience for his famous sermon of 1742, "Sinners in the Hands of an Angry God." Steeped in basic Calvinist beliefs in the power of God and the humility of man, Edwards promised immortal damnation to those who did not awaken from their secular complacency and try to seek God's grace through a conversion experience. The way to this experience, Edwards argued, however, was not through "enthusiasm" but through an emotional response to abstract ideas within an older, covenanted church. As you read this account of Edwards's life, ask yourself the following questions:

1. How did Edwards reconcile the Enlightenment and the Great Awakening?
2. Was Edwards more in agreement with John Winthrop or with Benjamin Franklin about man's relationship to God, and God's role in the world?
3. How representative was Edwards's theology compared with that of other famous preachers of the Great Awakening?
4. How did Edwards's congregation react to his ideas, and why did it react in this way?
5. How did Edwards's view of human beings limit his ability to understand and cope with his final illness?

MAPS AND FIGURES

Map 4.3 Religious Diversity, 1750 (p. 120)

By the middle of the eighteenth century, the development of numerous denominations had transformed the religious landscape of the English colonies in North America. This diversity would become the foundation for an almost inevitable separation between church and state, and for the emergence of a society tolerant of religious diversity. Examine the evidence presented on this map closely and ask yourself the following questions:

1. In what way does the distribution of the various denominations in the colonies in 1750 reflect the sequence in which the various groups came to the colonies?
2. In what way does the distribution of the various denominations in the colonies in 1750 reflect the impact of immigration to the colonies in the first half of the eighteenth century?
3. In what way does the distribution of the various denominations in the colonies in 1750 reflect the impact of the Great Awakening on religion in the colonies?

Map 4.4 European Spheres of Influence, 1754 (p. 133) and Map 4.5 The Anglo-American Conquest of New France, 1754–1760 (p. 135)

These two maps are closely related. The first map shows that the relative spheres of influence of the British and the French were shaped by historical precedent and geography. New France was centered in the St. Lawrence River Valley, the Great Lakes, and the Mississippi River Valley, while the British colonies were situated along the coast and were backed up against the Appalachian Mountains from Georgia to Maine. In a number of ways, these were separate and exclusive colonial worlds. As the English colonies continued to expand, however, and more colonists pushed west and north, they began to intersect with French claims. Disputes over these claims triggered the outbreak of war. Warfare occurred along the northern and western boundaries of the English colonies, where previous disputes had erupted, resulting in a predictable plan to invade Canada. As you look at these two maps, ask yourself the following questions:

1. What evidence on Map 4.4 allows you to predict where the points of tension would be?
2. How did the progress of the war follow the geography of posts, forts, and towns? What role did geography play in affecting strategy?
3. Why, if the war began over disputes involving the Ohio Company's claims near Fort Duquesne, do you think the British shifted their energy toward invading and taking French Canada? What does this say about Anglo-American perceptions of the structure of New France?

Figure 4.1 Population Growth, Wheat Prices, and Imports from Britain in the Middle Colonies (p. 114)

This chart presents data on economic activity and compares it with the population increase of the colonies. From this evidence, one can trace the course of economic development in the colonies during the eighteenth century. Look closely at the chronology presented and answer the following questions:

1. What was the general trend of wheat prices in the eighteenth century? How much did they increase in percentage terms between 1720 and 1770? What would cause such a price increase? Why would prices rise more in England than they did in the American colonies?
2. During the same period, what were the percentage increases in colonial population and imports from England to the colonies?
3. What does it mean when a country's imports increase at a faster pace than its population increases?
4. If the colonies were importing more per person, and imports were rising faster than wheat prices—the source of colonial income—how do you think the colonists paid for the difference? Was there anything wrong with this method of payment? What problems might it create in the future?

Figure 4.2 Increasing Social Inequality in Chester County, Pennsylvania (p. 115)

Economic development in a free marketplace tends to increase the unequal distribution of wealth within a society. Entrepreneurs who provide goods and services that are in high demand acquire a larger return on their work. As they increase their trade, their larger operation becomes more efficient. Acquiring money enables them to invest more in their operations and to further improve the profitability of their activities. Look closely at this chart and try to answer the following questions:

1. If wealth were equally distributed in Pennsylvania at any time in the century, what would the chart look like?
2. How does one calculate what percentage of the total wealth in a society is owned by the top 10 percent of taxpayers in that society?
3. What happened to the distribution of wealth over time? Why would this trend increase after 1760?

SELF-TEST

Multiple Choice

1. Land was the basis of life in the preindustrial world. As land became more scarce in colonial America, families devised new ways to transfer property to the next generation. They did this in *all* of the following ways *except*:
   a. Fathers granted each of their children a marriage portion upon reaching age twenty-three or twenty-five.
   b. Fathers granted a dower right to daughters who gained permission to marry by getting pregnant.
   c. Fathers willed land to one son and required that the land remain undivided and within the family.
   d. Fathers gave land to the oldest son and expected him to provide his siblings with cash or goods.

2. As plots of land decreased in size and yields declined, many farmers struggled to maintain a subsistence standard of living. Farmers used *all* of the following strategies *except* to:
   a. diversify their farming by planting a variety of crops.
   b. develop a system of barter exchange among households to generate income and acquire needed goods.
   c. develop new farm machinery to replace tools like the cradle scythe to increase yields.
   d. develop a mixed-crop grazing economy, mixing potatoes and grasses to reinvigorate the land and increase yields.

3. The material life of the average American farmer, limited as it was by what could be planted and harvested, was simple. On an average American farm, one would find *all* of the following *except*:
   a. colonial-style chairs and a dining-room table
   b. trenchers and noggins
   c. a one- or two-room house
   d. stools and benches

4. The largest group of new immigrants to British colonies in North America during the eighteenth century was the:
   a. Germans.
   b. Scots-Irish.
   c. Dutch.
   d. French Huguenots.

5. The diverse society of colonial Pennsylvania was characterized by:
   a. a fusion of different ethnic groups into a distinctive American mix.
   b. the dominance of all ethnic groups by the Quakers.
   c. most ethnic groups maintaining their own cultural identities by marrying within their own groups and preserving customs, resulting in a pluralistic society.
   d. continual ethnic conflict and discord.

6. *All* of the following were Enlightenment thinkers who directly influenced the intellectual climate of the American colonies *except*:
   a. John Locke
   b. Isaac Newton
   c. Jonathan Edwards
   d. Benjamin Franklin

7. The central premise of the Enlightenment was:
   a. Devotion and piety are the way to experience God's grace in a conversion experience.
   b. Human reason has the power to observe, understand, and improve the world.
   c. An activist God is involved in the everyday affairs of the world.
   d. Everyone's mind is a blank slate on which basic ideas or principles can be imprinted.

8. In the early 1700s, the middle colonies grew prosperous primarily because:
   a. artisans in New York and Philadelphia began to manufacture goods as part of an Industrial Revolution.
   b. the rise in wheat prices increased population and production and trade in wheat.
   c. the tobacco trade boomed as prices rose again.
   d. British merchants extended increasing credit to American colonists.

9. Someone who believes that God created the world but then allowed it to operate according to natural laws without intercession is a:
   a. humanist.
   b. Presbyterian.
   c. natural philosopher.
   d. deist.

10. The one criticism of traditional churches that devotees of the Great Awakening did *not* make was:
    a. Traditional churches relied on their own ministers, who had no clear methods or prescribed rules to lead members to a conversion experience.
    b. Members of traditional churches believed salvation could be achieved through good works without a conversion experience.
    c. Traditional churches charged membership fees that were difficult for yeomen farmers and laborers to pay.
    d. Established churches ministered only to the social elite and supported the increased competitive spirit and pursuit of wealth in society.

11. The French and Indian War was caused by:
    a. a border dispute over western lands in America among the British, the French, and the Indians.
    b. an effort by the French to gain the alliance of the major Indian tribes of the West.
    c. a struggle over control of the fur trade.
    d. British desire to remove the French in America as the main obstacle to British expansion.

12. The British passed the Proclamation of 1763, which temporarily barred Anglo-Americans from settling west of the Appalachians, because they wanted to:
    a. punish the western settlers, who had started the French and Indian War.
    b. develop the region as a vast Indian reserve.
    c. acquire imperial control of the western lands to prevent their control by individual colonies.
    d. address Indian concerns about control over western lands in the wake of Pontiac's rebellion, though they were not sure how to accomplish this.

13. American colonists were affected by the Industrial Revolution in Great Britain in *all* of the following ways *except*:
    a. Since British manufacturers were doing so well, they didn't need to sell to the colonies and Americans were allowed to manufacture their own goods.
    b. British merchants aggressively marketed manufactured goods in the colonies, triggering a consumer revolution.
    c. Americans increased agricultural exports to pay for the growing number of imported goods from Britain.
    d. Scottish merchants subsidized the production of American tobacco.

14. Land disputes erupted in several colonies in the late colonial period. The grievances at the center of these disputes included *all* the following *except*:
    a. foreclosures on farmers who went bankrupt through no fault of their own after the tobacco market declined.
    b. the efforts of landlords to reassert their proprietary right over lands.
    c. disagreements between western settlers and colonial leaders about Indian policy.
    d. insufficient available land in the western Carolinas upon which new arrivals could settle.

15. By 1750, the American colonies had become:
    a. a complex society with a large, diverse population and a sophisticated culture.
    b. a crude frontier society characterized by violence, social disorder, and a lack of culture.
    c. a homogeneous, content society culturally and intellectually dependent on England.
    d. a melting pot in which peoples from around the world created a completely distinctive society that was remarkably different from English society.

Short Essays

Answer the following questions in a brief paragraph.

1. What caused the crisis among freehold farmers in colonial America? How did they respond to it? (pp. 111–112)

2. In what ways were overcrowding and diversity transforming colonial society in the middle of the eighteenth century? (pp. 107–120)

3. How did the Quakers affect life in Pennsylvania? (pp. 115–118)

4. Why do you think American colonists became more receptive to the ideas of the Enlightenment in the mid-eighteenth century? What impact did this cultural movement have on the colonies? (pp. 121–123)

5. What were the causes and effects of the Great Awakening? (pp. 123–130)

6. In what ways did the pressure of increasing population on the supply of land contribute to the freehold crisis, social diversity, war with the French and Indians, internal conflicts, and the changing dynamics of economic development in colonial America? (pp. 109–141)

ANSWERS

Identification

1. freeholders
2. midwives
3. marriage portion
4. household production
5. cradle scythe
6. Quakers
7. Scots-Irish
8. Pennsylvania Dutch
9. Benjamin Franklin
10. enthusiasm
11. Jonathan Edwards
12. New Lights
13. George Washington
14. Pontiac
15. Regulators

Self-Test

Multiple Choice

1. b.	6. b.	11. a.
2. c.	7. b.	12. d.
3. a.	8. b.	13. a.
4. b.	9. d.	14. d.
5. a.	10. c.	15. a.

Short Essays

1. By the mid-eighteenth century, population pressure had divided lands so much that families were increasingly unable to provide for their children in traditional ways. In response, many New England farmers tried to introduce more currency into the economy, intensified their farming methods, developed household production, bartered for goods and services with other farmers, or established new towns on the frontier.

2. As immigration accelerated, the amount of available land decreased. Those who had land sought ways to make their production more efficient, to elevate their standard of living, and to distribute the land equitably to their children. Yet limited technology restrained the progress any individual family could make. The wheat trade and rising land prices differentiated wealth and land ownership even further in the next generation, enabling a class of agricultural capitalists to rise above yeomen farmers. Many others, facing traditional estates in New York, lost their lands, or never acquired land and were forced to settle for tenancy. Meanwhile, more diverse groups were entering the colonies, eroding the unified cultural outlook that had initially prevailed. As a result, colonial society became increasingly differentiated by wealth and divided by political tensions and social diversity.

3. The Quakers, having arrived in Pennsylvania first, had acquired control over Pennsylvania politics. In general, Quakers maintained control by instituting social and political policies that cultivated a strictly defined, self-contained, prosperous community. Therefore, even though they encouraged immigrants, and advocated religious toleration and a separation between church and state, they continued to exert considerable influence. Eventually, other groups would begin to oppose them, increasing political and social friction. Nevertheless, the Middle Atlantic colonies were able to develop an open political order that could generally navigate all the various social and political tensions inherent in a pluralistic society.

4. Pressures that threatened the freehold ideal, undermined social order, and thwarted individual action and initiative made many Americans receptive to the Enlightenment. Sensing that they needed to respond creatively to social and economic pressures, Americans embraced the rationalist ideas of the Enlightenment, which argued that through the scientific method one could analyze, understand, and change the natural and the human world. Enlightenment thinkers such as Benjamin Franklin established newspapers, founded institutions of learning, hospitals, and orphanages, and enhanced urban services in order to spread scientific and humanistic knowledge, improve the quality of civic society, and contribute to the progress of humanity. In doing so, they created a secular environment that welcomed rational critiques of society and politics and sought ways to reform both.

5. The pressures that threatened the freehold ideal, undermined social order, and thwarted individual action and initiative also made many Americans

receptive to the Great Awakening. Tapping the individualist impulse in American society, the traveling ministers triggered a revival in Calvinist ideas of committing oneself to faith, piety, prayer, and good works in order to achieve salvation. Their preaching prompted individual and group conversion experiences. Their influence spread across the colonies, as those moved by the Great Awakening reordered churches, challenged traditional clergy, questioned the values of the marketplace, established new colleges, and reinforced individualism in American culture.

6. Rapidly increasing population created an insatiable demand for land in colonial America. Population increase in settled areas, which left less and less land for children, threatened the freehold ideal. Many farmers were compelled to respond by changing their inheritance strategies, intensifying farming practices, limiting family size, and developing home production. As competition increased, farmers who responded were able to maintain their status, while those who did not struggled to avoid tenancy. Where immigration from Europe increased, land was settled by Scots-Irish, Germans, and other groups, each of whom cultivated their own social and cultural practices and resisted assimilation into society. So, too, as settlers and speculators pushed west, they demanded better treatment from eastern officials and creditors. When they pushed out onto Indian lands beyond the Appalachians, they caused border disputes with the Iroquois and the French that eventually led to war. In each case, colonial Americans' desire to make a living from the land created economic, social, and political tensions and drove the dynamics of change.

Chapter 5

Toward Independence: Years of Decision, 1763–1775

LEARNING OBJECTIVES

1. How did the Great War for Empire transform the relationship between the British and the American colonists?

2. The outcome of a political debate like that which developed between the American colonies and Great Britain in the 1760s is shaped by how members of both sides act in response to each other's ideas or actions. Either side can respond in a variety of ways, ranging from holding firm and resisting change to more flexible responses that seek a compromise, whether based on old or new and innovative actions or ideas. Assess the actions and responses of the Americans and the British to each other as their political debate escalated in a series of disputes and compromises. How creative or innovative was each side in attempting to find solutions?

3. Given the evidence from American activities between 1765 and 1775, how did the colonies transform a political dispute about particular issues into a broad-based resistance movement? What factors facilitated American efforts to establish a resistance movement?

CHAPTER SUMMARY

In the twelve years following the end of the Great War for Empire, prosperous, loyal American colonists became rebels. This dramatic change had two causes. Americans, used to ruling themselves, expected political autonomy and increasingly insisted on it. These expectations conflicted with British resolve, formulated during the war, to establish more rigorous imperial administrative control over the colonies. Disagreements about policy quickly evolved into ideological and political debates about the nature of the empire.

The crisis unfolded in four phases, each of which involved British action, American response, and British counterresponse. In each phase, the British maintained their position, while the American colonists, in both debate and political action, resisted the assertion of British power, claimed increasingly more rights, and organized in new ways to challenge British authority. Though initially the British sought compromise, with each creative American response they felt increasingly compelled to stand firm, thus gradually narrowing their options and reducing the chances of subsequent compromise.

The Reform Movement, 1763–1765 (pp. 146–152)

As it waged the Great War for Empire, the British government was transformed, through increasing expenditures supported by rising tax revenues, into an aggressive and powerful state. By asserting its authority through more activist administrative policies, it increasingly affected the lives of its citizens. When British political leaders began to follow through on their determination to reform the colonial administrative system, the American response triggered a political crisis.

Chapter Summary

The Legacy of the War

The Great War for Empire transformed the context in which the American colonies operated within the empire. No longer distant and indirectly regulated, the colonies had become central parts of the empire and would now come under more direct administrative control. Britain's experience in the war had convinced many British officials that a more rigorous administration of the colonies was needed both to control the empire and to generate funds to pay for the war, but also to clarify for Americans, who many feared already had too much autonomy and were drifting toward independence, their subordinate place within the empire. Assuming that their authority was accepted both at home and abroad, the British believed Americans, like British subjects, would submit to more active, aggressive government. The government tried to tighten administration of the Navigation Acts, impose higher duties on trade, and place British troops in the colonies. Colonists viewed this new assertion of power as an effort to subject them to imperial control and to second-class status.

British Reform Strategy

The British reform strategy was implemented by a new generation of officials who wanted to expand Britain's power over the colonies. Following the logic of the Navigation Acts, the ministers expanded the prohibition that Parliament had established in New England in 1751 against issuing paper currency to include all colonies, and shrewdly reduced trade duties on imported molasses while increasing enforcement. Americans quickly raised constitutional objections to these efforts, but the British rejected them on the grounds that Americans did not have the rights of traditional English subjects. In reality, the underlying issue was American displeasure with the increase in British authority.

The Stamp Act

Encouraged by the relatively mild American response to the Sugar Act, Parliament passed the Stamp Act in 1765. Though primarily a revenue act, the Stamp Act asserted Parliamentary supremacy over the colonies in all matters, and especially its right to tax the colonies.

The Dynamics of Rebellion, 1765–1766 (pp. 152–157)

The evolution of a political debate into a rebellion was determined by how the two sides responded to each other. Surprised by the colonists' aggressive response to the Stamp Act, the British initially sought compromise, while still committing themselves to pursuing a reform strategy. Renewed British efforts to tax and assert power over the colonies accelerated American efforts to intellectually and physically resist the British. These responses quickly evolved into a resistance movement that challenged British policy and authority. In the face of increasingly provocative American responses, the British felt they had no choice but to stand firm, thus narrowing their options and reducing the chances for subsequent compromise and resolution of the crisis.

The Crowd Rebels

British officials did not anticipate the strong American political response. Amid extensive public debate of the issue, the colonists rejected this assertion of Parliament's right to tax them, passing resolutions—one set drafted by an extraordinary meeting, the Stamp Act Congress—that rejected Parliament's power to tax while pledging their loyalty to the king. In addition to these debates, there was widespread popular resistance by street mobs and crowds across the colonies. These mobs, derived primarily from the middle and lower ranks of urban society, were aroused by fears of political oppression, economic self-interest, and religious passion. They intimidated and attacked Stamp Act officials and, in some cases, destroyed their property to force them either to leave town or to resign. Spurred by this violent response, merchants and lawyers spoke out against the tax and organized protests, and a nonimportation movement developed in towns across the colonies.

Ideological Sources of Resistance

By drawing on common law, rationalist thought, and radical Whig or republican political ideas, these elite leaders connected with the actions and ideas of the mob and transformed a specific tax protest into a resistance movement.

The Informal Compromise of 1766

The British, who were experiencing their own political turmoil in Parliament, responded to commercial self-interest and political expediency by repealing the stamp tax in 1766. Yet former prime minister George Grenville and other supporters of imperial reform won passage of an act asserting Parliamentary supremacy and administrative authority over the colonies, leaving the situation ambiguous.

The Growing Confrontation, 1767–1770 (pp. 158–164)

The ambiguity of the Stamp Act compromise left important constitutional issues unresolved, assuring that further efforts to tax the colonists would resurrect the same passions and violence and make it harder to resolve the crisis.

The Townshend Initiatives

The new British minister, Charles Townshend, reopened the debate by again seeking revenues in the colonies to pay for officials to enforce Parliamentary laws. He also passed legislation requiring American colonists to house and feed British troops stationed there.

America Again Resists

The Americans responded with more resistance and mob activity, and broadened the nonimportation movement, which gained considerable support from women. The British, out of patience and unable or unwilling to back down or compromise, sent troops to Boston in 1768.

The Second Compromise

The introduction of troops seemed to set the stage for an inevitable confrontation between the Sons of Liberty and British soldiers. However, domestic troubles and the impact of the American trade boycott caused the ministry to hesitate. Another new minister, Lord North, fearful of civil war and convinced that economic prosperity was more important than an assertion of authority, pushed for the repeal of the Townshend Duties and defused the crisis. For many, a period of harmony returned, and a resurgence of profitable trade between the colonies and Britain seemed to assure the continued existence of the empire. Not even mob violence in New York or the Boston Massacre of 1770 seemed to threaten the compromise. Radicals in the colonies, however, continued to debate sovereignty and organized correspondence committees to generate and spread anti-British propaganda during the lull.

The Road to Rebellion, 1771–1775 (pp. 164–173)

In spite of the compromise, rising tensions between the British and the Americans continued to fuel the development of an American resistance movement. When the British again tried to tax Americans, members of the movement responded by directly challenging British right to rule through the Boston Tea Party. After the British placed Boston under martial law, colonial American politicians met in a Continental Congress to formulate a political response, while across the colonies Americans reinvigorated the nonimportation movement and joined militia companies in expectation of British use of military force to assert their authority. Compromise failed, because neither side was willing or able to accept it.

The Compromise Overturned

In spite of the compromise, the actions of the rebels sustained the mutual distrust and anger that the disputes over taxation had caused. These tensions ensured that the next British action, the Tea Act of 1773, would be met with more resistance and propel the two sides to the brink of civil war. By reducing the tax on British East India tea, the British hoped to encourage Americans to import British tea. The Americans rejected this act as a ploy to make them accept the principle of taxation and symbolically resisted by staging the Boston Tea Party. The British, their patience exhausted, closed Boston Harbor, imposed martial law on Boston, annulled the colony's charter, and prohibited public town meetings. The Americans responded to the "Intolerable Acts" by forming a Continental Congress and preparing for war.

The Response of the First Continental Congress

The Continental Congress did seek compromise, but it also repudiated Parliamentary supremacy and began the nonimportation movement again. Though some British sought a compromise with the Congress, most felt that a third retreat was not possible. Americans must, Lord North decided, pay for defense and administration and acknowledge Parliamentary power.

The Rising of the Countryside

Meanwhile, colonists in towns across the countryside resisted British taxes, joined the nonimportation movement, produced "homespun" cloth, joined militia companies, and, in Massachusetts, organized extralegal assemblies.

The Failure of Compromise

When the British in Boston sought to extend their control into the countryside in April 1775, after a six-month stalemate, they met the armed resistance of a colonial militia—the Minutemen—at Lexington and Concord, thus initiating civil war.

Compromise failed because at each stage of the imperial crisis, the Americans responded aggressively and creatively, turning a political debate into a broad resistance movement. The British were forced to respond to events rather than to shape them. Over time, their ideological rigidity, and gradual loss of patience, made it increasingly hard for the British to compromise. Though a few British lawmakers did suggest colonial representation in Parliament and other compromises, these suggestions did not prevail among lawmakers, and Parliament was left no choice but to defensively harden its position and move toward the use of force.

EXPANDED TIMELINE

1754–1763 **British national debt doubles**
The cost of the British victory in the Great War for Empire was extremely high. To finance the war, the British doubled the national debt. Britain's administrative response to this financial crisis was to raise taxes at home and in the colonies.

1760 **George III becomes king**
In 1760, George III ascended the throne. Young and energetic, George III would support those who favored a more activist and expansionist colonial policy.

1762 **Revenue Act reforms customs service**
Toward the end of the Great War for Empire, determined to gain more control over the trading system in the American colonies, British officials began to press for legislative reforms that would plug loopholes and enforce the payment of duties. The first effort in this strategy was the Revenue Act. This legislation required customs officials to serve in the office to which they were appointed, rather than lease it to a deputy in return for cash payments, thereby placing more aggressive agents in the colonies.

Royal Navy arrests smugglers
In order to curb corruption and increase revenues in colonial trade, the British government instructed the Royal Navy to stop American merchants who were illegally trading grain with the French West Indies.

1763 **Treaty of Paris ends Great War for Empire**
Proclamation Line restricts settlement west of Appalachians
The Treaty of Paris confirmed the triumph of the British over the French in the Great War for Empire. The British acquired French Canada and all the French territory east of the Mississippi River, as well as Spanish Florida. Concerns over Indian occupation of the lands west of the Appalachians in the wake of Pontiac's uprising prompted British officials to issue the Proclamation of 1763, which prohibited British colonial settlement west of the Appalachians. To enforce the Proclamation, as well as to control the French population of Canada and safeguard Florida, the British placed a peacetime army of ten thousand men in the colonies.

George Grenville becomes prime minister
John Wilkes demands reforms in England
The new prime minister, George Grenville, strongly supported a more aggressive administrative policy over the colonies. He believed revenues from the Americans could be increased by closer regulation of colonial trade, and that Americans needed to submit to Parliamentary authority. Meanwhile in England, the increased taxes, government power, and fears of corruption generated political demands for a greater representation of the people in Parliament. The Radical Whig John Wilkes was the most outspoken critic of the government.

1764 **Currency Act protects British merchants**
Sugar Act places duty on French molasses
Colonists oppose vice-admiralty courts
To increase revenue from America and assert Parliamentary authority over the colonies, George Grenville won Parliamentary approval of both the Currency Act and the Sugar Act in 1764. The Currency Act prohibited the issuing of paper currency in all the colonies. The Sugar Act shrewdly lowered the duty on French molasses to enhance the competitiveness of British molasses, while increasing regulation of illegal trade through vice-admiralty courts. American colonists protested the act because they feared it would eliminate necessary trade with the French islands. They also questioned the constitutionality of the vice-admiralty courts. Mostly, they opposed this increased exertion of British authority.

1765 **Stamp Act imposes direct tax on colonies**
Quartering Act provides for British troops
Riots by Sons of Liberty
Stamp Act Congress
First nonimportation movement
To obtain even more revenue from the American colonies, Grenville gained passage of the Stamp Act, which imposed a tax on all legal documents, newspapers, and correspondence. To force colonists to pay for their own defense, he also gained passage of the Quartering Act, which required colonists to house and feed British troops in America. While urban street mobs, motivated by economic self-interest, and spurred on by religious enthusiasm and class animosity, rejected this assertion of authority with violence, political leaders called the Stamp Act Congress. Arguing that only elected representatives of the colonists could impose taxes, the delegates opposed the tax on constitutional grounds. Meanwhile, patriots

and their supporters organized a nonimportation movement against British goods. This combining of direct action and constitutional debates transformed the colonial response into a resistance movement.

1766 **First compromise: Stamp Act repealed and Declaratory Act passed**
A new prime minister, Lord Rockingham, opposed the Stamp Act. Caught between London merchants, who suffered at the hands of the colonial boycott and thus favored its repeal, and conservatives, who insisted that England respond to colonial resistance with force, Rockingham forged a compromise. The Stamp Act was repealed, and duties against colonial trade were reduced. At the same time, Parliament issued the Declaratory Act, which asserted its authority over the colonies. This ambiguous response allowed plenty of room for negotiation.

1767 **Townshend Duties on certain colonial imports
Restraining Act in New York temporarily suspends colonial assembly there
Daughters of Liberty make "homespun" cloth**
Influenced by George Grenville's persistent demand that America be tapped for more revenue, Charles Townshend recommitted the British government to this agenda. The Townshend Act levied a series of duties on trade goods imported into the colonies to raise revenue to pay for royal officials and support the military. Townshend also responded to New York's resistance to the Quartering Act by suspending its assembly until it submitted. In response, the colonists again refused to pay the duties, formed new political groups to organize resistance, and rejected Parliament's right to tax them. Meanwhile, American women responded to the second nonimportation movement by trying to replace imports with the home production of cloth, called "homespun."

1768 **Second nonimportation movement
British armies occupy Boston**
In response to the Townshend Duties, American patriots organized a second nonimportation movement. Deepening colonial resistance prompted the British to choose military coercion over debate and to send troops to Boston. Meanwhile, the boycott organized by the colonists against the British seriously began to cut into trade.

1770 **Second compromise: Townshend Duties repealed
Boston Massacre**
Lord North sought another compromise with the colonists. He decided to repeal all but the tax on tea, which he retained purely for symbolic reasons. In response, the Americans called off the boycott. A spirit of compromise prevailed even as the presence of British troops led to violence in both New York and Boston. In Boston, when street mobs harassed British troops, the troops fired into the crowd, killing five men. Though Boston rebels exploited the incident to broaden the movement against British rule, a spirit of harmony tended to suppress the deep passions and mutual distrust between the colonists and the British.

1772 **Committees of Correspondence formed**
Fearful of British efforts to increase power over them, the colonists formed numerous Committees of Correspondence. Committee members exchanged information and ideas regularly by letter from colony to colony and from the cities and towns to the countryside. These committees broadened the resistance movement even as compromise prevailed.

1773 **Tea Act assists British East India Company
Boston Tea Party**
Lord North revived American resistance by passing the Tea Act in 1773. Meant to help the East India Company by giving it a monopoly on tea sales in the colonies, it was viewed by the colonists as an effort to put American merchants out of business and enforce Parliament's authority to tax the colonies. Committees of Correspondence organized widespread boycotts and resistance to the shipment of tea to colonial ports. When the governor of Massachusetts maneuvered to force a shipment of tea into Boston, Boston Patriots stormed the ship and threw its cargo into the harbor.

1774 **Coercive Acts punish Massachusetts
Quebec Act offends patriots
First Continental Congress
Third nonimportation movement
Loyalists organize**
The British sought to punish the Bostonians by compelling them to submit to a series of Parliamentary acts. The Port Bill closed the harbor. The Government Act ended Massachusetts' political autonomy by annulling its charter and prohibiting public meetings. A new Quartering Act required colonists to accommodate more troops. The Justice Act took trials out of Massachusetts and moved them to other colonies. These acts, combined with the Quebec Act, which legalized Catholicism in Quebec, led to a broad-based call for a Continental Congress. Though many delegates sought compromise at the Congress, the majority stated its repudiation of Parliamentary authority and launched commercial warfare against Britain through a massive nonimportation movement. While the countryside prepared for armed resistance, the Massachusetts House defied British authority by continuing to meet outside Boston.

1775 **General Thomas Gage marches to Lexington and Concord**
When General Thomas Gage went into the countryside outside Boston to arrest colonial leaders and capture supplies, he encountered a countryside in rebellion. British troops did battle against colonial forces at Lexington and Concord. Debate and resistance had become civil war.

GLOSSARY

national debt Governments finance their operations either by taxation or by borrowing money. They usually borrow money from their own citizens by selling government bonds, Treasury certificates, or securities. Like all individuals or entities that borrow money, the government pays the lender interest, or a service charge on the money it borrows. The amount of money borrowed from the people and the interest paid annually for that money is the national debt. Though it is highly unlikely that the people of a country will call in the national debt and force their own government to pay the debt or go into bankruptcy, lowering the national debt is considered to be good policy. When the national debt is high, the government competes with others for money in the market, and thus forces interest rates up. Higher interest rates only increase the debt, while stifling the very economic growth that, through increasing tax revenues, would reduce it. In addition, raising taxes to pay the debt is never very popular because it involves taxing everyone to remunerate the relatively few who loaned money to the government. The British, faced with a doubling of the national debt during the Great War for Empire, discovered this when they chose to increase taxes on the American colonists. (p. 148)

excise levies One way that governments raise revenues is by increasing sales taxes on specific items. Usually these are luxury items, or items that are considered to be nonessential or even unhealthy, such as alcohol or tobacco. In colonial America, such sales taxes were imposed on essential and luxury colonial goods alike. (p. 148)

pensioners A pensioner is someone who receives a monthly payment (or "pension") for past government or military service from the government for as long as he or she lives. Critics of the British government charged that during the Great War for Empire the British bureaucracy had become bloated with thousands of such unproductive workers. (p. 148)

rotten boroughs In the late eighteenth century, members of the House of Commons in the British Parliament were elected as representatives from districts that had been established generations earlier. Over time, the population of various districts had increased or decreased as a result of economic development or decline. Parliament, however, had done little to maintain proportional representation, resulting in an increase in the disparity between the size of districts, or "boroughs," with a representative. Gradually, districts that had experienced major population loss became prey for aristocrats, rich merchants, or friends of a party who wanted power or "influence" in the House. Through influence, bribes, and payments, these individuals would control the voters and thus all but handpick those they wanted to become members of the House. Such districts where representation was corrupted by others' desire for political power were called, by critics of the system, "rotten boroughs." (p. 148)

legal tender Legal tender is the paper currency or coins issued and supported by a government with a promise to pay the value of the bill or coin on demand. Today, that promise is backed by both the word and the credit of the government. Thus legal tender must be accepted for payment of goods, services, debts, and all other transactions by everyone. Before modern countries went off the gold standard, this promise to pay the value of paper currency was a promise to pay in gold. The confidence in the currency was based on the confidence the holder of the currency had that the government could redeem its full value in gold. Great Britain circulated coins the size of which reflected their true value in gold, silver, or copper, as well as bills of exchange that traded at value. Paper currency issued by colonial governments, supported only by their word or credit, often lost its value, making British merchants loath to accept it. To limit its use, the British prohibited the issuing of paper currency in colonial America. (p. 149)

vice-admiralty courts The armed forces of most countries have special courts in which cases involving military personnel or issues pertaining to the military are tried. Usually, these courts operate by their own sets of rules and procedures, which are different from those of the judicial system. In the eighteenth century, cases involving the navy and the administration of the maritime empire were heard in the vice-admiralty courts. In these courts, rulings were made not by juries but by British judges, who were sympathetic to the strict enforcement of customs duties and other maritime regulations. (p. 150)

natural rights The Enlightenment emphasized the power of human reason and moral sense, and thus increasingly elevated man as a special being. Enlightenment thinkers held that each human being, by possessing these characteristics, had fundamental rights inherent to humanity and thus inalienable—unable to be taken away. These rights were life, liberty, and property. As a being with a free will, each individual had the right to own, control, and make his or her own life and to own the material fruits of his or her efforts. (p. 155)

common law Many laws are established not in statutes passed by a governing body but over time in the litigation of court cases on various issues. Past court decisions are reviewed for precedents that help establish a current course of action or behavior. Though all British subjects in the eighteenth century drew their rights from the common-law tradition, American colonists would particularly rely on this tradition to defend their rights against the Crown. (p. 155)

writs of assistance   In an effort to increase surveillance and prosecution of smuggling in the empire, Parliament granted customs officials the power to serve writs of assistance. These search warrants gave customs agents a blanket right to search and seize property as evidence from anyone they believed was withholding it. Such broadly construed search warrants were, and are, usually rejected on the grounds that they give the police or customs official too much authority over an individual and thus violate that person's right to property and to freedom from harassment. The power a search warrant gives the police remains a major rights issue today. Police officers are strictly limited in whom they can and cannot search, what they can and cannot do in a search, and what evidence from a search they can and cannot use in a case. (p. 155)

republicanism   A Whig believed that political power and legitimacy were vested equally in the king, the aristocracy, and the people. A republican argued that all power and legitimacy derived from the people and that government acquired legitimacy from the consent of the governed. Republicanism had developed in seventeenth-century England, and continued to gain British adherents or sympathizers, both at home and in the colonies, throughout the eighteenth century. (p. 156)

boycott   The power merchants possessed in politics has often made them the target of economic activities that indirectly seek to exert political pressure on the government. One of the most effective weapons that politically active people have is to refuse to purchase goods traded by merchants, or to refuse to use the service provided by a certain company or government, in order to inflict economic damage on that merchant or company and thus compel it to exert pressure on politicians to change the unpopular law. The boycott became a powerful weapon used by the American colonists to force the British to repeal taxation measures. (p. 156)

quartering   Before the development of modern military establishments in the nineteenth century, there was no separate government bureaucracy to house, feed, and clothe the military. Armies therefore, routinely had to request that local governments and populations provide them with supplies and housing—either local housing or barracks. When such offers of support failed to materialize, the national government often had to require local governments to provide aid. If and when this was not forthcoming, the army confiscated and occupied houses and buildings and foraged for food and supplies. (p. 159)

homespun   In support of nonimportation of British cloth, many women in the American colonies began to produce more yarn and cloth at home. The production of "homespun" gradually freed Americans from their dependence on British textile manufacturers. By rejecting British imports, and then reducing dependence on British manufacturers, the production of homespun highlighted the limitations that the Navigation Acts, by the third quarter of the eighteenth century, were placing on the economy of the colonies. It also pointed the way toward more serious import-replacement economic strategies undertaken twenty years later. (pp. 160–161)

loyalist   An American colonist who supported the continuation of British rule in the American colonies, and thus opposed the Revolutionary movement, was a loyalist. Many loyalists, caught between support for Britain and animosity from Patriots, chose to leave the colonies, often going to Canada. (p. 170)

extralegal   Something that is extralegal is outside the bounds of law. That does not necessarily mean it is illegal but, rather, that there are no statutes or laws that pertain to this development, activity, or forum. The colonists were regularly stepping outside the bounds of law to advance the Revolutionary movement. Street riots, resolutions from assemblies, assembly meetings after the assembly had been suspended, the Stamp Act Congress, and the First and Second Continental Congresses were all outside the bounds of English law and, thus, extralegal. (p. 172)

IDENTIFICATION

Identify by filling in the blanks.

1. To control the settlement of the country beyond the Appalachian Mountains, as well as to prevent Indian wars, the British established the _____ of 1763. (p. 148)

2. To control the colonial printing and circulation of paper money, Parliament passed the _____ in 1764, banning the use of paper money as legal tender in the colonies. (p. 149)

3. William Pitt's successor was _____. He had influence over the new king, George III, and was convinced that the British government

Features Exercises

needed to impose new taxes on the American colonies in order to pay for the national debt incurred by the Great War for Empire. (p. 149)

4. Since the Molasses Act of 1733, which had imposed a 6-pence duty on the importation of French molasses, American traders had taken to smuggling French molasses into the colonies. To encourage colonists to import British molasses, the _____ reduced the duty on French molasses to 3 pence, while increasing enforcement. (p. 149)

5. The prime minister who succeeded Lord Bute and initiated both the Sugar Act and the Stamp Act was _____. (p. 149)

6. The _____ required colonists to pay a tax on all legal papers, newspapers, playing cards, and other printed items. (pp. 150–151)

7. In response to the Stamp Act, street mobs formed Patriot groups to oppose enforcement of the act. They called themselves the _____. (p. 152)

8. In 1766, the British government repealed the Stamp Act, but then asserted its right of "full power and authority" to govern the colonists and pass whatever laws it chose to pass in the _____. (p. 157)

9. When a new minister replaced Grenville, he sought to continue the administrative effort to tax the colonists. The _____ of 1767 authorized taxes on paper, paint, glass, and tea imported into the colonies. (p. 159)

10. In 1767, when New Yorkers refused to quarter troops as required by the Quartering Act, Townshend passed the _____, suspending the New York assembly until it agreed to do so. (p. 159)

11. In 1768, after the assembly of Massachusetts had refused to accept the Townshend Duties, Lord Hillsborough, losing patience, decided to send British troops to _____ to force a showdown with the radical Patriots. (p. 161)

12. The British radical in the 1760s who called for reforms of the British system and who received much support in the colonies was _____. (p. 162)

13. Lord North managed a compromise by repealing all the Townshend Duties taxes except the one on tea. When the East India Company attempted to make a shipment of tea to Boston in December 1773, Patriots in Boston resisted by dumping the tea in the _____. (p. 165)

14. To display their contempt for the Coercive Acts, which essentially put Boston under military rule, Patriots referred to these measures as the _____. (p. 165)

15. In response to British force, residents of Massachusetts towns across the interior formed militia companies whose members pledged that they would be ready at a minute's notice to defend themselves against British troops. These local Patriot militias called themselves the _____. (p. 172)

FEATURES EXERCISES

American Voices

JOSIAH QUINCY JR., The Threat of Mob Rule (p. 154)

Mob violence was a traditional way for colonists who had no vote or say in politics to express their political will. The volatile nature of mobs, however, makes them an imprecise and often reckless way to express ideas or try to achieve goals. In this account, Josiah Quincy, a Whig supporter of the Patriot movement, provides a commentary on the mob that destroyed the house of Thomas Hutchinson. As you read this account, ask yourself the following questions:

1. What are Quincy's charges against the mob? Why does he think it went beyond acceptable behavior, even for a mob?

2. Why would the mob attack a man's property as opposed to the man himself?

3. Though Quincy criticizes the mob for excess, how does his report of Hutchinson's response the following morning indicate that the mob probably considered its night's work to have been a success?

4. Why does the author make a distinction between a "democratic state" and the "glorious medium" of the British constitution? Wasn't the British constitution democratic? Weren't Quincy and others in the movement in favor of democracy?

American Lives

George R. T. Hewes and the Meaning of the Revolution (pp. 166–167)

A variety of American colonists resisted British efforts to establish greater administrative control over the colonies in the 1760s. In order for those acts of resistance to develop into a revolutionary movement, however, the various participants—Whig leaders, merchants, assemblymen, farmers, and the artisans and workers in northern seaports—had to coordinate their actions and unify their ideas. The experience of George Hewes provides strong evidence of these dynamics. Hewes was an artisan-worker who was apprenticed early and struggled to establish himself. Sensitive about his class status, Hewes soon developed a republican view of colonial politics. He believed that the people were the source of legitimacy and power and should be involved as equals in home rule. As you read this piece, ask yourself these questions:

1. What rights did Hewes believe he had as a citizen?
2. How did his experience in the Boston Tea Party reflect the republicanism of the Tea Party supporters?
3. Why, in spite of his meager material gains, do you think Hewes supported the Revolution so strongly?

American Voices

ANONYMOUS BROADSIDE, MAY 18, 1775, "To the Associators of the City of Philadelphia" (p. 172)

Republicanism took strong hold among the sailors, workers, and artisans of the seaport colonial cities. Those who were republicans believed that not only are people the sources of the power and legitimacy to rule but that leaders should make an effort to equalize political opportunity by broad suffrage and by encouraging widespread political participation. Some republicans would gradually move toward more radical ideas about equalizing economic status as a means of assuring political equality. This broadside articulates the depth and direction of this more radical equalizing or "leveling" tendency. Read the piece and try to answer the following questions:

1. In what ways, in the views of this anonymous writer, were the republican Associators not republican enough?
2. How do his suggestions for a style of uniform indicate the direction of popular aspirations? Who usually wears such attire, and how is it different from what is generally worn by military men and women?
3. Embedded in the broadside are some fundamental principles of republican belief. What are they, and how does the writer's interpretation of these beliefs foreshadow the tendency among republicans to move increasingly toward democracy?

Voices from Abroad

LIEUTENANT COLONEL FRANKLIN SMITH, A British View of Lexington and Concord (p. 173)

In interpreting past events, historians try to figure out what really happened. They do this by evaluating different accounts of the same event. Often, some accounts seem more accurate than others. For historians, a "true and authentic" document is one that has certain characteristics: it corroborates other accounts; it tends to avoid rhetoric or exaggeration (an indication that it was written for a purpose); it accurately and reasonably portrays the goals, aspirations, actions, and responses of the participants; and it also accurately portrays the political, economic, cultural, and even spatial and environmental context in which the events described took place. As you read this account, ask yourself the following questions:

1. What is the tone of the report from the Patriot-controlled Provincial Congress? How does the British officer's report differ from the Provincial Congress's report?
2. What aspects of the British officer's report seem credible?
3. How does the officer's assessment of the Patriots' plans reflect a sound understanding of military planning and procedures?
4. In the two reports, who is to blame for starting the war? How much responsibility does the British officer accept for what happened?

MAPS AND FIGURES

Map 5.2 British Troop Deployments, 1763–1775 (p. 161)

As a result of the Great War for Empire, the British government decided to station 10,000 troops in the

American colonies. They did this to protect the borders of newly won territory and to enforce the prohibition of settlement beyond the Appalachian Mountains, both by placing troops along the frontier and in seaport towns. Analyze the data as it is presented on this map and try to interpret it without referring to the text. A battalion, represented by the largest circle, contained about 350 men. Smaller circles, each about one-half the size of the previous one, indicate corresponding numbers of men, from 175 to about 90, then 50, and finally 25. Using these numbers as guidelines, determine approximately how many troops are represented on this map. Having done this, answer the following questions:

1. How does the distribution of the troops reflect the British imperial policy of trying to increase authority over the American colonies?
2. Why are there so few troops along the frontiers?
3. Why are there troops in the South, along the Florida border, and the Gulf coast?
4. Why are so many troops located in and around Boston?

Figure 5.1 The Growing Power of the British State (p. 149)

Historians make generalized conclusions from evidence. In this case, the rising power of the British state is evident from the rising military expenditures and increased taxes, which required a larger bureaucracy to collect. This bureaucracy in turn increased general government expenditures. As you look at this chart, noting the changes from year to year, as well as the general upward trends, ask yourself the following questions:

1. Can you explain the reasons for the uneven ups and downs in military expenditures? How is that pattern different from patterns of military expenditures today?
2. Why did the number of tax collectors seem to grow steadily in the 1730s and 1740s? If this was occurring during a period of a "salutary neglect" policy in the colonies, what does the pattern indicate about the changing presence of government in different places in the empire?

Figure 5.2 Trade as a Political Weapon, 1763–1776 (p. 163)

Trade figures are some of the best historical evidence we have from the eighteenth century. The number of imports and exports arriving and leaving any port was recorded, and the figures from all ports were then added together to give approximate total figures for imports and exports between the colonies and Britain. We therefore have a good idea of the trend in exports from the colonies to Britain during the century, as well as in imports going to the colonies from Britain. Look at this chart closely and answer the following questions:

1. What does the regular excess of imports over exports for the colonies suggest about their economic situation?
2. If exports have been rising steadily, how does one explain a sharp change in imports over a two- or three-year period? Who or what factors might be responsible for such a rapid change?
3. Follow the ups and downs of imports and chronologically compare them with the passage of legislation. How closely are the two related? How strong is the cause-and-effect evidence? Is it stronger for one period than for another?

Table 5.2 Patriot Resistance, 1762–1775 (p. 171)

This chart breaks down the events that led to the Revolution as a series of actions and responses. If you read the list closely and think about how each side acted or responded to the other, you can get a much better sense of why events took the course they eventually did. As you read the list, ask yourself the following questions:

1. What is the general trend of British actions? Did they change, or were they consistent? Did British goals change or remain the same?
2. How does the pattern in American responses diverge from British responses? For example, compare and contrast British goals and demands in the Tea Act of 1773 through British policy in 1762 with colonial goals and demands during the Tea Party through American response to British legislation in 1762. Which side has changed more?
3. How do the American responses reflect the power of colonial assemblies and highlight the fact that the dispute was fundamentally a dispute over authority and representation within the empire between colonial assemblies and Parliament?

SELF-TEST

Multiple Choice

1. The leading political force behind the British desire to reassert authority over the American colonies in 1765 was:
   a. George III.
   b. General James Wolfe.
   c. Lord Bute.
   d. George Grenville.

2. The British ministry shrewdly drafted the Sugar Act of 1764 with the intention of:
   a. cutting off all colonial trade with the French West Indies.
   b. enforcing the 6-pence-per-gallon duty on French molasses as stated by the Molasses Act of 1733.
   c. allowing colonial trade with the West Indies and imposing a lower but more strictly enforced duty on French molasses.
   d. allowing colonial trade with the West Indies and imposing higher duties on French molasses.

3. The Americans responded to the Sugar Act of 1764 in *all* of the following ways *except*:
   a. Merchants opposed the new tariff and vowed to continue smuggling.
   b. Mobs rioted in the streets and boycotted molasses.
   c. Colonists objected to the empowerment of vice-admiralty courts established to enforce the duty because they had no trial by jury and were presided over by biased judges.
   d. Colonists objected to the act as a denial of some of their most basic rights.

4. When the colonists objected to taxation without representation, a debate developed over the nature of representation and the question of whether Americans were or should be represented in Parliament. By 1775, the colonists had decided the question by asserting:
   a. We are virtually represented in Parliament and do not want seats. Such seats would be redundant.
   b. Colonial representation in Parliament is impractical, given our distance from Britain and our distinct local interests. Colonial assemblies are separate and equal, and they alone have the power to tax the colonies. Parliament does not have supremacy over colonial assembles.
   c. Parliament can tax us only for external trade. For internal activities, we require representation to be taxed.
   d. We would like to form a large colonial assembly that would supersede Parliament's power in colonial affairs.

5. The Stamp Act Congress met in order to:
   a. humbly petition the king for repeal of the Stamp Act.
   b. issue resolves warning that if the Stamp Act was not repealed, riots and mob action against British officials would continue.
   c. propose a Continental Congress to prepare for a broad-based resistance movement.
   d. invite British leaders to seek a compromise by discussing new political arrangements between Britain and the colonies.

6. Urban mobs and organized groups like the Sons of Liberty were primarily made up of:
   a. criminals, transients, slaves, and other members of the urban "rabble" who wanted to vent their frustrations against local and British officials alike.
   b. elite merchants, lawyers, and businesspeople, who sought to set an example for the lower classes.
   c. small merchants, artisans, shopkeepers, and some farmers, as well as some apprentices, workers, day laborers, and sailors who wanted to participate in politics.
   d. loyalists who sought to sabotage the Patriot movement by infiltrating mobs.

7. Patriot merchants and lawyers who opposed the British drew their arguments directly from *all* of the following sources *except*:
   a. Enlightenment rationalism.
   b. common law.
   c. Radical Whig tradition.
   d. evangelical Christianity.

8. Among the various reasons the Stamp Act was repealed in 1766, the most important was that:
   a. it had failed to achieve its goals.
   b. the American boycott cut deeply into British exports to the American colonies.
   c. political squabbling among Whigs and Old Whigs in Parliament encouraged the Whigs to seek a compromise by repealing the act.
   d. Americans had placed political pressure on Britain to repeal the act.

9. The British responded to American challenges to their taxation efforts more harshly in 1768 than

they did only two years before for *all* of the following reasons *except*:
  a. Lord Hillsborough's patience was exhausted and he was under less pressure than George Grenville had been to find a compromise.
  b. The Massachusetts assembly had challenged Parliament's right to tax the colonies in all matters.
  c. An effective massive colonial boycott of British goods had raised the stakes.
  d. Colonial mobs called openly for independence.

10. In spite of the compromise over taxation worked out by Lord North in 1770, the Patriots continued to advance their movement by *all* of the following methods *except*:
  a. organizing committees of correspondence in towns and cities.
  b. using any relevant incident to propagandize against British threat to colonial liberties.
  c. continuing the boycott of British goods.
  d. organizing support for their resistance and establishing militia companies throughout the countryside.

11. Loyalists had a strong following among *all* of the following groups *except*:
  a. Regulators in the Carolina backcountry.
  b. Quakers and Germans in Pennsylvania.
  c. military and administrative officials, merchants with strong British contacts, members of the Anglican Church, and conservative lawyers.
  d. wealthy landowners across New York and the South who favored aristocracy.

12. The Patriots of Boston staged the Boston Tea Party because:
  a. they had a personal grudge to settle with Massachusetts governor Thomas Hutchinson and wanted to destroy the tea that had been consigned to his sons.
  b. Governor Hutchinson launched a scheme to have the army seize the tea for nonpayment of tax and then sell the tea and collect the tax, thus establishing the precedent of British right to tax the colonies.
  c. they wanted to contribute to the continuing nonimportation movement.
  d. they wanted to directly repudiate the leadership of Lord North and his support of the British East India Company.

13. The only mainland colony that did not send delegates to the First Continental Congress in Philadelphia in September 1774 was:
  a. Rhode Island   c. Georgia
  b. Maine   d. South Carolina

14. Thomas Gage marched into the countryside around Boston on April 18, 1775, in order to:
  a. attack and shut down an illegal Middlesex County assembly meeting in Concord.
  b. capture colonial leaders hiding in nearby towns and seize supplies.
  c. relocate his troops to provide better control over the region than was afforded by their location in Boston.
  d. seize storehouses and armories.

Short Essays

Answer the following questions in a brief paragraph.

1. What impact did the Great War for Empire have on British attitudes toward the American colonies? (pp. 145–152)

2. Why did American colonists object to rules, regulations, taxes, and enforcement that had become commonplace for citizens in Britain? What were the intellectual and political sources of their resistance? (pp. 148–156)

3. How did British action and American response in the Stamp Act crisis foreshadow the entire conflict? (pp. 150–157)

4. How did a political objection to taxation by some American colonists turn into a revolutionary movement? Between 1765 and 1775, how did the American Patriots broaden the movement and assure general support for their cause? (pp. 152–164)

5. Compare and contrast the first and second compromise in the crisis between the colonists and the British? How did each compromise deal with the major issues dividing the two sides? (pp. 156–168)

6. Why do you think the conflict finally erupted into bloodshed? Do you think one side is more responsible for the end of compromise and the beginning of civil war? Why, or why not? (pp. 164–173)

ANSWERS

Identification

1. Proclamation Line
2. Currency Act

3. Lord Bute
4. Sugar Act
5. George Grenville
6. Stamp Act
7. Sons of Liberty
8. Declaratory Act
9. Townshend Act
10. Restraining Act
11. Boston
12. John Wilkes
13. Boston Harbor
14. Intolerable Acts
15. Minutemen

Self-Test

Multiple Choice

1. d.
2. c.
3. b.
4. b.
5. a.
6. c.
7. d.
8. a.
9. d.
10. c.
11. b.
12. d.
13. b.
14. b.

Short Essays

1. The Great War for Empire left the British deeply in debt. The close interaction between American colonists and the British during the war had also highlighted social differences between them, and raised British concerns about the relative independence the Americans had gained from British authority. British officials believed that they needed to administer the colonies more aggressively, both to levy the taxes needed to pay for the war and to clarify to Americans that they were subordinate within the empire. The British assumed that the Americans, as faithful British subjects, would submit to imperial authority. The colonists refused to accept this effort to control and subordinate them to second-class status.

2. American objections were based on the idea that the right to taxation lies with the people who are being taxed. Because they were not directly represented in Parliament, the colonists argued, Parliament could not tax them. Resistance developed from the colonists' awareness of their natural rights, rooted in common law, the rationalist ideas of the Enlightenment, and Real Whig and republican political ideas.

3. The British tended to act without consulting or considering the colonists' response very closely. They also tended to base their actions on a straightforward understanding of authority. The Americans responded to British actions creatively and dynamically, and almost always surprised them. Rooted in popular resistance to authority, natural-rights philosophy, and the Enlightenment, American ideas and responses outpaced British action. The British were thus regularly outmaneuvered and left with fewer options to proceed.

4. The American response to the Stamp Act, the first in a series of taxes on the colonies, occurred on several levels—local, regional, and colonial-wide. Locally, the response of the people on the street, such as the Sons of Liberty, was quickly integrated into the goals and actions of the Whig majority, which was composed of merchants, professionals, and politicians. Together, they established committees to organize a boycott, organize local resistance, and correspond with other, similar committees elsewhere in the colonies. Through organization, communication, and effective propaganda, these committees formed the dynamic force of a revolutionary movement that gained more and more popular support.

5. The first compromise was ambiguous and sent mixed messages to both sides. The British repealed the Stamp Act for political reasons, not as a response to American intellectual and political protests. They then sent mixed messages by reasserting Parliamentary supremacy in the Declaratory Act. While the status of the colonies and the determination of the British remained uncertain, both sides claimed a victory of sorts. The second compromise did little to mediate the issues separating the two sides. Indeed, both sides had hardened, leaving fewer options. The Americans repudiated Parliament's right to tax them, while the British insisted they held such power. Unable to resolve their differences, both sides simply chose not to press the issue at that time. As a result, each side rejected offers from the other, and the two parties stood locked in opposition, with nothing resolved.

6. From the outset, the British were apparently less able to respond to new ideas and tended to back down in search of compromise. They would not

have been willing to act had the Americans been a little less adamant, aggressive, and creative. The dynamic American revolutionary movement forced the British into a tactical corner, eventually leaving them no real choice but to challenge American resistance. Though it was the British who finally lost their patience and took action against the Americans, it was the American colonists who had forced their hand.

Part Two

★

The New Republic, 1775–1820

Part 2 explores the evolution of the United States from the American Revolution to 1820. The Thematic Timeline (page 176) lists the main developments topically in five columns: Government, Diplomacy, Economy, Society, and Culture. Read the Timeline and the Part introduction together, beginning with the left-hand Timeline column.

The most fundamental development change in this period was the creation of state republican governments and a national republic. These developments are explained in paragraph two of the Part introduction.

During this period, the United States carefully navigated a foreign policy to stay clear of conflicts with European powers. In the Revolution and the War of 1812, the United States and Britain opposed each other in war. These events are interpreted in the third paragraph.

The third Timeline column charts the expansion of American commerce and manufacturing in these years. Economic growth and westward expansion laid the foundations for the development of a national economy. This development is summarized in paragraph four of the Part introduction.

Americans had to decide what their republican society would be like, what the ideals of liberty and equality should mean in practice. The Timeline lists the key advances in male suffrage, religious liberty, and other areas. But, as paragraph five of the Part introduction explains, women and African Americans were excluded from participating as equals in the republican society.

Fifth, the citizens of the new republic strove to establish a national cultural identity. And, despite their diversity, by 1820 a distinctive American character had emerged, as the last paragraph of the Part introduction explains.

Now, read the Timeline across to find out which events were occurring at about the same time. Note, in the period 1810–1820, for example, that the colonists' decision to wage war against Britain in 1812 was made while the federal government was dominated by the Jeffersonian Republican party.

Part Questions

After you have finished studying the chapters in Part 2, you should be able to answer the following questions:

1. How did the state constitutions and the Constitution of 1787 embody republican principles?

2. What are the most important differences between the Constitution of 1787 and the Articles of Confederation? What accounts for these differences?

3. Describe the role the United States played in the struggles among the European powers during this period. In what ways did the involvement of the United States in conflicts among European powers hurt or help it? Why did foreign-policy issues so sharply divide Americans?

4. How was the American economy transformed in the late eighteenth and early nineteenth century? How did different political parties think the government should support those changes?

5. How did the ideology of republicanism affect social relations in the early republic?

6. In what ways did the Revolutionary War, republican ideology, westward expansion, the Industrial Revolution, the War of 1812, and the Second Great Awakening shape the emergence of an American national identity?

7. How did the American Revolution, the ratification of the Constitution, the Industrial Revolution, and westward expansion affect the lives of native Americans and African Americans from 1775 to 1820? What role did these peoples play in shaping the emerging American identity?

Chapter 6

War and Revolution, 1775–1783

LEARNING OBJECTIVES

1. How was a dispute over taxation between the American colonies and Great Britain transformed within twelve years into a democratic revolution?

2. War is often determined by the resources the respective combatants have at their disposal. Compare and contrast American and British resources in the Revolutionary War. Which side seemed to have the advantage?

3. How did geography, manpower, and leadership affect military strategy in the American Revolution? Which was most important in affecting the outcome of the war?

4. How and why did the goals of the American Patriots in the resistance movement move from being moderate to more radical in the first two years of the war? Why did many Americans not support the movement?

5. The Revolutionary War tested the limits of republicanism against the force of classical liberalism. How does the apparent outcome seem to point the way to the subsequent development of American life?

6. Did the American Revolution trigger a social revolution? Why, or why not?

7. The Enlightenment and the Great Awakening impacted American culture throughout the eighteenth century. How did republicanism, a product of the Enlightenment, further affect American religion during the Revolutionary period?

CHAPTER SUMMARY

The American Patriots, having gained the advantage with the outbreak of fighting, convinced other colonists to fight for their freedoms by establishing a republic in which sovereignty would be placed in the people. In doing this, they challenged and redefined the traditional political and social order.

Toward Independence, 1775–1776 (pp. 180–183)

Though Patriots rejected Parliamentary supremacy and some argued for independence, most Americans retained deep loyalty to the king in 1775 and did not support independence. The outbreak of war and the Continental army's lack of success in the field, as well as Thomas Paine's pamphlet, *Common Sense*, eroded that loyalty and radicalized the majority of Americans to support the Patriots' political move toward independence.

From Confrontation to Civil War

Continued fighting after the battles at Lexington and Concord, Massachusetts, inspired a divided Second Continental Congress to organize a Continental army in May 1775 and initiate economic sanctions against Great Britain. While the fighting continued in Massachusetts, Congress sent contradictory resolutions to the king, one requesting that he repeal the legislation that had ignited the crisis, the second stating the colonists' case for taking up arms. Rather than exploit these divisions, King George declared the colonists to be in rebellion and vowed to crush their uprising. This threat, coupled with aggressive efforts by the governors of Virginia and the Carolinas to put down the rebellion, encouraged activists to call special conventions to declare themselves independent.

"Tis Time to Part"

Although most colonists remained loyal to the monarchy, politicians, ministers, and intellectuals began to argue against support for the monarchy. In January 1776, a recent immigrant, Thomas Paine, wrote the pamphlet *Common Sense*, in which he argued for Americans to reject the arbitrary powers of the king, as well as the monarchical and Parliamentary government of Great Britain, and move toward an independent republican government. A republic is a government without a monarch that derives authority and legitimacy from the people.

Independence Declared

Paine's pamphlet inspired increasing support for independence. In the Declaration of Independence, Thomas Jefferson legitimized a break with England by appealing to the natural rights that all people possess—life, liberty, and happiness. Rather than blame Parliament, as Patriots had done up to this time, Jefferson condemned the king as a tyrant because of his failure to restrain Parliament's repeated violations of the colonists' rights. On this basis, Jefferson argued, Americans were justified in breaking their allegiance to the king and creating an independent republic. The impact was immediate. Overnight, many Americans were radicalized, became republicans, and moved toward establishing republican institutions.

The Perils of War and Finance, 1776–1778 (pp. 183–191)

In response to the Declaration, Britain launched a full-scale war against the confederation of states. Heavily favored, the British prevailed in almost every battle. Only a few key victories and luck kept the Patriot cause alive.

War in the North

With a larger population and a larger, more professional army, the British had superiority in the field. This became apparent when, in 1776, British forces invaded and occupied New York City and the surrounding area, pushing the Continental army into Pennsylvania. Realizing the British army's advantage, in late 1776 Washington shifted his strategy from one of confrontation in the open field to one of surprise attacks. When the overconfident British let down their guard, Washington's army achieved small victories that boosted morale.

Armies and Strategies

The British sought to negotiate with the Americans or force them to surrender, rather than to destroy them. With an inexperienced, underfinanced, and undersupplied army of short-term enlistees, Washington had few strategic choices. His tactics grew increasingly defensive, as he sought to draw the British away from the coast and sap their morale. Given the poor condition of his forces, he was fortunate to have avoided defeat in the first year of the war.

Victory at Saratoga

The British grand strategy to isolate New England culminated in the 1777 campaign. But an overcomplicated plan, overconfidence, generals working at cross-purposes, and leisurely troop movements undermined the effort. While General William Howe moved slowly to take Philadelphia, troops under General John Burgoyne, moving north from New York City toward Canada, became bogged down. Without reinforcements, Burgoyne's troops were left exposed to thousands of American militiamen from New England, who converged on them at Saratoga, New York. The British defeat at Saratoga was a turning point in the war because it encouraged the French to join the Americans in their fight against the British. The British defeat also left the Indians who had become allied with the British isolated, forcing them to fight the Americans across New York on their own.

Wartime Trials

Trials during the Revolution were both personal and political. Because the war was fought on home ground, many Americans were killed and many others were assaulted or suffered deprivation and displacement. Both Congress and the states, reluctant to impose taxes for fear of weakening their authority, financed the war by borrowing money, selling Continental loan certificates, and issuing paper money. This policy of no taxation touched off the most rapid inflation in American history and, by setting self-interest against patriotism, undermined support for the Revolution. In the winter of 1777–1778, the army was caught between congressional insolvency and popular demoralization. Unable to acquire supplies from either Congress or the local population, the army suffered horribly. By winter's end, almost three thousand soldiers had died and another one thousand had deserted. Amid the gloom, Baron von Steuben imposed a standardized drill system and turned the survivors into a leaner, tougher professional army.

The Path to Victory, 1778–1783 (pp. 192–199)

The Americans blazed a path to victory by securing an alliance with France and then launching a guerrilla war against an invading British army in the southern states. Worn down by American forces in the Carolinas, General Cornwallis decided to march his army, the last major British force actively waging war, into Virginia. There, he was encircled by a rejuvenated American army under Washington, as well as by French forces and the French fleet, and forced to surrender. In a dramatic turnaround, the Americans had gained a military victory.

The French Alliance

Seeking revenge for their defeat in the French and Indian War, the French, early supporters of the American Revolution, formally entered into an alliance with the Americans and infused the Patriot cause with new life and money. As a result of both the French intervention and the growing costs of war to the British state, the war became increasingly unpopular in England. Initially, the British sought a compromise, but it was too late. Most Americans had, by 1778, embraced the Revolution and republican ideas. The British army was compelled to fight on, spreading many of its troops across the West Indies to protect the islands from French invasion, while shifting its strategy from isolating New England toward winning back the more valuable southern colonies. The war had become part of a larger struggle for maritime superiority.

War in the South

After reconquering Georgia, the British moved from one victory to another, until they were challenged by reenergized local militia forces in North Carolina. In what became a war of attrition, the British general Lord Cornwallis conceded the Deep South and marched into Virginia. While the British plundered eastern Virginia, Washington launched a major offensive against Cornwallis. American and French troops on land and the French fleet at sea encircled his forces and compelled Cornwallis to surrender at Yorktown. The British gave up active prosecution of the war and sued for peace.

The Patriot Advantage

Though weak in other respects, the American army had the advantage of fighting on its own territory. It also received enough support from local militias and, to a lesser extent, the population to survive at critical moments. To succeed, not only did the British have to win battles but they also had to win over the American population—something that was beyond their ability. George Washington provided confident, stable military leadership and always deferred to civilian authority. Later in the war, he also recruited such outstanding military men as Baron von Steuben and the Marquis de Lafayette to transform the Continental army into an efficient fighting force.

Diplomatic Triumph

Maneuvering between British and French interests, the Americans won a major victory at the bargaining table. Not only did the Treaty of Paris formally recognize American independence but it also ceded all the land east of the Mississippi River to the Americans, thus setting the stage for the opening of the West to American expansion and the creation of a large and powerful nation. The treaty was signed in September 1783.

Republicanism Defined and Challenged (pp. 199–207)

Republicanism was severely tested but had a major impact on social order during the war. Economic pressures during the war put self-interest directly at odds with public interest and thus undermined the influence of republican virtue. In contrast, the spread of republican ideas called into question the role of women, the existence of slavery, and the organization of religion.

Republican Ideals and Wartime Pressures

Although the Declaration of Independence articulated the individual freedom and civil rights of every citizen, republican theory argued that each individual had certain responsibilities to the common good. The Revolutionary War severely tested this patriotism against individual self-interest. Soldiers, though lauded for their self-sacrifice, were condemned and punished for attempted mutinies motivated by their frustration over harsh conditions and lack of material rewards from Congress. Officers wanted lifetime pensions; soldiers, back pay and clothes. Among civilians, economic opportunities for short-term profit, amid the general economic distress and deprivation created by the war, prompted many to reexamine the nature of republican virtue. In most cases, self-interest tended to triumph. In response to the desperate need for clothing and supplies, American women dramatically increased their production of cloth. Many others filled in for their absent men by assuming farm production as well. Taught from childhood to be selfless, few women suffered tension between civic virtue and self-interest.

Meanwhile, the government's financial problems further tested republican virtue. As government-issued currency depreciated, even patriotic citizens would not accept it, and Congress was forced to remove it from circulation. Many speculators had bought up the Continental bills from farmers and artisans who were no longer able or willing to hold the depreciating currency. While speculators profited, farmers, artisans, and soldiers paid in personal sacrifices for the Revolution. While it seemed to some that self-interest had triumphed over virtue and patriotism, many kept faith that republican values would sustain the new republic.

The Loyalist Exodus

The war disrupted the lives of tens of thousands of people. Armies marching back and forth across states caused the colonists to live in fear and polarized public opinion. Both Loyalists and Patriots organized into political committees and local militias and actively opposed or fought each other, depending on which troops were in their area. Fearful Loyalists migrated to Canada, Britain, and the West Indies. Although some local Patriot governments seized Loyalist land, buildings, and goods, many officials opposed the confiscation and redistribution of Loyalist property. Because republican merchants and professionals in some cities replaced the departing Loyalists in the local economic structure, the Loyalist exodus did not cause a major change in society.

The Problem of Slavery

Slaves took part in the fight for independence on their own terms. Thousands of slaves responded to Lord Dunmore's offer of freedom if they would fight with the British, while thousands more evacuated with the British troops when they left Charleston. Other slaves who were Loyalists fled to Canada. Still others negotiated with their masters, remaining loyal during the war in return for their freedom after the war. In the northern states, thousands of free blacks fought with the Patriots.

As Americans professed belief in a free, egalitarian society, they were forced to question the existence of slavery in what became an intense debate. Quakers and other religious groups openly supported emancipation. Northern states moved toward abolishing slavery, while several southern states permitted masters to manumit their slaves, resulting in the freeing of about ten thousand. But these developments were short-lived. Most southern whites did not want a biracial society and advocated legislation that made it more difficult to manumit slaves, thus slowing the emancipation of the slaves who were working for their freedom. In response to growing frustration, slaves in Virginia planned a revolt in 1800. When whites discovered and suppressed the uprising, the debate over emancipation ended. Southern whites reaffirmed their commitment to slavery, regardless of how much it contradicted republican ideals.

A Republican Religious Order

Republican theory affected religious life as Anglicans renounced their allegiance to the king, the head of the Church of England. Virginia, New York, and New Jersey passed laws to establish religious freedom, making all churches equal by supporting none financially. Established churches remained in New England and in the Deep South. But everywhere, freedom of religion spread, republican principles liberalized religious ideas, and religious participation was increasingly viewed as a voluntary activity. Americans were creating a new republican order.

EXPANDED TIMELINE

1775 **Second Continental Congress meets**
Though the Second Continental Congress was divided between Patriots, who wanted independence, and conservatives, who preferred reconciliation with Great Britain, it did organize a Continental army, name George Washington as commander, and authorize the invasion of Canada.

Battle of Bunker Hill
The Continental army took over the waging of the war, which through the early summer of 1775 had been fought by militiamen from Massachusetts. They had withstood three assaults from British troops before giving up their position outside Boston at Bunker Hill in June 1775.

Congress submits Olive Branch petition
Meanwhile, moderates in Congress who favored reconciliation with England pushed through the Olive Branch petition to King George, in which they pledged

their obedience and asked him to repeal oppressive Parliamentary legislation. King George rejected the petition, declared the Americans "traitors," and vowed to crush the rebellion.

Lord Dunmore's proclamation offers freedom to slaves
When Patriots took over the Virginia assembly, the governor, Lord Dunmore, took refuge on a ship and organized two Loyalist military forces. One of these consisted of slaves, to whom he had offered freedom if they would join the Loyalist cause.

American invasion of Canada
Meanwhile Congress, hoping to unleash a popular rebellion in French Canada, authorized a military invasion of Canada. Though one small American force captured Montreal, another failed to take Quebec, and the effort failed when the French expressed no interest in joining the American rebellion.

1776 **Patriots and Loyalists skirmish in South**
When the Loyalist governor of North Carolina launched a military effort to suppress the rebellion there, Patriot militias rose up and defeated his troops and then established an independent Congress controlled by Patriots.

Thomas Paine's *Common Sense*
Early in 1776, Thomas Paine's pamphlet *Common Sense* gave a boost to the Patriot cause by persuasively attacking the monarchy and advocating the creation of an independent republic. By weakening Americans' loyalty to the Crown and presenting a plan for a new government, Paine dramatically increased support for independence. The rising tide of support for independence encouraged Patriots in North Carolina and Virginia to call on the Continental Congress to consider a resolution for independence.

Declaration of Independence (July 4)
In the Declaration of Independence, Jefferson, appealing to the natural rights of the governed, blamed the king for abridging the rights of his subjects and declared him a tyrant. The document justified the creation of an independent American republic.

British general William Howe defeats General George Washington in New York
In August, British forces under General William Howe easily outmaneuvered Washington's inexperienced forces before New York, allowing the city to be occupied by the British for the rest of the war. American forces narrowly missed being captured twice, and were forced to retreat north into New York. The British moved from one victory to another against the inexperienced American army, and by year's end had pushed Washington's troops across New Jersey into Pennsylvania.

Virginia Declaration of Rights
Republican ideas quickly began to influence American social and cultural life. In the Virginia legislature, Patriots who were advocates of the Enlightenment pushed through a resolution declaring religious freedom for all Christians.

1777 **Patriot women become important in war economy**
American women responded to wartime shortages and inflation by dramatically increasing their production of homespun cloth. Women filled in for those men who were absent due to war service and ran shops and farms across the colonies. Women generally experienced an increased sense of involvement in public affairs, prompting some of them to claim more rights in the new republic.

Howe occupies Philadelphia
The British launched a new campaign in 1777 to invade Canada and cut New England off from the other colonies. General Howe, however, moved south and, after defeating Washington's troops yet again at Brandywine Creek, occupied Philadelphia.

General Horatio Gates defeats British general John Burgoyne at Saratoga
Howe's occupation of Philadelphia left General John Burgoyne, who was bogged down in the Hudson Valley, without support. Burgoyne was forced to surrender to Horatio Gates and thousands of American militiamen at Saratoga, New York.

Continental army suffers at Valley Forge
Severe inflation of paper currency
Congress, reluctant to raise taxes, issued paper currency to finance the war. But the money quickly depreciated, making it nearly impossible to acquire supplies just as Washington's army went into winter camp at Valley Forge, leaving the men without provisions and forcing them to endure incredible hardship.

1778 **Franco-American Alliance (February 6)**
Lord North seeks negotiated settlement
British begin southern strategy; capture Savannah
The American victory at Saratoga reassured the French that the British could be beaten and encouraged them to sign a treaty of alliance with the Americans. Lord North, eager to forestall such an alliance, tried one last time to negotiate a settlement with the Americans, but it was far too late. As a result, the British, now wary of French designs on the rich West Indies colonies, spread out their troops and concentrated on trying to recover the rich southern colonies, where they believed there was considerable Loyalist sentiment and a good chance of victory.

1780 **Sir Henry Clinton seizes Charleston (May 12)**
French army lands in Rhode Island
In response to the successful British capture of Charleston and Camden, American militia and regular

forces intensified their efforts to defend the South. While American forces increased their harassment of British forces and eventually prevailed at Kings Mountain, North Carolina, the French landed in Rhode Island and, by posing a threat to British troops in New York, forced the British to again shift their strategy.

1781 **Lord Cornwallis invades Virginia; surrenders at Yorktown**
Lord Cornwallis, stymied in North Carolina, headed northeast into Virginia. Meeting little opposition, his forces and those led by Benedict Arnold ransacked the countryside. Meanwhile, Washington, taking advantage of French troops and the arrival of the French fleet from the West Indies, launched a major offensive against Cornwallis. By means of vigorous troop movement, Washington was able to coordinate his arrival at Yorktown with the arrival of the French fleet. Surrounded, Cornwallis had no choice but to surrender.

Loyalist immigration
The war polarized popular opinion and increased Patriot harassment of Loyalists, forcing many to leave the country by 1781.

Partial redemption of Continental currency at 40 to 1
Unable to tax the states, the Congress was compelled to finance the war by issuing bills of credit, or paper money. Many states also issued paper money. The flood of currency, combined with a loss of faith in the ability of the government to redeem the currency for gold or silver at value, touched off the worst inflation in American history. By 1781, it took forty dollars of Continental currency to acquire a dollar in gold or silver. When merchants began to refuse the currency, civilian patience and morale eroded, threatening the social order.

1782 **Slave manumission in Virginia (reversed, 1792)**
The presence of British troops in the South increased the number of slaves who sought refuge behind British lines and escaped to freedom. Some masters, seeking the loyalty of their slaves, bought that loyalty with promises of future freedom. Others sensed the implications of republican theory and freed their slaves or allowed them to work to free themselves. In 1782, the Virginia legislature passed an act that officially permitted masters to free their slaves, leading to the manumission of at least ten thousand slaves by 1792. In 1792, rising resistance to the manumission of slaves resulted in the state legislature's rescinding the law.

1783 **Treaty of Paris (September 3) officially ends war**
Maneuvering around French delay tactics and taking advantage of British political interest in signing a treaty quickly, American diplomats managed to acquire both recognition of American independence and land rights to all the territory between the Appalachian Mountains and the Mississippi River, thus establishing the basis for a large and powerful nation.

1786 **Virginia Bill for Establishing Religious Freedom**
Republican theory permeated American life, changing people's attitudes toward religion. Many state legislatures passed laws separating church and state and making all churches equal before the law by providing no government support for any denomination.

1800 **Gabriel Prosser's conspiracy in Virginia**
By the 1790s, the tide had turned against the emancipation of slaves in the South. When Virginia officials discovered plans for a slave rebellion, led by Gabriel Prosser, they suppressed the uprising and executed Prosser and thirty of his followers, thus reaffirming the southern commitment to slavery and white supremacy.

GLOSSARY

pacifist A pacifist is someone who does not believe in the use of violence, including war, to mediate disputes. The Quakers were pacifists and opposed the Revolution on principle. (p. 181)

republic A government or state without a monarch that derives authority and legitimacy from the people. (pp. 182–183)

mercenary A professional soldier who fights for money rather than in defense of his own nation or principles. The British army hired thousands of German mercenaries to fight in the Revolutionary War. (p. 184)

outflanked When two armies face each other in battle, one of them may send forces to the right or left of the opposing lines. If the first army then successfully attacks from the side, it has outflanked its opponent. The British troops routinely outflanked the Americans because the British were better-trained soldiers and were able to move more quickly in large numbers. (p. 186)

redeeming currency Before the twentieth century, when a government issued currency, the currency represented a certain actual amount of gold and silver. To redeem a currency, the government would purchase the notes for gold or silver, or for some other paper money backed by another source. This system assured the value of the currency by giving people who held the notes the confidence that they could, if they wished, actually get the promised amount of gold or silver. The government would also accept this currency in payment of taxes due, thus giving it value. (pp. 189–191)

republican virtue This trait was embodied by individuals who acted collectively in the interests of all, or in the public interest. Thomas Paine, Benjamin Rush, and other Patriots believed that each citizen had a responsibility to contribute to the "public good" of the republic. (pp. 199–202)

classical liberal *Liberal* means "free." A classical liberal argues that each individual should be free to act according to his or her "self-interest." As a result, classical liberals believed government should not restrain trade, control prices, or have any right to take away personal property or abridge individual liberties. Patriot financier Robert Morris and Benjamin Franklin supported this view of economic behavior by opposing price controls in Pennsylvania. (p. 201)

depreciation A loss in value. When people become less confident that currency issued by a government or bank will be retrievable in gold or silver or accepted for payment for the amount of the note, its purchasing power, or value, begins to decline. As the value of notes declines, it takes more notes to purchase an item, touching off inflation. Inflation further depreciates the value of the note. By accepting a note, letting it depreciate, and then cashing it in or spending it for less than it was worth when one received it, one is paying a small "tax" to the government. This process amounts to a tax because one accepts government currency at one value and then spends it at a lower value, thus freeing the government of an obligation to repay the notes at their original value. This provides the government with money and thus indirectly supports the financing of the war. (p. 202)

manumission When masters set their slaves free, they literally "let go from the hand," or manumitted, them. (p. 204)

self-purchase One way for slaves to gain their own freedom was to work for wages and then use that money to buy themselves from their masters. (p. 205)

IDENTIFICATION

Identify by filling in the blanks.

1. In the summer of 1775 the Second Continental Congress, seeking reconciliation with King George III, passed the _____, which the king rejected. (p. 180)

2. _____, in response to the House of Burgesses' seizing authority in Virginia, formed two military forces, one white and one black, composed of slaves whom he offered freedom if they would join the British side. (pp. 180–181)

3. Thomas Paine was the author of _____, a political pamphlet that encouraged Americans to break their ties with the king and declare their independence as a republic. (p. 182)

4. In both the Declaration of Independence and his earlier pamphlet, _____, Thomas Jefferson made a case for blaming the king for the crisis, thereby allowing him to declare George III a _____ unfit to rule a free people. (p. 182)

5. General George Washington's primary opponent, and the formulator of the cautious British strategy in the early years of the war, was General _____. (p. 185)

6. The British again defeated the Continental army by outflanking it at the Battle of _____, south of Philadelphia, in September 1777. (p. 188)

7. The American victory under the leadership of Horatio Gates at the Battle of _____ in 1777 was the turning point of the Revolutionary War. (pp. 188–189)

8. Patriots in towns across the North organized _____ to collect taxes, send food and clothing to the Continental army, and impose fines on or jail Loyalists. (p. 189)

9. One of the three American diplomats who negotiated the Treaty of Alliance with France in 1778 was _____, who was already famous in the new United States as a publisher, scientist, Enlightenment thinker, and politician from Philadelphia. (p. 192)

10. The French aristocrat who aided the Continental army as a member of Washington's staff, encouraged the French to offer stronger military support, and then led forces in Virginia against Cornwallis was _____. (p. 194)

11. The "financier of the Revolution," who tried to keep the financial system of Congress afloat, was _____, a Philadelphia merchant. (p. 201)

12. In 1779, in Philadelphia, the Committee on Prices invoked the traditional idea of a _____ to prevent profiteering by city merchants. (p. 201)

13. In 1783 Washington had to use his personal authority to thwart a potentially dangerous mutiny among his officers at _____. (pp. 200–201)

14. In 1800 a Virginia slave, _____, was executed along with thirty of his followers for planning an uprising. (p. 206)

15. In 1786 the Virginia legislature passed a Bill for Establishing Religious Freedom, written by _____. (p. 207)

FEATURES EXERCISES

American Voices

THOMAS PAINE, Common Sense (p. 184)

Thomas Paine wrote his famous pamphlet, *Common Sense*, in simple language to persuade the average American who was loyal to the Crown to break that loyalty and support a republican government. In his arguments, Paine assures the average reader by using familiar ideas, experiences, and phrases to suggest a new interpretation or viewpoint. Aware that people resist because they fear that which is new, he also offers them models developed from familiar institutions. By portraying republicanism as a bridge between the past and the future, Paine imbued the American Revolution with republican spirit, a higher moral dimension, and historical purpose. As you read excerpts from *Common Sense*, ask yourself the following questions:

1. Paine holds what theory about the British constitution?
2. How does he coax the reader to favor the republican part of the constitution?
3. How does he apply republican ideas to institutions that colonists are familiar with to suggest what a republic might look like?
4. To assuage concerns about the lack of a king (which many people saw as essential for order), Paine declares that in America "law is king." What does he mean? How does the image of law as king ease concerns about disorder under a republican government?

Voices from Abroad

BARONESS VON RIEDESEL, The Surrender of Burgoyne, 1777 (p. 190)

General John Burgoyne was noted for fighting with style, rather than speed and tactical maneuver. While marching through New York toward Canada in 1777, Burgoyne's forces, burdened by a long supply train that included much food and wine, and harassed by American militia, became bogged down. Many of his troops were German mercenaries, among them General von Riedesel. The general's wife, Baroness von Riedesel, kept a journal of their progress. As you read this record of their advance, ask yourself the following questions:

1. What evidence of Burgoyne's slow progress and conservative tactical movements does Baroness von Riedesel provide?
2. What were some of her criticisms of Burgoyne? Were her views shared by others?
3. In what ways does the constant danger described by von Riedesel further highlight Burgoyne's predicament?

American Lives

The Enigma of Benedict Arnold (pp. 196–197)

Throughout the war, many Patriots—from farmers and merchants to soldiers and officers in the Continental army—struggled with the conflict between civic duty and private self-interest. By 1778, Benedict Arnold had established a distinguished record of service in the Patriot cause, rising to be a major general in the Continental army. He then fell into debt and became involved in shady financial schemes. Facing congressional investigation and a possible court martial, he switched sides and sought fame and fortune in the service of the British army. Arnold committed treason neither because he was disgusted with Congress and embittered at his lack of recognition nor because he believed the British cause was right. Rather, he selfishly sought his own material advancement. For him, self-interest prevailed over civic duty, earning him the disdain and contempt of both sides in the war.

As you read "The Enigma of Benedict Arnold," ask yourself the following questions:

1. What were Benedict Arnold's military achievements for the Patriot cause? What does his behavior reveal about his character?

2. What hint does his behavior as commander in Philadelphia in 1778 indicate about the real motives for his subsequent treason?

3. What action of Arnold's was treasonous?

4. What does Arnold's career as a British general tell you about his military skills? Why, in spite of his success, was he never popular among the British?

American Voices

BENJAMIN BANNEKER, On Jefferson and Natural Rights (p. 205)

In this account, Benjamin Banneker, a free black farmer, challenges Jefferson's suggestion, in *Notes on Virginia,* that African Americans were an inferior race. Jefferson believed African Americans had human moral sense and thus possessed natural rights. He also believed, however, that they were mentally, physically, and culturally inferior and was therefore pessimistic about the ability of whites and blacks to live peacefully together. As you read Benjamin Banneker's letter to Thomas Jefferson, ask yourself the following questions:

1. How does Banneker use Jefferson's own arguments against him?

2. Drawing on the Enlightenment rationalism to which Banneker and Jefferson both subscribed, how does Banneker make the point that blacks and whites are equal? How does he play to Jefferson's sense of rationality to try to convince him that he is wrong?

3. Having argued for equality, how does Banneker highlight an apparent contradiction or paradox to further move Jefferson from his position? Is he charging Jefferson with hypocrisy?

MAPS AND FIGURES

On the map shown below, locate the following places: Boston, New York, Philadelphia, Saratoga, Brandywine Creek, Camden, and Yorktown.

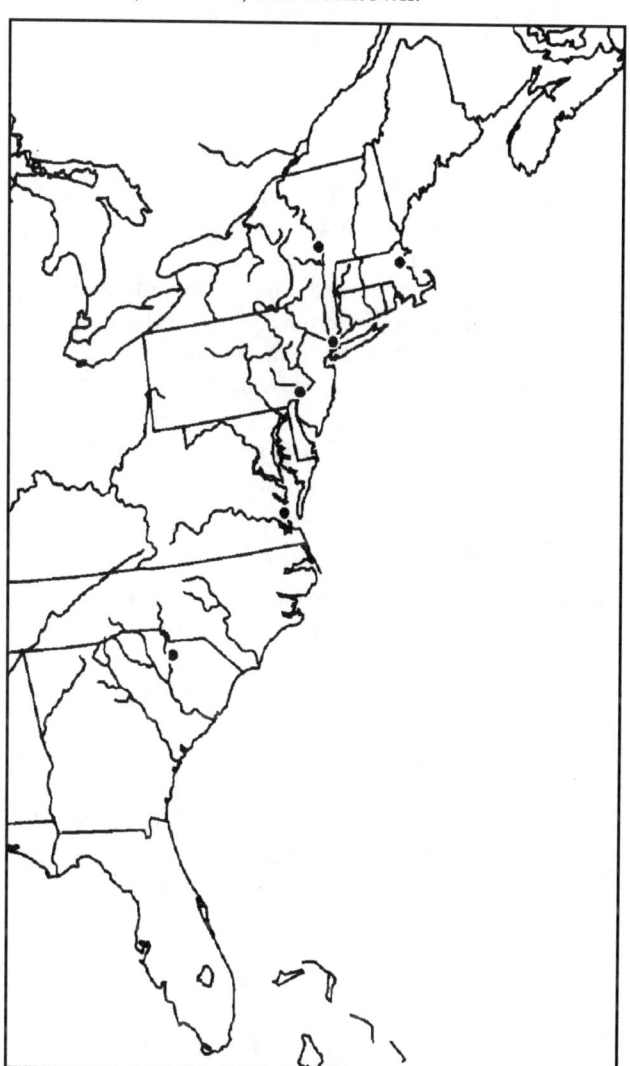

SELF-TEST

Multiple Choice

1. King George responded to the Olive Branch petition by:
   a. sending diplomats to America to begin negotiations.
   b. receiving the petition, considering it carefully, and deciding that he must continue the military effort to quell the rebellion.
   c. ceasing hostilities while trying to decide what to do.

d. refusing to receive the petition and issuing a Proclamation for Suppressing Rebellion and Sedition.

2. The British had the advantage over the Americans in *all* of the following areas *except*:
   a. professionally trained soldiers.
   b. supplies and weaponry.
   c. support of the local population.
   d. financial resources.

3. Despite overwhelming superiority, the British failed to win the war in its first year for *all* of the following reasons *except*:
   a. General William Howe had the authority to negotiate and wanted the surrender of the rebels rather than their defeat.
   b. they were restrained by distance from their sources of supply.
   c. they tried to evade the rebels but kept being drawn into open battle.
   d. they failed to encourage Loyalists to support the British army.

4. General Howe advanced on Philadelphia in 1777 rather than reinforce Burgoyne up North because he:
   a. believed that by taking the capital he would draw Washington into a battle and end the war with a major victory.
   b. believed that if Philadelphia was taken, the middle colonies would fall and divide New England from the South.
   c. believed that by going to Philadelphia he would force Washington to keep some troops in the middle colonies, and thus limit those that could be sent against Burgoyne in the North.
   d. preferred Philadelphia to New York because it had a larger Loyalist population.

5. The British lost the Battle of Saratoga for *all* of the following reasons *except*:
   a. they failed to receive support from Howe's army.
   b. the Iroquois joined the Americans.
   c. they traveled with a heavy baggage train and became bogged down in the wilderness.
   d. they faced the large forces of the American militia.

6. To finance the war, Congress did *all* of the following *except*:
   a. levy heavy taxes against the people.
   b. issue Continental loan certificates.
   c. borrow from the French and the Dutch.
   d. print paper money.

7. The French alliance affected the American cause in *all* of the following ways *except*:
   a. it provided badly needed funds and improved the supply of goods to the army.
   b. the French officers and advisers eclipsed Washington as commander of the Continental army.
   c. the extra funds allowed Congress to give pensions to the officers.
   d. the French provided manpower and a navy, enabling the American-French forces to outnumber and overpower the British.

8. The British responded to the French alliance by altering their military strategy in the following way:
   a. They put more troops in all the colonies and escalated their war effort.
   b. They pulled troops out of the colonies entirely and launched an invasion of France.
   c. They made remarkable constitutional concessions and sued for peace.
   d. They concentrated troops on defending the British West Indies and launching an invasion of the richer southern colonies.

9. *All* of the following are accurate descriptions of the final defeat of Cornwallis's troops *except*:
   a. Cornwallis moved north into Virginia and then marched east onto the York peninsula.
   b. Washington's and Rochambeau's armies marched south from New York in the fall.
   c. The Americans and French won a great, open-field battle outside Yorktown by tactically outmaneuvering Cornwallis's army.
   d. The French fleet gained control of the waters of Chesapeake Bay, cornering the British by sea.

10. The terms of the treaties of Paris and Versailles in 1783 included *all* of the following *except*:
    a. the return of Canada to the French.
    b. Americans' control of the land between the Appalachian Mountains and the Mississippi River.
    c. recognition of the new American republic by Britain.
    d. the transfer of Florida from Britain to Spain.

11. American women contributed to the war effort by doing *all* of the following *except*:
    a. supervising hired laborers and slaves.
    b. producing increased amounts of homespun.
    c. making clothing for the troops.
    d. involving themselves in politics.

12. During the Revolution, thousands of slaves gained their freedom in *all* of the following ways *except*:

a. independently launching an insurrection against their masters.
   b. striking bargains with their masters, including the promise that if they remained loyal they would be freed after the war.
   c. manumission by their masters, who felt that slavery was a contradiction of republican ideals.
   d. seeking refuge behind British lines.

13. An established church is one that:
    a. has a majority of the population as members.
    b. is supported financially and legally by the government.
    c. has a charter from the government.
    d. is established by a congregation as a church.

14. Which of the following did not characterize the new republican religious order?
    a. attempts to separate church and state.
    b. the increased prevalence of deism.
    c. the increase of secularism across society.
    d. elimination of religious requirements for voting or political office.

Short Essays

Answer the following questions in a brief paragraph.

1. Why did Thomas Paine write the pamphlet *Common Sense*, and what did he argue in it? (pp. 181–182)
2. Why did the first year of the war go so badly for the Americans? (pp. 183–187)
3. How did the victory at Saratoga manifest British weaknesses and American strengths in the war as a whole? (pp. 188–189)
4. Why was the Continental Congress so unsuccessful in financing the war? (pp. 189–191)
5. What were France's motives for deciding to join the Americans in the war against Great Britain? Which motive was most important? (pp. 192–195, 198)
6. Compare and contrast how the military and civilians tried to live up to the ideals of republicanism. (pp. 199–202)
7. How did republican ideals affect the role of women in American society? (pp. 201–202)
8. How were Loyalists treated by Patriots and state governments during the war? (pp. 202–203)
9. How did the American Revolution affect slavery? (pp. 203–206)
10. Did the Revolution increase or decrease the power of organized religion in the United States? Explain. (pp. 206–207)

ANSWERS

Identification

1. Olive Branch petition
2. Lord Dunmore
3. *Common Sense*
4. *Summary View of the Rights of British America*; tyrant
5. William Howe
6. Brandywine
7. Saratoga
8. Committees of Safety
9. Benjamin Franklin
10. the Marquis de Lafayette
11. Robert Morris
12. just price
13. Newburgh, New York
14. Gabriel Prosser
15. Thomas Jefferson

Maps and Figures

For New York, Philadelphia, Saratoga, Brandywine Creek, and Boston, see Map 6.1 (text p. 185). For Camden (N.C.) and Yorktown, see Map 6.2 (text p. 186).

Self-Test

Multiple Choice

1. d.
2. c.
3. c.
4. a.
5. b.
6. a.
7. b.
8. d.
9. c.
10. a.
11. c.
12. a.
13. b.
14. c.

Short Essays

1. Thomas Paine sensed that the American people needed to be convinced of the legitimacy of breaking from the Crown. Paine equated monarchy with tyranny and argued that the people should rule themselves in a republican system.

2. Washington had had no time to train the ragtag, militia-based Continental army. As a result, the Americans were no match for the professionally trained army that the British were able to put in the field. Time and again, Washington's forces were outflanked and forced to retreat. Only the speed with which they retreated and luck kept them from being caught and forced to surrender. Washington had also not yet formulated his defensive and evasive strategy.

3. The British command was initially timid and slow in fighting the Americans. British forces easily outflanked the Americans at Fort Ticonderoga but failed to capture the army. Over-elaborate strategy and the need to wait for slow baggage trains hindered the British effort. The Americans relied on surprise, fighting from the forest, and on the participation of local militias to increase the size of their force.

4. Having initiated a Revolutionary War based on the grievance of unjust taxation, Patriot politicians were reluctant to tax the people directly. Instead, the Continental Congress requisitioned funds from the states but received little. The Congress borrowed money from the French and the Dutch and sold loan certificates to wealthy Americans. But as costs escalated beyond available funds, resources ran out and Congress was forced to print paper money to finance the war effort.

5. The French sought revenge against Great Britain for their defeat in the Seven Years' War, which resulted in the loss of Canada and some islands in the Caribbean. They wanted to regain lost territory and reestablish a naval presence on the North Atlantic. In strengthening the challenge to British rule in North America and severing its lucrative empire, the French also sought to spread British forces thin and reduce Great Britain's power in international affairs. Revenge was their primary motive.

6. Many Americans considered private property to be the basis of happiness and self-interested action to be healthy behavior. Republicanism rested on the premise that, for government by the people to work, the people had to exercise public virtue by acting selflessly and contributing to the public good. For men, this conflict between self-interest and public virtue existed in both civilian and military life. Hardships in the field led many soldiers to mutiny, and officers demanded pensions. Economic hardship convinced many civilians to act in their own self-interest rather than contribute to the war. Accustomed to self-sacrifice, women experienced little tension between self-interest and republican virtue.

7. Women were not included in the Founding Fathers' discussions of liberty and justice for all. Women were expected to continue to carry out traditional family roles and to defer to their husbands or male relatives in matters of politics and public life. Nevertheless, they were affected by the war and contributed to the war effort. During the war, women organized drives to gather goods for the army, produced homespun cloth and clothes for the soldiers, supervised workers, and ran the farms in their husbands' or sons' absence.

8. Committees of Safety forced people to take loyalty oaths or face penalties, fines, and jail terms. Some formed Patriot groups and engaged in direct actions against Tories, many of whom they forced to leave their homes. Governments often rented out or confiscated and resold Loyalist property, though in most places property was confiscated only to the extent that creditors needed to be paid off, and the rest reverted to widows or kin of the Loyalists.

9. The establishment of republican governments committed to individual rights and equality intensified the debate about slavery. As the contradiction of slavery within a republic became apparent, many northerners used religious and secular ideas drawn from the Enlightenment to argue for the abolition of slavery. So, too, some planters in the South moved away from slavery by allowing slaves to buy their freedom or by manumitting their slaves. But both developments struggled against a pervasive fear among whites that blacks would compete for jobs and housing, seek more civil rights, and escalate social and political tensions. Even southerners who were sympathetic to arguments against slavery resigned themselves to the argument that slavery was a "necessary evil" to maintain social order. When Virginia authorities uncovered a conspiracy by Gabriel Prosser to launch an uprising, and arrested and then executed Prosser and thirty of his followers, the debate over slavery in the South ended.

10. The effect of the Revolution on organized religion varied from state to state. In general, though, state legislatures passed laws that made all churches equal before the law and gave support to no particular church. This decreased the role of established churches.

Chapter 7

The New Political Order, 1776–1800

LEARNING OBJECTIVES

1. Americans assumed that the new national government would be a republic or a democracy. Compare and contrast a republic and a democracy. What are the basic similarities and differences?

2. How republican or democratic were the new state constitutions formed in the 1770s and 1780s? Were they more one than the other?

3. How republican or democratic was the new federal Constitution ratified in 1789? Was it more one than the other?

4. What role did compromise play in the new Constitution?

5. What roles did the following men play in establishing the republican constitutional order of the United States by 1800: Thomas Jefferson, George Washington, Alexander Hamilton, and James Madison?

6. What impact did the French Revolution have on internal politics and foreign policy in the first decade of the republic?

7. At what point do you think the American Revolution finally ended? What criteria are you using to make your judgment?

CHAPTER SUMMARY

The republican ideals of the Declaration of Independence and George Washington's insistence on military deference to civilian rule assured that the new government of the United States would be a republic. A republic is a government or state without a monarch that derives authority and legitimacy from the people. How the government of the republic would be organized, implemented, and run on the state and federal levels absorbed the energies of a remarkably creative group of politicians and thinkers for more than twenty years. Although this process would become increasingly conflict-ridden as these men emphasized different elements and values based on social and political self-interest, they nevertheless managed to create a new republican constitutional order in which power could be transferred peacefully from one party to another.

Creating New Institutions, 1776–1787 (pp. 212–222)

From 1776 to 1787, the states of the new nation created first individual state constitutions and systems of government, then two different systems of national government. At stake in developing state systems of government was the question of how much power should be held by regular citizens and how much by a traditional, ruling elite. The Articles of Confederation, adopted as a national system of government in 1777, and the Constitution of the United States, which supplanted them in 1787, were also attempts to deal with the question of how power should be divided between ordinary citizens and the elite, as well as how it should be divided between the states and the national government.

The State Constitutions: How Much Democracy?

While the Revolutionary War raged, politicians debated how democratic the new republican state constitutions should be. Radical Patriots were populists. They wanted state governments to be directly controlled by the people. They formed extremely democratic governments, the most democratic of which was in Pennsylvania, where a unicameral legislature was elected through universal suffrage for white males. Moderates and conservatives, led by John Adams, believed government should be run by wealthy men possessing "civic virtue." Too much democracy, they feared, would lead to chaos and tyranny of the masses. To limit democracy, Adams proposed a government in which power was divided between differing governing bodies that would check and balance each other, and thus prevent the tyranny of one group over others. In various states, checks on popular rule included property restrictions on suffrage, and granting veto power to the governor, while direct election of the governor checked the power of the elite. Balances included the division of legislatures into two bodies (one of which apportioned seats on the basis of population to provide more direct representation by the people), and of government into three branches. In doing so, they established republican governments with democratic elements that would become models for the federal Constitution.

Republicanism challenged the belief that only men could be involved in politics. Elite women were quick to point out that republicanism applied to women as well and argued for increased public rights and equality before the law, while challenging the assumptions on which women's secondary status was based. Likewise, the republican belief in an educated citizenry encouraged many women to acquire an education. Women's advances in pursuit of education laid the groundwork for subsequent challenges to their status as second-class citizens in the republic.

The Articles of Confederation

The Articles of Confederation, ratified in 1781, cautiously established the first national government by confirming the operations of the Confederation Congress, which, since its formation as the Continental Congress, had formed an army and a navy for defense, declared independence and war, established diplomatic relations with other countries, and adjudicated disputes among a loose association of states. Congress's inability to tax or enforce requisitions from the states weakened its ability to rule. Moreover, the necessity of unanimous votes for approval of amendments weakened the Congress's power and thwarted efforts to reform the Articles. Ironically, faced with bankruptcy, Congress innovatively exerted the power the Articles gave it to initiate and control the sale of western lands as a means of enhancing its power and easing its fiscal difficulties. Congress acquired control over a national domain of public lands west of the Appalachians from the Treaty of Paris and various land cessions from individual states. It then established an efficient system for surveying and selling western lands to speculators and settlers. Once an area was settled, Congress organized and supervised territorial governments to administer the population. When the population in these territories reached sixty thousand, Congress allowed territorial residents to write a republican constitution and apply for admission to the Union as a state equal with the others. Through this achievement, the Articles of Confederation turned Americans' attention to the West and laid the groundwork for the creation of a dynamic republican society and polity.

The Postwar Crisis

After the war, worthless currency, large state debts, and the disruption of trade plunged America into a recession. Creditors urged politicians to pass laws that would limit the use of paper money and impose higher taxes to accelerate debt repayment. In some states the debtors resisted such measures, which would have made repayment more difficult for them, and prodebtor legislation was passed. In Massachusetts, where such prodebtor legislation was not enacted, merchant and landowner creditors in the East pressed farmer debtors in the West to the brink of bankruptcy. The farmers resisted, and a popular movement coalesced into a full-scale uprising, in which an army of disgruntled farmers challenged state authority. Though it was put down, this movement, known as Shays's Rebellion, provided evidence of growing discontent and shocked many Patriots enough to encourage them to press for a stronger central government.

The Constitution of 1787
(pp. 222–230)

Forged out of long debates about political ideas and power, the Constitution created a republican national government that creatively responded to the concerns of various interests while addressing the issue of state versus federal power.

The Rise of a Nationalist Faction

In response to Shays's Rebellion, the lack of power of the central government, and the financial weakness and prodebtor policies of several states, a group of nationalists decided to take action. While most Americans remained primarily loyal to their states, many former military officers, government officials, and diplomats during the Revolution had developed a national view of politics. Worried about a lack of national power, growing financial woes, and public discontent at the state level, these nationalists arranged a trade convention in 1786. At the convention, commissioners from only five states called for a meeting to review issues about the Articles. In response, supporters in Congress pushed through a resolution calling for a national convention to revise the Articles of Confederation.

Drafting a New National Constitution

Fifty-five delegates arrived at the national convention in Philadelphia in 1787, committed to strengthening the central government. After agreeing that a simple majority of votes, one from each state, would decide an issue, and deciding to debate in secret, the delegates considered James Madison's Virginia Plan. Madison's plan proposed a central government in which national power was drawn directly from the people. Three separate branches of government based on specific functions—executive, legislative, and judicial—would check and balance each other to maintain republican order. After a series of compromises concerning the nature of representation in the two houses of the legislature, how to determine representation, the power of the judiciary, voting rights, states' role in national elections, and the status of slavery, and following a decision on enhancing the fiscal power of the central government, the plan was approved and offered to the people for ratification.

The Debate over Ratification

In the debate that followed, those who favored the Constitution, including many nationally known leaders who had been active in the Revolution, called themselves Federalists and argued for the benefits of a stronger central government. But the outcry against the proposed Constitution by Antifederalists, a diverse group that distrusted central power and mercantile elite rule and feared that it would encroach upon state powers, appealed to fears of central power and disorder. Antifederalists charged that this new central power would restore the high taxes, oppressive bureaucracy, and standing armies they had just thrown off in the Revolution, eliminate state governments, and threaten the natural rights of the people. *The Federalist* argued that checks and balances within the system, the size of the republic, and the republican virtue of the people themselves would restrain the central government and safeguard liberty. To allay the fears of many Antifederalists, the Federalists added a Bill of Rights to the new Constitution. In 1789, after a series of very close votes, the Constitution was ratified by nine of the thirteen states. The new Constitution created a strong national republican government that balanced federal power against the power of the states, returned more creditors and merchants to power at the expense of artisans and yeomen farmers, yet checked elite power with a directly elected legislature, and assured the people that their rights would be protected in a Bill of Rights. In doing so, it balanced various political interests and ended the Revolutionary era.

The Constitution Implemented

Once voters had elected the members of the first Congress and George Washington as president and John Adams as vice-president, each proceeded to establish how the different branches would operate. Washington drew on the Articles of Confederation to establish precedents for the executive branch. He reestablished executive departments and secured control of them by personally appointing secretaries as members of his cabinet of advisors. Congress organized the judicial system in the Judiciary Act of 1789 by creating a national Supreme Court with three circuit courts that heard cases on constitutional appeals from thirteen federal district courts, one for each state. By giving the president the power to execute laws, and the judiciary the power to interpret the meaning of the Constitution, these actions created the two forces that would check and balance legislative power and thus balance the government. Finally, Congress passed the Bill of Rights promised by the Federalists in the ratification conventions, which safeguarded the people's liberties and, by assuaging Antifederalists, broadened political support for the new government.

The Political Divisions of the 1790s (pp. 230–244)

The general wording of the new Constitution, however, still left the implementation of critical national powers open to different interpretations. Alexander Hamilton's efforts to establish a national fiscal policy and enhance central power triggered an acrimonious political debate between two developing factions, Federalists, led by Hamilton, and Republicans, led by Thomas Jefferson. These divisions were exacerbated by conflicting opinions on the French Revolution, which broke out in 1789. Out of this debate emerged two very different visions of how democratic the new republic would be.

Hamilton's Program

Alexander Hamilton believed, like other supporters of the Constitution, that a strong central government must rest on a solid financial foundation. He sought to lay this foundation by redeeming the credit of the Confederation, creating a national debt, and establishing a national bank that could regulate or stimulate the economy. In particular, he hoped the government would stimulate manufacturing so that the United States could achieve economic self-sufficiency. These powers, he argued, were implied by the Constitution when it empowered Congress to make all laws "necessary and proper" to run the country. Hamilton articulated a "loose" interpretation of the Constitution. At every step, Madison and Jefferson opposed Hamilton. His policies, they argued, favored wealthy creditors and speculators, increased central power, and supporteded industrialization at the expense of artisans, farmers, and debtors, states' rights, and agricultural development. His policies also exceeded, they believed, the powers strictly delegated to the central government by the Constitution.

Jefferson's Vision

Thomas Jefferson believed Hamilton's program exceeded the powers articulated by the Constitution, arguing, according to a "strict" constructionist view, that Congress could do only what the Constitution specifically said it could do. More important, Jefferson feared Hamilton's programs on moral and ideological grounds. Jefferson imagined American democracy as a yeoman republic in which economic and political power were widely dispersed, social differentiation was limited, and yeomen farmers ruled themselves through nearby state governments. A national debt would create a class of wealthy speculators whose political power endangered democratic equality. A debt would also increase the central government's power to tax citizens, undermining their autonomy and liberty. Speculators would resist policies that assured the availability of land in the West for continued settlement by yeomen farmers.

War and Party Politics

War in Europe increased prices for grain and cotton and set in motion a boom in farming and trade. Commerce brought prosperity to American ports. The American merchant fleet quickly became one of the largest fleets in the world. However, this increase in trade brought more Americans directly in contact with the belligerents, threatening to embroil the United States in a war. Americans generally favored the republicanism of the French Revolution, but conservative Federalists were appalled by the execution of the king, political terror against members of the aristocracy, and the abandonment of Christianity. The Federalists increasingly favored a pro-British neutrality, whereas the Republicans favored neutrality with a French bias.

For five years American politicians maneuvered between pro-British and pro-French policies. In response to the United States apparently pro-French actions, the British began seizing American ships. To avert war, America and Britain negotiated Jay's Treaty, securing a pro-British policy, with considerable criticism from Republicans. Meanwhile, a domestic rebellion against a new tax on whiskey erupted in Pennsylvania, where armed rebels justified their resistance with ideas from the French Revolution. To uphold the power of the federal government, Washington raised an army and suppressed the rebellion.

By 1796, two distinct parties had formed and begun mobilizing support among voters. The Federalists were primarily merchants and grain farmers who supported a strong central government and a pro-British foreign policy. The Republicans, a diverse coalition of farmers and southerners, supported the states' rights, limited central government, and were pro-French. In the national elections, a flaw in the electoral-college process resulted in the election of John Adams, a Federalist, as president and Thomas Jefferson, a Republican, as vice-president, creating a divided administration. After the election, French arrogance toward diplomats of the Adams administration increased the danger of war against France. But Adams maintained neutrality, while Congress authorized American ships to attack French shipping. Thus America found itself in an undeclared war against France.

The Crisis of 1798–1800

To quash partisan Republican criticism of his pro-British undeclared war against France, the Adams administration pushed through legislation increasing residency requirements for immigrants, limiting free speech, and deporting foreigners, actions that alienated many Federalist supporters and increased Republican support in the election of 1800. A tie in the electoral college between Thomas Jefferson and Aaron Burr threw the election into the House of Representatives. Ironically, Alexander Hamilton, who was more opposed to Burr than to Jefferson, persuaded key Federalists not to vote for Burr and thus gave the election to Jefferson, ushering in a more democratic and republican administration. In spite of party strife and threats of civil war, the new republican constitutional order ultimately worked, allowing a peaceful transfer of power. The success of the Republicans, and their desire to return to the promises of the Declaration of Independence and a strict interpretation of the Constitution, amounted to, as Jefferson called it, the "Revolution of 1800."

EXPANDED TIMELINE

1776 **Pennsylvania's democratic constitution**
Although popular sovereignty was established in the Declaration of Independence and everyone assumed that the national government of the new United States would be republican, it was up to the states to decide how their own governments would be organized. Radicals in Pennsylvania offered the most democratic plan, creating a unicameral assembly that ruled without a council or a governor.

John Adams, *Thoughts on Government*
John Adams offered a more conservative system, which was still republican but less democratic. He wanted to emulate the mixed system of the British by establishing three separate branches of government, each with a single function; these branches would use checks and balances to restrain each other and maintain liberty. This system was instituted in Massachusetts and some of the other states because it was similar to the government the people were used to and limited the excesses of direct democracy.

Propertied women vote in New Jersey (until 1807)
The New Jersey constitution of 1776 granted the vote to all property holders. When free black men and unmarried women began to exercise the vote, the state closed the loophole in 1807 by abolishing property as the basis for suffrage and limiting the vote to white men only.

1777 **Articles of Confederation (ratified 1781)**
The Articles of Confederation created a national government centered in Congress. The Articles did not grant the federal government the right to tax, form a judiciary, control interstate commerce, or compel the states in any way. However, they were effective in terms of diplomacy and in organizing the acquisition, survey, and sale of western lands.

1779 **Judith Sargent Murray, "On the Equality of the Sexes"**
Judith Sargent Murray challenged contemporary assumptions about the inferiority of women. She argued that women were intellectually equal to men but that their training was less rigorous, resulting in apparent inequality. Women's equality made them fit to assume an equal position in society.

1780s **Postwar commercial recession**
Creditor-debtor conflicts in states
The loss of trade monopolies established by the British Navigation Acts left Americans with few markets after the war. In addition, state governments were caught in the middle between creditors and debtors over debts accumulated during the war years. Debt compelled states to raise taxes and limit paper money, putting the squeeze on debtors. As creditors pressured debtors for payment, the debtors also appealed to state governments for economic relief and legal protection.

1781 **Bank of North America chartered by Congress**
Robert Morris became superintendent of the finances of the Articles of Confederation and, shocked at the national government's financial weakness, sought to undertake a program to improve its financial stability and authority. His plan was to establish a national bank to issue notes to stabilize the currency, and then to create a national debt by spreading war debts among the states, controlling the foreign debt, and imposing national import duties. Congress chartered the bank but resisted Morris's efforts to establish a national debt. As a result, the Articles of Confederation lacked a financial foundation upon which to establish its authority.

1784–1785 **Political and Land Ordinances outline policy for new states**
In its search for funds, the government of the Articles of Confederation turned to western lands. After considerable efforts, it gained control of western lands from individual states, initiated a policy to acquire lands from the native Americans, established the grid system for surveying and selling western lands to generate revenue, and provided for the orderly organization of western territories and their admission as equal states into the Union.

Thomas Jefferson, *Notes on the State of Virginia*
Thomas Jefferson articulated his vision for a democratic republic of yeomen farmers in a book he wrote on the economic, social, political, and institutional organization of his home state of Virginia. Strong foreign markets for American farm produce and an expansive western land policy, which Jefferson helped establish, moved his vision closer to reality in the 1790s.

1786 **Annapolis commercial convention**
Shays's Rebellion in Massachusetts
Organized resistance to procreditor policies arose in Massachusetts, where the government did not pass prodebtor legislation. Farmers and artisans, unable to pay their debts, refused to let creditors foreclose and organized meetings and an army to resist efforts by the state to enforce procreditor laws. Shays's Rebellion, under the leadership of Daniel Shays, ultimately succumbed to cold weather and political pressure. It did, however, convince some nationalist

observers that chaos could result from a weak central government. To amend the Articles of Confederation, nationalists convened a meeting to discuss tariff and taxation issues at Annapolis, Maryland, and then called for a constitutional convention in Philadelphia the following summer.

1787 **Northwest Ordinance**
Following on the Land Ordinance of 1784, the Northwest Ordinance provided for the sale of lands, the establishment of territories, and the admission to the Union of three to five free states north of the Ohio River.

Philadelphia constitutional convention
At this meeting to reform the Articles of Confederation, James Madison offered a comprehensive restructuring of the government in a proposal known as the Virginia Plan. The Virginia Plan established the supremacy of the national government over the states and checked its power by creating three functional branches of government that would check and balance each other. This conservative revision was reshaped through a series of compromises on issues that were of concern to various interest groups.

1787–
1788 **Ratification conventions**
The Federalist **(John Jay, James Madison, Alexander Hamilton)**
The nationalists, who called themselves Federalists, argued that a powerful central government would strengthen the United States and restore public credit and property rights. Their opponents, who called themselves Antifederalists, feared central power, the control of government by mercantile elites, and the weakening of state governments.

The Federalists focused on allaying the fears of Antifederalists in a published series of essays called *The Federalist*. Though James Madison supported federal supremacy and the direct power of the central government over individuals, he argued that the system of checks and balances would restrain government power and that the size and diversity of America would prevent any party from gaining domination. In a series of very close debates at ratification conventions, the Constitution passed and became law.

1789 **George Washington inaugurated as first president**
Washington established executive departments and appointed secretaries of foreign affairs, finance, and war to run them. He also set protocol on the relationship between the president and Congress and determined how the president would present himself in public.

Judiciary Act establishes federal court system
Congress organized the judicial system by creating a national Supreme Court with three circuit courts that heard cases on appeal from thirteen federal district courts, one for each state.

Outbreak of French Revolution
The French Revolution, inspired in part by the American Revolution, overthrew the monarchy in France, a development with which most Americans sympathized.

1790 **Alexander Hamilton's program: redemption and assumption**
Alexander Hamilton, secretary of the Treasury, offered a three-part program to restore public finances. The federal government would pay off, or redeem, securities and bonds issued during the Revolution, assume the debts of the states, and establish a national bank with the power to tax and issue currency.

1791 **Bill of Rights ratified**
The first ten amendments to the Constitution were passed to mollify Antifederalist fears that the central government would encroach on the liberties and rights of the people. The passage of the Bills of Rights increased support for the Constitution and enhanced its legitimacy.

1792 **Mary Wollstonecraft,** *A Vindication of the Rights of Woman*
Women remained a marginal group, as men ignored the ideas of women like Judith Sargent Murray. A more radical critique, written by the British republican Mary Wollstonecraft, argued for the legal and political equality of women. Though she gained a widespread hearing, many Americans were shocked by Wollstonecraft's sexually free life-style. Most men disregarded her argument.

1793 **First French Republic; Louis XVI executed**
Democratic-Republican party founded
War between Britain and France; Washington's Proclamation of Neutrality
In France, the change from a constitutional monarchy to a republican Directory that executed the king polarized American opinion. Federalists agreed with the British that the French had gone too far toward anarchy. Meanwhile, Republicans under Madison and Jefferson remained sympathetic, though concerned about the radical direction of the Revolution. When Britain went to war against France, Washington and the Federalists tried to remain neutral; this became difficult when the British began seizing American ships.

1794 **Whiskey Rebellion**
As national politics became polarized, some people in Pennsylvania reacted to the passing of a national tax on distilled spirits by forming an assembly and arming themselves. President Washington raised an army and put down this rebellion.

1795 **Jay's Treaty**
To avert war with Britain, John Jay was sent to negotiate a treaty that established American neutrality in exchange for allowing the British to seize French goods on American ships and compensating the British for losses during the Revolution. In return, the British agreed to withdraw their troops from forts in the Northwest, to stop supporting the Indians, and to redress American merchants' losses incurred through illegal British seizure of their goods.

Two organized parties offered slates of candidates in the 1796 election. The Federalist John Adams was elected president, but Thomas Jefferson, a Republican, was elected vice-president, creating a divided administration.

1798 **XYZ Affair (1797) prompts war with France**
In response to America's pro-British policy, the French began to attack American ships. When John Adams's attempts to negotiate were rebuffed and three agents of the French foreign minister asked for a loan and a bribe from American diplomats, an action Americans considered an insult to their honor, Americans prepared for war and joined the British in attacking French ships. Although President Adams averted a full-scale war, the United States was involved in a quasi-war with France for two years.

Alien, Sedition, and Naturalization Acts
Kentucky and Virginia Resolutions
Adams sought to quell opposition by pushing through the Alien and Sedition Acts, which increased residency requirements for citizenship, threatened foreigners with potential deportation, and prohibited criticism of the administration's policies. The Republicans attacked these acts as encroachments on individual liberties and asserted the rights of the states to nullify national laws in the Kentucky and Virginia Resolutions.

1800 **Jefferson elected in "Revolution of 1800"**
Taking advantage of the opposition to the Alien and Sedition Acts and Federalist war policies, the Republicans carried the election of 1800. However, Aaron Burr of New York and Thomas Jefferson of Virginia tied in the electoral-college vote for president, throwing the election into Congress. After numerous votes and a growing threat of civil war, Alexander Hamilton convinced several Federalists to give Jefferson the election. Constitutional procedures thus led the nation through a political stalemate and permitted the peaceful transfer of power. Jefferson called this the "Revolution of 1800" because the ascendancy of the Republicans ensured a return to the initial principles of the Declaration of Independence and the Constitution.

GLOSSARY

populist A populist is someone who believes that political legitimacy and power lie in the hands of the average people. In the Revolutionary era, Radical Republicans were populists. (p. 212)

unicameral A one-house assembly is referred to as unicameral. Considered efficient and democratic, this type of assembly can pass legislation more quickly and with less consideration. Pennsylvania had a unicameral assembly during the Revolution. Today, only Nebraska has a unicameral state legislature. (p. 212)

civic virtue Republican theory argues that each individual should act not only in his or her self-interest but also in the interests of all, or in the public interest. Each citizen has a responsibility to contribute to the "public good" or the public life of the republic. To act for or contribute to the public good of one's town or city is civic virtue. (p. 213)

mixed government John Adams's plan called for a mixed government of three branches, each representing one function: executive, legislative, and judicial. Their interaction would maintain a balance of power and ensure the legitimacy of governmental procedures. (p. 213)

bicameral A bicameral congress or assembly has two houses, usually a lower house elected by popular vote and an upper house representing those of wealth or property. Different qualifications, procedures, term lengths, and means of election differentiate the two and ensure that each piece of legislation is reviewed and debated by two different groups. (p. 213)

checks and balances Assigning different functions and procedures to different branches of government allows each branch to limit the actions of the others in a system of checks and balances. This ensures an equal balance of governmental functions and maximizes liberty. (p. 213)

companionate marriage Republicanism advocated equality and freedom for all people. Women drew power from these ideas to press for legal equality in marriage, increased education, and a greater share in the decision making in marriage. Even though men retained power as the patriarchs, they increasingly viewed their wives as equal companions and friends rather than as inferior and dependent partners. (p. 216)

franchise In the early national period, the franchise, or right to vote, was limited by property restrictions, but later all white men over age twenty-one were given the vote. The term *suffrage* also refers to the right to vote. (p. 216)

tariff A tariff is a tax added to the cost of an imported item, raising its price and making local products more desirable. Tariffs are intended to give a price advantage to domestic producers over foreign producers. (p. 220)

electoral college As set forth in the Constitution, the president was to be elected indirectly. A group of electors, usually politicians, were appointed each election year to vote for the president and the vice-president. This was done to give the states some power in the choosing of a president. Because the president would be elected by state votes, rather than by the popular vote, even close popular votes would become clear majorities in the electoral college. (p. 224)

cabinet Washington organized bureaucratic departments to carry out the work of the executive branch and appointed secretaries to run those departments. Those secretaries, who constituted a small group of the president's close advisors on matters of policy, were called his cabinet, a term still used today. (p. 229)

national debt By borrowing money from the people through the sale of bonds, a government accumulates a debt to the people, or a national debt. Hamilton believed that developing a national debt to finance government would create ties of loyalty between the government and the financial community. (pp. 230–233)

redemption Governments routinely borrow money by selling securities or bonds. Brokers and bankers trade these securities in the marketplace, their value determined by the soundness of the government and by market demand for the security. When one presents the security to the government for payment, one *redeems* the security for its market or face value. A key component of Alexander Hamilton's financial program in the 1790s was the redemption of millions of dollars of securities issued by the Confederation. (p. 230)

assumption Hamilton also wanted the federal government to assume the debts of the states by buying the debts and repaying creditors. The national government quickly "funded" a national debt while relieving the state governments of their debts. (p. 232)

strict interpretation A strict interpretation of the Constitution argues that the national government can do only what is explicitly stated in the Constitution, leaving to the states all powers not expressly mentioned. Jefferson and Madison argued for this interpretation. (p. 232)

loose interpretation A loose interpretation of the Constitution argues that the national government may do whatever is "necessary and proper" to carry out its functions. Hamilton argued that although the Constitution did not explicitly state that the government had the power to establish a national bank, in Article 1, section 8, it did give Congress the power to make "all laws necessary and proper" to carry out the Constitution and thus implied that the government had the power to establish a national bank. (p. 232)

faction A faction is a small political group organized around a single issue or person. Factions often become the foundation for political parties. In the eighteenth century, factions were considered dangerous because they undermined the ability of a party to rule and thus threatened public order. Disagreement over Hamilton's financial program divided the Federalists into two factions, each of which would form into a political party by 1796. (p. 233)

yeomen farmers Jefferson believed that American society was based on the work of independent yeomen farmers who owned their land and planted crops for a market. (pp. 234–235)

party A party is an organized political movement that establishes a platform of issues based on distinct principles, holds caucuses to select candidates, and runs campaigns. By 1796, the two factions that had emerged in the course of the debate over Hamilton's financial program had developed into separate political parties, Republicans and Federalists. (p. 239)

states' rights This is an interpretation of the Constitution that argues that the states hold the ultimate sovereignty and have power over the federal government. It was expressed in the Virginia and Kentucky Resolutions and formed the basis for resistance by the South against attempts to control slavery. (p. 240)

IDENTIFICATION

Identify by filling in the blanks.

1. The author of *Thoughts on Government*, a treatise on the formation of state constitutions, was _____. (p. 213)

2. A radical view of women's rights was articulated by the English republican author _____ in *A Vindication of the Rights of Woman*. (p. 215)

3. A 1776 law inadvertently gave the vote to widows and single women of property in the state of _____ until it was rescinded in 1807. (p. 216)

4. _____ argued in "On the Equality of the Sexes" that women were intellectually

equal to men and needed only training and education to show it. (p. 216)

5. Thomas Jefferson wrote the _____, which made provisions for the admission of new states in the western territories. (p. 220)

6. In 1786, _____ led a pro-debtor revolt against the government of Massachusetts. (pp. 221–222)

7. Thomas Jefferson missed the Philadelphia convention of 1787 because he was serving as the American minister to _____. (p. 223)

8. In 1786, a group of nationalists called for reform of the Articles of Confederation at a commercial convention in _____. (p. 223)

9. As part of the constitutional compromise over slavery, Congress was denied the power to ban the slave trade for _____ years after ratification of the Constitution. (p. 225)

10. _____ of Massachusetts, who had been an influential leader of the Patriot movement in Boston before and during the Revolutionary War, opposed the new Constitution. (p. 227)

11. Supporters of the Constitution, such as James Madison, John Jay, and Alexander Hamilton, published a series of articles called _____. (p. 227)

12. Hamilton's three-tiered program to revive the finances of the United States involved the paying off of old government securities, the _____ of state debts incurred during the war, and the chartering of a national bank. (pp. 230–233)

13. Those who adopted a _____ interpretation of the Constitution based their argument that Congress should make "all laws which shall be necessary and proper" on Article 1, section 8. (p. 232)

14. In 1798 the Adams administration, through the _____, abridged the rights of free speech by prohibiting malicious criticism of administration policies and limited the rights of foreigners. (pp. 239–240)

15. The man who was prevented from becoming president after he had tied with Thomas Jefferson in the electoral college in 1800 was _____. (p. 241)

FEATURES EXERCISES

American Voices

ABIGAIL AND JOHN ADAMS, The Status of Women (p. 215)

Republicanism argued that all power derived from the people and that government acquired legitimacy from the consent of the governed. Each free person possessed the natural rights of life, liberty, and property. Once such powerful ideas took hold among the people, it would be hard to limit their impact on all social and political relationships. Just as republicanism illuminated the hypocrisy of slavery, so, too, did some women use republican ideas to comment on their own social status. To Abigail Adams, the strong and outspoken wife of John Adams, a delegate to the second Continental Congress from Massachusetts, republicanism could hardly be an idea that pertained only to men. In particular, she objected to the legal and social dependency and inequality of married women and to women's lack of access to education.

As you read "The Status of Women," ask yourself the following questions:

1. How are the difficulties Abigail Adams and other women of her generation faced evident in her husband's response? How does his response suggest the possibility of change?

2. What was the primary impact that republicanism would have on the status of American women? In what ways do Abigail Adams's complaints and suggestions anticipate this result?

3. Who do you think won this exchange? Why?

American Lives

Gouverneur Morris: An Elitist Liberal in a Republican Age (p. 218)

The career and life of Gouverneur Morris, the son of a New York aristocrat, indicates how members of the colonial elite responded to the Revolution and to republican social theory by shifting the basis of their leadership from lineage to personal achievement. Making use of his good connections, Morris was able to amass a considerable fortune in business, which allowed him to claim elite status on the basis of work and achievement rather than family heritage. His ideas reflected the values of emergent capitalism, which emphasized the free individual in the economy and promised to provide a new theory of social order based on individualism.

As you read "Gouverneur Morris," ask yourself the following questions:

1. How does one reconcile Gouverneur Morris's aristocratic beliefs with his willingness to support the Revolution?
2. What other Founding Fathers shared Morris's political and social views?
3. How can someone who is suspicious of majority rule and believes in a property requirement for voting or political participation advocate freedom or equal rights for all?
4. How did Morris's career indicate changes in the definition of elite status in society?

American Voices

ROBERT YATES AND JOHN LANSING, A Protest against the Philadelphia Convention (p. 225)

Opposition to the Virginia Plan and its design to create a strong central government began as soon as James Madison introduced it to the constitutional convention in Philadelphia. Within a few months, opponents of the plan began to call themselves Antifederalists, continuing their opposition even when the plan was amended by a series of compromises that balanced the power of both small and large states. Yates and Lansing felt that any formation of a central government at some distance from the people or the states would corrupt the leaders, causing them to consolidate power at the expense of the liberty of the people. Representative government must, they argued, be run by those who are in direct and regular contact with the will of the people. The more distant the representatives and leaders were from the people, the more likely they were to abridge the people's rights. As you read "A Protest against the Philadelphia Convention," ask yourself the following questions:

1. In what ways were the ideas of people like Robert Yates and John Lansing shaped by their colonial experience in the Revolutionary War?
2. What experience indicated to them that a "consolidated" central government tended to deprive states of their "most essential rights of sovereignty"?
3. How would James Madison, in *The Federalist*, later respond to Yates and Lansing's fears that the extensive territory of the United States precluded the possibility of an effective central government?
4. How would Yates and Lansing's fellow delegate from New York, Alexander Hamilton, counter their arguments?
5. In what ways would Yates and Lansing's ideas lead to the Republican Party and the Kentucky and Virginia Resolutions of 1798?

New Technology

Machine Technology and Republican Values (pp. 234–235)

Thomas Jefferson believed in the moral superiority of independent yeomen farmers and argued that they were the best hope for a successful democratic republic. Yet he recognized that the lack of industrial development in America threatened to make Americans subject to foreigners and became convinced of the need to develop American manufacturing. He sought to develop manufacturing without its negative consequences—concentration of power in the hands of a few, the impoverishment of the workers, and their living and working in horrible conditions—all of which would undermine democracy. He argued that the household, farm, and plantation could become small manufactories, providing everything that Americans needed. How slave labor on a plantation worked to support democracy, Jefferson did not explain. Nor was he able to explain how a small-scale system of household production, using primarily manual power, could compete against large firms using water- and steam-driven engines and more efficient processes of production.

As you read "Machine Technology and Republican Values," ask yourself the following questions:

1. Why did industrial technology tend to impoverish workers?
2. Jefferson wanted to achieve industrial production by means of farm labor. To what extent was this feasible? In what ways was it not feasible?
3. Were there ways to develop industry without creating the same conditions that existed in England?

Voices from Abroad

WILLIAM COBBETT, Peter Porcupine Attacks Pro-French Americans (p. 238)

In this essay, William Cobbett, the British journalist who wrote under the name Peter Porcupine, responds to an inflammatory definition of loyalty to the republican cause that based loyalty on whether one supported the French Revolution. Cobbett expresses anger that some American republicans have championed the French Revolution simply because it is a republican movement, without seeming to consider its horrors. Such partisan judgment, Cobbett argues, is what led to the excesses of the French Revolution, and, he argues, there is no reason that similar republicans could not move toward such extremes in the United States as well. As evidence for this, he notes the public attacks on George Washington, which he sees as similar to those made against the king of France.

As you read "Peter Porcupine Attacks Pro-French Americans," ask yourself the following questions:

1. Why does Cobbett attack the French Revolution? What are his political motives?
2. What evidence does Cobbett present to indicate the possibility that radical republicanism could result in similar events in the United States?
3. Why does Cobbett believe the Federalists had a better plan for a republic?

MAPS AND FIGURES

Map 7.2 Ratifying the Constitution (p. 229)

The geographic patterns of support and opposition to the ratification of the Constitution tell us a lot about the self-interest, values, and attitudes that affected people's viewpoints. Look at this map closely and describe which people from which areas seem to support or oppose the ratification. Then ask yourself the following questions:

1. What were the geographic patterns governing support of and opposition to the Constitution? Who supported the ratification? Who opposed it?
2. From what you know about the experiences of people in each area, what factors account for these patterns?

Map 7.3 The Election of 1800 (p. 241)

Examine the patterns of support for Federalist and Republican candidates in the election of 1800. After looking at this map closely, ask yourself the following questions:

1. Where was Thomas Jefferson's support strongest? Why?
2. Where were the Federalists' support strongest? Why?
3. How does the relative balance of support for Republicans and Federalists suggest which party seems to be on the rise?
4. How does the pattern of support for the Republicans and the Federalists in 1800 compare with the support for and opposition to the Constitution in 1787–1789 (see Map 7. 2)? Can you explain the similarities and differences?

SELF-TEST

Multiple Choice

1. In deciding who should rule, the answer that most state constitutions gave was:
   a. the same people who had ruled before the war.
   b. the same people, with more yeomen farmers, middling farmers, and artisans.
   c. fewer people than before the war.
   d. the same people who had ruled before the war minus the Loyalists.

2. Since the new governments would be republican, the general conclusion was that there should be:
   a. as much direct democracy as possible, with a unicameral house and no governor or council.
   b. very little democracy, with a strong governor and an elite council.
   c. a moderate amount of democracy, with separation of powers and checks and balances.
   d. a minimum of democracy in a mixed system limited by strict property requirements for voting.

3. The Articles of Confederation are best characterized as a:
   a. failure in foreign affairs.
   b. success in managing western lands and establishing the framework of a dynamic society.

c. success in managing the financial affairs of the nation.
   d. success in negotiating grievances among states.

4. The land policy of the Confederation Congress accomplished *all* of the following *except*:
   a. establishing friendly relations with native Americans.
   b. persuading the states to give up their claims and place western lands in the public domain.
   c. organizing the survey of public lands by means of a grid system.
   d. establishing procedures by which new territories in the West could become states.

5. A postwar crisis developed for *all* of the following reasons *except*:
   a. state governments were burdened by war debts and were forced to raise taxes.
   b. American trade, no longer protected by the Navigation Acts, slumped.
   c. political struggles developed between creditors and debtors.
   d. the British threatened to invade America from Canada.

6. The nationalists took *all* of the following assertive actions to ensure the drafting of a new constitution *except*:
   a. calling for a convention in Philadelphia to consider revision of the Articles of Confederation.
   b. accepting the work of the convention and sending the Constitution to the states for ratification.
   c. specifying that the Constitution would go into effect if nine states ratified it.
   d. offering to the convention not a revision of the Articles of Confederation but a completely new constitutional framework.

7. Which of the following was not at the Philadelphia convention?
   a. Benjamin Franklin
   b. George Washington
   c. James Madison
   d. John Adams

8. The Constitution offered to the states for ratification in 1787 represented a compromise on *all* of the following issues *except*:
   a. representation of the states in the two houses of Congress.
   b. representation of African American slaves in the South.
   c. the extension of the judiciary into the states.
   d. the creation of a national government whose authority would be the supreme law of the land.

9. Who among the following former Patriots was *not* an Antifederalist?
   a. Robert Morris
   b. Samuel Adams
   c. George Mason
   d. Patrick Henry

10. The Federalists won ratification for *all* of the following reasons *except*:
    a. they included men who had fought in the Revolution and achieved fame and respect.
    b. they stood confidently for the future of the nation.
    c. they included many shrewd politicians who promised special favors in return for votes in state ratification fights.
    d. They were able to organize effectively, pay for campaign events, and buy newspaper space.

11. The immediate impact of the passage of the Bill of Rights was to:
    a. begin an era in which individuals could seek redress against the federal government through the Supreme Court.
    b. enhance the legitimacy of the Constitution by allaying the concerns of the Antifederalists.
    c. lead to a broadening of suffrage to include women and free African Americans.
    d. trigger a fierce debate about the powers of the Constitution.

12. In his financial program, Hamilton wanted to:
    a. empower the central government by connecting its interests to those of the elite.
    b. outperform Thomas Jefferson in the cabinet and succeed Washington in 1796.
    c. subvert the Constitution and revert to a government much like the British system.
    d. broaden the powers of the federal government as stated in the Constitution.

13. Among the following ideas, the only one Thomas Jefferson did *not* believe in was:
    a. a strict reading of the Constitution.
    b. a democratic republic rooted in an agrarian yeoman farming population.
    c. rapid settlement of the West by farmers and the admission of new territories into the Union.
    d. the abolition of slavery in the South.

14. Jay's Treaty included *all* of the following terms *except*:
    a. a return of property confiscated from Loyalists during the Revolution.
    b. acknowledgment of the British right to remove French property from American ships.

c. repayment of prewar debts to British merchants.
d. removal of British forts in the West.

15. The Republicans won the election in 1800 because:
   a. John Adams's administration had enacted the Alien and Sedition Acts.
   b. the Federalists were divided by internal disputes.
   c. the Republicans nominated Thomas Jefferson, a very popular candidate.
   d. Alexander Hamilton supported Thomas Jefferson.

16. The instability of government during the 1780s was reflected in the frequency with which extralegal procedures and meetings occurred both within and outside government. Which of the following actions was *not* extralegal?
   a. the call by nationalists at the Annapolis convention for a convention to revise the Articles of Confederation.
   b. meetings among farmers in western Massachusetts in 1786 to protest high taxes and aggressive creditors.
   c. the decision among the members of the constitutional convention to require only nine of the thirteen states to ratify the Constitution in order for it to go into effect.
   d. a 1792 assembly in Pittsburgh to protest Hamilton's excise tax on whiskey.

Short Essays

Answer the following questions in a brief paragraph.

1. How did the colonial experience affect the structure of the state governments that were organized during and after the Revolutionary War? In general, were they more republican than democratic or more democratic than republican? (pp. 212–214)

2. Why were the rights of women ignored during a revolution that was fought for the liberty, freedom, and equality of all? (pp. 214–216)

3. Why were the Articles of Confederation weak? (pp. 216–222)

4. What did the nationalists, who later called themselves Federalists, hope to achieve by revising the Articles of Confederation and establishing a new central government based on the Constitution of 1787? (pp. 222–223)

5. How and why did the Antifederalists lose the ratification debates in 1787 and 1788? (pp. 226–228)

6. Why did both Washington and Adams, as well as the Republicans, consider it imperative to remain neutral and avoid war with either France or Britain in the 1790s? Given this general agreement, how do you account for the acrimony of the political debates of the 1790s? (pp. 236–240)

7. Was the "Revolution of 1800" really a revolution? In what ways was it not a revolution? (pp. 240–241)

ANSWERS

Identification

1. John Adams
2. Mary Wollstonecraft
3. New Jersey
4. Judith Sargent Murray
5. Ordinance of 1784
6. Daniel Shays
7. France
8. Annapolis, Maryland
9. twenty
10. Patrick Henry
11. *The Federalist*
12. assumption
13. loose
14. Alien and Sedition Acts
15. Aaron Burr

Self-Test

Multiple Choice

1. b.	7. d.	13. d.
2. c.	8. d.	14. a.
3. b.	9. a.	15. a.
4. a.	10. c.	16. b.
5. d.	11. b.	
6. d.	12. a.	

Short Essays

1. Colonial governments were modeled on the government in Great Britain; each had an assembly, a council, and a governor representing the sovereignty of the people, the nobility, and the king, respectively. The structure was familiar, as were the checks and balances that limited the power of each branch and ensured liberty for all. Having just thrown off a central power, however, several states empowered the legislatures and broadened suffrage to make the government more democratic, while others maintained a powerful governor or developed a judiciary to make sure that unbridled democracy was checked by republican procedures. While all the new state governments were republics, they varied in the degree to which they tried to limit democracy.

2. Gender relations in the eighteenth century were based on the notions that men were intellectually superior to women and that only men could be economically independent. Women, it was argued, lacked the intelligence and independence of men and therefore could not be full-fledged citizens. For this reason, as well, they could not be given the right to vote, and their complaints about political or social inequality could not be taken seriously.

3. Because the Articles of Confederation did not establish coercive power of the national government over the states, they could not create a coherent public policy. In addition, because the Articles did not include the power to tax, the national government could not fund programs without requisitioning or borrowing from the states. As a result, the government was chronically short of revenue, though the sale of public lands eventually eased this problem. Lacking funding, Congress was unable to launch national programs or finance the military and diplomatic corps. In consequence, the central government was weak and inefficient.

4. The nationalists wanted a stronger central government that could have power over the states and prevent the interstate squabbles and disputes that threatened the Confederation. Such a government would create a new national realm, a nation, which could take its rightful place among other nations of the world. That many nationalists had served in the Revolution or had been diplomats and seen how important it was for a nation to have a strong central structure only deepened their interest in establishing a new national framework.

5. The Antifederalists were a diverse group reacting to actions already taken by the assertive nationalists. As a result, they were less organized and slower to bring their forces together. Moreover, in their arguments, the Antifederalists failed to provide an alternative to the weak government under the Articles. Driven by fear for the future rather than by expectation and hope, they viewed the plans of the Federalists with suspicion. Thus they argued defensively and negatively. In the final debates, they had less to bargain with because they had little to offer. The Federalists, in contrast, offered a new Constitution, a new nation, and a more secure government.

6. The United States benefited enormously from maintaining neutrality and trading with both the British and the French. After years of economic uncertainty, the prosperity of the 1790s established the nation on a firmer footing. In addition, for a new, uncertain country to ally itself with great powers would have endangered its independence, no matter which side it chose. It was important, as George Washington argued, to stay clear of another country's disputes and act in self-interest. Washington feared that, given the fragility of the new republic, any dispute or disagreement that caused people to choose sides would threaten national independence and unity with the possibility of civil war. Articulating a clear national self-interest would, Washington believed, cultivate national unity. Ironically, the debate over involvement in foreign affairs in the 1790s created intense passions that intensified the friction between factions, or evolving parties, and thus threatened national unity itself.

7. The transfer of power from the elite, aristocratic Federalist Party to the agrarian Democratic-Republican Party was as much of a change of ruler as the Revolution had been. For Jefferson, the election of 1800 meant the Republicans could eliminate some of the centralist policies of the Federalist era, reducing the size and power of the federal government, strengthening the states, and broadening democracy. This transfer of power was revolutionary because it marked a rare moment in history when a total change in government was effected in a peaceful and orderly fashion. Yet, because it occurred according to procedures spelled out in the Constitution, Jefferson's election simply confirmed and validated the political system established by the Constitution in 1787. Much of how that system operated had been established by Washington and Adams. Jefferson simply continued the same government under the same Constitution. Presidents elected in the United States today generally do the same thing, transferring political power from one person or party to another without violence or revolution.

Chapter 8

Westward Expansion and a New Political Economy, 1790–1820

LEARNING OBJECTIVES

1. What roles did migration to the West, presidential leadership, and innovative public policy play in shaping the new American republic? Was any one factor more important than the others?

2. Why did Americans migrate to the West? What impact did westward migration have on the nation as a whole?

3. What were the causes of the War of 1812, and what was the role of the Republican leadership in events leading to the war? Did Republican leadership decisions cause the war, or did events shape Republican leadership?

4. Laws can affect how people will behave economically. How did the state commonwealth system affect the development of the American economy? How did national policy affect the economy?

CHAPTER SUMMARY

In the decades immediately following the Treaty of Paris, the pressure of America's growing population in the East, together with economic forces, drove Americans across the Appalachian Mountains and into the West in search of land. President Thomas Jefferson and the leaders of the Republican Party viewed westward migration as a positive development. Though many farmers in the East had responded to a declining standard of living with home production, the barter system, and more intensive agricultural practices and thus remained yeomen farmers, many others had been forced into tenancy or into the cities, thus threatening the yeoman ideal at the core of Republican ideology. By moving west, yeomen farmers not only escaped the overcrowded and depleted lands of the East but also preserved the yeoman ideal as the foundation of the republic. Republican policies of aggressive land acquisition through purchase or diplomacy, easier land-purchase policies, proactive transportation and trade policy, active defense of national boundaries, and an expansionist Indian policy all aimed at maintaining the yeoman-farmer basis of the republic. Both national and state governments encouraged capitalist economic development for "the public good" through a commonwealth system of law and policy that privileged private activity for a public purpose over individual self-interest and, thus, stimulated economic growth.

Westward Expansion (pp. 246–253)

Between 1790 and 1820, millions of Americans in both the North and the South migrated into the interior West. In spite of native American resistance, which the government subdued through military action, treaties, and attempts at assimilation, Americans brought their economic, social, and political beliefs, practices, and institutions west and transformed the life of the entire nation. When settlers were faced with transportation limitations that threatened their progress, state and federal governments stepped in to finance roads and transport systems, enabling

107

yeomen farmers and entrepreneurs to continue the conquest of the interior.

Native American Resistance

As the pace of immigration onto the lands acquired in the Treaty of 1783 increased, native American resistance intensified. To secure the land for American settlers, the U.S. government fought a series of battles against the Indians, forcing them in treaties to cede claims to their lands in the Northwest Territory, as well as across Tennessee and parts of Mississippi and Alabama. Once the native Americans had been subdued, some government officials favored a policy that sought to assimilate them into American life. Many native peoples rejected white missionaries, sometimes by moving or by reasserting their identity through religious and cultural revival.

Settlers, Speculators, and Slaves

Native American resistance did little to deter Americans in both the South and the North from migrating to the West. In the South, an increase in the demand for cotton, the region's new cash crop, combined with efficiencies in production created by Eli Whitney's invention of the cotton gin, provided the impetus for westward migration. Speculators from the South bought vast tracts of Tennessee, Kentucky, and territory to the west and south and sold it to slaveowning planters, who brought slavery west with them. Northern speculators and yeomen farmers alike poured out of New England, often in large associated groups of relatives or church members, and moved into the Northwest Territory. Meanwhile, the loss of rural population compelled farmers back East to further intensify their efforts to increase yields. By opening new lands to production and reinvigorating the potential of long-settled lands, westward migration boosted the entire economy.

The Transportation Bottleneck

The vast extent of the territory across which Americans migrated expanded the reach of U.S. markets and compelled government officials to develop aggressive policies to support better means of transportation. Inland waterways were crucial to navigation, and entrepreneurs sold property in riverside towns for premium prices, increasing these towns' importance. State governments supported turnpike construction, improvement of rivers, and the building of inland canals. For many westerners, life on the frontier nevertheless meant self-sufficiency, limited trade, and isolation from the national market.

The Republicans' Political Revolution (pp. 253–265)

The West played an important role in Republican policy. By the 1820s, Republican policies favoring western expansion, small government, and states' rights had made good on the party's promises in the "Revolution of 1800."

The Jeffersonian Presidency

As president, Jefferson aimed to reduce the size of the national government, lessen the influence of the northeastern merchants and creditors in the national government, and cultivate the yeoman-farmer ideal through westward expansion. He cut the national debt by almost half, reduced the size of military and government bureaucracy, liberalized naturalization laws, abolished excise taxes, and allowed the Alien and Sedition Acts to expire. He also sought to reduce the power of the judiciary, even though he did not move aggressively to remove Federalist judges who dominated the federal court system.

Jefferson and the West

To encourage western settlement, Jefferson favored lowering the price of federal lands to make them available to yeomen farmers. When France decided that it no longer wanted to control the vast territory of Louisiana, Jefferson adjusted his strict constructionist view of the Constitution and argued that the use of presidential power to purchase the territory and thus expand the national domain and open more land to potential settlement was legitimate. When Jefferson and Napoleon had completed the deal to purchase the Louisiana Territory, doubling the size of the country, Jefferson funded an expedition by Meriwether Lewis and William Clark to explore the new region. Fearing that western expansion would diminish the power of the Northeast, some New England Federalists, as well as former Vice-President Aaron Burr, talked of secession. Burr's involvement in a scheme to separate western territory from the country resulted in his being tried for treason. He was acquitted.

Conflict with Britain and France

The outbreak of war between France and Britain threatened the neutrality of the young republic. Although both countries restricted American free trade, Americans were especially incensed by the British impressment of American citizens, seized aboard American ships, into the British navy. When

Chapter Summary

a British warship attacked the U.S. Navy vessel *Chesapeake,* Jefferson imposed an embargo on all American ships, forbidding them to leave port or trade with either belligerent, in an effort to peacefully coerce both governments to change their policies. In the end, the embargo hurt Americans more than the British or French, neither of whom changed their policy. Continued public discontent forced Jefferson's successor, James Madison, to repeal the embargo, although he tried to continue to limit trade with France and Britain.

Meanwhile, with British support, Shawnee chief Tecumseh and his brother, the prophet Tenskwatawa, revived the Western Confederacy of the 1790s. American settlers and territorial militias responded by fighting the Indians, culminating in an American victory at Tippecanoe. At the same time, Americans demanded that the British respect American sovereignty in the West. Republican congressmen from the West, eyeing the addition of Canada and Florida to the American domain, argued that the United States was bound by national honor to fight to gain British recognition of American sovereignty in the West, neutral rights on the Atlantic, and respect for the United States as an independent nation. A divided Congress reluctantly voted to declare war against Britain.

The War of 1812

The War of 1812 was almost a disaster for the United States. Militarily unprepared, short of funds, and divided, the Americans failed to invade Canada in 1812, were helpless against British naval power, and suffered the humiliation of a British invasion that culminated in the burning of Washington in 1814. As a British blockade stifled trade, opposition to the war in seaport cities increased. Though by the end of 1814 the Americans had gained control of the Great Lakes, defeated the Western Confederacy, repulsed a British invasion at Baltimore, and, after the war was actually over, defeated British troops at New Orleans, neither American nor British leaders saw anything to gain by continuing the war. A peace negotiated by Albert Gallatin, Henry Clay, and John Quincy Adams restored prewar conditions and left unresolved issues open. From 1817 to 1819 Adams, as secretary of state, would negotiate the acquisition of Florida and the clarification of the border between the United States and New Spain and Canada, further expanding the nation's westward ambitions. Meanwhile, Andrew Jackson's victory at New Orleans over the British, which he followed in 1817 with an unauthorized military attack on Florida, transformed the war into a defining event that ended American dependency on Britain, increased national pride, and unified the nation.

The Capitalist Commonwealth (pp. 266–275)

During the early 1800s, the American republic gained economic independence from Great Britain as many of its workers shifted from agriculture to commerce, banking, and rural manufacturing. To develop commercial and industrial activity, banks increasingly created and supplied capital, and those with wealth reinvested in the economy and tried to shape its policies. This focus on the accumulation and investment of capital for economic return transformed the mercantilist agrarian economy into a capitalist economy. Even so, the ideology of republicanism influenced some lawmakers to try to steer some of this development for private gain toward activities that favored the public good.

A Merchant-Based Economy: Banks, Manufacturing, and Markets

The accumulation and investment of capital that drove economic development derived from the expansion of American trade after the Revolutionary War. As American merchants pursued more extensive trading connections, they were compelled to enlarge partnerships and seek more credit from the nation's fledgling banks. In response, a banking system, led by a national bank with branches in major cities, was established. The national bank lasted until 1811, when Madison decided to let it lapse. Its close left the needs of American entrepreneurs in the hands of weaker and more volatile state banks. Meanwhile, entrepreneurs, lacking sufficient capital to invest in large factories, developed an outwork system of manufacturing. This system, which took advantage of an excess labor supply and local networks of barter and exchange, involved manufacturers hiring women to produce finished goods from the raw materials delivered to each house or transferred from one house to another. Innovative organization, marketing, and technology led to an increase in production and sales, which drew more competitors and interested investors into manufacturing. The profits from this increased productivity and rising real incomes set in motion an engine of capital development that would transform the country.

Public Policy: The Commonwealth System

State governments took the lead in stimulating the economy and encouraging large-scale manufacture and capital investment. The chief instruments of what came to be called the "commonwealth" system were corporate charters that granted companies monopolies, protected investors through limited liability, and allowed companies to claim eminent domain in carrying out their projects. By encouraging companies to undertake projects for "the public good," the commonwealth system privileged private activity that had a public purpose and, thus, stimulated economic growth.

The Law and the Commonwealth: Republicans versus Federalists

American economic growth under state mercantilism generated economic and legal controversy in the early 1800s, bringing to the fore conflict between the proponents of Federalist and Republican philosophies. Both Federalists and Republicans espoused the commonwealth system to stimulate the economy, but in different ways. The Federalist program involved national tariffs to protect home production and the creation of a national debt funded by a central bank. The Federalists also believed that each individual maintained traditional property rights rooted in common law. The Republicans supported the federal financing of internal improvements to foster economic development. Law, they argued, derived from the will of the people. According to Republicans, sometimes the broader good of the people, defined as social utility, superseded individual property rights in economic development.

Federalist Law: John Marshall and the Supreme Court

During his thirty-four-year tenure as Chief Justice of the United States Supreme Court, John Marshall brought traditional Federalist principles to bear on the Supreme Court's rulings. The Marshall court delivered opinions with far-reaching consequences for the development of the country. By emphasizing judicial authority, national supremacy over states' rights, and a static rather than a dynamic definition of property rights, the Court strengthened the power of the federal government and slowed the pace of economic growth. In a series of important cases, Marshall's defense of contracts and property struck down the right of states to tax all institutions within their borders, upheld contracts against state efforts to rescind them through new legislation, and defended property rights by ruling that private corporations had the right to govern themselves and avoid government regulation. In so doing, Marshall perhaps unwittingly unleashed the power of corporations to operate independently across state lines, thus laying the legal and political economic foundations for the Industrial Revolution.

After 1821, increasing numbers of Republican appointments to the Court diminished Marshall's power, contributing to a more general erosion of Federalist influence and paving the way for more aggressive economic development during the cycle of Republican ascendancy that followed.

EXPANDED TIMELINE

1787 **Northwest Ordinance**
The Articles of Confederation Congress gained control of western lands, organized a system of land distribution, and developed a program for the admission of new states into the Union. The Northwest Ordinance of 1787 divided the region north and west of the Ohio River into a grid of sections and townships, established price limits and minimum sizes for federal lands, and stipulated that eventually five new states would be formed from this region.

1790s **Turnpikes and short canals are built**
To facilitate farmers' access to regional, national, and international markets, states made the construction of turnpikes and canals a top priority in the 1790s.

Rural outwork system begins in shoes and textiles
The introduction of rural manufacturing and production through outwork marked an early stage in the transformation of the American economy. In addition to growing grain and raising livestock, farmers began to produce raw materials for manufacture, such as milk for cheese and hides for leather goods. Rural manufacturing helped encourage the development of a market economy in the United States. It also provided the raw materials and manpower that enabled some manufacturers to develop the outwork system of production. In Massachusetts, manufacturers employed farmers and their family members working in their homes to make boots and shoes.

State mercantilism emerges: corporate charters
In their efforts to attract new enterprises and expand their economic bases, many states devised plans to make the incorporation of businesses easier. Corporate charters provided businesses with greater legal protection (limited liability) and with advantages not granted to individuals (the right to take property under eminent domain). State mercantilism facilitated the expansion of state and national economies and the development of a market economy.

1790–1791 **Little Turtle defeats American armies**
The westward migration of Americans met considerable native American resistance. When American settlers streamed into southern Ohio, the Miami chief Little Turtle launched attacks to repulse American forces.

Expanded Timeline

1791 **First Bank of the United States (1791–1811)**
As secretary of the Treasury under George Washington, Alexander Hamilton advocated the creation of a national bank, the Bank of the United States, to serve as the fiscal agent for the new nation. After successfully countering critics, who believed the bank was unconstitutional, Hamilton won the president's support and congressional approval for the bank. The bank's twenty-year charter expired in 1811, but during its lifetime it provided economic support for a growing economy.

1792 **Kentucky joins Union; Tennessee follows (1796)**
Migration east into Kentucky and Tennessee was so extensive between the 1770s and the 1790s that both territories, administered by Virginia and North Carolina, respectively, qualified for statehood.

1794 **Battle of Fallen Timbers; Treaty of Greenville (1795)**
In retaliation for their defeat of Little Turtle, a large American force pursued and engaged the allied Western Confederacy in present-day Ohio. Though defeated, the Western Confederacy remained strong. The United States sought a compromise peace in which it recognized Indian ownership of the trans-Appalachian West and renounced claims based on conquest. In return, the Indians ceded land in Ohio and ports on the Great Lakes, acknowledged American sovereignty over the Northwest region, and agreed not to ally themselves with the British.

Lancaster Turnpike Company chartered
During the nineteenth century, the United States experienced a transportation revolution that encouraged the movement of people into developing regions in order to stimulate the growth of the economy. The building of hard-surfaced roads like the Lancaster Turnpike in Pennsylvania was an important part of this revolution. The Lancaster Turnpike Company, which received a monopoly charter, not only made a profit for investors, but also reduced transport costs, increased trade and travel, and sparked a turnpike-construction boom, each of which enhanced the public good. State support of the Lancaster Turnpike Company provided a good example of the role states played in encouraging private enterprise and spurring economic development.

1795 **Massachusetts Mill Dam Act promotes industry development**
Under the commonwealth economic system, states tended to give priority to public good rather than to private interests. A reflection of this new attitude, the Mill Dam Act allowed mill owners to flood farmlands contiguous to their mills in return for "fair compensation" to the landowners whose farms were flooded. The Massachusetts legislature judged that more people would be served by the output of the miller than by that of the farmers whose land was lost.

Pinckney's Treaty with Spain allows U.S. use of Mississippi River
As American settlement pushed west, more American farmers and merchants wanted to use the Mississippi River, the border with Spanish Louisiana, for trade. The Spanish accommodated American interests by signing a treaty giving Americans the right to ship exports from the West, down the Mississippi River, and through the Spanish port of New Orleans.

1801 **Spain restores Louisiana to France**
American access to New Orleans was threatened when France coerced Spain into selling Lousiana and Napoleon ordered Spanish officials to restrict American trade. The Americans entered into negotiations with Napoleon, with a goal of purchasing the port of New Orleans.

John Marshall becomes Chief Justice
Shortly before he left office, President John Adams appointed John Marshall as Chief Justice of the Supreme Court. For the next three decades, Marshall used the Court as a forum to assert the power of the federal government and ensure its supremacy over the states. Long after the Federalist Party was dead in national politics, Marshall applied the Federalist doctrines of judicial review, federal power, and property rights to interpret the laws of the United States.

1801–
1807 **Treasury Secretary Albert Gallatin reduces national debt**
Republicans believed that the national debt established by Alexander Hamilton enabled northeastern creditors and merchants to exert considerable control over the national government. Jefferson's conservative treasurer, Albert Gallatin, carefully controlled government expenditures to reduce the national debt by almost half during his presidency. In so doing, Gallatin helped fulfill a Republican promise to reduce the influence of the elite and increase the influence of the people in American life.

Seizures of American ships by France and Britain
As early as 1801, British ships began attacking neutral American ships and impressing American sailors, who the British alleged were deserters, into the British navy.

Handsome Lake revives traditional beliefs
In response to the continued pressures of American life on the traditional culture of the Iroquois tribe, the prophet Handsome Lake initiated a revival of traditional beliefs to reinvigorate tribal life.

1803 **Louisiana Purchase; Lewis and Clark expedition**
American diplomats Robert Livingston and James Monroe purchased the entire territory of Louisiana from the French, doubling the size of the United States and dramatically expanding the republican

vision of a yeoman republic. At Jefferson's request, Meriwether Lewis and William Clark set out on an expedition of exploration across the Louisiana Territory and beyond, all the way to the Pacific Ocean.

Marbury v. Madison asserts judicial review
Marbury is one of the landmark decisions of the Supreme Court, marking the first time the Court overturned a federal law—or, in this instance, a section of a federal law—as unconstitutional. This power of judicial review allows the Court to restrict the power of the executive and legislative branches and serves as a critical check within the system of checks and balances in the American government.

1807 **Embargo Act cripples American shipping**
After the British attacked the American ship the *Chesapeake* and either killed or wounded twenty-one men, Jefferson and his secretary of state, James Madison, devised an embargo on American shipping, forbidding American ships to leave port or trade with any other nations. The self-imposed embargo hurt the American economy and was widely hated. Madison repealed the embargo and, instead, prohibited trade only with France and Britain. Americans' frustrations with British and French violations of their neutrality grew.

1809 **Tecumseh and Tenskwatawa mobilize Indians**
Tecumseh and his brother, the prophet Tenskwatawa, revived the Western Confederacy among Indians across the Northwest and then tried to extend it to the South. When the confederacy increased attacks against American frontier settlements, forces under Governor William Henry Harrison attacked Tenskwatawa's home village in Indiana. When the War of 1812 broke out, Tecumseh sided with the British.

Congress bans importation of slaves
In accordance with the compromise on slavery in the Constitution, Congress banned American participation in the foreign slave trade in 1809. From that time on, all slaves in the Southwest were drawn from the East. This increased the domestic slave trade.

1810s **Expansion of slavery into Old Southwest**
The development of cotton as a cash crop in the South increased the demand for good land and thus set in motion the migration of slavery to the Old Southwest. Within two decades, thousands of whites and their slaves had moved to Alabama and Mississippi, enabling those regions to become states in 1817 and 1819, respectively.

Fletcher v. Peck extends contract clause
The *Fletcher* decision prohibited the state of Georgia from reclaiming land granted to the Yazoo Land Company by the state legislature. The Supreme Court granted the right of a new legislature to rescind a law passed by a previous legislature but denied the right to rescind a contract executed under law. This ruling endorsed traditional concepts of property rights and contracts.

1811 **Battle of Tippecanoe**
American troops led by William Henry Harrison defeated Tecumseh's Western Confederacy at Tenskwatawa's sacred town at Tippecanoe, Indiana. Evidence of British support inflamed "war hawks" in Congress to call for a war against Britain to end British encroachment on American sovereignty in the West.

1812– **War of 1812**
1815 The United States' Declaration of War against Britain followed a lengthy period of rising tensions over Britain's practice of impressment, violations of American neutrality, and disregard for American sovereignty. The expansionist goals of western war hawks in Congress, who imagined an American realm that included Canada, Florida, and more western lands, added further impetus to the call for war.
  American forces briefly entered Canada and defeated the Western Confederacy at the Battle of the Thames, in which Tecumseh was killed. Nevertheless, American forces withdrew. Meanwhile, the British navy quickly gained control of the seas, harassing American shipping and threatening American coastal ports. An American victory on Lake Champlain, which prevented a British invasion of the Hudson River Valley, and the defeat of the British-supported Creek Indians by a militia led by Andrew Jackson, were the only American successes in a year of military defeat and stalemate. The British invaded and burned Washington, D.C., before being repulsed at Baltimore. British and American diplomats entered into negotiations to end the war in August. By December, they had agreed on a treaty that restored conditions to what they had been before the war and left unresolved issues to future discussions. Andrew Jackson's brilliant victory over seasoned British troops at New Orleans after the treaty had been signed and the war was over, made him a national hero overnight and boosted American morale.

1817– **British-American agreements establish U.S.-**
1818 **Canadian boundary**
John Quincy Adams emerged as a skilled negotiator for the United States during the treaty negotiations at Ghent in 1814. Three years later, he negotiated a peaceful resolution to British and American disputes on the Great Lakes by limiting naval forces on the lakes and establishing the 49th parallel as the border of the United States and Canada from the Lakes to the Rocky Mountains.

1817– **Era of Good Feeling during James Monroe's**
1825 **presidency**
The absence of Federalist opposition led observers to

refer to James Monroe's administration as the Era of Good Feeling. In fact, regional interests and personalities were already emerging to create factions that would undermine party unity within a decade.

1819   **Adams-Onís Treaty: Florida annexed, Texas boundary defined**
After Andrew Jackson made an unauthorized military expedition into Florida, John Quincy Adams negotiated American acquisition of the entire peninsula from Spain. Spain's cession of Florida to the United States ended more than three hundred years of Spanish control over Florida (except for British control from 1767 to 1783).

McCulloch v. Maryland **enhances power of national government**
In *McCulloch*, the Marshall court affirmed the power of Congress to take any actions deemed "necessary and proper" to carry out its responsibilities. The Court specifically ruled that the state of Maryland did not have the authority to tax the national government, in this case the Bank of the United States. Arguing that Congress lacked the authority to create the bank in the first place, lawyers for the state of Maryland maintained that the state did indeed have the right to tax a federal entity operating there. Marshall noted that the "elastic clause" in the Constitution gave the federal government the power to establish a national bank. He also noted that because "the power to tax involves the power to destroy," a state's taxing a federal entity gave the state power over the federal government, which ran counter to the Constitution.

Dartmouth College v. Woodward **protects corporate property rights**
When the state of New Hampshire tried to convert Dartmouth College into a public institution, the college sued. Its lawyers argued that the college had been formed by a contract with the king, and that contracts could not be tampered with by any state. The state argued that such a change in the college would be for the public good. Marshall agreed with the college, arguing that "a contract within the letter of the Constitution, and within its spirit also," is inviolable and could not be impaired or overturned by a state law. Where *Fletcher* gave protection to individual property rights, *Dartmouth* guaranteed the protection of corporate property rights. At a time when states were becoming more involved in economic expansion under the commonwealth system, *Dartmouth* checked the growing power of the state.

GLOSSARY

assimilation   A social policy advocating that people who are different from the majority in a culture should adopt the values and behaviors of people in the dominant culture. Some Americans in the nineteenth century favored attempts to assimilate Indians into American life through religion, farming, patriarchy, and individualism. (pp. 247–248)

speculators   A speculator is someone who enters a market to buy an item not to use or improve it but to resell it at a higher price. In the early trans-Appalachian West, speculators with social connections to government officials acquired huge parcels of western land. Government regulations permitting purchases of a minimum size of 23,040 acres, in half the townships and of 640 acres elsewhere allowed only wealthy speculators to enter the market. They then sold it to subsequent settlers. (p. 248)

crop rotation   Different crops use and return different nutrients to the soil. In the late eighteenth century, farmers recognized that when they planted a different crop rather than the same crop each year, the crop yields increased. British reformers introduced this method widely in the East to increase crop yields. (p. 250)

turnpike   A turnpike is a privately built and maintained road on which the owner charges travelers a fee or a toll. (p. 252)

patronage   As early as the eighteenth century, British politicians recognized that patronage, the power to appoint individuals to many posts in the royal and colonial bureaucracy, gave them the power to influence the policy and operations of an office or a government. Such appointments also allowed politicians to reward their political supporters. Thus patronage became an important currency, which allowed politicians to consolidate their political power and influence. (pp. 253–254)

townships   The Northwest Ordinance divided the Northwest Territory into uniform units called townships. Each township, modeled on a New England town, was 6 miles square. There were thirty-six sections in a township, each one mile square. (p. 254)

secession   The exact nature of the contract that bound individual states to the larger union of states called the United States remained unclear to early Americans. In the early nineteenth century, a number of disgruntled members of the system suggested that a state or a group of states could voluntarily leave, or secede from, the Union. Aaron Burr in 1805 and a number of Federalist delegates at the Hartford Convention of 1814, mostly from New England and New York, suggested that secession might be the best way for New England states to maintain their power in the face of western expansion. (pp. 257–258, 264)

impressment Impressment is the act of physically removing a sailor from a ship and forcing him into naval service. The British Royal Navy, claiming that American ships were staffed by deserters from the Royal Navy, routinely impressed American sailors between 1802 and 1811. Their actions played a role in leading to war between the two nations. (p. 258)

embargo An order issued by a government prohibiting the departure or entry of ships into ports within its territory. An embargo is somewhat different from a nonimportation act in that it prohibits the arrival or departure of ships, as opposed to the goods in those ships. (p. 259)

capital Capital is money or wealth that can be invested in economic activity, financial institutions, material supplies, machinery, or infrastructure, enabling economic activity to proceed more efficiently or productively. Financiers accumulate capital through profits on business ventures and savings. The accumulation, use, and investment of capital is the central defining aspect of capitalism. (p. 266)

political economy The political economy is the realm in which governmental policies affect economic growth and development. Individuals who operate in the economy and, at the same time, enter politics or try to influence politicians to develop governmental policies favorable to their economic activities are acting within a political economy. In the early republic, Americans were divided between a political economy that empowered states to issue charters and monopolies and abridge property rights, if necessary, for the public good, and those who favored a free-market economy, in which each individual's property and contracts were inviolable and everyone competed equally. (p. 266)

outwork or putting-out system During the sixteenth century, English merchants supported the production of goods through an outwork system, using people in the countryside to produce textiles that the merchants in turn could sell in the market (see Chapter 1, text p. 32). The outwork system developed in the United States after the War of Independence. Farm families and rural artisans produced various goods, including tinware, cheese, cloth, and shoes the merchants sold in both domestic and overseas markets. This system created new job opportunities in rural America but cost some farmers their economic freedom because of their growing dependence on the merchants who sold their outwork and their transformation into consumers. (p. 268)

preindustrial Reliance on production done by hand rather than by machinery is a chief characteristic of preindustrial manufacturing. Most manufacturing in the United States at the beginning of the nineteenth century remained preindustrial. (p. 269)

corporate charters During the colonial era, private investors in England often promoted the establishment of colonies through trading companies or joint-stock companies that were chartered by the Crown. Support from the government translated into a greater likelihood of success. The same system was used by state governments in the United States to encourage economic development. States awarded corporate charters to private businesses, assuring them of legal protection and an economic advantage over other businesses. In turn, these state-chartered corporations provided help to the states—for example, by building roads, bridges, and canals that encouraged expansion of the market economy. (p. 270)

limited liability The establishment of joint-stock companies in England in the early 1600s facilitated the founding of colonies in America. A joint-stock company brought together several investors who shared risk and gained profit in proportion to their share of the total investment (see Chapter 1). The idea of limited liability evolved in the nineteenth century to mean that the personal assets of shareholders could not be sold to cover the debts of a corporation. Each individual could be held accountable for debts only to the extent of his or her investment in the corporation. (p. 270)

commonwealth *Commonwealth* refers to the public welfare, or the good of the people. State governments advocated the commonwealth system to achieve economic growth by granting corporate charters to private companies whose activities were of benefit to the public. State governments granted charters particularly to companies that built roads and canals, and gave them considerable power to carry out their projects. In so doing, the state acted for the improvement of the commonwealth, or the public good. (pp. 269–270)

eminent domain This principle grants a government legal control of all property within its sovereign jurisdiction, with the power to take and use property for public purposes, provided that compensation be given for the property taken. The government can take land even if the owner does not want to surrender title to the property. Under the early nineteenth-century system of state mercantilism, states granted this power to private corporations, which, like the states themselves, could seize property for public projects like roads, bridges, and canals. (p. 270)

precedent In jurisprudence (law), this term describes a previous case that can serve as a model for judgment in a current case. By using previous rulings to provide a justification or a rationale for a decision, judges can maintain consistency and continuity over a long span of time. Precedent was the foundation of common law, a conservative approach to law that was advocated by Federalists. (p. 272)

common law   Common law was established case by case, precedent by precedent, over time. It was considered by conservatives to be unchanging and venerable and the foundation of jurisprudence. Common law was rooted in traditional rural life and became the core of Federalist conservatism. (p. 272)

social utility   Favoring changes that provide the greatest good for the greatest number of people, state governments with Republican leanings often emphasized public good over private interest under the commonwealth system, judging the value of their legislation and rulings according to the number of people affected. This approach flew in the face of traditional attitudes, which had favored the good of individuals, but it served the needs of the growing young nation. (p. 272)

judicial review   In the American federal system of government, the concept of checks and balances is paramount, ensuring that none of the three branches of government can dominate or control the others. For the judicial branch—that is, the courts—the key check is the power of judicial review, or the power to judge the constitutionality of laws passed by Congress and executive orders issued by the president. This power is implicit within the Constitution but came into practice in 1803 with the Supreme Court's ruling in *Marbury v. Madison*. (pp. 273–274)

contract clause   Under the Constitution, Article 1, section 10, states are prohibited from passing laws "impairing the Obligation of Contracts." The founders endorsed the contract clause in order to void state laws that protected debtors at the expense of their creditors. During John Marshall's tenure as chief justice, the Supreme Court expanded the scope of this clause. This prohibition of congressional impairment of contracts became the means the justices used to protect property owners and corporations against intrusion by state legislatures. The result—in *Fletcher v. Peck* (1810) and *Dartmouth College v. Woodward* (1819)—was a check on state mercantilism. (p. 275)

IDENTIFICATION

Identify by filling in the blanks.

1. In the 1790s, a confederation of Indian tribes throughout the Great Lakes led by _____ defeated American forces led by Josiah Hamar and General Arthur St. Clair. (p. 246)

2. Despite a defeat in the Battle of Fallen Timbers in northern Ohio, the Western Confederacy remained strong enough to forge a compromise treaty with the Americans in 1795 at _____, Ohio. (p. 246)

3. _____ was a prophet and a spiritual leader who developed a dualistic religious faction to reinvigorate tribal life. (p. 248)

4. The three Republican presidents of the "Virginia Dynasty," who held the office from 1801 through 1825, were _____, _____, and _____. (p. 253)

5. The Federalist Supreme Court justice who sat on the Court from 1801 through 1825 and shaped American law by advocating judicial supremacy, supremacy of national over state laws, and static property rights was _____. (pp. 253, 272–273)

6. Jefferson's secretary of the Treasury, Albert Gallatin, believed that the _____ was an "evil of the first magnitude." (p. 254)

7. In 1803 the American minister to Paris, Robert Livingston, called the _____ "the noblest work of our lives." (pp. 256–257)

8. Lewis and Clark reached the Pacific Ocean by crossing the Rocky Mountains and descending the _____ River. (p. 257)

9. In 1804, after he killed Alexander Hamilton in a duel, _____ became involved in a plan to arrange the secession of Louisiana from the Union, an act for which he was tried for treason but acquitted. (p. 258)

10. The aggressive governor of the Indian territory who acquired millions of acres from the Indians and finally led an expedition to defeat the Western Confederacy at the Battle of Tippecanoe in Indiana in 1811 was _____. (p. 259)

11. Although it was fought after the Treaty of Ghent, which ended the War of 1812, was signed, the American victory at the Battle of

_____ made the American leader _____ a national hero. (pp. 264–265)

12. The skilled secretary of state who had helped negotiate the Treaty of Ghent in 1814 and negotiated one treaty acquiring Spain and another with Britain, establishing the boundary with Canada, was _____. (pp. 264–265)

13. State governments encouraged investment in corporations by guaranteeing investors the protection of their personal property from creditors of the corporations. This protection was called _____. (p. 270)

14. John Marshall expressed his belief in the supremacy of the Court to interpret national law, or judicial review, in the celebrated case _____. (pp. 273–274)

15. John Marshall established his defense of property rights on the basis of the inviolability of a contract in a landmark case concerning a New England college's status in _____. (p. 275)

FEATURES EXERCISES

American Voices

REUBEN DAVIS, Settling the Southwestern Frontier (p. 251)

The nature of frontier society fascinated early Americans and still intrigues Americans today. Did frontier society represent a "new" social order with new structures, behaviors, and attitudes, or was it a composite of various social influences brought to the frontier from different regions—an "old" society relocated on "new" ground and rearranged? As you read "Settling the Southwestern Frontier," ask yourself the following questions:

1. Which aspects of the social arrangements Davis describes were "new," and which aspects were familiar and traditional?
2. To what extent did interaction with the native Americans make settlers like Reuben Davis more accepting or less tolerant of native Americans? What is the source of the race hatred he notes?
3. In Davis's account of his frontier experiences, does individualism or cooperation seem to have had the most influence in ordering frontier society?

American Lives

Tenskwatawa: Shawnee Prophet (pp. 260–261)

As the pressure from American settlers intensified, native Americans across the West faced a desperate struggle for survival. While some native Americans succumbed to U.S. aggression, others exhorted their fellow tribe members to reverse the cycle by resisting. Warriors such as Pontiac, Little Turtle, and Tecumseh organized confederations and tried to resist American encroachment militarily. Others recognized a deeper, spiritual malaise as the core of the crisis, and sought, almost like a Protestant evangelical minister, to stir up a spiritual revival among the tribal members, exhorting them to reform themselves and seek renewal. Often, these revivalists presented themselves as prophets and formed new religions to draw converts. The Shawnee Indian Tenskwatawa was one of numerous prophets who emerged seeking regeneration of the native peoples through spiritual renewal. As you read "Tenskwatawa, Shawnee Prophet," ask yourself the following questions:

1. What was the experience that caused Tenskwatawa to emerge from the person Lalawethika?
2. What did Tenskwatawa believe contact with white culture and society had done to Indians? What did he urge as a solution?
3. How did Tenskwatawa use the culture that he opposed to promote his cause?
4. Why did Tenskwatawa change the focus of his movement from spiritual regeneration to military defense? Could he have kept the two approaches separate? In what way did this fusion of strategies undermine the movement?

American Voices

CHIEF SHABONNE, The Battle of Tippecanoe, 1811 (p. 262)

In 1811, William Henry Harrison defeated a force of Shawnee and allied tribes of the Western Confederacy at Prophetstown on the Tippecanoe River, the village of the prophet Tenskwatawa. Harrison, governor of the Indiana Territory, was a shrewd, hard, and tested leader who had pursued a consistent policy against the

Indians. In contrast, the Potawatomi chief Shabonne's interview indicates that the agendas of Indian allies were divided, the young warriors underestimated or did not respect the American threat, and the Prophet asserted influence through inflated rhetoric and extravagant promises.

As you read "The Battle of Tippecanoe," ask yourself the following questions:

1. How was Tenskwatawa's view of white men responsible for the Indians' dangerously unrealistic or naive views?
2. What was Chief Shabonne's view of William Henry Harrison? What aspect of Harrison's character did he see that others apparently did not?
3. How and why did the Prophet seek to influence the women of the tribe?
4. What does this account say about the nature of Tenskwatawa's movement?

Voices from Abroad

ALEXIS DE TOCQUEVILLE, Law and Lawyers in the United States (p. 273)

How is social order established and maintained in a democracy? From the formation of state constitutions in the eighteenth century to the present, this has been a central question for observers of American life. For Alexis de Tocqueville, a Frenchman whose generation was only thirty years removed from the rigid hierarchical society in which everyone—the monarch, the aristocracy, and the people—had a place and was expected to maintain it, this concern was especially critical. After the structures of traditional social order had been destroyed in the Revolution, how would social order be maintained? As republican ideals penetrated into every social relation, the question became increasingly urgent. One answer, Alexis de Tocqueville suggested, was lawyers, who both practiced law and dominated the political system.

As you read "Law and Lawyers in the United States," ask yourself the following questions:

1. According to Tocqueville, did lawyers create order because of who they were or because of what they did? How did being a lawyer order one's behavior?
2. Why did Tocqueville believe lawyers were implicitly Republicans, able to inculcate order in much the same way as the rich, aristocrats, or the king had done?
3. According to Tocqueville, how did popular concern with law, legal procedures, government operations, and politics in a democracy reinforce the tendency toward social order?

MAPS AND FIGURES

Map 8.2 Land Divisions in the Northwest Territory (p. 255)

1. In what ways does the grid system facilitate land description and sales?
2. What image does the checkerboard pattern of land distribution project about economic and social activity and relationships?
3. What does a checkerboard pattern say about the cultural values and attitudes of the people who employ it?

Map 8.3 The Louisiana Purchase, 1803 (p. 257)

1. How did the addition of the Louisiana Purchase affect the total size of the United States?
2. Judging by their route, what was Lewis and Clark's primary means of transportation?
3. Which contemporary states lie within the Louisiana Purchase?

SELF-TEST

Multiple Choice

1. American Indian policy from 1790 to 1820 included *all* of the following *except*:
   a. assimilation of Indians into American culture.
   b. acknowledging Indian ownership of western lands.
   c. allowing native peoples, as independent nations, to negotiate and establish alliances with any other country.
   d. coercing and bribing native Americans to cede vast tracts of western lands to the Americans.
2. Americans migrated to the West for *all* of the following reasons *except*:
   a. to acquire a farmstead and an independent life as yeomen farmers.
   b. to escape slavery.
   c. to increase their capital and income in order to achieve social mobility.
   d. to establish new yeoman farming communities.

3. Jefferson's presidency was characterized by:
   a. a massive government bureaucracy to provide work for unemployed Americans.
   b. smaller government, less national debt, more states' rights, and an expansive western policy.
   c. a clean sweep of all Federalist officeholders from office.
   d. a neutral policy with France and Britain, reinforced by laws that limited the naturalization of foreigners and punished critics of the government.

4. The Constitution says nothing about the acquisition of territory being part of federal power. Thomas Jefferson justified his acquisition of Louisiana as:
   a. part of the treaty-making power granted to the president by the Constitution.
   b. a justifiable overreaching of presidential authority because it fit so well with his dream for the West.
   c. a routine matter involving the minister to France, and thus part of the power of diplomacy granted to the president.
   d. a case in which the "necessary and proper" clause applied to presidential powers.

5. The Embargo of 1807 was:
   a. a solid success, hurting British trade and compelling the British to be more conciliatory toward American shipping.
   b. moderately effective, if only because it encouraged American home production and stimulated industrial development.
   c. an imaginative and naive failure that hurt Americans more than anyone else.
   d. an act of economic aggression that plunged the United States into war against Britain.

6. The United States *officially* declared war on Great Britain in 1812 because:
   a. the war hawks wanted more land in the West and they wanted Britain out of the way.
   b. the British refused to alter their policy of ignoring American neutrality and impressing Americans into the Royal Navy.
   c. Americans felt that Great Britain did not respect them as an independent country.
   d. the British had blockaded American ports, causing economic distress throughout the country.

7. In regard to the War of 1812, the American people were:
   a. unanimously in favor of the war as a means of restoring national pride.
   b. divided on the basis of the very different interests of the North and South in regard to western economic development and the expansion of slavery.
   c. deeply divided along party lines; the Federalist merchants in the Northeast were opposed, while most Republicans supported the war.
   d. divided within the Republican Party between the war hawks in the West, pacifists in the middle colonies, and indecisive planters in the South.

8. The Treaty of Ghent:
   a. restored prewar borders and left unresolved issues open to further debate.
   b. established the 49th parallel as the border between Canada and the United States west of the Great Lakes.
   c. granted Florida to the United States.
   d. compelled the British to pay damages to the United States for the impressment of Americans and for damage to American ships.

9. The "commonwealth" system involved *all* of the following policies *except:*
   a. corporate charters with limited liability.
   b. monopoly charters with eminent domain for transportation projects.
   c. high tariffs against imports.
   d. judicial support of corporate activity on the basis of "social utility."

10. *All* of the following were advantages to state corporate charters *except:*
    a. limited liability for shareholders.
    b. tax exemptions and monopoly privileges.
    c. the ability to amass greater working capital.
    d. guaranteed exemption from federal prosecution even in interstate trade.

11. One of the early successes in solving transportation problems in the United States was the construction of the Lancaster Turnpike in 1794 in:
    a. Pennsylvania.   c. Virginia.
    b. New York.   d. North Carolina.

12. Under the terms of the Massachusetts Mill Dam Act of 1795:
    a. the state set a fair market price for mill goods.
    b. mill owners could flood farmlands adjacent to their mills if they paid "fair compensation" to the farmers.
    c. farmers could sue mill owners for triple damages if they overcharged for mill products.
    d. Massachusetts and Connecticut agreed not to place dams anywhere along the Connecticut River.

Answers

13. In *Fletcher v. Peck,* John Marshall contributed to the emergence of a national capitalist economy by:
    a. declaring federal law supreme, allowing anyone to do business anywhere under the umbrella of federal law.
    b. assuring state operators that the Supreme Court could declare any state law unconstitutional.
    c. confirming the legal right of eminent domain so long as the project was for the public good.
    d. expanding the contract clause to include state grants and charters, thus securing the validity of contracts across state lines and encouraging companies to do interstate business.

14. The Supreme Court upheld the constitutionality of the Bank of the United States in the case of:
    a. *Marbury v. Madison.*
    b. *Fletcher v. Peck.*
    c. *McCulloch v. Maryland.*
    d. *Cohens v. Virginia.*

15. *All* of the following describe the ideas and principles of Chief Justice John Marshall *except* that he:
    a. was a loose constructionist.
    b. used the contract clause to defend property rights.
    c. claimed the right of judicial review.
    d. believed in the "commonwealth" system.

Short Essays

Answer the following questions in a brief paragraph.

1. Compare and contrast western settlement in the Northwest and the Southwest. (pp. 246–249, 254–258)

2. What were the key aspects of Republican policy in the early republic? Why did Republicans pursue these objectives? (pp. 253–258)

3. How did native Americans fare under Republican policy? How did they respond? (pp. 259–262)

4. What were the causes of the War of 1812? What did the war achieve for the United States? (pp. 262–265)

5. In what ways was the American political economy of the early nineteenth century a mix of Republican and Federalist philosophies? How did the Constitution contribute to this mix? (pp. 271–275)

ANSWERS

Identification

1. Little Turtle
2. Greenville
3. Handsome Lake
4. Thomas Jefferson, James Madison, and James Monroe
5. John Marshall
6. national debt
7. Louisiana Purchase
8. Columbia
9. Aaron Burr
10. William Henry Harrison
11. New Orleans; Andrew Jackson
12. John Quincy Adams
13. limited liability
14. *Marbury v. Madison* (1803)
15. *Dartmouth College v. Woodward* (1819)

Self-Test

Multiple Choice

1. c.
2. b.
3. b.
4. a.
5. c.
6. b.
7. c.
8. a.
9. c.
10. d.
11. a.
12. b.
13. d.
14. c.
15. d.

Short Essays

1. Settlers were driven to the Northwest and the Southwest by similar motivations. They wanted more land to improve their economic and social status. In the Northwest and the Southwest, settlers aggressively sought to remove the native peoples from their lands. The government pushed Indians off their lands through bribes, deceit, war, and treaties. Once the Indians had been removed, speculators purchased vast tracts of frontier land in order to sell it to settlers. The Northwest was settled by independent farmers

who migrated west to escape the crowded lands in the East and to preserve the yeoman ideal. Yeomen farmers also settled the Southwest. They were quickly followed, however, by elite planters who carried slavery to the West. Both sought new land on which to plant the South's new cash crop, cotton. In both cases, entire communities, groups, and families often made the move together, simply relocating old communities on new ground.

2. Republicans sought to reduce the size of the national government, lessen the influence of the northeastern merchants and creditors in the national government, and cultivate the yeoman-farmer ideal through westward expansion. They did this by cutting the national debt by almost half, reducing the size of military and government bureaucracy, liberalizing naturalization laws, abolishing excise taxes, and allowing the Alien and Sedition Acts to expire. Republicans also fostered westward migration by supporting lower prices and allowing land to be sold in parcels that were small enough for yeomen farmers to afford them. Republicans also wanted to reduce the power of the federal judiciary in order to limit federal power.

3. The American government first employed military action to bring the native Americans to the negotiating table. In the Northwest, Little Turtle initially defeated American forces. In time, however, he was defeated and forced to cede lands in Ohio to the Americans. A decade later, Tenskwatawa and Tecumseh resisted American settlement. Again, American forces defeated the native Americans militarily and forced them to cede vast tracts of land. Meanwhile, some government officials favored a policy that sought to assimilate the native American into American life. Most native Americans resisted such efforts by moving west, rejecting white missionaries, or reasserting their identity through religious and cultural revivals.

4. The war was caused by a combination of factors. Americans were exasperated with Britain's refusal to respect American neutrality and with its impressing Americans into the Royal Navy. The United States gave these as the official reasons for going to war. But war hawks were pushing for more land in the West and thus supported Indian removal. British efforts to control the native Americans, and their continued presence along the frontier, convinced many Americans that Britain did not respect the United States as an independent country.

5. Both the Federalists and the Republicans were divided between those who advocated economic development through the commonwealth system, which supported private activity undertaken for the sake of the public good, and those who maintained a traditional defense of individual property rights. Those in favor of the commonwealth ideal supported changes in statute law that gave priority to public needs over private interests, rejecting traditional common-law principles, which discouraged economic development and challenged the concepts of state mercantilism. Those who believed in a free competitive market felt that states had no right to favor or interfere with property. Because the Constitution assured different types of leadership could coexist in the executive, legislative, and judicial branches, Federalist John Marshall served as Chief Justice of the United States Supreme Court during a long period of Republican presidencies. Marshall opposed the commonwealth system by asserting judicial authority, national supremacy over states' rights, and a static definition of property rights. As a result, the political economy of the period was a mix of ideas.

Chapter 9

The Quest for a Republican Society, 1790–1820

LEARNING OBJECTIVES

1. How did republicanism affect American society after the Revolution? How did its ideas change personal behavior?

2. Where and how was the spread of republicanism circumscribed and resisted?

3. How did evangelical Christianity affect American society after the Revolution? How did it become a force for social change?

4. How might an American middle-class woman living in the North in 1825 experience and understand her life differently from a similar woman living thirty years earlier?

5. How did early Americans reconcile the ideal of republicanism with the slave system in the South? How did the response of African American slaves to their enslavement help shape southern society?

CHAPTER SUMMARY

By the 1820s, two ideological forces that had emerged in the eighteenth century—republicanism and evangelical Christianity—had exerted influence on nearly every social structure to transform American society into a republican and predominantly Christian society. In the North, the expansion of a democratic-republican polity eroded traditional patriarchal family and social relations, redefined the role of women, and transformed the way children were reared and educated. In the South, republicanism enabled slaveowners to describe themselves as free men with a moral purpose, but it did little to transform social relations or the lives of African American slaves. Ironically, evangelical Christianity reinforced new social roles and behavior in the North as well as traditional ones in the South.

Democratic Republicanism (pp. 280–290)

Republican ideals were employed to broaden the franchise, increase social and geographic mobility, reorganize families, and democratize education, institutions, and professions. Everywhere, the "ordered liberty" of elitism, hierarchy, and tradition was in retreat.

Social and Political Equality for White Men

Republican ideas encouraged states to broaden the franchise by abolishing property qualifications for voting and officeholding. By the 1810s, most states had universal suffrage for all male taxpayers, while several others pushed toward universal suffrage for white males. Widespread emphasis on social mobility also enhanced the status of the legal profession, which relaxed its standards for admission to the bar in order to allow more people to practice law.

Republican Women: Marriage and Motherhood

By emphasizing equal natural rights and individual achievement, republicanism eroded traditional family relationships. Having less farmland to give to their children, parents lost control over their children's life decisions. Individualism, and sentimentalism, a nineteenth-century cultural movement emphasizing the importance of feeling, also eroded parents' control over their children by encouraging young people to marry for love rather than for convenience or financial stability. Though republicanism would not dramatically change gender roles, women were affected by ideas of individualism and self-achievement. In addition, the Christian male clergy increasingly advanced the idea of women as cultivators of virtue, a role many women accepted even as it limited them. They were thus accorded the role of "republican mother" to morally rear and educate their children to be good citizens. The desire among women to parent children more intensively, as well as to do more than bear and nurture them, encouraged many couples to reduce the size of their families by means of birth control or abstinence. In addition, many couples increasingly shared duties and responsibilities and viewed each other as "companions."

Rearing and Educating Republican Children

Republican ideology promoted education and self-reliance, and these ideas affected family relations. While many parents continued to rear their children with strict Calvinist discipline, many others began to allow their children considerable leeway in exercising independence and self-reliance. In the 1820s, reformers successfully campaigned for state funds for more public schools and improved instruction, although most students left school after the primary grades, where the emphasis was on basic skills and patriotic instruction. During this period, a distinctive American literature began to develop, celebrating American characters and themes to promote shared cultural ideals.

Slavery and Aristocratic Republicanism in the South
(pp. 291–303)

The reinvigoration and expansion of slavery to the Southwest highlighted the limits of republicanism and gave it an aristocratic flavor. Sectional differences over the expansion of slavery intensified political tensions between North and South and threatened national unity. Meanwhile, slaves in the South tried to live their lives as best they could by constructing an African American society and culture, shaping the nature of their work, and resisting the most oppressive aspects of the system.

Sectional Contrasts and Conflicts

Southern society, because of its commitment to slavery, remained more stratified than did northern society. To maintain control, slaveowners established themselves as a power elite at the top of a hierarchical society that was divided by class and race. Within such a social structure, republicanism's call for equality and social mobility had little impact on providing opportunity, education, or equality for poor whites and African American slaves. The expansion of slavery to the Southwest aggravated political tensions between North and South. Though politicians from the two regions were still able to compromise through the 1820s, that task would become more difficult as the social and cultural differences between the two regions sharpened.

African American Society and Culture

The end of the slave trade, the spread of slavery to the Southwest, and the emergence of a free black population led to an increasingly distinct and unified African American society and culture in the United States. African American life in slavery was made up of family-centered communities tied to each other by the cultural traditions of their African past. More stable families and communities were able to resist and endure oppression more effectively. Although slaves continued to suffer abuses such as the sale and separation of families, beatings to make them work, and the sexual assault of women, both slaves and community leaders, influenced by evangelical Christianity and republicanism, questioned or resisted these abuses more often. Some slaves exerted slightly more control over the terms of work, material maintenance, and their own lives. Though a few slaves did revolt or escape, for most this was not possible, and they tried to make the best of the situation on the plantations on which they were born. Outside of slavery, a growing free black community emerged in the urban North and South. Though free blacks were segregated and discriminated against, and performed the most menial tasks in the economy, some of them did become craft workers or shopkeepers and established churches, schools, associations, and social-welfare programs. Symbols of freedom to their enslaved brethren, free blacks were viewed as threats to the social order by the majority of whites.

The Southern Social Order

The shrinking minority of white southerners who held slaves and controlled power viewed themselves as a "natural aristocracy"—that is, a group who believed they were meant by nature to rule. To assert this supremacy, they lived lavishly and tried to justify their social power by pretending to be moral and benevolent elites. They maintained power over poor whites through race solidarity, even as they forced the poor whites into tenancy, provided few opportunities for advancement, and dominated politics. In such an oligarchy, there was little chance for republican social and political equality to develop.

Protestant Christianity as a Social Force (pp. 303–309)

A new wave of religious revivals transformed American life, adding a moral dimension to republicanism.

The Second Great Awakening

The growth of republicanism had a profound impact on religious expansion in the early 1800s. An upsurge of Protestantism, spurred by a new spirit of revivalism, swept across the country, especially the frontier regions of the South and the West. The Second Great Awakening witnessed a shift from old-line denominations to evangelical churches and from competition to cooperation among ministers and local congregations. The Methodists, Baptists, and Presbyterians, all denominations with strong democratic cultures, recorded the most significant gains in membership. Methodists and Baptists were especially successful in attracting members among the black slave population of the South by providing spiritual solace for their enslavement. Meanwhile, more established denominations from the colonial period—Episcopalians, Congregationalists, and Quakers—declined in relation to other denominations.

Emphasizing faith and the power of free will to effect one's salvation, the Second Great Awakening suffused republican society with deepening humanistic impulses, free-will individualism, and a growing optimism in the power of human action. Gradually, evangelical Protestants would apply their missionary zeal and spiritual and moral intensity to American politics and the development of national identity.

Women's New Religious Roles

New evangelical Protestant thought that argued that women, not men, were primarily responsible for establishing a moral and virtuous society, gave women a range of new opportunities in organized religion. They became actively involved in church affairs, maintained moral households, reared moral children, and exerted their personal moral influence on their husbands, thus contributing to public life by elevating its moral character. Expectations that they should play a higher moral role in society stimulated a movement to provide better education for women, increased the number of women teachers, and even encouraged some women to advocate moral and social reform by preaching or speaking in public. The Second Great Awakening thus infused republicanism with moral power and optimism, and broadened the framework of women's lives.

EXPANDED TIMELINE

1782 **St. Jean de Crèvecoeur, *Letters from an American Farmer***
In the half-century after America won its independence, many aristocratic Europeans traveled to the United States to study the new republic and compare the new nation with Europe and European institutions. One of the first, St. Jean de Crèvecoeur, praised the United States for establishing a democratic social order that allowed people to succeed on the strength of their own abilities rather than be locked into a predetermined social position by birth and family status.

1787 **Benjamin Rush, *Thoughts on Female Education***
A shift in Christian thought encouraged some writers, such as Benjamin Rush, to argue that women should be educated to be agreeable companions to their husbands and "republican mothers."

1790s **Parents limit family size**
At the turn of the nineteenth century, the United States experienced a sharp decline in the birth rate. Many people chose to marry later in life and to have smaller families. This change grew out of economic reality: With less good land available, parents were less likely to have large holdings to pass on to their children. Accordingly, they limited family size to ensure an adequate inheritance to all their children.

Second Great Awakening
From the 1790s to the 1830s, the Second Great Awakening inspired an upsurge of revivalism and church growth. Old-line denominations fell out of favor, as evangelical churches, led by Baptists and Methodists, spread Protestantism from New England to the South and into the frontier regions. In the climate of republicanism, the Second Great Awakening promoted democracy and friendly competition among the churches and helped create a truly American form of Protestantism.

"Republican motherhood" defined
Around 1800, a change in Christian thought led Americans to view women as morally superior to men. Ministers began to encourage women to influence the

moral character of society. They urged women to become "republican mothers," who gave their children proper moral instruction in order to establish in them the solid foundation upon which they would become republican citizens.

1800s **Rise of sentimentalism and republican marriage system**
The predominance of republican values (especially support for greater democracy), increasing economic pressures on families, and the rise of sentimentalism, a cultural movement that emphasized feelings and emotions over reason, dramatically altered attitudes toward marriage in the United States. As people placed greater emphasis on emotion, young men and women selected their own partners for love instead of parents arranging marriages for their children. Republican marriages decreased parental control over children but actually increased the power of husbands over wives, who could no longer turn easily to their parents for support.

Women's religious activism and female academies
In the early 1800s, new ideas that argued that women were morally superior opened many opportunities for women in church work. Outnumbering men in many denominations, women assumed a greater share of the responsibility for leadership and won the right to have "mixed" prayer sessions, which both men and women attended together, in some churches. A few women, such as Jemima Wilkinson, achieved fame as revivalists. Women also practiced religious activism in their homes. As "republican mothers," American women shouldered the burden of guiding their children both morally and spiritually.

Spread of evangelical Baptists and Methodists
The growth of republicanism had a profound effect on denominations, such as the Baptists and Methodists, that promoted democracy in church matters. Revivalism swept across the frontier regions of the country, stirring up audiences "as if by a storm," and brought huge gains in membership among whites and African Americans. The religious tone of the country changed dramatically, with evangelical churches becoming dominant in numbers and influence.

Beginnings of benevolent reform
Linking salvation with social reform through the concept of benevolence, followers of the Second Great Awakening organized churches, charitable organizations, schools, and interdenominational societies to spread their vision and reform society. This large religious movement added an intense religious aspect to politics and national identity.

Chesapeake blacks adopt Protestant beliefs
After 1800, thousands of blacks across the South embraced the Protestant evangelical ideas of Methodists and Baptists, giving them a particular interpretation. Blacks focused primarily on God's justice and viewed themselves as an oppressed people who had a special relationship with God. By emotionally focusing on preparing their souls for the ultimate freedom of salvation, African Americans affirmed their equality with whites and took some solace in the injustice of their enslavement.

1807 **New Jersey excludes propertied women from suffrage**
In 1776 the republican members of the New Jersey state legislature, acting on republican ideas, granted suffrage to all property holders in the state. Because most women could not hold property, this excluded them. However, many widows, as well as free blacks, who could and did hold property, recognized the loophole and became active participants in electoral politics in the state. In 1807, the state legislature, again following republican ideas, eliminated the property-holding requirements to vote and adopted universal suffrage for all white males. In doing so, they excluded women and blacks from citizenship and the vote. As republican theory broadened to include all white men, it clarified its gender and racial limits.

1810s **Expansion of suffrage for men**
In response to republican ideals, northern states expanded political democracy. Maryland (1810), and the new states of Indiana (1816), Illinois (1818), and Alabama (1819) all provided for broad male suffrage in their constitutions.

Slavery defined as "necessary evil"
As slavery was reinvigorated and then extended to the Southwest by the increasing demand for cotton, political tensions between the South and the North increased, forcing southern planters to justify slavery. Initially, though many planters had qualms about slavery, they viewed it as a "necessary evil" that maintained white supremacy, their standard of living, and prevented racial war. By the 1820s, many planters would portray themselves as "natural aristocrats" who ruled over their slaves with disinterested benevolence.

Expansion of cotton South and domestic slave trade
The increased demand for cotton from mills in New England and Great Britain drew planters and their slaves to the West and Southwest in search of new land. As settlement spread across the Old Southwest, cotton production soared. The expanding demand for workers in the cotton belt increased the domestic trade in slaves from the Old South to the new states of Alabama, Mississippi, and Arkansas.

1819–1821 **Conflict over admission of Missouri**
Diverging political views between North and South made it harder to compromise on the issue of slavery. After lengthy dispute, a political compromise allowed

Maine to enter the Union as a free state, and Missouri as a slave state to maintain the balance of power between North and South in the Senate. Slavery was prohibited in the Louisiana Territory north of the southern boundary of Missouri.

1820s **Reform of public education**
Women become schoolteachers
In the early 1800s, prominent Americans began to promote a wider distribution of knowledge to create a "republic of letters." In the 1820s, these calls for change led to increased public funding for the primary grades. Educators expanded school curriculum and raised standards for teachers. The idea that women were morally superior and, as "republican mothers," should exert a moral influence on their children and therefore on society, was accompanied by a rising expectation that women be educated. As more women attended academies and seminaries, the moral imperative of "republican motherhood" was expanded to include influence over children in school. As a result, more women became public school teachers.

GLOSSARY

ordered liberty In the eighteenth century, republicans believed that all men were created equal and that political power was held by the people. Fearing an excess of democracy, however, they believed that liberty would be safeguarded or more "ordered" if the "people" included only adult males with property, and if they would defer to the wisdom of a traditional elite to rule. Gradually, ordinary men began to realize that this view of republicanism was too elitist and narrow. Arguing that all men were equal and had a right to social mobility, republicans expanded suffrage and access to government office to all white men. (p. 280)

deferential The politics of the eighteenth century assumed that elite men, having status, experience, wealth, and time, could best represent the people. It was expected, therefore, that the people would be deferential, or conform to, this expectation and elect their social superiors as their political leaders. This idea was rejected by republicans in the early nineteenth century. (p. 281)

sentimentalism A cultural attitude, spawned by the Romantic movement in Europe in the late 1700s, that emphasized feelings and emotions rather than reason and logic. Love became as important in marriage as financial considerations; and religion became more emotional, encouraging a revival of religious fervor called the Second Great Awakening. (pp. 282–284)

companionate marriage Empowered by republican ideas, women pressed for legal equality in marriage, increased education, and a greater share in the decision making in marriage. Even though men retained power as patriarchs, they increasingly viewed their wives as equal companions and friends rather than as inferior and dependent partners. (p. 284)

demographic transition A significant shift in the size of the population owing to a sharp change—a rise or a fall—in either the birth rate or the death rate is referred to as a demographic transition. Around the turn of the nineteenth century, the United States was one of the first countries in the world to experience this transition when the birth rate began to decline dramatically. In some urban areas the decline over a half-century was 50 percent among white women. Smaller families meant reduced population pressure in settled areas and greater opportunities for social and economic stability. (p. 284)

Republican motherhood The idea that women's moral superiority gave them a special role to play in the republic in providing their children with moral and religious education. (p. 285)

primogeniture The legal practice of transferring most or all of one's wealth to one's first (i.e., *primo*) or oldest son (i.e., *geniture*—to issue forth from) only. In the early nineteenth century, republican Americans increasingly felt this was unfair. As a result, most state legislatures rejected the practice by passing laws requiring the equal distribution of estates. (p. 287)

dower right When a woman in eighteenth-century America married, she surrendered her property to her husband. In compensation, she received the right to use (but not sell) a third of her husband's estate if he died. She received this right only if she remained an unmarried widow, however. Upon her death, the property returned to the family. Even as state legislatures moved to eliminate primogeniture, they maintained the dower right for widows. (p. 288)

chattel slavery By definition, a "chattel" is a possession that is movable. In the early nineteenth-century Americas, such possessions included slaves, who could be moved or sold at will by the owner or master. In time, the word *chattel* became synonymous with *slave*. In spite of this legal definition of slavery, nineteenth-century masters were never able to exert total control over their slaves in the same way they could over other property. (p. 297)

natural aristocracy Wealthy southern slaveholding planters in the early republic presented themselves as a social elite who had achieved status and therefore had the right to rule society. (p. 302)

noblesse oblige An aristocratic style of leadership that feigns disinterest in one's own affairs and concern for the well-being of others. Southern planters who cultivated the air of noblesse oblige tried to create the appearance that such behavior was a natural part of the social order. (p. 302)

benevolence Broadly conceived as the desire to do good for others, benevolence became a seminal concept in American religious thinking during the Second Great Awakening. Rejecting the Calvinist notion of predestination in favor of universal salvation, promoters of benevolence suggested that people who had experienced saving grace could inspire others to find salvation. Some acted individually; others worked through benevolent organizations that aspired to reform society. (p. 307)

calling A protestant idea that each person is given an indication of what she or he is meant to do on earth by God. To follow one's "calling" imbues that occupation with spiritual purpose and meaning. Preachers of the Second Great Awakening encouraged women to recognize their special moral calling. (p. 308)

seminaries An educational institution, especially one that includes religious training. In the early nineteenth century, the education of women dramatically expanded with the opening of numerous schools for young women. These schools were called female academies, or seminaries. (p. 309)

IDENTIFICATION

Identify by filling in the blanks.

1. The republican idea of _____ encouraged most states to broaden the franchise to include all white men by eliminating property requirements. (p. 281)

2. Born out of the Romantic movement in Europe in the late 1700s, _____ celebrated the role of feeling rather than reason as the best way to understand the experiences of life. (p. 282)

3. The noble republican ideal that encouraged individuals to make their spouse a best friend was known as "_____" marriage. (p. 284)

4. At the turn of the nineteenth century, the United States faced a sharp decline in the birth rate, which is known as a _____. (p. 284)

5. In his *Thoughts on Female Education* (1787) _____ argued that a woman should receive an education so that she can be an agreeable companion for a sensible man. (p. 285)

6. In contrast to the traditional strict, authoritarian approach to child rearing rooted in _____ ideas, affectionate rationalists encouraged a more lenient approach to raising children. (pp. 289–290)

7. The "blue-backed speller" that attempted to standardize vocabulary and grammar for the American people was written by _____. (p. 290)

8. The American writer of the early 1800s who enthralled readers with tales of Dutch-American life in works such as *Diedrich Knickerbocker's History of New York* was _____. (p. 290)

9. During the Second Great Awakening, the most spectacular growth in membership was experienced by the _____ and _____ churches, making them the largest religious denominations in the United States. (p. 305)

10. Across the West, the Second Great Awakening was spread by ministers who traveled from place to place to hold revivals, earning them the name _____. (p. 305)

11. During the Second Great Awakening a new sect known as _____ flourished in New England. It rejected the Calvinist concept of predestination and advocated salvation for all people. (p. 304–305)

12. One of the most articulate ministers of the Second Great Awakening, who emphasized the power of each free-will individual to shape his or her own salvation, was _____. (p. 307)

13. Protestants who believed in a single, "united" God were called _____. (p. 307)

14. Founded in Great Britain, the _____ sect migrated to America with Mother Ann Lee in the 1770s, leading to the establishment of communities in several states. (p. 308)

15. The first institutions of higher education for women were called female academies, or _____. (p. 309)

FEATURES EXERCISES

American Voices

ELIZA SOUTHGATE, The Dilemmas of Womanhood (p. 284)

Republicanism democratized society and encouraged people to live their lives based on self-interest rather than live lives determined by their birth into a particular social class, as they would have done in the eighteenth century. Educational opportunities also expanded, and schools began to open to girls as well as boys. Young women learned about equality, although they frequently continued to play subordinate roles. In this selection, Eliza Southgate writes of the dichotomy between equality and subordination.

As you read "The Dilemmas of Womanhood," ask yourself the following questions:

1. In what aspect of a woman's life was "inequality of privilege" between men and women most telling?
2. Why did this inequality between men and women seem not to bother Southgate?
3. In what ways did she see men and women as equals? Could men and women be equal and still find "harmony" in their lives? Or was inequality preferable?

New Technology (pp. 286–287)

Women's Health and Fertility: From Folk Remedies to Pharmacies

In the last decades of the eighteenth century American women, responding to changes in life-style as well as to new cultural forces, began to reduce the number of children they had. A general cultural environment influenced by Enlightenment rationalism, republican egalitarianism and freedom, evangelical Christian morality, and sentimentalism seemed to focus more attention on the quality, emotions, and satisfactions of parenting than on the number of children one had. There is evidence that in the last third of the eighteenth century, more American women than ever before were aware of ways to break the continual cycle of sexual relations, pregnancy, birth, and nursing that had always defined their adult lives. These methods accompanied a gradual increase in the knowledge of the female reproductive system. Since eighteenth-century women were unclear about the timing and nature of conception and its impact on menstruation, many women confronted with a late period, considered themselves "obstructed" or "ill" rather than pregnant and took an herbal potion to clear the "blockage" from the womb. When women who knew they were pregnant had problems and took the same kinds of medicine, particularly savin, to clear the womb, they understood more clearly that it worked as an abortifacient. By trial and error, women came to understand that regular use of herbal potions enabled them to avoid pregnancy and limit the size of their families.

As you read "Women's Health and Fertility," ask yourself the following questions:

1. How might each of the major cultural developments of the time—Enlightenment rationalism, republican egalitarianism and freedom, evangelical Christian morality, and sentimentalism—have affected women's understanding of their bodies?
2. How could women who gave birth so often—an average of nine times—know so little about human physiology?
3. Why didn't these women use other forms of birth control?
4. From the evidence in the text, at what point does it seem apparent that women were deciding to include herbals as a regular part of a birth-control strategy? What explains this effort to turn reproductive biology into planned behavior?

American Voices

JACOB STROYER, A Child Learns the Meaning of Slavery (p. 297)

Though African Americans born into slavery in early America never knew freedom, certain incidences of slave life made one's lack of freedom painfully clear. As children, slaves were generally unsupervised by their owners. Only after age six were they integrated into the daily regimen of the owner's farm or plantation. As a boy, Jacob Stroyer, the author of this piece, expressed an interest in a certain kind of work, and when he succeeded in being assigned to that work, Stroyer no doubt felt a sense of satisfaction and achievement. Therefore, the first time that an overseer whipped him for not controlling a horse came as a profound shock to him.

As you read "A Child Learns the Meaning of Slavery," ask yourself the following questions:

1. Why was Stroyer, a young slave, angry when his overseer whipped him? How did his reponse indicate that he did not understand the power of the master over the slave?

2. Explain Stroyer's father's response. What did the father fear or understand that his son did not?

3. What did the father see as his role? What explains the different responses of Stroyer's father and mother to their son's anger? How does religion help Stroyer's father cope with slavery?

4. From this episode, what can you infer that Jacob Stroyer "learned" about slavery?

American Lives

Richard Allen and African American Identity (pp. 300–301)

After the Revolution, slavery was abolished in the free states of the North. In Philadelphia, a large free black community developed and forged a distinctive identity that was separate from the white community. Though they opposed racism and segregation in white churches, free blacks founded their own churches, institutions, schools, and newspapers. Richard Allen founded the African Methodist Episcopal Church. The church gave voice to the concerns of the black community and provided the groundwork for African Americans to found and develop other institutions of their own. Members of the free black community in Philadelphia actively petitioned for the end of slavery and the slave trade, opposed the capture of escaped slaves, and rejected the colonization in Africa of free blacks—views that they expressed openly in the nation's first black newspaper.

As you read "Richard Allen and African American Identity," ask yourself the following questions:

1. Why was religion so important to Richard Allen?

2. Why was the Methodist Church more appealing to free blacks than the Episcopal or Quaker churches?

3. Why did Richard Allen found the first independent black denomination in the United States? Why did he choose Philadelphia? Could he have founded such a church in New Orleans or Charleston?

4. Why did Allen initially support the American Colonization Society? Why did he change his mind?

Voices from Abroad

FRANCES TROLLOPE, A Camp-Meeting in Indiana (p. 306)

As the Second Great Awakening swept across the frontier, preachers adjusted to the dispersed population by riding a "circuit" from place to place. Occasionally, a number of preachers would gather at one location and have a "camp meeting." People from the surrounding region would flock to this site to hear a series of preachers, not unlike stump speakers in politics who talked for hours, hoping that as many visitors as possible would have a chance to hear them. A combination of emotional preaching day and night (requiring illumination by large bonfires), large crowds of frontier people, and a rural site in the woods, intensified the experience. Almost immediately, the synergy of these conditions generated a high degree of crowd excitement, sweeping like waves over the crowds, becoming, in a way, the dynamic of the revival itself. Serving both the spiritual and the social hunger of frontier life, these camp meetings became extraordinary events in the region and were the means by which the Second Great Awakening spread far and wide. Through the eyes of English traveler Frances Trollope, these meetings even seemed strange.

As you read "A Camp-Meeting in Indiana," ask yourself the following questions:

1. How did the site itself and the time of night at which Trollope arrived add to the exotic quality of the meeting?

2. What evidence does Trollope's account give that camp meetings generated crowd dynamics that exerted immense pressure on the participants?

3. What does it suggest about camp meetings and the Second Great Awakening that Trollope says little, if anything, about the preachers' message? Why does she focus entirely on the site, the arrangement, the images, the sounds, and the feelings of the event?

4. Do camp meetings seem to have served a social purpose on the frontier? Is there any evidence that such a purpose enhanced their popularity?

MAPS AND FIGURES

Map 9.1 The Expansion of Voting Rights for White Men, 1800–1830 (p. 282)

1. By the turn of the nineteenth century, American territory east of the Mississippi River had been carved into territories and states. On the map above, locate and identify the three regions that were territories rather than states.

2. By 1830, all but six states had eliminated property ownership as a qualification for voting for white men. On the map above, locate and identify those six states:
   a. two states of the Old South
   b. one state in the new West
   c. one state in the mid-Atlantic
   d. two states in New England

Map 9.5 Ethnicity and Religion in Eastern Pennsylvania and New Jersey, circa 1780 (p. 307)

1. How does the pattern of denominational diversity reflect the pattern of ethnic diversity?

2. What traditional Protestant denominations were in a distinct minority in this region?

Table 9.3 African American Naming Patterns (p. 296)

1. Look closely at the pattern of names given to babies of slaves on a plantation in South Carolina between 1793 and 1828. What development in family life among African Americans do the patterns indicate?

SELF-TEST

Multiple Choice

1. Republicanism affected the breadth of democracy in *all* of the following ways *except*:
   a. deferential politics and social behavior declined.
   b. all or most white males in most northern states were given the vote.
   c. free blacks were given the vote in all northern states.
   d. a loophole was closed and women were excluded from the vote in New Jersey.

2. Originating in the Romantic movement in Europe, sentimentalism altered the behavior of Americans in *all* of the following ways *except* by:
   a. emphasizing romantic love in marriage.
   b. encouraging people to respond emotionally to evangelical preachers.
   c. increasing the expression of emotion in political discourse.
   d. compelling some guilty masters to free their slaves.

3. The new republicanized and sentimentalized view of marriage included *all* of the following ideas *except*:
   a. one married for love, not simply for wealth or prospects.
   b. the ideal of "companionate marriage."
   c. women began to view themselves as having a moral role in the home.
   d. couples began having more children.

4. Men and women achieved "demographic transition" by *all* of the following *except*:
   a. delaying marriage and thus reducing the years for giving birth.
   b. marrying not for love but for money and social status.

c. abstinence from sexual intercourse.
d. using primitive means of birth control that prevented or prematurely ended pregnancy.

5. The concept of "republican motherhood" constituted:
   a. a revolutionary departure for women.
   b. a limited revision or enhancement of traditional ideas that had a real impact on how women viewed themselves and behaved.
   c. a rationalization of patriarchy to placate angry women.
   d. an ideal image that was more rhetoric than reality.

6. Republicanism transformed parenting for some couples by encouraging them to:
   a. intensify discipline on fewer children.
   b. let children run free, with no supervision.
   c. emphasize self-control, self-responsibility, self-education, and independence.
   d. focus entirely on religious instruction.

7. Most families in African American slave societies were characterized by:
   a. stable relationships, defined by extended family relations and regulated by taboos against incest.
   b. short-term marriages routinely broken by the sale or death of the husband and wife.
   c. low birth rates due to overwork and lack of community support.
   d. naming practices determined entirely by slaves' white masters, with little regard for African family identities.

8. Most slaves resisted the system of work, forced separations, or abuse by the master in *all* of the following ways *except:*
   a. destroying tools or buildings.
   b. mass slave revolts.
   c. slowing down in the pace of work and general resistance to demands.
   d. feigned illness.

9. Free blacks living in the North in the early nineteenth century were:
   a. treated as social equals, with the full range of civil rights due any male citizen.
   b. allowed to vote and go about routine activities of life without segregation or discrimination but otherwise treated as second-class citizens.
   c. discriminated against in the job market and given the most menial jobs, not allowed to vote, and segregated in churches, schools, and public life.
   d. assumed to be runaway slaves and continually in danger of being sent South.

10. The denominations that were most affected by the Second Great Awakening and experienced increases in memberships were those that:
    a. welcomed new immigrants into their congregations.
    b. emphasized emotional preaching rather than intellectual sermons.
    c. denied an individual's ability to affect his or her salvation.
    d. had hierarchical clerical structure.

11. Through the influence of the rationalist movement, which emphasized the individual's ability to shape his or her own salvation, many New England Congregationalists in the early nineteenth century became:
    a. Universalists.   c. Unitarians.
    b. Presbyterians.   d. deists.

12. The idea of "republican motherhood" was formulated by:
    a. republican political theorists who wanted to assure the republican virtue.
    b. evangelical Protestant ministers who articulated the moral superiority of women.
    c. feminist writers who argued for women's rights.
    d. evangelical Christian women who wanted to use their moral superiority to exert an influence on public life.

13. The most famous Unitarian minister of the early nineteenth century was:
    a. Jonathan Edwards.
    b. Samuel Hopkins.
    c. William Ellery Channing.
    d. Lyman Beecher.

14. Women responded to the Christian view of their moral superiority in *all* of the following ways *except:*
    a. attending "promiscuous" services that allowed men and women to worship together.
    b. avoiding expression of emotions or feelings in religious services or at camp meetings.
    c. emphasizing female moral virtue and postponing sexual intercourse until marriage.
    d. joining women's church and reform organizations to take a morally active role in public life.

15. The outspoken female leader of a new sect that fused Calvinist and Quaker ideas with a view of universal salvation similar to that of the Universalists was:
    a. Jemima Wilkinson.
    b. Ann Lee.
    c. Eliza Southgate.
    d. Mary Wollstonecraft.

Short Essays

Answer the following questions in a brief paragraph.

1. How did republicanism affect the lives and roles of women in the North? (pp. 282–288)
2. Why did republicanism tend to encourage more education for women? (pp. 289–290)
3. How did slaveowning planters, who were a minority of the white population in the South, manage to rule as natural aristocrats without being challenged by other whites? (pp. 302–303)
4. How did the dynamics of slave society and the impact of republican ideology gradually alter the nature of slavery? (pp. 294–302)
5. Why did the Second Great Awakening have its greatest effect on congregations with republicanized cultures? What does this say about the interaction between the two cultural movements? (pp. 304–308)

ANSWERS

Identification

1. popular sovereignty
2. sentimentalism
3. companionate
4. demographic transition
5. Benjamin Rush
6. Calvinist
7. Noah Webster
8. Washington Irving
9. Baptist; Methodist
10. circuit riders
11. Universalism
12. Lyman Beecher
13. Unitarians
14. Shaker
15. seminaries

MAPS AND FIGURES

Map 9.5

1. Although German settlers dominated eastern Pennsylvania and New Jersey, they were nevertheless only one of a variety of ethnic groups in the area. English-born Quakers, Presbyterians, and Methodists mixed with Dutch Reformed congregations from Holland. In addition to this ethnic diversity, there was considerable denominational variety among the Germans. Along with the Lutherans, German congregations included the Dutch Reformed, German Baptists, German Reformed, Mennonites, Moravians, and Roman Catholics.
2. There were only a few Anglican and Methodist congregations. There were no Congregationalist churches. The German Mennonites, of whom there was just one congregation, were a distinct minority everywhere.

Table 9.3

1. There was a pattern of naming female babies after the mother's parents, and male babies after the father or the father's father. Naming children after a previous generation fixed identity and acknowledged ties of biological kinship. The patterns also indicate stable marriages and extended family connections. Such names bound generations together and emphasized how grandmothers and grandfathers helped define girls and boys.

Self-Test

Multiple Choice

1. c.	6. c.	11. c.
2. d.	7. a.	12. a.
3. d.	8. b.	13. d.
4. b.	9. c.	14. b.
5. b.	10. b.	15. a.

Short Essays

1. Women began to redefine their role as "republican mothers." Through the cultivation of virtue, women acquired the moral power to claim some rights in marriage, and transformed parenting by viewing themselves as the moral educators of their children. Women also began to play a more active role in church life and in maternal and reform associations.
2. Increased expectations by political theorists and ministers that women should play a higher moral role in society, though still circumscribed by gen-

der attitudes, stimulated a movement to provide better women's education. More education encouraged women to enter teaching and even to advocate moral and social reform by preaching or speaking.

3. Southern elites maintained power over poor whites by encouraging racial solidarity. They threatened that unless poor whites remained content as tenants they would fall to the status of the slaves. Hence southern aristocrats provided few opportunities for the advancement of poor whites and continued to dominate politics.

4. African American life in slavery was made up of family centered communities tied by cultural traditions to their African past. Stable families and communities were able to resist and endure oppression more effectively. As slaves acquired a stronger solidarity and a cultural identity, they were better able to control their own lives, exerting more control over the terms of work and slowly improving their material comfort. They also developed strategies to respond to and resist continued abuses by whites, such as sale and separation from their families, being beaten to make them work, and the sexual assault of women. Though some slaves did revolt or escape, for most this was not possible and they tried to make the best of the situation on the plantations on which they were born. In general, these developments occurred not because republicanism or evangelical Christianity had made masters more sensitive and thus unable to tolerate abuses as they had in the past but because slaves had created a distinct society.

5. Both republicanism and evangelical Christianity emphasized free will and man's role in shaping his own life and salvation. These analogous views of reality made evangelical Christianity more individualistic and denominational organizations more democratic. Evangelical Christianity influenced republicanism by giving it a moral and a religious dimension.

Part 3

Economic Revolution and the Sectional Strife, 1820–1877

Part 3 covers American history from the early Industrial Revolution to the end of Reconstruction. The Thematic Timeline (p. 312) lists the main developments under five topical headings: Economy, Society, Government, Culture, and Sectionalism. Read the Timeline and the Part introduction together, beginning with the left-hand Timeline column.

The first column traces the main stages of the most transforming development of this period, the Industrial Revolution and economic shift to a market system. The significance of a changing economy is explained in the first two paragraphs of the Part introduction.

Another consequence of the new, industrialized economy, as documented in the second column of the Timeline, was the emergence of a new class structure. Social structure was altered even more dramatically by the end of slavery. Paragraph three of the Part introduction discusses these developments.

Third, as the nation expanded westward, political life became more democratic. Paragraph four examines the impact of democratization on the American party system.

Fourth, social and economic changes produced a wide variety of reform movements, ranging from tranquil utopian communities to abolitionism's fervent challenges to the established order. The fifth paragraph of the Part introduction explains the significance of reform in the antebellum and Reconstruction eras.

The final column, Sectionalism, traces the struggle between North and South throughout this period, from the compromises and crises of the prewar period, through the establishment of the Confederacy, and the readmission of the southern states to the Union. The last section of the Part introduction outlines the causes of the Civil War and assesses the accomplishments and legacy of Reconstruction.

Now read across the Timeline, looking for relationships among events that took place during the same period. The entries for the 1850s, for example, suggest a connection between the publication in 1852 of the powerful antislavery novel *Uncle Tom's Cabin* and events that took place later in the decade—the Kansas-Nebraska Act, the *Dred Scott* decision, and John Brown's raid—all of which heightened the sense of crisis prior to the Civil War.

Part Questions

After you have completed studying the chapters in Part 3, you should be able to answer the following questions:

1. What circumstances explain the rapid spread of the Industrial Revolution in the northern United States? Why did the same thing *not* happen in the South?

2. Explain how the introduction of the market system influenced the structure of American society.

3. Compare and contrast the reform objectives of the Benevolent Empire and the calls by transcendentalists and other utopians, woman-suffrage advocates, and abolitionists for radical change in American society. What did each of these reform movements accomplish?

4. What explains the democratic movement in American politics and the rise of Andrew Jackson?

5. Describe American expansionism from the acquisition of Florida (1819) to the Mexican War and the adventurism of Franklin Pierce. Why did the United States pursue an expansionist foreign policy during these years? What were the consequences?

6. Why did slavery become an increasingly divisive issue after 1820? In framing your answer, consider social and economic realities, the power of abolitionist and proslavery arguments, and the cohesiveness of the national parties.

7. How do you explain the Union victory in the Civil War?

8. Why did the North not take full advantage of its victory during Reconstruction?

Chapter 10

The Economic Revolution, 1820–1860

LEARNING OBJECTIVES

1. How and why did changes in technology and the organization of production increase productivity in the Industrial Revolution?

2. How did increased productivity affect the dynamics of the American marketplace?

3. What changes occurred in transportation from 1820 to 1860? How did improvements in transportation expand markets and generate industrial development?

4. How did productivity contribute to increasing differentiation between social classes?

5. How did different groups involved in economic activity respond to the Industrial Revolution?

6. In their response to the Industrial Revolution, did Americans draw on cultural values already in place or did they invent new class cultures? How did these responses affect class relations?

7. How did the Industrial Revolution make Americans more responsive to a revival of evangelical Christianity and moral reform? How did this response affect class relations?

CHAPTER SUMMARY

The reorganization and mechanization of the production of goods triggered an Industrial Revolution in the United States between 1820 and 1840. As more goods flooded the market, the states and the federal government launched ambitious programs to build roads, canals, and railroads to expand the marketplace across the nation. By 1840, towns and cities, providing market access as well as labor and capital, emerged as the market exchange and production centers of the Industrial Revolution. While the Industrial Revolution drew most Americans into the same market, however, it did not distribute the material benefits of increased productivity and income equally. A distinct class structure arose in which the business elite, the middle class, and the working class lived unmistakably separate lives. In response to concerns and fears of disorder, middle-class men and women launched a broad-ranging campaign of moral and institutional reform called the Benevolent Empire.

The Rise of Manufacturing
(pp. 316–326)

American manufacturers responded to British industrial production by developing their own kinds of factories. Drawing on an abundance of natural resources, excess labor on farms, access to water power, and a pool of mechanical skill and innovative ideas among American workers, American manufacturers brought everything under one roof in large, efficient factories that made it possible for them to compete with the British. When they faced further competition, manufacturers sought tariff protection, and aggressively pursued further technological and organizational innovation. In so doing, they steadily undermined workers' status and elicited a range of responses from workers that eventually developed into a workingman's movement.

Division of Labor and the Factory

The Industrial Revolution in America was concentrated in the Northeast, where the first factories brought workers together in one place and applied the principle of division of labor. In divided labor, each worker had a specific task to do in the process of production, thus enhancing workers' specialized skills while accelerating production. Both organizational and technological innovations dramatically improved output.

The Textile Industry and British Competition

The American textile industry made dramatic gains in productivity by combining new technology with the division of labor. American manufacturers, taking advantage of abundant natural resources—wool, cotton, and the availability of power from the fall line—constructed large factories in which labor was divided, and built and installed machinery based on superior British technology brought to the United States by British mechanics. Still finding it difficult to compete against established British mills, which were able to pay workers far less, American manufacturers sought tariff protection. They also improved on British technology and aggressively tried to lower the cost of labor by hiring women and girls, whom they could pay less than men.

The leader in these developments was the Boston Manufacturing Company. Founded in 1814, the company opened a textile plant in Waltham, Massachusetts, that was the first in the United States to consolidate all the operations of making cloth under one roof. The mill recruited its work force from among the girls and young women of New England farm families. Other textile manufacturers employed entire families. The availability of this cheap work force enabled American textile mills to overtake British manufacturers. It also made it possible for New England manufacturers to best other American textile producers.

American Mechanics and Technological Innovation

Craft workers contributed to the Industrial Revolution inventions that improved American manufacturing. The development of a machine-tool industry in which machine parts could be made interchangeable through precision craft work, such as that carried out by Eli Whitney in the production of firearms, allowed mechanized innovation to transform American manufacturing.

Wage Workers and the Labor Movement

As the number of Americans working for others for wages grew and as independent artisans were forced to abandon their crafts for semiskilled or unskilled work dependent on others, these workers organized to protect their own interests. Responding to managers who strove to increase productivity by reorganizing and dividing labor, reducing required skills, quickening the pace of work, demanding longer hours, or introducing new machine technology to replace employees, workers formed unions, fought for the ten-hour day and better wages, criticized the industrial order, and demanded a just return on the value their labor added to society. Through strikes, unions won some concessions. But, in general, workers lacked the capital, managerial skills, and education to significantly relieve their plight and alter their position.

The Expansion of Markets
(pp. 326–333)

Migration to the West

In the 1820s, the state and federal governments began to support the construction of roads, canals, and railroads to enable producers and consumers to participate in a larger marketplace. The continuing migration of Americans across the West created much of the pressure for an expanded market. Three great streams of immigrants moved into the Southwest and the Northwest. One stream moved from coastal Georgia and Carolina into the Southwest, expanding the cotton kingdom. Another stream from Virginia and Kentucky surged west into the Ohio River Valley, seeking better land or escape from the planter-dominated slave states. Yet another major stream moved from New England across New York and into the northern parts of Ohio, Indiana, Illinois, Iowa, and Wisconsin in search of better farmland. Having moved west, these people demanded connections to the national market, enabling farmers to acquire new machinery and implements that would, in turn, enhance their ability to provide raw materials for factories and food supplies for urban populations, as well as markets for manufactured goods.

The Transportation Revolution

Economic expansion, both industrial and agricultural, was made possible in part by transportation improvements that included better roads and new waterways. The most important new waterway was the Erie Canal, between Albany and Buffalo, New York. This publicly funded project stimulated the economic development of the entire region it traversed and drew the West into the national market. It also set in motion a canal-construction boom. The steamboat transformed western development by increasing the speed and reducing the cost of water transportation. The construction of interstate railroads, supported by the Supreme Court ruling *Gibbons v. Ogden*, which allowed corporations to operate and trade goods freely across state lines, was under way by 1830. By the 1850s, the railroad had opened new regions to settlement, increased the speed of transport while reducing its cost, and provided a new demand for iron that stimulated further economic growth and development. These developments in the Northeast and West stood in increasingly stark contrast to the South, where traditional production and transportation methods remained in place.

The Growth of Cities and Towns

Economic expansion and the growth of trade stimulated the pace of urban growth in the United States. Cities that were manufacturing centers and those located at transportation junctions flourished. During the 1820s and 1830s, New York City became the nation's most important economic center—thanks, in large part, to the construction of the Erie Canal, which connected the city to the interior of the continent.

Changes in the Social Structure
(pp. 333–343)

The Industrial Revolution raised the standard of living of most Americans, but it also increased the distance between social classes and encouraged class antagonisms. In doing so, it challenged America's republican ideals.

The Business Elite

Though the uncertainties of the capitalist market ruined some businessmen, many advanced in wealth and status and emerged as a new elite who lived lives that separated them from the middle and working classes. They did this by moving to houses on the edge of towns and cities, cutting themselves off from social interaction with other classes, and setting themselves apart by increased material consumption.

The Middle Class

Though some managers gained enormous wealth, establishing themselves as a social elite, most joined the growing ranks of entrepreneurs, merchants, and professionals, who considered themselves to be members of a rising urban middle class. Middle-class families combined increased income with the ideological emergence of women as moral paragons to create a private domestic realm that was separate from the public world of work. New building techniques, better means of providing heat and water, and a larger choice of household goods enabled middle-class women, who had more time and leisure as birth rates continued to drop, to establish increasingly comfortable, even luxurious, homes. The middle-class home became a symbol of self-discipline, morality, achievement, and success that stood in stark contrast to the disorderly world of the new working class. Leisure and increased education also led to an explosion in reading, both of religious work and fiction, much of which celebrated the work ethic.

The New Urban Poor

Forced into low-paying, insecure jobs, many workers crowded into boardinghouses and small, unsanitary apartments in distinctive working-class neighborhoods. Unlike middle-class families, the working poor were often forced to send their children to work in order to make ends meet. Amid increasing social disorder and violence fueled by a rising tide of alcohol consumption, working families struggled to establish an orderly, private home life.

The Benevolent Empire

Acting in response to their fears of social disorder, middle-class men and women launched a broad-ranging campaign of moral and institutional reform that historians have called the Benevolent Empire. On one front, they established organizations that encouraged individuals to discipline themselves, avoid vice and drink, and keep the Sabbath. On another, they organized and provided institutions that could ameliorate the condition of the working class; these included homes of refuge, orphanages, asylums, aid societies, clubs, and charitable organizations.

Revivalism and Reform

Charles Grandison Finney, the most important Protestant revivalist of the 1830s, preached a religious message that aided reform efforts. Finney taught that each person possesses a free will, which he or she should use to accept God's saving grace. At his dramatic revivals, members of the middle class and some of the poor found moral strength. By highlighting an individual's moral condition, Finney converted both the rich and the poor and aligned them with middle-class moral respectability. Converts pledged to reform their own lives and those of their workers, especially by curtailing alcohol abuse. They hoped to create a society based on Protestant evangelical principles. This form of revivalism swept through communities from New England to the Ohio River Valley. As it spread, it strengthened the campaign of the American Temperance Society and encouraged adherence to the work ethic.

Immigration and Cultural Conflict

Fleeing conditions at home and attracted to the opportunity presented by open land or industry in the United States, waves of immigrants from northern Europe arrived during the 1840s and 1850s. The largest group was the Irish. Fleeing famine in Ireland, they arrived in the eastern coastal cities and took the lowest-paid, hardest work. Most of the Irish were devout Catholics who turned to the Catholic Church for support in their hard lives. To aid its Irish parishioners, the Church helped build an institutional network of churches, societies, schools, newspapers, and organizations that shaped a new Irish American identity and provided Irish Americans with the institutional skills to acquire political power. The rising tide of immigration, and the growth of the Catholic Church touched off a wave of anti-Catholic sentiment, nativist organizations, and riots and violence. Class and ethnicity differences threatened to divide northern society, even as the majority of white Americans held fast to the shared values of individualism, capitalism, and democratic republicanism.

EXPANDED TIMELINE

1782 **Oliver Evans develops automated flour mill**
Oliver Evans, a Delaware inventor, applied the idea of the division of labor and the use of technological advances to the process of flour milling, and built the first machine-driven flour mill in the United States.

1790 **Samuel Slater opens spinning mill in Providence, R.I.**
Samuel Slater, a British mechanic, immigrated to America in 1789 and the next year sparked the beginning of the Industrial Revolution in the United States by building a machine-driven cotton mill in Providence, Rhode Island.

1793 **Eli Whitney manufactures cotton gins**
Whitney's cotton gin revolutionized cotton production. Later, he pioneered the construction of machine tools, which made it possible to manufacture products with interchangeable parts, the crucial first step toward mass production. In 1798, Whitney secured a federal contract to manufacture ten thousand muskets.

1807 **Robert Fulton launches the *Clermont*, the first steamboat**
The inventor Robert Fulton applied the use of steam power to a piston-driven engine that could propel a boat along a body of water. Much faster and more reliable than sailing vessels, the steamboat dramatically reduced transportation costs on inland rivers.

1810s **Cotton Kingdom begins in Old Southwest**
The rising demand for cotton from cotton mills in England and then New England increased the demand for new lands. Plantation owners and their slaves migrated to the Old Southwest in search of land. Mississippi and Alabama became states in 1817 and 1819, respectively.

1814 **Boston Manufacturing Company opens cotton mill in Waltham, Massachusetts**
The Waltham mill combined innovations in technology—Paul Moody's high-speed power loom—with innovations in organization. It was the first plant in America to combine all the operations of cloth making under one roof. The mill operators also hired young women workers, a strategy called the Waltham plan.

1817 **Erie Canal begun; completed in 1825**
The state-funded Erie Canal proved to be an immediate success. It dramatically reduced the cost of transport of goods across New York State, stimulated economic development, and quickly paid for itself. Its success touched off a canal-building boom.

1820 **Minimum federal land price reduced to $1.25 per acre**
Between the 1790s and 1820, public lands had been relatively inexpensive at $2.00 per acre. In 1820, the Republicans lowered the price to $1.25 per acre. The new, lower price meant that a greater number of farmers could acquire western lands; combined with a rapidly growing population, it spurred the westward migration.

1820s **Women become textile operatives**
Building-trade workers seek ten-hour day
In order to compete against the British, the Boston Manufacturing Company lowered the cost of labor by hiring women and girls to work in its mills. It paid them better than what other women were paid, and provided them with housing and social support. For most other workers, however, industrialization and urbanization increased competition and therefore meant longer hours. In response, many workers, including those in the physically taxing buildng trade, joined a movement that demanded a ten-hour day.

Rise of Benevolent Empire
In response to the growing social disorder among the working class, many middle-class Americans, influenced by evangelical Christian revivals, created a series of new reform organizations that used systematic tactics to combat social evils.

1821 **End of Panic of 1819; fifteen-year boom begins**
The Industrial Revolution touched off a rapid increase

Glossary

in capital investments by those seeking to make money in the broadening marketplace. As investment pushed the market ahead, speculation often took over, creating an excess supply of goods, services, or capital. These booms were followed by corrections, or busts of panic, in which investments, production, and prices were brought back into alignment with actual demand. The first boom of the 1810s ended with the panic of 1819. After the panic, investors returned to the market and set off a rapid expansion of industrial activity, canal construction, and land development that accelerated production and kept it apace with rising consumption through 1837.

1824 **Congress raises tariffs; raised again in 1828**
In 1824, to protect American manufacturing the federal government expanded the list of imported items that would be taxed to include iron, woolens, cotton, and hemp. In 1828, it increased the tariff rate on each of these kinds of goods.

Gibbons v. Ogden **promotes interstate trade**
The Supreme Court struck down a state-granted steamboat passenger-service monopoly, opening up business competition and facilitating interstate commerce.

1830s **Expansion of western commercial cities**
Industrialization and the expansion of canals and transport by steamboat led to the development of inland trading cities that emerged as dynamic centers of regional commerce.

Union movement; class-segregated cities
In response to longer hours, worsening conditions, lower wages, and less skilled jobs, workers across the East formed unions to challenge their employers. As the Industrial Revolution differentiated wealth, people of different classes separated themselves from each other and lived in class-segregated neighborhoods.

Growth of temperance movement
In 1832, evangelical Christians gained control of the American Temperance Society and adopted revival methods to spread their efforts to reduce alcohol consumption.

Creation of middle-class culture
In response to the Industrial Revolution, the growing ranks of entrepreneurs, merchants, and professionals began to consider themselves members of a rising urban middle class. Drawing on republicanism, individualism, and evangelical Christianity, the members of this group created a distinctive middle-class culture based on the values of equality, hard work, self-control, and gentility.

1830 **Charles Grandison Finney begins Rochester revival**
Employing an emotional style of preaching in revival meetings, Charles G. Finney had already achieved considerable success in revitalizing evangelical Christianity in smaller towns and villages of New York. In 1830, he brought his methods to Rochester, and touched off a great revival that lasted six months, continuing into 1831. In time, his revival movement would spread to other cities in the North.

1837 **Panic of 1837; seven-year recession begins**
When the British government cut the flow of specie and credit from Britain to the United States, the American economy was compelled to make up the loss by drawing on its own specie and capital reserves. This touched off a general contraction, which led to a financial panic that closed banks and factories, bankrupted businesses, stopped canal construction, and dried up the markets for raw materials. As production and investment plummeted, unemployment increased, throwing the United States into a seven-year recession.

1840s–1850s **Irish and German immigration; ethnic riots**
In the 1840s, a wave of immigrants from Ireland and Germany, escaping famine and political turmoil, arrived in the United States. Their arrival increased ethnic tensions, which led to a number of urban riots.

Expansion of railroads
By the early 1850s, another product of industrial technology, the railroad, was beginning to transform the American economy. Able to transport goods faster, in greater bulk, and to places canals and rivers could not serve, the railroad broadened existing markets into a national marketplace.

Rise of machine-tool industry
Machine technology also continued to transform American industry. As machine tools became more precise, machinery used in industrial production became faster and more efficient. Able to produce more items with interchangeable parts, American industry had outcompeted British industry by the 1850s.

1857 **Financial panic after fourteen-year boom**
Overexpansion of the railroad system, combined with rampant land speculation and investment led, in 1857, to another excess in supply over demand. A financial panic ended the economic expansion that had begun in the early 1840s.

GLOSSARY

productivity The amount of work completed by a worker during a given time frame. From the late eighteenth century on, manufacturers in the Industrial Revolution employed new organizations of workers and machinery to dramatically increase productivity. (p. 315)

division of labor In the craft shop, each worker performed all the tasks necessary to produce a finished good by himself. In a factory, the manager assigns each worker a single task in the process. This division of labor into different tasks improved efficiency and productivity. (p. 316)

outwork The outwork system developed in the United States in the late eighteenth century. The manufacturers organized the supply of raw materials and provided for the final finishing of products at one location. For the intermediate stages, they hired rural artisans and individuals in farm families to perform various tasks in the production process. Drivers carried raw materials or partially finished goods from one household to the next. In this way, manufacturers produced a variety of goods, including tinware, cheese, cloth, and shoes, without ever investing in a large centralized manufactory. This system created new job opportunities in rural America but cost some farmers their economic freedom because of their growing dependence on the merchants who sold their outwork. (p. 316)

mechanics In a preindustrial society, goods necessary to daily life, such as boots, shoes, barrels, glass bottles, soap, candles, pots and pans, furniture, and clothing, were handmade by skilled craft workers and artisans. During the early Industrial Revolution, skilled workers performed more specific tasks in the production process. In particular, skilled workers who built and improved machinery were called mechanics. (p. 317)

machine tools The most important contribution of American mechanics to the Industrial Revolution was the invention of machine tools—machines that could be used to produce other machines. Machine tools were eventually able to cut machine and product parts that were so precise they were interchangeable—that is, any part could be used to fit into any product or machine with minimal adjustment. This greatly lowered the costs of machine production. (p. 321)

strike A strike is a refusal to work until their demands are met by members of a group of workers who have formed a union. The union empowered workers by allowing them to present their grievances collectively against a factory owner, rather than as individuals, whom owners could easily ignore or fire. The strike was the union's most common pressure tactic. (p. 322)

labor theory of value The belief that the value of a finished good, as indicated by its unit price, should reflect the labor that went into making it. Those who articulated this theory believed that the value of a finished product was mostly in the labor, although the price set usually represented the factory owner's costs for management or marketing expenditures or his desired profit margin. The difference between what a worker received for his or her work on a product and what he or she put into it in terms of labor was usually great, indicating the degree to which the factory owner had exploited the worker by undervaluing his or her labor. (p. 326)

balloon frame Before the nineteenth century, all wooden houses were built in the same way. Large corner posts and sometimes a center post or two were set vertically in the ground to form a rectangle. These posts supported beams from corner to corner that were connected by elaborate joints to form the framework of the walls. Other beams from the center of each wall to the opposite side framed the ceilings and floors. The walls were then filled in with plaster or mud and straw material or, as in New England, covered with cut boards called clapboards. Improved planning mills and stronger nails enabled builders in the 1830s and 1840s to replace the thick posts and beams with numerous 2-inch-thick-by-four-inch-wide pieces of lumber (called two by fours) that were nailed to each other to form a frame, and then filled in with vertical pieces of lumber called stud boards, which were nailed from ceiling to floor several inches apart and secured by crossties. The walls were then raised and nailed together to form a box frame. Because these new buildings could be constructed in a short time and were both light and strong, contemporaries referred to this method of construction as balloon-frame construction. It enabled builders to meet the rapidly increasing demand for housing in America's growing cities. As a result, balloon-frame construction has been the dominant method of American residential-house construction from the 1830s to the present. (pp. 332, 335)

coitus interruptus In the 1820s through the 1850s, middle-class couples sought to have fewer children, employing various methods of birth control. The only manufactured birth-control device available was an animal-skin condom. Many couples tried to engage in sexual intercourse in which the man withdrew before achieving orgasm. This interruption of sexual intercourse was called "coitus interruptus." Many women induced abortions by taking abortifacient pills that were available on the market. Given these limited, marginally successful, and often dangerous options, many couples decided that abstinence was the only sure way to have fewer children. (p. 335)

benevolence Broadly conceived as the disinterested desire to do good for others, benevolence, a key idea of the Second Great Awakening, encouraged many evangelical Christians to create a wide range of reform and charitable organizations. These organizations are known as the Benevolent Empire. (p. 337)

temperance Abstention from alcohol. In the 1830s, a temperance movement was one of the major campaigns of Benevolent Empire reformers. (p. 340)

nativism Nativism is the desire to keep foreigners out of one's country. Some native-born Americans organized to resist the influx of immigrants into the United States during the 1830s. (p. 342)

IDENTIFICATION

Identify by filling in the blanks.

1. The dramatic gain in productivity that occurred in American industry during the Industrial Revolution was due to the combination of _____ and _____. (p. 317)

2. In 1824, the federal government began to protect American manufacturing from foreign competition by imposing an import tax, or _____, on manufactured goods. (p. 319)

3. One of the most important keys to success for textile manufacturers was the ability to acquire British _____ and cheap _____. (p. 319)

4. In 1814, _____ formed the Boston Manufacturing Company and built a textile factory at Waltham. (p. 319)

5. The paternalistic system that provided boardinghouses and supervision for young women textile workers is known as the _____. (pp. 319–320)

6. The _____ in Philadelphia supported the development of mechanical skills and knowledge. (pp. 320–321)

7. Congress significantly encouraged western expansion by reducing the price of _____ in 1820. (p. 327)

8. The federal government's most important contribution to the transportation revolution was _____. (p. 328)

9. Governor DeWitt Clinton of New York was the leading force behind the plan, funding, and completion of the _____ across the state from Albany to Buffalo. (p. 328)

10. The first American steamboat was built by _____. He navigated it up the Hudson River in 1807. (p. 330)

11. Houses built by the new, efficient construction methods of the 1830s, involving the use of stud boards and crossties, were known as _____ houses on account of their lightness. (p. 335)

12. Benjamin Franklin's widely read *Autobiography*, published in 1818, extolled the business-class values of _____, _____, _____, and _____. (p. 336)

13. To promote proper observance of the Sabbath, _____ and other Protestant ministers founded _____ in 1828. (p. 339)

14. The most influential Protestant revivalist in the 1830s was _____. (p. 339)

15. In 1832, evangelicals gained control of the _____ and achieved success through the use of revival methods. (pp. 340–341)

FEATURES EXERCISES

New Technology

Cotton Spinning: From Spinsters to Machines (p. 318)

The reorganization of work and new technology had particular impact on the production of thread and cloth. From earliest times, spinning had been repetitive drudge work that was learned fairly easily. The simplicity of the tasks involved made this kind of work especially adaptable to machine technology. Carding machines, spinning jennies, and spinning frames were mechanized and replicated so that one person could produce many times an individual's previous output.

As you read "Cotton Spinning: From Spinsters to Machines," ask yourself the following questions:

1. How did the spinning jenny differ from the spinning wheel? How did a worker operate a spinning jenny?

Chapter 10: *The Economic Revolution, 1820–1860*

2. What advantages did the water frame possess over the spinning jenny?

3. What steps were involved in operating a water frame?

4. Why was the thread produced by the water frame so useful in American textile manufacturing?

5. What effect did the mechanization of the textile industry have on other industries?

American Voices

LUCY LARCOM, Early Days at Lowell (p. 321)

Early industrialists tapped the underused labor on farms to provide workers for their textile mills. At Lowell, Francis Cabot Lowell hired farm girls between the ages of ten and twenty-five to do the work. By hiring female operatives, Lowell thought he would have a more orderly, attentive work force that would benefit from the work not only financially—he paid them more than they would have earned as servants or outwork laborers—but also in terms of building character and self-esteem. To assure that they were protected and would not be morally compromised, the women lived under a strict routine of discipline. Lowell attempted to build the Industrial Revolution upon a cooperative republican social order.

As you read "Early Days at Lowell," ask yourself the following questions:

1. What evidence is there that Lucy was alienated by the work environment?

2. In what ways did she struggle against the work regime?

3. How do Lucy's comments about the girls with whom she worked confirm both of Lowell's expectations about hiring farm girls?

4. How do Lucy's comments about the girls with whom she worked provide evidence of the beneficial impact of work on these young women?

5. What career choices did these young women have? In what sense did mill work offer the women opportunity?

6. Based on this account, how did the coming of industry *not* seem to violate the Jeffersonian vision of America?

American Lives

Eli Whitney: Machine Builder and Promoter (pp. 324–325)

From his youth on a farm to his efforts later in his career to manufacture goods with interchangeable parts, Eli Whitney understood the economic forces that drove the engine of change. As a farm boy he understood that he could profit more by providing needed repair services to local farmers than by farming. When imports were shut off during the Revolution, Whitney saw his chance and began manufacturing substitutes. He prospered in a monopoly market. When he was thrown out of business by competition, instead of quitting he improved his market position by acquiring the education he needed. Again, while visiting a plantation in Georgia, he quickly recognized that the slow cleaning process prevented cotton production from developing to its full potential. He built a machine to clean cotton that was so simple that everyone copied it. Later, he recognized that American industry would grow if it developed even more intensive labor-saving machinery. This would require a machine-tool industry capable of producing interchangeable parts. Whitney pursued this technology in the manufacture of guns and made it a model for breakthroughs in other lines of production that increased efficiency and output and enabled American producers to outcompete the British.

As you read "Eli Whitney: Machine Builder and Promoter," ask yourself the following questions:

1. What problems was Whitney attempting to solve when he devised the cotton gin and machine tools?

2. Why was Whitney unable to profit from his inventions?

3. How did Whitney's career map the changes that were taking place in the American economy?

4. How did Whitney's response to different career situations reflect the nature of the marketplace?

Voices from Abroad

FRANCES TROLLOPE, American Workers and Their Wives (p. 338)

As managers reorganized labor and transformed work by installing machines, the skills needed to perform work declined. As a result, wages declined for most workers. Long hours and little pay transformed workers' lives into a daily struggle to support themselves. Women found these pressures doubly hard, for they were expected to work while maintaining the household as best they could. Frances Trollope, a social commentator from England, considered this double burden on women to be unfair.

As you read "American Workers and Their Wives," ask yourself the following questions:

1. Why does Trollope compare the English peasant with the American worker?
2. How does she think the life of the American worker generally compares with that of the English peasant?
3. Why are tobacco and alcohol such a problem in America?
4. Why would there be more sickness in the United States than in England?
5. How trustworthy do you think Trollope's comparisons are? What point is she trying to make?

American Voices

JOHN GOUGH, The Vice of Intemperance
(p. 342)

In response to the disruptions and stresses of the Industrial Revolution, many people increased their consumption of alcohol. Sharing a drink with friends often facilitated sociability and provided social relief from one's everyday work concerns. For many, however, social drinking could quickly degenerate into binge drinking—drinking to become intoxicated. Today, we recognize that alcoholism is a disease that requires treatment. In the nineteenth century, however, temperance reformers viewed drinking as a moral issue and believed that with regard to drink, as with vice in general, every person was corruptible and could fall into intemperance or, alternatively, choose to stop drinking.

As you read "The Vice of Intemperance," ask yourself the following questions:

1. What is Gough's purpose in telling the reader or listener of his suffering?
2. What motivates Gough to quit drinking?
3. What does Gough's "slumbering demon" suggest about his condition?

MAPS AND FIGURES

1. Locate the following on the outline map above:
   a. The four largest American cities in 1840 (p. 333)
   b. Six of the most important manufacturing sites in 1840 (p. 333)

2. Trace the three streams of westward migration (by using arrows). (p. 327)

3. Trace the route of the Erie Canal. (p. 329)

SELF-TEST

Multiple Choice

1. One consequence of the Industrial Revolution in America during the 1830s and 1840s was that it:
   a. raised the standard of living of all Americans.
   b. increased the standard of living of most Americans.
   c. eased tensions between rich and poor.
   d. encouraged a more equitable distribution of wealth.

2. British textile manufacturers were able to outcompete American manufacturers because they possessed *all* of the following advantages *except:*

a. low shipping rates.
b. low interest rates.
c. low wages.
d. abundant cotton production at home.

3. *All* of the following are true of Oliver Evans's flour mill *except:*
   a. it demonstrated the efficiency of new organizational techniques.
   b. it required fewer workers to operate.
   c. it ran on water power.
   d. it became a model for flour milling in the United States.

4. The Waltham and Fall River plans were devised to provide employees for the first textile factories because:
   a. young men had better opportunities in farm or construction work.
   b. young women were eager to leave their families to work.
   c. laws prohibited the use of children as workers.
   d. women and children were not capable of using the heavy machines in the earliest factories.

5. The development of machine tools is significant because they:
   a. facilitated the repair of complicated equipment.
   b. produced machines that made standardized parts rapidly and cheaply.
   c. produced machines that could be run by women and children factory workers.
   d. were of higher quality than similar British equipment.

6. The primary industrial activity that occupied the energies of the inventor Eli Whitney was the manufacture of:
   a. cotton gins.
   b. cotton and woolen cloth.
   c. farm machinery.
   d. firearms.

7. Cities such as Buffalo, Chicago, and Detroit grew rapidly in the 1830s because:
   a. their location facilitated the use of water power in factories.
   b. their mayors and other city officials used public funds to build new ports and harbors to increase trade.
   c. they were located where goods had to be transferred from one mode of transportation to another.
   d. they facilitated the transfer of goods between the East and the West.

8. New York City's economic advantages included *all* of the following *except:*
   a. many enterprising merchants.
   b. a fine harbor.
   c. the fact that it was the state capital.
   d. the Hudson River–Erie Canal network.

9. When southern cotton producers moved West, they moved primarily to:
   a. southern parts of Ohio, Indiana, and Illinois.
   b. Mississippi, Alabama, Arkansas, and Louisiana.
   c. northern parts of Ohio, Indiana, and Illinois.
   d. Missouri, Nebraska, Michigan, and Wisconsin.

10. The growth of farming in the West was significant to the country's industrialization for *all* of the following reasons *except:*
    a. farmers grew or raised cheap raw materials for industrial production.
    b. western farms increased opportunities for young men in farm work.
    c. farmers provided inexpensive food for factory workers and other urban residents.
    d. farmers bought equipment produced in eastern factories.

11. The free workers who faced the worst working and living conditions were:
    a. mill hands.
    b. mechanics.
    c. day laborers.
    d. canal-boat crews.

12. The rise of the business class changed the social order by:
    a. creating greater differences between agricultural and industrial workers.
    b. stimulating religious-reform groups that tried to stop factory workers from drinking alcohol.
    c. increasing the differences between manufacturers and their employees.
    d. providing the middle class with new manufactured products.

13. The Benevolent Empire tried to do *all* of the following *except:*
    a. end alcohol abuse.
    b. rescue prostitutes from degradation.
    c. ensure that convicts were more harshly punished.
    d. improve care for the mentally ill.

14. One key to Charles Grandison Finney's revival success was that he rejected:
    a. the emphasis on original sin.
    b. free will.

c. the need for God's grace.
d. the importance of preaching.

15. A major result of the growth of revivalism and reform was:
   a. a decrease in prostitution in the new urban centers.
   b. greater religious tolerance for all Christian denominations.
   c. an increased emphasis on nonmaterial values among the business class.
   d. a belief among members of the business class in their own moral superiority.

Short Essays

Answer the following questions in a brief paragraph.

1. What caused the Industrial Revolution in the United States? Why did the textile industry, once it became established, lead the Industrial Revolution in the United States? (pp. 317–320)
2. What role did American mechanics play in advancing the Industrial Revolution in the United States? (pp. 320–322)
3. How did the Industrial Revolution create a working class? (pp. 322–326)
4. Why did migration to the West continue to increase even as the Industrial Revolution took off? How did increased agricultural production in the West cause cities to develop? (pp. 326–333)
5. How and why did state and federal governments contribute to the transportation revolution? (pp. 328–332)
6. How did Americans of different groups respond to the Industrial Revolution? How did these responses alter the structure of American society? (pp. 333–337)
7. What was the connection between the Industrial Revolution and the spiritual response of members of the business class? (pp. 337–341)
8. In what ways was the emergence of the middle class a response to the emergence of an urban poor and increased immigration to American cities? (pp. 341–344)

ANSWERS

Identification

1. new organizational techniques; technological innovations
2. tariff
3. technology; labor
4. Francis Cabot Lowell
5. Waltham plan
6. Franklin Institute
7. federal land
8. the National Road
9. Erie Canal
10. Robert Fulton
11. balloon-frame
12. hard work; saving; temperance; honesty
13. Lyman Beecher; the General Union for Promoting the Observance of the Christian Sabbath
14. Charles Grandison Finney
15. American Temperance Society

Self-Test

Multiple Choice

1. b.
2. d.
3. a.
4. a.
5. b.
6. d.
7. c.
8. c.
9. b.
10. b.
11. c.
12. c.
13. c.
14. a.
15. d.

Short Essays

1. Americans' desire to provide goods for themselves, rather than trading goods made by other countries, combined with new means of production to trigger the Industrial Revolution. Merchants went into manufacturing with the capital acquired from trading, and used their knowledge of business to reorganize labor and to introduce machinery. The manufacture of such finished goods as shoes and clothes, which are not easily

convertible to assembly-line production required more complex machinery to facilitate. Textiles, however, were only moderately difficult to produce and thus their production could be more easily mechanized.

2. American mechanics essentially invented the machine-tool industry. For mechanization and assembly-line production to really work, manufacturers needed precisely made machines that could operate at high speeds. To keep those machines running efficiently, one needed to be able to make repairs quickly. This required easily replaceable parts. By creating machine tools, mechanics played a critical role in advancing the Industrial Revolution.

3. As the process of manufacturing was broken down into multiple steps by division of labor and mechanized, workers were reduced to machine tenders and wage earners. As they experienced reduced skill training and pay, work routinization and acceleration, and a decline in living conditions, workers' concerns, complaints, and responses became increasingly alike. From this shared experience and collective response to their situation, a new life-style and consciousness developed.

4. The Industrial Revolution triggered increased specialization in all areas of the economy. As workers moved into cities, they took specialized jobs in the service, mercantile, or industrial sectors of the economy. Instead of producing food, they were now demanding it. Thus urbanization increased the demand for food and stimulated more agricultural production in both the East and the West. As agricultural production expanded, prices declined, creating more competition and forcing more farmers to maximize their efficiency in order to stay in business. Those who moved West sought to own more land and increase their productivity, which better-quality land in the West enabled them to do easily. As agricultural productivity in the West increased, more and more eastern farmers, unable to compete, turned to garden farming or moved into the cities. Thus the Industrial Revolution contributed to the emergence of the West as the breadbasket of the national economy.

5. When industries increased their output, they soon produced more than the local markets could support. To expand their sales and profits, they needed to be able to market their goods across greater distances. Improving transportation made this expansion of markets possible. The government helped improve transportation and expand the marketplace by funding the construction of roads, canals, and railroads. Better transportation was an essential component of increasing productivity, advancing the Industrial Revolution and increasing the per-capita wealth of Americans. Supporting transportation improved the welfare of the population and fostered political stability.

6. The middle class intensified their values of self-discipline, self-control, and morality to establish themselves as the driving force of social change. The working class viewed themselves increasingly in opposition to mainstream values and the system, while the elite established themselves in a geographically and culturally distinct sphere. The result was increased class friction and a declining sense of social cohesiveness.

7. Discipline, self-control, and morality, which were essential to responding aggressively to the changes wrought by the Industrial Revolution, encouraged people to focus on their spiritual lives. They were therefore ripe for emotional conversion experiences that would enhance their social roles and their sense of self.

8. The middle class viewed the disorder and immorality of the working class as a fate they could suffer if they did not discipline themselves and remain focused on their ideological and moral agendas. Concern for the lost souls of those living immoral lives also motivated them.

Chapter 11

A Democratic Revolution, 1820–1844

LEARNING OBJECTIVES

1. How did the broadening of suffrage in the 1820s through the 1840s transform the role and function of parties in the political system?

2. In what ways was the "democratic revolution" revolutionary?

3. How did individuals who wanted to be elected to office in the 1820s through the 1840s change their campaign strategies as a result of the increased size and diversity of the voting public?

4. Why, in spite of the increasing diversity and size of the American electorate in the 1820s through the 1840s, did only two major political parties develop? What do you think this says about the changing role of parties in American politics and society during the period?

5. How did the shift in political issues that concerned the major parties in the 1820s through the 1840s reflect changes in American society? What does this relationship tell you about the purpose of political parties in the American system?

CHAPTER SUMMARY

Geographic expansion, rapid economic development, and the broadening of suffrage eroded the traditional social and political order of the United States. The broadening of suffrage undermined the operations of traditional parties in which a small group of elites decided who would run for office. Parties were compelled to organize more effectively to get votes from a larger, more diverse voting population. Party organizers established platforms that spelled out the party's stand on political issues, democratized the process by which candidates were selected, and organized more aggressive campaigns involving newspaper crusades, mass meetings, speeches, and parades to put their candidate before the people. Effective organization enabled parties to establish political order within an increasingly dynamic and diverse society. Whether or not parties would be able to maintain order as the American economy and society continued to experience rapid change and political issues became more sectional was unclear in the early 1840s.

The Rise of Popular Politics, 1820–1829 *(pp. 348–354)*

The expansion of suffrage gave ordinary men considerable power. As the Republican Party splintered into personal factions, leading to the election of John Quincy Adams, supporters of Andrew Jackson responded by forming the Democratic Party. While John Quincy Adams ruled as a paternalist aristocrat, Jackson's party responded to the larger voting public by establishing a platform, democratizing the selection of candidates, disciplining legislators to vote the party line, and getting out the vote through an aggressive campaign. By seeking votes from a wide variety of social and economic groups, the Democrats secured the election of westerner Andrew Jackson and ushered in a new era of popular politics.

The Decline of Notables and the Ascent of Parties

The expansion of the franchise ushered in a democratic revolution in American politics. As ordinary white men acquired the right to vote, they elected men from their own classes, putting many of the old elite "notables" out of office. The new participants brought their own concerns to the political arena, and in the process revised state constitutions and reformed political parties. New parties emerged to organize this popular involvement into focused political programs. Parties developed state and national organizations to establish platforms, pick and campaign for candidates, create party discipline and loyalty, and reward supporters with appointments to government offices.

The Election of 1824

The rise of democracy coincided with the division of the dominant Republican Party into separate factions supporting regional candidates for president in 1824. The campaign was waged among five regional candidates: John Quincy Adams from the Northeast, William Crawford and John C. Calhoun from the South, and Henry Clay and Andrew Jackson from the West. When the very popular Andrew Jackson finished first in the electoral college, Henry Clay, horrified at the prospect of Jackson, whom he considered a "military chieftain," becoming president, threw his support behind Adams. Adams's decision to reward Clay with the office of secretary of state led Jackson supporters to charge Adams and Clay with a "corrupt bargain." In response, Democrats formed a new opposition party in support of Jackson and set in motion the emergence of a new party system.

The Presidency of John Quincy Adams, 1825–1829

Oblivious to the new style, organization, and rhetoric of democratic politics, John Quincy Adams sought to govern as a traditional paternalist member of the elite. By embracing the key aspects of Henry Clay's American System—protective tariffs, internal improvements, and a national bank—Adams drew criticism and opposition from a variety of sources. Most members of Congress opposed the program because they felt that it exceeded the role of the national government. With the help of support from Jackson forces, however, Adams did manage to impose higher tariffs on imported manufactured goods. Because the South faced little competition from foreign cotton production, and because tariffs would raise prices for all their imports, southerners strenuously opposed the tariff. Their opposition to Adams drew them to Jackson, even though he also supported a tariff.

Adams and the Jacksonians in the Election of 1828

With support from the West and the South, Jackson advocates reorganized and launched an aggressive campaign to elect their candidate. Calling themselves Democrats, they appealed to a wide variety of social groups who were wary of or hostile toward the Industrial Revolution, elitism, and accommodation to Indians. Adams, aloof and passive, was unwilling to respond by mounting a campaign of his own. On the strength of a dramatic increase in voter turnout, Jackson, vowing to democratize American politics, swept into office.

The Presidency of Andrew Jackson, 1829–1837 (pp. 354–365)

Andrew Jackson used his personal power to carry through the mandate of the people to destroy the main aspects of Henry Clay's American System and reduce the size of the government.

Jackson's Agenda: Patronage and Policy

As president, Jackson translated popular will into policy by an adept use of personal advisors, skillful political strategy, and broad support within government secured by patronage. The two toughest issues he faced were the tariff and the national bank.

The Tariff and Nullification

When Congress failed to repeal the tariff of 1824 in 1832, southerners rose in protest against the tyranny of federal power. In South Carolina, a convention was held in which the members declared that federal law was null and void in South Carolina, and that if the government tried to collect the tariffs the state would secede from the Union. Arguing that sovereignty was vested in the states, John C. Calhoun, the author of the nullification decree, asserted the rights of state governments over the federal government.

While Jackson supported states' rights and wanted to limit the power of the federal government, he also recognized that federal power served its purpose in maintaining the Union. He pursued a centrist position on the two critical issues of the tariff and the national bank. Sharing the views of the majority of Americans, he asserted that the federal government had power over state governments and that no state could nullify federal laws or leave the Union. Meanwhile, he pursued a compromise on the tariff, mollifying many supporters of states' rights.

The Bank War

Jackson was also skilled at gaining support not through compromise but by taking a firm stand on a political issue. Though he had some reservations about a national bank, Jackson was reluctant to reduce its power for fear of empowering state banks, which he blamed for general financial instability. However, when two political opponents sought to lure Jackson into an unpopular veto by proposing to recharter the bank early in the election year of 1832, Jackson not only vetoed the bank but turned the issue into an ideological referendum on states' rights and the egalitarian power of the people, winning wide popular support. With Van Buren as his running mate in 1836, Jackson launched a brilliant campaign against Clay, who advocated the American System. Sweeping to an impressive victory, Jackson followed through on his promises and used presidential power to destroy the second United States Bank.

Indian Removal

Jackson did not hesitate to use military force to hasten the removal of the Indians to lands west of the Mississippi. Committed to open lands for white settlers, and a confirmed opponent of Indian claims to sovereignty and ownership of the land, Jackson pushed through the Indian Removal Act of 1830. This legislation offered Indians lands west of the Mississippi in exchange for their lands in the East. Approximately seventy Indian peoples accepted these terms and moved west. The Cherokee, who had developed cultural and political institutions drawn from American models, were forced off their lands. Twice they appealed to the Supreme Court to clarify their tribal status as distinct political communities. Even though John Marshall agreed with the Cherokee in the second case, Jackson pressed forward with the removal of the tribe from Georgia in 1838 to the new Indian Territory in Oklahoma. The Sac and Fox Indians, from Illinois, were also removed to Oklahoma after their defeat in the Black Hawk War.

The Jacksonian Legacy

While dismantling key aspects of federal power such as the bank and tariffs, Jackson stood firm for the Union and asserted federal power over the Indians. Most important, he empowered the president as the democratic representative of the people. His appointee as Chief Justice of the Supreme Court, Roger B. Taney, persuaded the Court to reduce the power of corporations, undermine monopolies, favor market competition, and enhance the regulatory powers of the states. Jacksonian Democrats likewise encouraged the expansion of democracy in all aspects of state government.

Class, Culture, and the Second Party System (pp. 366–375)

The development of the Whig Party, in response to Jackson's Democratic Party, established what historians call the Second Party System. The two parties represented two distinctive class cultures that supported very different policies.

The Whigs and Their Outlook

Though they supported policies that equalized opportunity, the Whigs believed that those in the social elite who had achieved success should guide national policy in order to encourage economic development. The party was made up of a variety of factions. Among northern Whigs, those elites were primarily members of the burgeoning middle class. In the South, the planter elite was divided between Democrats and Whigs. For some Whigs the rise of the middle class was evidence that the economy provided opportunity for all. For others, elite rule was maintained at the expense of workers, propertyless whites, and slaves. Either way, most Whigs supported national policies to encourage economic development.

In the mid-1820s, the development of a strongly religious political movement against the Masons, a fraternal order of deists, broadened the agenda of the Whig Party and gave it a moral dimension. Anti-Masons articulated a Christian ethos of moral self-discipline as the basis of personal achievement and social mobility. They supported equal opportunity by helping people to achieve this behavior through temperance and moral reform. In 1836, they supported several candidates against Martin Van Buren, who, as the champion of individual rights, small government, and freedom, maintained wide appeal. Even though the Whigs lost in 1836, they established themselves as a strong second party.

Labor Politics and the Depression of 1837–1843

Amid the rising prosperity of the 1830s, many industrial workers experienced stagnant wages and longer workdays. In response to these inequities caused by the Industrial Revolution, workers demanded shorter, ten-hour workdays, better working conditions, and the reorganization of factories. As economic development and inflation increased the gap between rich and poor, they focused their critique on the growing inequities and increasing dependence of the working class by opposing all the policies and institutions—monopolies, tariffs, banks, debtors' policies—that contributed to economic differentiation. During the 1830s, most workers were absorbed into the Democratic Party.

The British decision to cut off the export of capital and specie to the United States triggered a run on banks, the drying up of capital, cuts in production, and massive layoffs and unemployment that became known as the Panic of 1837. The depression undercut middle-class progress and devastated the labor movement.

"Tippecanoe and Tyler Too!"

Martin Van Buren was committed to a laissez-faire policy of limited government financial intervention in response to economic downturns as well as to the Specie Circular, which required purchases of public land to be in gold and silver. Van Buren, therefore, bore the brunt of criticism and blame for the continuing depression. The Whigs capitalized on the erosion of Van Buren's working-class support by arguing that aggressive government policy in support of internal improvements, a national bank, and protective tariffs would get the country back on its feet. As the Democrats had done in 1828, the Whigs nominated a western military hero—William Henry Harrison—for president and launched a massive political campaign using all the new electioneering methods to attract voters. The 1840 campaign was the first campaign in which two well-organized parties competed for votes. Drawing on support from the wealthy elite, the Whigs prevailed only six years after being organized.

When Harrison died only a month into office, he was succeeded by John Tyler, a southern Whig and former Democrat who did not share the views of northern Whigs. Acting more like a Democrat than a Whig, Tyler vetoed various Whig efforts to implement the American System. Tyler's gutting of the Whig agenda, combined with Democratic success in attracting a wave of Irish immigrants arriving in America, enabled the Democrats to quickly reemerge as the majority party. Nevertheless, two strong parties now competed actively for the loyalties of the people in a political system that was more responsive to the popular will than ever before.

EXPANDED TIMELINE

1810s — **Revisions of state constitutions and expansion of voting rights**
Martin Van Buren's political innovations
In the 1810s, new western states and several states in the East extended suffrage to all adult men. The increased size of the electorate forced states to democratize representation and officeholding, allowing more ordinary men to enter government. As this happened, parties increasingly had to organize platforms, meet in caucuses to choose candidates, mount campaigns to get candidates elected, control legislators, and distribute government jobs to maintain party loyalty. Martin Van Buren of New York was an innovator of many of these new political strategies and tactics.

1825 — **John Quincy Adams elected president by House; advocates Henry Clay's American System**
John Quincy Adams was elected president, even though Andrew Jackson received more popular and electoral-college votes, because when no candidate had the majority, the election was decided by the House. Henry Clay threw his support, and thus his electoral-college votes, to Adams because Adams supported Clay's American System. Adams also made Clay secretary of state. This was a serious political mistake because it allowed the Democrats to claim that a "corrupt bargain" had been made and thus gained an issue around which they could organize opposition to Adams.

1827 — **Philadelphia Working Men's Party organized**
The first workers' party was formed by workers in Philadelphia. The party advocated the abolition of private banks and proposed that higher taxes be imposed on the rich to help pay for a system of free public schools that would allow workers to gain the education they needed to become members of the propertied classes.

1828 — **"Tariff of Abominations" raises duties on imported materials and manufactures**
By the late 1820s, both the Republicans and the Democrats in the North favored some kind of tariffs to protect American manufacturers from British competition, though they differed in the reasons for their support and in what imports should be taxed. Under democratic control, Congress passed the Tariff of 1828. Southerners, gaining nothing and facing increased prices from the tariff, called it the Tariff of Abominations. This presented Jackson, who supported tariffs, with a serious political problem that had to be addressed.

The South Carolina Exposition and Protest **challenges idea of majority rule**
In response to the tariff, John C. Calhoun published a tract in which he asserted that states have the right to nullify acts of Congress and to secede from the Union.

1830 — **Andrew Jackson vetoes extension of National Road**
True to his belief that the federal government should not support internal improvements, Jackson vetoed a bill passed by Congress to extend the National Road.

Indian Removal Act
To satisfy white southern settlers, Jackson attempted to compel southern native Americans to give up their lands and move west of the Mississippi.

Expanded Timeline

1831 ***Cherokee Nation v. Georgia*** **denies Indians' claim of national independence**
As white settlers encroached on the vast lands owned by the Cherokee, many mixed-bloods adopted European practices. They resisted Andrew Jackson's policy of Indian removal by claiming that they were a "foreign nation" under the supervision of the Supreme Court. John Marshall rejected the argument, denying the Indians' claim of national independence.

1832 **Bad Axe Massacre of Sauk and Fox by American troops**
As part of his removal policy, Jackson sent American troops to oust Black Hawk and members of the Sauk and Fox who supported him from their ancestral lands. Rejecting Black Hawk's offer of surrender, American forces massacred most of his warriors at Bad Axe in Wisconsin Territory.

Jackson vetoes Second Bank bill
When, for political reasons, Henry Clay and Daniel Webster convinced the director of the Bank to put its charter up for renewal to lure Jackson into an unpopular veto, Jackson countered by portraying himself as a defender of states' rights and democracy against a burgeoning federal government and the interests of "special privilege." Jackson's attack on the Bank carried him to victory in 1832.

South Carolina nullifies Tariff of 1832
A state convention in South Carolina defied the federal government by nullifying the Tariff of 1828 in South Carolina. Rather than confront South Carolina, Jackson engaged in a debate in which he supported the Union over states' rights.

1833 **Force Bill and Tariff Act**
Balancing coercion with compromise, Congress passed the Force Bill, which gave the federal government the power to enforce federal laws, while Jackson negotiated a compromise by reducing tariff rates. In response, South Carolina backed down and the crisis was defused.

1834 **Whig Party formed by Henry Clay, John C. Calhoun, and Daniel Webster**
Congressional opponents to Jackson's policies and his high-handed tactics came together in 1834 to form a new party. This party, made up mostly of Republicans who supported Henry Clay's American System, called themselves Whigs in reference to the politicians who opposed King George III in the eighteenth century.

1835 **Roger Taney named Supreme Court Chief Justice**
As Chief Justice of the Supreme Court from 1801 to 1835, John Marshall expanded and defended the power of the Court, supported the power of the federal government over states' rights, and maintained a static view of property rights. His death in 1835 gave Andrew Jackson a major opportunity to change the course of the Supreme Court. He made a crucial decision to appoint Roger B. Taney, a strong anti-monopolist and states' rights advocate, to succeed Marshall. In doing so, he shaped the course of politics for thirty years, as Taney reversed or modified most of Marshall's decisions.

1837 ***Charles River Bridge Co. v. Warren Bridge Co.*** **undermines legal position of chartered monopolies**
Taney indicated his ideas in a case in which the Charles River Bridge Company demanded a monopoly right to bridge the Charles River. Taney argued that the state, keeping the well-being of the citizens or the public good in mind, had the right to limit the monopoly and allow other companies to build competing bridges. This undermined the legal support of monopolies.

Panic of 1837 begins depression of 1837–1843
The British decision to curtail the shipment of specie—i.e., gold and silver—to the United States caused a severe shortage of money. This shortage forced many companies into bankruptcy and triggered a financial and economic downturn that lasted for six years.

1838 **Trail of Tears: Thousands of Cherokee die on forced march to new Indian Territory**
As part of Jackson's Indian removal policy, the U.S. Army forced 15,000 Cherokee to march in winter 1,200 miles to Oklahoma Territory. More than 3,000 Indians died along the way.

1840 **Independent Treasury Act**
Arguing that the nation's financial reserves should be above politics, Van Buren passed legislation to remove specie from Jackson's various "pet banks" and place it in federal vaults. By taking yet more money out of circulation and limiting loans from those banks, the act actually delayed recovery.

Whig victory in "log-cabin" campaign
Taking advantage of deepening opposition to Van Buren's insufficient response to the financial crisis, the Whigs nominated a military hero, William Henry Harrison, for president. Playing on his western background, Whigs portrayed Harrison as a man of the people who had been born in a log cabin. In fact, Harrison was the son of a rich planter and an inexperienced politician as well. Nevertheless, the Whigs waged an aggressive campaign, using many of the new Democratic tactics, and Harrison was elected.

1841 **John Tyler succeeds William Henry Harrison as president**
The Whig victory was short-lived. After only a month in office, Harrison died. He was succeeded by John Tyler, a southern Whig who agreed with Jackson on most issues and, as president, acted more like a Democrat than a Whig.

Preemption Act promotes purchase of federal land
Tyler and the Whigs agreed that offering western lands at a lower price would accelerate settlement. When the Whigs passed the Preemption Act, Tyler signed the bill into law.

1842 ***Commonwealth v. Hunt* legitimates trade unions**
Even as the financial crisis of 1837–1843 undermined the union movement, the Massachusetts Supreme Court ruled that unions were legal organizations. By declaring unions legal organizations and arguing that strikes were legal, the Massachusetts Supreme Court gave legitimacy to the labor movement and improved its long-term prospects.

GLOSSARY

republicanism To the generation of the Founding Fathers, republicanism meant that all political power derived from the people and that government acquired legitimacy from the consent of the governed. They developed a variety of political strategies and frameworks to ensure, however, that the power of the people was indirect and balanced by various interest groups in society. By the 1820s, the procedures established by the Founding Fathers to assure ordered liberty seemed conservative and designed to maintain the rule of a property-owning elite. (p. 347)

democracy The Founding Fathers feared democracy, or direct rule by the people. Although they accepted the premise that all men are equal in natural rights, they believed that the direct expression of the self-interest of the people had to be balanced and checked by the interests of men of property. By the 1820s, many Americans had come to believe the idea that the best government was that which most directly reflected the will of all the people. (p. 348)

deference The belief that some people are destined by reason of their social class, status, or wealth to hold government office, and some are meant to be ruled. The latter, recognizing this fact, are expected to accept it and elect the former. In doing so, they "defer" to these people. Popular politics in the 1820s overturned these assumptions. (p. 348)

franchise The right to vote. In the early nineteenth century, most new states and several older states extended the franchise to all adult males. (p. 348)

squatters A squatter is someone who settles on land to which he does not have a title or deed of ownership. Some squatters across the West were transients who tried to survive by living off the land. Many squatters, however, settled on a plot of land that had not yet been surveyed or placed on the market in hopes that they could eventually acquire full title to the land. (p. 349)

political machines In the early nineteenth century, American political parties developed into organizations run by professional administrators for the purpose of maintaining the administration or party's power. To contemporaries, these organizations seemed so much like the machines that facilitated industrial production that they generally referred to them as political machines. (p. 349)

platform One of the central purposes of political parties is to take the wide variety of opinions and views among the members of the party and draw up a generalized statement of what the party stands for, what its general views on key issues are, and what policies the party candidates, if elected, will attempt to implement. In the early nineteenth century, politicians increasingly established platforms to create a unified set of party ideas and goals to present to the electorate in campaigns. (p. 349)

patronage Elected officials often consolidated their political power by appointing to various government offices people who had been loyal supporters of the party. Such salaried appointments created an incentive for party members to provide service to the party organization. They also ensured that party members would follow and vote for the party line, thus strengthening party discipline by assuring that political strategies pursued by elected officials from the party would be carried out by appointed officials. (p. 349)

party discipline A party had discipline when its leaders could instruct members on how to vote and were then assured that legislation, once enacted, would be fully endorsed by elected officials from the party. Party discipline was maintained by getting out the vote, by patronage, and by mounting organizational support of candidates. If a member failed to toe the party line or follow through on what was expected of him, it could cost him support, further access to patronage, and, in time, his position. By assuring that the platform promised by a party would be carried out, discipline strengthened the effectiveness of political parties and democracy. (p. 349)

caucus A meeting among political leaders and operatives of a party is called a caucus. Such meetings were usually called to make decisions on the slates of candidates and on various planks of the party platform. Party discipline was maintained by making party members accept the majority decisions of the party caucuses. (p. 349)

American System Henry Clay argued that the national government should be actively involved in promoting and investing in economic development. He proposed to carry out this policy by supporting and regulating a national bank and employing its funds, as well as those derived from high tariffs, to stimulate manufacturing and to subsidize internal improvements. Through an activist government, Clay envisioned creating an expansive economic system that offered a broad range of the people economic and social mobility. (p. 350)

corrupt bargain When no candidate for president in the election of 1824 received a majority of votes in the electoral college, the decision fell to Congress. Henry Clay had finished fourth and was himself out of the picture, as was the third candidate, William Crawford, who had suffered a stroke. Clay therefore used his power as Speaker of the House to sway other representatives, deciding which of the first two candidates, Andrew Jackson or John Quincy Adams, would be president. Abhorring Jackson as a crude westerner, Clay threw his support to Adams. Adams, in gratitude, appointed Henry Clay secretary of state in his administration. To Jackson's supporters, it looked as if Adams had made a "corrupt bargain" with Clay, promising him a cabinet post in return for his support, though the charge was probably unfounded. In response to this charge, an opposition emerged that would become the Democratic Party. (p. 351)

negative campaigning In a democracy, political campaigns focus on each candidate's ideas and views on important issues. In addition to or in place of presenting their own ideas, however, some candidates criticize their opponent's ideas, attack his or her character, and attempt to undermine voter confidence in that person's ability to hold office. Jackson supporters in the 1828 campaign personally attacked John Quincy Adams's character more than they opposed his political ideas, and thus introduced to American politics the practice of "negative" campaigning. (p. 353)

self-made man In the traditional society of the eighteenth century, most people were born into a relatively permanent social position. By the nineteenth century, the cultural focus on individualism and social mobility emphasized each individual's role in achieving social status through his own efforts. Those men who achieved their social status through what seemed to be entirely their own self-discipline, hard work, and morality were increasingly described as "self-made" men. (p. 353)

Kitchen Cabinet The presidential cabinet was made up of the various secretaries of the executive departments. These secretaries were expected to run their departments as well as to provide the president with advice. When Jackson became president, he relied more on the counsel of a group of close advisors and friends who gathered around him informally than on his formally appointed advisors. These informal advisors were called a Kitchen Cabinet, evoking the practice of meeting in an informal place, such as around the kitchen table. (p. 355)

rotation in office The belief that no one should hold any political office for an extended period of time. The Democrats believed that an official should hold an office only for a certain period of time before relinquishing it to someone else. In this way, no official became too entrenched or acquired too much power, and was compelled to return to the people, as Jackson remarked, to "making a living as other people do." The policy of rotation also enabled elected officials to use the patronage system to its fullest political advantage. (pp. 355–356)

spoils system Jackson used the principle of rotation of office to create the spoils system. The spoils system is based on the idea that when a party wins an election, it has the right to remove all officeholders from the opposition party and replace them with appointees from the newly elected party. Hence the party that wins the election is able to dispense to its membership the "spoils" of victory. (p. 356)

nullification Arguing that sovereignty lay not in the people as a whole but in the people "acting through their state governments," John C. Calhoun asserted that state sovereignty was superior to federal power and, therefore, if a state convention objected to a federal law, it could declare that law unconstitutional and thus null and void within the bounds of the state. The act of declaring a federal law null and void in a state is nullification. (p. 356)

specie, or **hard money** The real value of money used to be in the actual value of the amount of gold or silver in a coin. Such "hard" money, the actual gold and silver coins, is also called specie. Banks issued notes based on the amount of specie they held. Most people used a bank's currency for trade and transactions without worrying about the actual gold or silver that currency represented. When a person wanted specie in return for currency, he or she redeemed the currency at a bank for gold and silver coin. (p. 358)

pet banks To destroy the Second Bank of the United States, President Andrew Jackson had the secretary of the treasury, Roger B. Taney, remove government funds from the Bank and deposit them in state institutions. Critics of Jackson's actions called these state banks "pet banks." (p. 360)

mixed-bloods Children of an Indian parent and a white European-American parent are referred to as mixed, or mixed-blood, people. In Latin America, these people are called mestizos, or "mixed." Mixed-bloods among the Cherokee in the 1820s and 1830s favored assimilation with white culture even as they advocated creating a strong national identity for the Cherokee people. (pp. 360–361)

closed shop When a union gains control of a workplace, it often imposes a closed-shop rule. This means that the employers may hire only workers who are members of the union. Owners resisted these efforts throughout the 1830s and were in favor of keeping an open-shop system of employment. (pp. 371, 372)

suspension of payments In the 1830s, many private banks issued banknotes that they agreed to redeem in specie, at any time, for the note's full value. Because only a fraction of the people who used a bank's notes to carry on trade and business redeemed their notes, issuing banks issued far more notes than the amount of specie they had on hand to support that issue. The danger was that some economic upheaval would result in more people demanding redemption of their notes than there was specie in the vault to redeem them. To avoid a rush and the complete draining of its specie reserve, a bank would be forced to suspend payments. If a bank suspended payments and failed to reopen, it failed. When this happened, all its currency as well as all deposits with the bank became worthless, a total loss to both holders of banknotes and depositors. When, in 1837, the British cut off the supply of specie to the United States, a shortage of specie touched off runs against several banks, forcing them to suspend payments. The suspension of banks in New York triggered a general suspension of banks throughout the country known as the Panic of 1837, which sent the country into a six-year recession. (pp. 371–372)

bullion Bullion is gold and silver that is formed into bars and ingots that have been weighed and tested by the government or a bank. A bank's gold and silver supplies were often held in this form rather than as specie. (p. 372)

IDENTIFICATION

Identify by filling in the blanks.

1. Henry Clay advocated a program of government support to spur economic development through banks and internal improvements called the _____. (p. 350)

2. The chief architect of the emerging system of party organization was _____. (p. 353)

3. To formulate policy, Andrew Jackson relied on a close set of personal friends as his advisors. These friends became known as his _____. (p. 355)

4. Andrew Jackson's vice-president and a supporter of the theory of nullification was _____. (p. 357)

5. _____ of Massachusetts ardently defended the Union in a famous speech in his 1830 debates with Robert Y. Hayne by proclaiming, "Liberty *and* Union, now and forever, one and inseparable!" (p. 358)

6. The conservative leader of the Second United States Bank, who limited expansion in the West and restrained the money supply in the 1820s, was _____ of Philadelphia. (p. 359)

7. Sequoyah was the mixed-blood offspring of a white fur trader and an Indian woman. He was part of a small group that developed a system of writing his native language and published a newspaper in Georgia for the _____ tribe. (p. 361)

8. In 1832, American forces massacred hundreds of the warriors of chief Black Hawk, thus ending his resistance, in what was known as the _____ in Wisconsin Territory. (p. 362).

9. In May 1838, the forced expulsion of the Cherokee Indians from Georgia to the new Indian Territory, in what later became Oklahoma, was remembered by the Indians as the _____. (p. 363)

10. When Chief Justice John Marshall died in 1835, Andrew Jackson appointed his secretary of the treasury, _____, to the Supreme Court. In his twenty-eight years as Chief Justice, he would reverse and alter many of Marshall's fundamental legal views. (p. 364)

11. When a group of congressmen opposed Andrew Jackson's aggressive use of presidential power to establish his policies in 1834, they likened him to King George III and called him "King Andrew I." Comparing their opposition to Jackson to that of the Americans against George III sixty years earlier, they named their opposition group the _____ Party. (p. 366)

12. The Whig Party acquired a strong moral reform plank when it was joined by members of a party in the North that had established itself in opposition to a rationalist, deist sect that had been in existence since colonial times. These people were called _____. (p. 367)

13. Taking advantage of the fact that the public blamed Democrat Martin Van Buren for the Recession of 1837, the Whigs nominated a winning presidential candidate, _____, a military hero known for his victory at Tippecanoe, Indiana, against the Indians in 1812. (p. 373)

14. When the new Whig president died a month after taking office, a former Democrat who did not support Clay's American System became president. The presidency of _____ undermined Whig rule almost as soon as the party had achieved success. (p. 374)

15. In 1841, Congress passed the _____, which favored western settlement by dramatically reducing the cost of public land. (pp. 374–375)

FEATURES EXERCISES

American Voices

MARGARET BAYARD SMITH, Republican Majesty and Mobs (p. 355)

The election of Andrew Jackson by the "people" regardless of rank or distinction struck Margaret Smith as an extraordinary event. Smith marveled at the order of Jackson's inauguration, and at the sense of majesty it created. But her concerns about democracy immediately came to the fore when the people became less orderly at the reception. As you read "Republican Majesty and Mobs," ask yourself the following questions:

1. What impressed Margaret Bayard Smith at the inauguration? To what extent was it the people rather than the ceremony that elicited this response?

2. What is it about democracy that impresses the author?

3. What qualms about democracy did the people's less than orderly behavior at the White House reception create for Smith? What deeper concerns did her expression reflect?

4. On the whole, did Smith approve or disapprove of the day's activities? Was she optimistic or pessimistic about democracy?

Voices from Abroad

ALEXIS DE TOCQUEVILLE, Parties in the United States (p. 361)

Alexis de Tocqueville observed American life during the 1830s and, in an attempt to understand what ailed democracy in France, analyzed American democracy in considerable detail. He was especially concerned with how the people acted politically, seeking to understand what made American democracy work. As you read, "Parties in the United States," ask yourself the following questions:

1. According to Tocqueville, what are great parties? How does contrasting political parties in America with great parties help him to understand the purpose of American parties?

2. What are the people's ultimate goals, in Tocqueville's view?

3. In what ways do Tocqueville's conclusions about political parties still ring true today?

American Voices

BLACK HAWK, A Sacred Reverence for Our Lands (p. 363)

In the 1830s, the pace of American settlement in the West increased dramatically. As a result, the pressure on Indians to leave their ancestral lands, reinforced by Jackson's removal policy, intensified tremendously. To many Indians, the faster the process occurred, the more shocking and bewildering it seemed. In this piece an Indian chief discusses this pressure and his response, as opposed to that of other members of the tribe. As you read "A Sacred Reverence for Our Lands," ask yourself the following questions:

1. What procedure did the whites follow in acquiring and using Black Hawk's land?

2. How were the whites able to go among the Indians in the village and begin planting without resistance from the Indians?

3. What is Black Hawk's general view of whites?

4. Why did Black Hawk pursue a policy of passive resistance?

5. What was the basis of Black Hawk's claim that the ground was sacred?

American Lives

Frances Wright: Radical Reformer
(pp. 368–369)

The Industrial Revolution caused dramatic social change in the United States in the 1820s through the 1850s. In response, many Americans felt that they had to redouble their efforts to curb social disorder by advocating reform. While some sought to achieve moral reform through evangelical Christianity, others pursued social reform based on the republican ideas of the Enlightenment. Frances Wright was a radical English reformer who saw great promise in American society. She pursued a utopian vision of American society that eliminated class rule, sexism, and racism through a universal system of education marked by republican ideas, socialism, and feminism. Though her public talks attracted considerable crowds, workers and middle-class Americans alike eventually rejected her ideas.

As you read "Frances Wright: Radical Reformer," ask yourself the following questions:

1. What were the major influences that shaped the ideas of Frances Wright?
2. How did Wright try to put her ideas into practice?
3. Why were her ideas eventually rejected by reformers from both the middle class and the working class?

MAPS AND FIGURES

Map 11.4 Anatomy of a Panic: Bank Suspensions in May 1837 (p. 372)

The arrows on this map indicate the spread, or diffusion, of the bank panic of May 1837 across the United States. The dynamics and speed of the diffusion of an event or news across the country in the days before today's nearly instantaneous high-speed information system depended on the means of transport. In 1837, there were no telegraphs. The fastest means of conveyance were a few short railroads that ran at about 10 or so miles an hour, steamboats that could travel 7 miles an hour, and the horse and carriage or wagon, which traveled at around 3 to 5 miles an hour. Something that happened in New York, therefore, would not be heard about in St. Louis until nearly twelve days after it had occurred. Likewise, someone in New York who wanted to know how someone in St. Louis had reacted to the news of what had happened in New York twelve days earlier would have to wait another twelve days. For New Yorkers to fully experience impact, result, and reaction, therefore, took nearly a month. As you look carefully at this map, ask yourself the following questions:

1. Given the flow of arrows from one point to the next on the map, determine how the American banking system was organized? Who loaned money to whom?
2. How do you explain the different timing of the flows to the South and West?
3. How does such a rate of news transmission affect how people respond to news?
4. Explain the major gaps in the flow of news and information?
5. How does this map reflect the achievements of the Industrial Revolution through 1837?

SELF-TEST

Multiple Choice

1. The democratization of politics in the 1820s was the result of *all* of the following *except*:
   a. extension of franchise to women.
   b. removal of property requirements for voting.
   c. direct popular election of most offices.
   d. development of modern political parties.

2. In the election of 1824, who swung the votes in the House of Representatives to John Quincy Adams?
   a. Daniel Webster.   c. William Crawford.
   b. John C. Calhoun.   d. Henry Clay.

3. As president, John Quincy Adams supported *all* of the following *except*:
   a. Indian removal from lands desired by white settlers.
   b. government support of internal improvements.
   c. protective tariffs for manufacturing.
   d. a national bank to stabilize currency and promote economic growth.

4. In the election of 1828, Andrew Jackson drew support from *all* of the following groups *except*:
   a. western settlers.
   b. northern manufacturers.
   c. urban workers.
   d. southern farmers.

5. Jackson's practice of appointing loyal members of his party to public offices became known as:
   a. the caucus system.
   b. the spoils system.

c. patronage.
   d. the rotation system.

6. In his Supreme Court decisions regarding the Cherokee and the state of Georgia, Chief Justice John Marshall stated that:
   a. the Indians were blocking the advance of civilization and should give up their lands and move west.
   b. the Cherokee were such successful farmers and had assimilated into American life so well that they should be able to keep their lands like any settlers.
   c. the Indians should be removed for their own good to protect them from settlers.
   d. the Cherokee constituted a domestic dependent nation with rights to their own land.

7. President Jackson decided to veto the rechartering of the Second Bank because:
   a. he believed it undermined the interests of "special privilege" and monopoly.
   b. he preferred to use his "pet banks" at the state level to do government business.
   c. he wanted to make the Bank a political issue against the Whigs.
   d. he believed it was financially reckless and unstable.

8. Which group seemed to benefit most from the tariffs of 1828 and 1832?
   a. northern manufacturers.
   b. southern planters.
   c. southern yeomen farmers.
   d. urban workers.

9. In his view of states' rights, John C. Calhoun believed that:
   a. each state legislature should be consulted when national laws were passed.
   b. a state convention in any state could be called to declare a federal law null and void in all the states.
   c. each state supreme court had the power to determine whether a federal law would be law in that state.
   d. a state convention in any state could declare a federal law null and void in that state alone; such a decree would stand only until the Constitution was amended by three-fourths of all the states to give the federal government the power to carry out the nullified law.

10. Andrew Jackson's legacy included *all* of the following *except:*
    a. he increased the power of the presidency.
    b. he turned back the influence of the Marshall court and its defense of federal power and monopoly property rights.
    c. he weakened the Union and advocated states' rights.
    d. he made the political system more democratic.

11. The Whig Party included *all* of the following groups *except:*
    a. evangelical Protestant middle-class northerners.
    b. northern elite businessmen.
    c. southern planters and some nonslaveholding whites.
    d. northern immigrants and workers.

12. Workers in the north responding to increasing prosperity in the 1830s demanded *all* of the following *except:*
    a. shorter work hours.
    b. a return to the artisan republic.
    c. closed shops.
    d. increased wages.

13. The Panic of 1837 was caused by:
    a. Martin Van Buren's laissez-faire policies.
    b. the Bank of England's decision to curtail shipments of specie to the United States.
    c. overspeculation in western lands.
    d. rich bankers and merchants reducing the supply of credit.

14. The "log-cabin" campaign was most noteworthy for:
    a. negative campaigning.
    b. low voter turnout.
    c. lack of party discipline among the Democrats.
    d. the use of modern campaign tactics by the Whigs.

15. Whig success was undermined almost as soon as it was acquired because:
    a. William Henry Harrison, as a military man, had no political experience.
    b. the Democrats controlled Congress, thus thwarting all Whig efforts to pass their program.
    c. William Henry Harrison died only a month into office and was succeeded by John Tyler, a southern Whig who was really a Democrat and thus undermined Whig programs.
    d. northern Whigs refused to allow the passage of the Redemption Act

Short Essays

Answer the following questions in a brief paragraph.

1. In what ways did the expansion of democracy in the 1810s under Republican leadership contribute to the emergence of a new kind of political leadership in the 1820s and 1830s? (pp. 348–349)

2. How did Andrew Jackson transform American democracy? (pp. 354–365)

3. What were the major planks of the Whig platform? (pp. 366–367, 370)

4. What were some of the causes and consequences of the Panic of 1837? (pp. 370–372)

5. Which coalition party was stronger and more successful during the 1830s and 1840s? Which party contributed most to the "democratic revolution"? (pp. 372–375)

ANSWERS

Identification

1. American System
2. Martin Van Buren
3. Kitchen Cabinet
4. John C. Calhoun
5. Daniel Webster
6. Nicholas Biddle
7. Cherokee
8. Bad Axe Massacre
9. "Trail of Tears"
10. Roger B. Taney
11. Whig
12. Anti-Masons
13. William Henry Harrison
14. John Tyler
15. Preemption Act of 1841

Self-Test

Multiple Choice

1. a.
2. d.
3. a.
4. b.
5. b.
6. d.
7. c.
8. a.
9. d.
10. c.
11. a.
12. c.
13. b.
14. d.
15. c.

Short Essays

1. As more and more white men received the vote, the range of views and interests became too diverse for any single individual to address. In response, political parties organized more effectively to unify ideas, get out the vote, and control party members. They established platforms, ran slates of candidates, campaigned, and, once their candidates had been elected, enforced party discipline through the patronage system.

2. Jackson enhanced the power of the presidency through his personal authority. With the advice of his Kitchen Cabinet and his use of the spoils system, he gained support for his legislative programs. Jackson skillfully played opposing sides against each other to establish a middle ground on issues such as states' rights versus the Union, the bank, and property rights. He also left a legacy by appointing a Supreme Court justice who gradually repealed most of the decisions made by John Marshall. In general, Jackson transformed the president into a force of change from the federal government that brought government closer to the people.

3. The Whigs emerged as an opposition party to Jackson's powerful leadership of the Democrats. The Whigs proposed to employ Clay's American System to increase opportunity and assure social mobility. They enhanced these goals by accepting a strong evangelical Christian reform agenda as part of the party platform.

4. The British, in an effort to improve their economy, cut loans and capital outflow to the United States. This compelled American producers and merchants to use specie from their local banks to pay for their imports. The run on banks with lower specie reserves across the country predictably forced many closures. The closing of banks starved the economy of capital, forcing manufacturers and consumers alike to retrench and cut back. Manufactories closed, putting thousands out of work. Without income, workers refrained from spending money. As consumption dropped, more layoffs followed, and prices fell lower still. While the government pondered what action to take, the experience undermined the unions and increased support for anyone but Van Buren, whom the public blamed for the recession. The election of Harrison, a Whig, had little long-term impact on the domination of the Democratic Party, however, when he died a month into office.

5. The Democrats drew on broad-based support from immigrants, workers, westerners—especially farmers—as well as southerners. Though diverse, a common stand against big government, the bank, and tariffs encouraged them to work together between 1828 and the late 1840s. In contrast, a small group of New England senators set up a party based on opposition to Jackson, support for Clay's American System, and the Anti-Masons' moral reform. In time, the Whigs, who came from different regions and occupations, disagreed fundamentally about basic planks in their platform on the power of the federal government, equality of opportunity, tariffs, and Indian policy. In contrast to the Democrats, there were major differences of opinion among various groups in the Whig Party.

Chapter 12

The Ferment of Reform, 1820-1860

LEARNING OBJECTIVES

1. How did social change affect the way people viewed themselves and their relationship to society in mid-nineteenth-century America?

2. What were some of the common ideas, tactics, and goals shared by all reformers of American society in the nineteenth century? In general, did these reformers accept or reject the basic premises of American social order?

3. Did individualism contribute to reform in American society in the early nineteenth century or did it reinforce the status quo?

4. What impact did communalism, feminism, and abolitionism have on American society before 1850?

CHAPTER SUMMARY

While the Industrial Revolution, territorial expansion, and increasingly democratic politics opened new opportunities for many Americans, they also increased social differentiation by class, wealth, gender, and race. Reform movements grew out of this rising tension between increased opportunity and the diverging interests of the new industrial order. By calling into question basic assumptions about society, reform movements prompted a wide debate about the American social order. Reformers believed the changes they called for would improve society, but others were fearful of the threat these changes posed.

Individualism (pp. 380-384)

The notion of being a free individual, liberated from traditional social ties and institutions, transformed the lives of countless Americans. The intellectual excitement of individualism generated several waves of reform movements.

Emerson and Transcendentalism

In 1832, the Unitarian minister Ralph Waldo Emerson left his pulpit to celebrate the individual as a being free of tradition and custom, self-reliant and nonconformist. Emerson believed in the ability of people to attain, through solitude and the contemplation of nature, a mystical union with "currents of Universal Being." Emerson's challenge to traditional religion and his emphasis on the individual became popular as he toured the North delivering public lectures to thousands. Emerson was more radical than many people realized; his pantheism was outside Christian doctrine, and he criticized the new industrial society for its shallow exaltation of material consumption. He became the leader of a new intellectual movement known as transcendentalism.

Emerson's Literary Influence

A generation of young intellectuals responded to Emerson's call to create a genuinely American literature characterized by an emphasis on democracy and individual freedom. Henry David Thoreau, who tried to live a life of absolute simplicity during his stay at Walden Pond, told a story of radical nonconformity and a search for spiritual meaning in nature, distant from society's demands. Walt Whitman's exuberant poetry elevated the individual and the common person almost to divinity. Whitman's exultant democracy challenged traditional social barriers and the restraints that traditional religion imposed on individual expression. In contrast, the novels of Nathaniel Hawthorne and Herman Melville criticized excessive individualism as having a destructive impact on society. Their gloomy visions did not find popular audiences until years later.

The Brook Farm Experiment

Some transcendentalists tried to create ideal communities called utopias that encouraged individualism and personal freedom and set an example for the larger society. Brook Farm, founded in Massachusetts in 1841, was the most famous of these; its intellectual community included Emerson, Hawthorne, the editor Margaret Fuller, and other noted transcendentalists. Young Bostonians found the environment stimulating, but Brook Farm never established an economic base and declined by 1846. In the 1850s, transcendentalists became less radical and joined mainstream New England culture.

Communalism (pp. 384–390)

Although many transcendentalists gave up their attempts at comprehensive reform with Brook Farm's decline, others sought to reform society along socialist lines, celebrating individualism within the context of a larger social community.

The Shakers

The Shakers came from England in 1774, led by their founder, Mother Ann Lee. They believed that God was both male and female, and the leadership in their communities thus included men and women. They also welcomed African Americans into their communities. Shakers believed in celibacy, and practiced strict separation of the sexes. Their structured communities also embraced abstinence from alcohol, tobacco, politics, and war. Flourishing during the 1820s and 1830s, these communities attracted people who agreed with the Shaker belief that sin is a product of society. Nevertheless, their commitment to celibacy and their limited resources led to the gradual decline of Shaker communities.

The Fourierist Movement

In an effort to combat the capitalist wage-labor system, the Frenchman Charles Fourier established communal phalanxes that were cooperative work and living units in which all residents held shares, thus owning all property in common. Laborers received the bulk of profits from production in the community. Arthur Brisbane brought this idea to the United States, helping to create about a hundred such communities in the North and the Midwest. Like other utopian communities, however, phalanxes had problems supporting themselves.

Noyes and the Oneida Community

Inspired by Charles Finney, and convinced that communal societies needed strong religious discipline, John Humphrey Noyes sought to establish his own version of a utopian community. Noyes was one of the leading "perfectionists" of his day. Believing that the Second Coming of Christ had already occurred and that people could, therefore, aspire to freedom from sin, he sought to create a community in which people would face no barriers to salvation. The major barrier, he believed, was marriage, which promoted exclusiveness and jealousy. Noyes therefore created a community in Oneida, New York, that practiced "complex marriage," the belief that every person was married to every other person. Oneida residents also practiced community ownership of property. The Oneidians' sexual practices scandalized society, forcing Noyes to flee prosecution. Both Shakers and Oneidians tried to free individuals from the sinful effects of society. In particular, they felt that traditional gender relations were a corrupting force in society.

The Mormons

Joseph Smith, inspired by religious revelations, founded the Mormon Church in New York. Deeply critical of society's growing emphasis on individualism, Smith forged a strong hierarchical community of religious faithful who owned private property but acted in unison with church authority. When Smith and the Mormons were persecuted in the East, Smith led his followers west to Illinois to find a haven in the wilderness. There, he established a Mormon community, which in its size, wealth, and power generated considerable antipathy from nearby settlers. When Smith instituted the practice of polygamy—a man's having more than one wife—within the community, animosity boiled over into war and he was murdered by members of a mob in 1844. Brigham Young took over the Mormon leadership, as he led more than ten thousand people to establish disciplined communities in Utah, where they made innovations in the areas of irrigation, communal labor, and water rights. Appointing Young as governor of Utah Territory, Congress rejected a Mormon petition to create a Mormon state extending from Utah to the Pacific. President James Buchanan, pressured by Christian churches and Republicans who denounced polygamy, precipitated the bloodless "Mormon War" in 1857-1858 when he sent federal forces to Utah. For political reasons, however, Buchanan withdrew, leaving the Mormon leadership free to continue to develop its hierarchical, conservative communities in Utah Territory for another generation without federal interference.

The Women's Movement (pp. 390-396)

Women's involvement in reform movements, particularly abolitionism, led many women to insist on their political and social equality with men.

New Social Roles for Women

While the Industrial Revolution created a new industrial society that seemed to exclude women from paid employment, middle-class women restricted to the home became guardians of family and religious morality precisely because they were outside the commercial world. At the same time, evangelical religion emphasized that women's salvation and social responsibilities were as important as those of men. From this elevated position, many women became ardent reformers who sought to rid society of the evils of industrialism. They formed societies to attack prostitution and to improve the conditions in hospitals, jails, and other social institutions.

The Influence of Abolitionism

A few women abolitionists, such as the Grimké sisters, came to equate traditional female roles with slavery. Among the male abolitionists who accepted this equation was William Lloyd Garrison, who insisted on "universal emancipation" for enslaved men and all women. Women's experiences within the abolitionist movement taught them organizational and political skills that they carried over to the women's rights movement.

The Program of Seneca Falls

Most women were not so radical as to challenge the institution of marriage or women's traditional role within it but, rather, chose to focus on women's legal position. In 1848, Elizabeth Cady Stanton and Lucretia Mott, leading female abolitionists, called the first United States convention to address women's rights, in Seneca Falls, New York. Basing their program on the republican principles of the Declaration of Independence, they asserted women's full equality with men. After Seneca Falls, national women's rights meetings became annual events. Susan B. Anthony joined Stanton in the 1850s, creating effective political lobbying campaigns for women's rights. Their only legislative accomplishment was the revision of states' property laws, allowing married women to keep their own property and working women to keep their own wages. Other women, such as Harriet Beecher Stowe and Sojourner Truth, criticized slavery for its destruction of families, black and white.

Abolitionism (pp. 396-403)

Among reform movements, the drive to end slavery emerged predominant in the 1840s and 1850s. In the 1830s, northern whites shifted their efforts from accepting slavery as a "necessary evil" to recognizing that it was a sin that should be ended. They pursued four strategies to achieve their goals as well as to broaden the movement: supporting African colonization, promoting and aiding slaves in their efforts at escape or rebellion, appealing to the Christian conscience of slaveowners, and advocating a free-soil policy that prohibited slavery in all new territories.

African Colonization

The American Colonization Society, founded in 1817, hoped to gradually emancipate slaves by compensating their owners and then sending the former slaves, as well as free northern African Americans, to a colony in Africa. White northerners, with a racist opinion of blacks as degenerate, found colonization attractive because it promised to remove African Americans from American society. Southerners felt that colonization was necessary to prevent a race war. Popular among many people who disliked African Americans but opposed slavery, the American Colonization Society established the colony of Liberia on the western coast of Africa but sent only 1,400 African Americans there.

Slave Rebellion

Most African Americans considered the United States to be their home and denounced colonization as well as slavery. Free African Americans in the North published newspapers and pamphlets supporting immediate abolition. David Walker's pamphlet exhorting slave rebellions to end slavery began to reach the free black community in the South and triggered the rebellion led by Nat Turner in Virginia in 1831.

White southerners' fears of slave uprisings increased after Nat Turner's rebellion and led them to pass tougher slaves codes, enact harsher laws restricting slaves' activities, and prohibit anyone from teaching slaves to read, thus limiting the ability of slaves to acquire any news of abolitionism that might influence them to revolt.

Evangelical Abolitionism

Evangelical religions inspired many young men to call for the end of slavery as a Christian duty. William Lloyd Garrison founded the antislavery paper *The Liberator* in 1831 and the New England Anti-Slavery Society in 1832, both of which demanded immediate abolition. He attacked colonization as racist and assailed the Constitution as "an agreement with Hell" because it recognized slavery. Garrison's radicalism attracted a loyal few but repelled most. In contrast, Theodore Dwight Weld was a more moderate abolitionist. Weld preached antislavery in churches throughout the North and the Old Northwest. He believed opposition to slavery was a Christian's moral duty. His sermons and writings gave wide publicity to the cruelty of slavery.

Weld, Garrison, and the wealthy Tappan brothers helped found the American Anti-Slavery Society in 1833; through religious revivals and mass communications, they hoped to create a public climate that was hostile to slavery. They also sought to help slaves who wanted to escape from the South through the "underground railroad." Finally, they planned to have local antislavery groups pressure Congress through petitions against slavery. Thousands of middle-class men and women responded to these strategies with passion. Thoreau's works extolling nonconformism and radical responsibility aided their efforts. Inspired, women abolitionists founded their own antislavery societies.

Opposition and Disunity

Some northerners sympathized with the southern argument, fearing that an attack on slavery might become a more general attack on private property. The economic self-interest of northern textile manufacturers who depended on southern cotton led them to fear abolition activities. Wage earners, too, feared competition for their jobs from freed slaves. The result was that northern mobs attacked abolitionist speakers. Meanwhile, southern leaders moved from defending slavery as a "necessary evil" to asserting it as a "positive good," arguing that slavery benefited slaves by protecting them from the harshness of an industrial society. Southern ministers also cited the biblical command that servants should obey their masters. Southern legislatures passed harsh laws against abolitionist activity in the South. In the national House of Representatives, southerners succeeded in passing a "gag rule" that prohibited the acknowledgment of antislavery petitions. Internal divisions developed among abolitionists over whether to focus on abolitionism alone or to place it within a broader campaign for the reform of American society. The violence against abolitionism and the suppression of free speech led many Americans to fear that abolitionism might undermine social order and threaten the unity of the nation.

In the 1840s, evangelical abolitionists turned to practical politics, seeking the support of moderate voters. Garrison, who had become more committed to broad-based social transformation, precipitated a split in the antislavery movement. Many of those who disagreed with Garrison turned their attention to electoral politics through the newly organized Liberty Party.

EXPANDED TIMELINE

1817 **American Colonization Society founded**
Northerners who wanted to remove free African Americans from northern society and southerners who felt that blacks could not cope in a free society joined to create the American Colonization Society, whose goal was to send African Americans back to Africa. Its supporters eventually founded the colony of Liberia.

1829 **David Walker's *Appeal* encourages slave revolts**
This pamphlet by a free African American living in Boston advocated and threatened a slave rebellion. When the pamphlet began to reach southern free African Americans, the white South's fear of slave violence increased. Walker and other African American abolitionists called a national convention at which free blacks condemned northern discrimination as well as slavery. They advocated legal means to improve their situation.

1830 **Joseph Smith publishes *The Book of Mormon***
Responding to angelic revelation, Smith told of Christ's visit to the Western Hemisphere. His book became the founding doctrine for the Church of Jesus Christ of Latter-Day Saints, Mormonism.

1831 **William Lloyd Garrison begins *The Liberator*, an antislavery weekly**
Garrison's paper gave him a national forum in which to demand an immediate end to slavery and condemn colonization. Garrison's passionate abolitionism led him to criticize the Constitution because it recognized slavery. *The Liberator* made him a leader among radical abolitionists and helped to convince white southerners that the North was hostile to them.

Nat Turner's rebellion
Turner, an educated, favored slave with deep Christian beliefs, felt that he had been entrusted with a divine

mission to organize a slave rebellion. He and his small force killed almost sixty white southerners before they dispersed and were hunted down by the militia. White southerners reacted by passing harsher laws to maintain slavery and by using terror as a deterrent to other would-be rebels.

1832 **Ralph Waldo Emerson resigns his pulpit**
Emerson's resignation marked the beginnings of the transcendentalist movement, as he left organized religion and chose to emphasize individuality, self-reliance, dissent, and nonconformity in his popular public lectures and writings.

New England Anti-Slavery Society founded
William Lloyd Garrison founded this organization to press politically for the immediate abolition of slavery. The group embraced his radical approach to reform.

1834 **New York Female Moral Reform Society established**
From their position as society's moral guardians, women reformers attempted to protect the home through public action. The New York Female Moral Reform Society was the first major women's organization that tried to end prostitution. Women reformers also tried to improve the conditions in mental asylums and jails.

1836 **House of Representatives adopts gag rule**
The "gag rule" allowed southern congressmen to table all antislavery petitions so that they could not be debated or even acknowledged. This suppression of free speech shocked many northerners.

1840 **Liberty Party runs James G. Birney for president**
Founded by moderate abolitionists who had split with Garrison, the Liberty Party was the first political party to focus on abolition. It was relatively unsuccessful until it changed its emphasis to criticizing slavery as a threat to republican ideals.

1841 **Transcendentalists found Brook Farm, a utopian community**
Brook Farm was an attempt by transcendentalists to create a society based on individual self-realization and harmony, as opposed to conformism and commercialism. The enterprise failed for many reasons, particularly because of its inability to achieve economic self-sufficiency.

Dorothea Dix promotes investigations for the insane
Dix's work started with her investigation into the conditions in a Massachusetts jail for women. She went on to reform thousands of prisons and asylums for the mentally ill.

1844 **Margaret Fuller's *Woman in the Nineteenth Century***
Fuller's work, which asserted women's equality with men, was based on the transcendentalist faith in individualism.

1845 **Henry David Thoreau withdraws to Walden Pond**
Thoreau's experiences while living on Walden Pond became the basis for *Walden*, in which he celebrated simplicity and a nature mysticism that exalted self-discovery over the demands of a civilized society.

1846 **Mormons trek to Salt Lake under Brigham Young**
Seeking religious independence and physical safety, Brigham Young assumed leadership from the murdered Joseph Smith and led more than ten thousand Mormon followers across the plains from Illinois.

1848 **John Humphrey Noyes founds Oneida community**
Oneida was a utopian community based on cooperation and Christian ethics. Noyes believed that perfection—freedom from sin—was possible and attempted to achieve this goal through his advocacy of "complex marriage," which became a scandal to mainstream society.

Seneca Falls convention proposes women's equality
This first meeting of women's rights supporters outlined a program for equality that was rooted in the republican ideology of the Declaration of Independence.

1851 **Herman Melville's *Moby Dick***
This American classic attacked individualism and self-reliance, the transcendentalists' creed, as dangerously mad.

Susan B. Anthony joins movement for women's rights
With experience in antislavery and temperance reform movements, Anthony committed her organizational talents to the women's cause. She helped organize a network of women across New York State who involved themselves in politics to advocate legal rights for women.

1852 **Harriet Beecher Stowe's *Uncle Tom's Cabin***
Stowe's emotional book criticized slavery for its destruction of the slave family and the degradation of slave women. In the North, it became one of the most popular books of its day.

1855 **Walt Whitman's *Leaves of Grass***
Whitman published the first edition of his poetic celebration of individualism and American democracy.

1858 **The "Mormon War" over polygamy**
Pressured by churches and political opponents who opposed the Mormon practice of polygamy, President Buchanan sent federal troops into Utah after removing

Brigham Young as territorial governor; however, he withdrew the troops in the face of Mormon refusal to end polygamy, fearing that forcing the issue might require him to force the end of slavery, too.

GLOSSARY

individualism In the early nineteenth century, more Americans found that they were on their own socially, and able to pursue their self-interest free from the ties and constraints of social classes, groups, families, and institutions. Though some observers worried that this was itself a cause of social disorder, others saw in it a chance for people to achieve a deeper understanding of the self and a heightened ability to develop their talents and ideas. This view of the self was increasingly called individualism. (p. 380)

Romanticism Romantics believed that true insight and understanding of the human soul or spirit came not from reason but from passions, emotions, and intuitions. Transcendentalists in America employed these ideas to tap into the mysterious intuitive powers of the self, and thus liberate and empower the self to take an active role in shaping the world. Many reformers were inspired by these ideas to commit themselves to morally reform society. (p. 380)

Unitarian Unitarians, deriving their ideas from rationalist deists, believed that God is a single being. They did not accept the Christian story of God the Father, the Son, and the Holy Spirit and thus moved outside the mainstream of American Christianity. Ralph Waldo Emerson was a Unitarian minister until he resigned his position in 1832 and gave up organized religion in favor of personal contemplation and moral insight. (p. 380)

materialism The philosophical belief that physical matter is the only reality and that all ideas and concepts are rooted in and can be understood in terms of that material reality. Transcendentalists such as Ralph Waldo Emerson were idealists who believed that behind the concrete world one could comprehend through the senses was an ideal world of universal ideas and concepts. (p. 381)

pantheism The idea that the world around us is God. Having created it, God is nature itself. Emerson saw God as represented by, or reflected or saturated in, nature. This implied that God may exist apart from nature, an idea that Christians accepted. (p. 381)

transcendentalism Transcendentalists believed that each individual had an inner, intuitive power that, if tapped, allowed one to go beyond normal experience to acquire some mystical knowledge of oneself and the world. One accessed this intuitive power through contemplation of the God-saturated world of nature, in which one could recognize the mystic harmony that exists between oneself and the soul of nature, or the "currents of Universal Being." Transcendentalist intellectuals such as Emerson and Thoreau emphasized the search for such meaning through the expression of one's individuality in self-reliant and nonconformist ways. (p. 381)

American Lyceum The American Lyceum was a speakers' bureau that sent ministers, transcendentalists, and scientists all across the North on speaking tours. It did much to spread transcendentalism and reform movements. (p. 381)

socialism The general political theory that argues that the means of production, distribution, and ownership of property should be shared by a collective entity or government or distributed equally or equitably among the members of a society. In such a system, there is no private property. Communal groups such as Brook Farm, the Shakers, the Fourierists, and the Oneida community were all socialists. (pp. 384–390)

celibacy The practice of abstaining from sexual intercourse. Mother Ann Lee Stanley, the founder of the Shakers, believed sexual gratification was the source of all corruption and prohibited sexual intercourse among the members of her communities. (p. 385)

phalanx A phalanx was the name given to a cooperative community in the American Fourierist movement, in which all members were shareholders in the community's property and laborers received the largest portion of the community's earnings. Phalanxes spread from Massachusetts to Michigan during the 1840s. (p. 386)

perfectionism Perfectionists held the religious belief that people could be perfect, or free from sin, because the Second Coming of Christ had already occurred. Perfectionism was an evangelical movement that impelled reformers to attempt to correct social wrongs. (pp. 387–388)

complex marriage John Humphrey Noyes led his Oneida community in the practice of complex marriage, based on the belief that all members of the community were married to one another. In his community, Noyes sought to free women from ownership by men and to give all members the freedom to pursue sexual fulfillment, which, through birth control and self-restraint, he hoped would not lead to procreation. Through sexual control, Noyes sought to achieve social control of the community. (p. 388)

counterculture Something that is countercultural exists or acts in opposition to the mainstream values of a society or culture. Counterculture activities posit an alternative way of doing things, a different set of values, or a new social structure. Reform movements, like those of the mid-nineteenth century, are often countercultural. (p. 388)

polygamy The practice of one man's having two or more wives at the same time. Some Mormons practiced polygamy until it was abolished in 1890. (p. 389)

moral reform One of the first reform movements in which women publicly participated, moral reform attempted to end prostitution and to protect single women, among other goals. The first moral-reform society was founded in New York City in 1834 and quickly became a national organization. (p. 391)

colonization The American Colonization Society, founded in 1817, supported the movement to end slavery by sending free African Americans to Africa. Supporters of colonization included those who wanted to end slavery as well as those who were concerned chiefly with removing blacks from white society. (p. 396)

abolition The immediate and uncompensated end of slavery. (p. 400)

gag rule Southerners achieved passage of a "gag rule" in the House of Representatives, an informal procedure that enabled congressmen to ignore antislavery petitions by tabling them as soon as they were received. The gag rule infuriated northerners, who saw in it a violation of freedom of speech. (p. 403)

IDENTIFICATION

Identify by filling in the blanks.

1. The leading spokesman for transcendentalism, a former minister who moved to Concord, Massachusetts, was _____. (p. 380)

2. The _____ spread public awareness of transcendentalism by arranging speaking tours for its spokespeople. (p. 381)

3. Henry David Thoreau named his most famous book after _____, where he went to experiment with a life of simplicity. (p. 382)

4. The feminist author of *Woman in the Nineteenth Century*, who in 1844 proclaimed a new era of gender relations, was _____. (p. 382)

5. The novelist Nathaniel Hawthorne set his book *The Blithedale Romance* in the utopian community of _____. (p. 384)

6. Phalanxes were based on the ideas of the French utopian _____. (p. 386)

7. The founder of Oneida, John Humphrey Noyes, sought to organize his community through the practice of _____. (p. 388)

8. After the murder of Joseph Smith, _____ led settlers to the Great Salt Lake. (p. 389)

9. Middle-class women built a common identity around the concept of _____. (p. 391)

10. Through their experiences in the _____ movement, the Grimké sisters came to assert the equality of men and women. (p. 392)

11. Women at the Seneca Falls convention based their declaration of principles on the _____. (p. 393)

12. The activities of American Colonization Society supporters led to the creation of the African nation of _____. (p. 397)

13. In his *Appeal . . . to the Colored Citizens*, _____ justified and advocated slave rebellion, which terrified white southerners. (p. 399)

14. The major financial backers for the American and Foreign Anti-Slavery Society were the brothers _____. (p. 400)

15. Henry David Thoreau claimed that citizens could transcend their complicity in slavery and redeem the state through _____, also the title of his essay. (p. 401)

16. The _____ prevented antislavery petitions from being debated in Congress. (p. 403)

FEATURES EXERCISES

Voices from Abroad

The Mystical World of the Shakers (p. 386)

The Shakers were a sect derived from the Quakers. They sought to live orderly, peaceful, and sinless lives through ascetic discipline and meetings at which members were encouraged to experience the inner light. But rather than sit quietly like the Quakers, the Shakers felt that more movement and the expression of emotion would enable them to experience this "gift." As you read this account of a Shaker service by a British visitor, ask yourself the following questions:

1. How did the Shakers alter the Quaker service? To what purpose?
2. How were Shaker practices similar to or different from those of evangelical Christians during the Second Great Awakening?
3. How and why did the Shakers add Indian ritual to enhance their own service?
4. What did the writer think was "American" about the Shaker service?

American Voices

An Illinois "Jeffersonian" Attacks the Mormons (p. 390)

The Mormons moved west in 1839 and established a settlement at Nauvoo, Illinois, on the Mississippi River. In a few years, immigration made Nauvoo one of the largest towns in the region. Mormon leadership exerted theocratic rule over the town and the people. From the start, the Mormons were unwelcome neighbors, and frictions between them and American "gentile" settlers increased. As you read "An Illinois 'Jeffersonian' Attacks the Mormons," ask yourself the following questions:

1. What does this person think of the Mormon Church? Why?
2. What are his political objections to their activities?
3. Does he charge the Mormon leadership with any crime?
4. Given what he says about what the Mormons have allegedly done to deserve his "condemnation," what is this Jeffersonian's view of how society and politics should work?

American Lives

Dorothea Dix: Public Woman (pp. 394–395)

Dorothea Dix was the foremost social reformer of the nineteenth century. She began by organizing and running "charity schools" for indigent children and became interested in providing Sunday school for women in prison. This led to a growing interest in the treatment of people living in insane asylums, which resulted in her launching a movement to improve asylums and prisons across the country. During the Civil War, Dix became Union superintendent of nurses, making her the highest-ranked woman in the federal government. As social reformer, lobbyist, activist, and feminist, Dix was, in many ways, ahead of her time.

As you read "Dorothea Dix: Public Woman," ask yourself the following questions:

1. In what ways did Dix's early experiences prepare her for her reform activities in the 1840s and later?
2. What tactics did Dix employ in her reform efforts? How were they different from the tactics of many of her contemporaries?
3. What led Dix to believe that federal activism was necessary to improve care for mental patients?
4. What role did outside national issues have in shaping Dix's career as a reformer?

American Voices

LUCY STONE, The Question of Women's Rights (p. 398)

The early feminist movement, though grounded in the principles of the Declaration of Independence and essential rights due to all people, pursued the issue of women's rights through very practical issues of law and opportunity. In this talk, Lucy Stone articulates this practical approach by drawing on her personal experience as a woman living in the United States in the 1850s. For her, it was a society and a system that was full of roadblocks, in which she had to make decisions based on a lack of property and income that led to disappointment.

As you read "Lucy Stone, The Question of Women's Rights," ask yourself the following questions:

1. What experiences have made Lucy Stone a "disappointed" woman? What is the nature of her disappointment?
2. According to Stone, how did contemporary society "pervert" marriage?
3. According to her discussion, what was the life expectation of most middle-class white women in antebellum America?
4. What does Stone mean when she says that "the question of Women's Rights is a practical one"?
5. In Stone's view, how do women's rights help men?

SELF-TEST

Multiple Choice

1. Ralph Waldo Emerson encouraged listeners and readers to seek transcendence to a higher reality because he wanted them to:
   a. experience an evangelical Christian conversion experience.
   b. join moral-reform movements for temperance, maintaining the Sabbath, and the abolition of slavery.
   c. celebrate and energize individualism.
   d. vote for the Democratic Party.

2. Critics of transcendentalism such as Nathaniel Hawthorne and Herman Melville focused on:
   a. the perils of excessive individualism.
   b. scandals in the private lives of prominent transcendentalists.
   c. the emphasis on destabilizing social reform among the transcendentalists.
   d. the lack of financial stability within transcendentalist communities.

3. Brook Farm appealed primarily to:
   a. religious zealots.
   b. New England intellectuals.
   c. farmers and craft workers.
   d. perfectionists.

4. Arthur Brisbane promoted the concept of the phalanx in:
   a. *Self-Reliance.*
   b. *Democracy in America.*
   c. *The Dial.*
   d. *The Social Destiny of Man.*

5. Ideas that the Shakers supported include *all* of the following *except*:
   a. celibacy.
   b. abstention from alcohol.
   c. complex marriage.
   d. abstention from politics and war.

6. Perfectionists believed that freedom from sin was possible:
   a. if people isolated themselves from society.
   b. if people practiced celibacy.
   c. because Christ's Second Coming had already occurred.
   d. for communities that practiced group ownership of property.

7. Congress rejected a Mormon petition to create a new state extending to the Pacific Ocean called:
   a. Nauvoo.   c. Moroni.
   b. Carthage.   d. Deseret.

8. Moral reform was primarily a women's movement to:
   a. end prostitution.
   b. restrict the consumption of alcohol.
   c. enforce Sabbath rules.
   d. work for antislavery.

9. Both an abolitionist and a supporter of women's rights, the author of *Uncle Tom's Cabin* was:
   a. Lucy Stone.
   b. Elizabeth Cady Stanton.
   c. Sarah Grimké.
   d. Harriet Beecher Stowe.

10. Before the Civil War, women in the state of New York achieved *all* of the following *except* the right:
    a. of widows to their property after their husbands' death.
    b. of working women to collect their own wages.
    c. to vote.
    d. to bring suit in court.

11. Supporters of the American Colonization Society were prompted by *all* of the following reasons *except* the:
    a. desire to remove free African Americans from the North.
    b. belief that African Americans were inferior.
    c. belief that blacks should live in equality with whites.
    d. desire to avoid a race war in the South.

12. *All* of the following were directly influenced by Charles Finney, the evangelical Christian preacher who touched off a major revival across New York State during the Second Great Awakening to become a minister or a reformer *except*:
    a. Theodore Dwight Weld, abolitionist.
    b. Joseph Smith, Mormon leader.
    c. John Humphrey Noyes, founder of the Oneida community.
    d. Dorothea Dix, reformer.

13. The abolitionist strategies to eliminate slavery in America included *all* of the following *except*:
    a. encourage slaves' to escape to the North or to Canada.
    b. purchase slaves' freedom through a massive program of remuneration to southern masters.
    c. convince people of the evil of slavery through mass propaganda and publicity.
    d. use political pressure to pursue antislavery legislation.

14. Southerners responded to the abolitionist movement and to fears of slave rebellion in *all* of the following ways *except*:
    a. toughening slave codes.
    b. ending the foreign slave trade.

c. defending slavery as a "positive good" rather than a "necessary evil."
d. limiting slave movements and prohibiting them from reading.

15. The more successful tactic of the American Anti-Slavery Society in affecting public opinion was to:
    a. donate substantially to the American Colonization Society.
    b. pressure Congress through petitions.
    c. mail abolitionist pamphlets throughout the country.
    d. hold dramatic public meetings with passionate speakers.

16. Many northerners were troubled by abolitionist tactics for *all* of the following reasons *except:*
    a. freed slaves might take the jobs of northern wage earners.
    b. Christian doctrine appeared to support slavery.
    c. abolitionists actively involved women in the movement.
    d. many northerners feared racial mixing.

Short Essays

Answer the following questions in a brief paragraph.

1. How did Emerson think the individual should respond to the society the Industrial Revolution had created? (pp. 380–381)
2. Why was individualism so deeply rooted in different aspects of American social reform? How did the transformation of individualism from the 1820s through the 1840s change American society? (pp. 380–384)
3. In what ways did Thoreau, Whitman, Poe, and Hawthorne either support or criticize individualism? (pp. 382–384)
4. Why did so many utopian communities adopt communal ownership of property as opposed to private property? Doesn't this contradict the main individualistic tendency of the time? (pp. 384–390)
5. How did early feminists argue for women's rights? What issues were most important to them? (pp. 390–396)
6. What were the attitudes of white southerners and northerners outside the abolitionist movement toward abolitionism? How did they gradually change? (pp. 402–404)
7. Which of the abolitionist's strategies undertaken to achieve their goal was most effective? Why? (pp. 400–401)

ANSWERS

Identification

1. Ralph Waldo Emerson
2. American Lyceum
3. Walden Pond
4. Margaret Fuller
5. Brook Farm
6. Charles Fourier
7. complex marriage
8. Brigham Young; Mormon
9. separate domestic sphere
10. abolitionist
11. Declaration of Independence
12. Liberia
13. David Walker
14. Arthur and Lewis Tappan
15. civil disobedience
16. gag rule

Self-Test

Multiple Choice

1. c.	7. d.	13. b.
2. a.	8. a.	14. b.
3. b.	9. d.	15. c.
4. d.	10. c.	16. b.
5. c.	11. c.	
6. c.	12. d.	

Short Essays

1. For Emerson, the erosion of traditional constraints on the individual presented each person with an opportunity to achieve individual freedom. He encouraged people to rise above the daily pressures of work and their preoccupation with material consumption to try to achieve a spiritual sense of oneness with nature. In this way, he believed individuals could tap their deeper intuitive powers and gain the moral and spiritual insight to live fuller, more fulfilling lives.

2. Individualism, or the liberation of the individual from social ties and institutions, was deeply rooted in a variety of cultural responses to the social changes caused by the Industrial Revolution. Emerson encouraged people to seek their intuitive moral powers. At the same time, competition in the marketplace prompted many people to pursue moral perfection through self-discipline. Likewise, evangelical Christians encouraged individuals to take control of their salvation by seeking a mystical union with God through a conversion experience. In each realm, individuals sought a heightened state of moral awareness and thus tended to pursue social reform. Individualism transformed American society from a traditional society in which individuals acted according to the expectations of family, class, and institutional agendas to a dynamic society in which the individual was both the source of social order and the driving force behind social change.

3. Thoreau and Whitman argued that the individual who broke away from tradition and social restraints could through contemplation or action achieve a deeply fulfilling nonconformist life. Though both admitted that this effort could fill one with anxiety and pain, they also promised that a happier life would follow. Poe and Hawthorne were less optimistic. They believed that the individual, cut free from the social order, would be unable to control his or her passions and thus either become obsessed with him or herself to the exclusion of others or be so wracked with guilt for violating the social order that he or she would suffer intensely and ultimately be destroyed.

4. The social organization and practices of utopian social communities, in general, reflected the tensions and strain traditional people felt in an increasingly individualist, industrial society. They believed that individual self-interest, the possession of private property, unequal social and labor relations, and sexual desire were the sources of most social inequality, discord, corruption, and evil. Most people tried to neutralize the negative effect of these desires and passions on social relations through the communal ownership of property as well as communal work routines and social activities. The Shakers tried to eliminate the inequities caused by sexual difference by practicing celibacy. The Fourierists tried to eliminate the burden of domestic duties on women. The members of the Oneida community practiced complex marriage, in which all individuals were married to one another and were free to pursue sexual fulfillment without the restraints of a monogamous relationship. Though it seems as if members of utopian communities surrendered their individuality to a higher common purpose, many argued that, in fact, members of these communities, liberated from social forces that created inequality and corruption, were more free to pursue happiness and perfection. Communalism, therefore, was a direct result of the individualistic impulses that were transforming American society.

5. Women's enhanced moral role at home and their central role in social-reform efforts elevated their public status in American life. As some women who were involved in female moral reform shifted their attention to the issue of abolitionism, they became increasingly frustrated by the discrimination they faced and began to challenge the lower status of women. Most women's rights activists called for full and equal rights for women. Reformers fought for and won laws that gave married women legal rights over their property. They also fought for the passage of laws that gave women the right to their earnings from work, the right to custody over their children, and the right to sue and testify in court. After achieving these goals, women's rights activists began a long campaign to gain the right to vote.

6. Most white southerners and northerners opposed abolition. In the North, many felt that the attack on slavery would lead to a larger challenge to property rights. Others feared labor competition from freed blacks, declining wages, racial mixing, the decline of family order, and social disorder in general. In the South, whites opposed abolitionism as a direct attack on property and social order and defended slavery as a "positive good." Over time, more northerners gradually became convinced of the moral injustice of slavery and grew more sympathetic to the abolitionist cause, while southerners only became more adamant in their opposition.

7. Abolitionists employed three main strategies to achieve their goal of abolition: they sought to influence public opinion through a massive literature campaign; they pressured Congress and state legislatures with petitions, and they organized a network to help slaves escape from the South. In the 1830s and 1840s, the literature campaign created tensions within and outside the movement and caused a broad-based resistance to their efforts. Meanwhile, Congress tabled all petitions concerning slavery from 1836 through 1844. By the 1840s, about one thousand slaves a year were escaping to freedom with the aid of abolitionists. In real terms, therefore, the last strategy had the greatest impact, though, in relation to the total number of slaves, it was still very limited and did little to advance the cause of abolition.

Chapter 13

The Crisis of the Union, 1844–1860

LEARNING OBJECTIVES

1. How and why did Americans find it harder to compromise politically after 1840?

2. Did the politicians of the 1840s and the 1850s formulate policies that shaped the course of events, or did they simply respond to the unfolding of events as shaped by the people?

3. How and why did the Mexican War begin? Were the reasons for beginning the war valid?

4. How and why did the Compromise of 1850 undermine the stability of the American political party system?

5. In what ways did the Supreme Court contribute to the developing crisis between the North and the South?

6. How does a party like the Whigs fall apart? How does a party like the Republicans develop and evolve? How did the demise of an established party and the appearance of a new party affect the political system?

CHAPTER SUMMARY

By the 1840s, economic growth and social reform had made the North and the South increasingly different economies, societies, and cultures. When these emerging differences intersected with ambitions over the control of the West, sectional differences became different visions of the American future. In the political struggle to determine the course of expansion and the social and institutional development of the new territories, residents of both North and South increasingly viewed the prospects for their region as dependent on keeping up with the other region. The passions of increasing sectionalism would end the Second Party System and endanger the Union.

Manifest Destiny (pp. 408–414)

The push of American settlers into the Mexican province of Texas, as well as into Oregon and California, encouraged expansionists to dream of an American nation that stretched all the way to the Pacific. As Americans considered the potential size of the nation, politicians began to articulate expansion policies to pursue their political ambitions. Such policies, they hoped, would unify both their parties and the nation. But rising popular enthusiasm for expansion inevitably involved the question of whether slavery would expand, too. As a result, the issue of slavery again entered the national political debate, and sectional agendas began to prevail over national ones, threatening the stability of the Union. The question of Texas and the expansion of settlers in California and Oregon set in motion a series of events that would unravel the Compromise of 1820 and embroil the nation in sectional conflict.

The Independence of Texas

In 1835 American settlers in Texas, who outnumbered Mexicans by more than eight to one, rose up in a short but bloody rebellion against Mexico to gain their independence. When the citizens of the Republic of Texas voted by plebiscite for annexation to the United States, they placed American politicians in a predicament. Many feared that if the United States accepted Texas's request, a war with Mexico would follow. More important, they feared that the expected American victory would bring Texas into the Union as a slave state, thus unraveling the Missouri Compromise of 1820 and destabilizing national politics.

The Push to the Pacific

In the 1840s, more Americans came to believe that the nation had a Manifest Destiny to extend its domain to the Pacific and thus draw parts of Mexico and Canada into the republic. Settlers heeded the call by migrating overland to Oregon and, to a lesser extent, to California. An American presence in Oregon, California, and Texas compelled the national government to settle the issue of the boundary between Oregon and Canada and address the interest of Americans migrating into Mexican territory in California in joining California to the United States.

The Fateful Election of 1844

Popular enthusiasm for expansion of the national boundaries became the central issue of the election of 1844. Southern Democrats led by James K. Polk sought the annexation of Texas. When the Whig candidate Henry Clay wavered on the question of Texas, northerners who had opposed previous efforts to annex Texas on the grounds that annexation would expand slavery shifted their support to other candidates. Polk, ambitious politically and ardently expansionist, won the election. Democrats overrode Whig opposition to a new slave state with a joint resolution of Congress calling for annexation. Political compromise had been sacrificed to ambition and expansion.

War, Expansion, and Slavery, 1846–1850 (pp. 414–425)

American success in the Mexican War led to the annexation of a vast region of the Southwest to the United States. The war and the annexation of territory destabilized both parties. Only after a complex set of six legislative acts among political parties increasingly divided over the issue of slavery, was a compromise reached. But the cost was high. The Compromise of 1850 ended the Missouri Compromise and increasingly sectionalized political views on slavery.

The War with Mexico, 1846–1848

Having acquired Texas, James Polk was now determined to add the Mexican provinces of New Mexico and California to the United States. When an effort to purchase the provinces failed, Polk fomented rebellion in both regions, and then sent the American army to the Mexican border to provoke a fight. While American settlers in California rose in revolt, the army invaded New Mexico and, then, upon facing unexpected resistance, approved a military strike deep into Mexico. Following the route of Cortés, American troops seized Mexico City and forced Mexico to cede New Mexico and California to the United States.

A Divisive Victory

Instead of unifying the nation behind a fight between democracy and a corrupt weak regime, the war divided the country and American politics. Whigs and Democrats disagreed both on which territory to annex to the United States and on whether slavery should be allowed in the new territory. The expansionist President Polk, who had dreamed of taking "All Mexico," compromised and purchased only New Mexico and California from Mexico. But the addition of this vast territory to the United States only heightened northerners' fears of a "Slave Power" conspiracy. In response, many northerners joined the Free Soil Party, which viewed slavery as a threat to free republican institutions. When David Wilmot, a northern Democrat, offered an amendment that would prohibit slavery in the new territories acquired from Mexico, northern Democrats drifted into the Free Soil Party, or joined "conscience Whigs," who opposed the expansion of slavery. Pressed on the issue, the Democrats remained vague about the expansion of slavery in the election of 1848. The Whigs managed to smooth over sectional differences within the party by nominating the southerner, Zachary Taylor, who, as a military hero, had national appeal. Because the Free Soil Party drew enough votes away from the Democrats, Taylor was elected. Now southerners feared that many northerners were determined to end slavery. Increasing fear in both North and South that the other side sought either to expand or end slavery changed the dynamics of American politics.

1850: Crisis and Compromise

The California gold rush, which drew eighty thousand immigrants to the territory in 1849, accelerated the change in political dynamics. Zachary Taylor, seeking to attract Free Soilers and northern Democrats to the weak Whig Party, supported California's quick admission to the Union as a free state. Though Taylor assured them that he would protect slavery, southerners feared that the entrance of California would tip the balance of national power in favor of the North and threaten the future of slavery. When, in exchange for accepting California as a free state, southerners demanded much stronger federal support of slavery, politics hit an impasse. With strong opponents on both sides, the debate led to a series of legislative acts but left both sides uneasy. The admission of California as a free state and the abolition of slavery in Washington, D. C., convinced many southerners that northerners were committed to ending slavery. The passage of the Fugitive Slave Act and the establishment of the idea of popular sovereignty, which allowed a territory's residents to decide whether that territory would be slave or free, convinced many northerners that southerners had gained a permanent advantage by turning back the Missouri Compromise. The emotional, mostly negative responses to the Compromise, pointed the way to more political conflict.

The End of the Second Party System, 1850–1858 (pp. 425–434)

Resistance to the compromise of 1850 further divided Americans along sectional lines. Northern resistance to the Fugitive Slave Act coalesced sectional opposition to slavery. Northern Whigs could no longer operate within a party that included southern Whigs, and the national party fell apart. Former northern conscience Whigs, as well as northern Democrats, Free Soilers, and members of the short-lived Liberty and Know-Nothing parties, coalesced into the Republican Party, a northern party that stood for limiting the expansion of slavery while allowing it to survive in the South. Democrat James Buchanan was faced with the balancing act of maintaining a compromise between southern interests and free soil. The *Dred Scott* decision, which voided the Missouri Compromise, as well as Buchanan's effort to bring Kansas in as a slave state, however, only deepened the split in his own party and the nation.

Resistance to the Fugitive Slave Act

Northerners challenged the Fugitive Slave Act through argument, propaganda (exemplified by Harriet Beecher Stowe's book, *Uncle Tom's Cabin*), extending legal rights to fugitives, and noncompliance with federal law. These activities helped intensify northern opposition to slavery and made the act a "dead letter."

The Whigs' Decline and the Democrats' Diplomacy

The Whig Party, already weakened by the deaths of Henry Clay and Daniel Webster, was divided and ultimately undermined by the Fugitive Slave Act, as massive numbers of southerners left its ranks. In the election of 1852, the equally divided Democrats finally compromised on Franklin Pierce. Pierce swept the election, but then launched an expansionist foreign policy that further inflamed northerners' fears of an expansionist South.

The Kansas-Nebraska Act and the Rise of New Parties

The increasing polarization between North and South came to a head in 1854 over the status of slavery in the new territory of Nebraska proposed by Senator Stephen Douglas of Illinois. Southerners, who wanted assurance that slavery could be extended into the territories, objected to Douglas's plan out of fear that residents could declare a territory free. To curry their favor, Douglas proposed that slavery be determined by popular sovereignty, and that the territory be divided into Kansas and Nebraska, giving the southerners a better chance of controlling the more southern territory, Kansas. At the same time, Douglas tried to assure northerners that popular sovereignty could work in their favor. But many northerners saw the act as a clear attempt to extend slavery into the territories and abandoned the Whig Party for the newly formed Republican Party. The Republicans stood for individual liberty, capitalist enterprise, and the social mobility of the self-made man, to which they felt the expansion of slavery was a threat. Popular sovereignty touched off a bloody civil war in Kansas between pro- and antislavery forces. The anger over the violence in Kansas enhanced the Republican Party's power, as did its call for prohibition of slavery in all the territories as the only way to limit "Slave Power." Though Democrat James Buchanan won the election of 1856, the extent of support for the Republicans—a party with no southern contingent—pushed the Union to the edge of dissolution.

Buchanan's Failed Presidency

Before Buchanan could do anything as president, the Supreme Court, led by Chief Justice Roger B. Taney, pushed the nation further from compromise in the *Dred Scott* decision. Responding to the question of whether a former slave was made free by escaping to a free state, Taney argued that not only were slaves not citizens but that due process could never take away anyone's property, thus invalidating any law that had prohibited slavery in any territory. By voiding the Missouri Compromise and declaring the Republican platform unconstitutional, the Democrat-dominated Supreme Court confirmed the Republicans' worst fears. When Buchanan tried but failed to gain the admission of Kansas to the Union as a slave state, he further divided his party and the nation.

Abraham Lincoln and the Republican Triumph, 1858–1860 (pp. 434–437)

Lincoln was a self-made former state legislator, congressman, and lawyer whose early career embodied Whig and, later, Republican values. In his earlier speeches, especially in the Lincoln and Douglas debates in Illinois, Lincoln articulated the Republican position on slavery and his vision for the nation. Elected as a sectional candidate in 1860, Lincoln found himself president-elect of a deeply divided and confused nation.

Lincoln's Early Career

A chief spokesman for the Republican view was Abraham Lincoln. Aroused by the Kansas and Nebraska Act, Lincoln returned to politics to play a key role in the development of the Republican Party.

The Republican Politician

Lincoln was convinced that a "Slave Power" conspiracy to open the territories to slavery existed. On this premise, he played a strong role in establishing the Republican platform, calling for the prohibition of slavery in the territories followed by gradual emancipation of slaves. Through his simple rhetoric and skillful debating style—highlighted by his debates with Stephen Douglas in 1858—Lincoln played a key role in drawing all the various anti-Nebraska elements into the Republican Party and edging it toward national power. He also helped splinter the Democratic Party by forcing Douglas to revise his view of popular sovereignty, making him admit that settlers of a region might legitimately refuse to accept slavery, a view that cost him much radical and even moderate southern Democratic support. Southern fears of a gathering abolitionist conspiracy against slavery were exacerbated by John Brown's raid on a federal arsenal at Harpers Ferry, Virginia. Though Republicans tried to disavow a connection between Brown's raid and their platform, most observers in both the North and the South recognized the logical connection. So, too, was Virginia's execution of Brown taken as an expression of the state's determination to defend slavery. When Lincoln, arguing a moderate Republican line, defeated the divided Democratic Party in the election of 1860, he found himself president-elect of a nation in which the logic of events imperiled the future of the Union.

EXPANDED TIMELINE

1836 **Texas proclaims independence from Mexico**
Thousands of Americans who had settled in Texas fought a brief but bloody rebellion against Mexico and declared their independence as the Republic of Texas. Though the republic sought annexation to the United States right away, this would not occur for nine years.

1842 **Overland migration to Oregon begins**
Many Americans, inspired by the dream of a continental nation, migrated across the Great Plains and the Rocky Mountains to the fertile lands of Oregon. The American presence in the territory increasingly necessitated a clarification of the ownership of Oregon and its boundary with Canada.

1844 **Fate of Texas and Oregon dominate presidential election**
Because many northerners were being expansionist by calling for the ousting of the British from Oregon, southerners believed they could now pursue an expansionist policy of annexing Texas without being concerned about sectional discord. James K. Polk supported both, but by forcing through the annexation of Texas, he set off a sectional dispute over slavery.

1845 **John O'Sullivan coins term *Manifest Destiny***
Many Americans began to express expansionist dreams, supported by a sense of cultural and racial superiority, that the American republic should expand all the way to the Pacific Ocean. These dreams were supported simply by the belief that such expansion was the obvious, or manifest, destiny of the republic. The phrase *Manifest Destiny*, coined by a New York journalist, stuck.

Texas admitted to Union as a slave state
Encouraged by his election in 1844, James K. Polk, a Democrat, pursued Democratic policy in favor of annexation of Texas. Unable to acquire the necessary two-thirds majority in Congress, Democrats passed the annexation as a joint resolution. The annexation of Texas brought the divisive issue of slavery to the national level.

John Slidell's diplomatic mission to Mexico fails
Following his successful annexation of Texas, Polk pursued his ambition to further enlarge the American republic by exploring various strategies to acquire New Mexico and California. Polk sent John Slidell on a secret mission to purchase the territories from Mexico, but he really hoped that Mexican response would trigger a war. The Mexicans obliged by not only refusing Slidell's offer but by declaring the annexation of Texas illegal. Polk then had American forces build a fort on the Rio Grande to provoke a military response. Again, the Mexicans obliged by attacking American forces.

Expanded Timeline

1846 — **United States declares war on Mexico**
Oregon treaty ratified; 49th parallel becomes boundary
When Slidell's mission failed, Polk fomented rebellion in both New Mexico and California and provoked Mexico to respond militarily, leading to a declaration of war. To avoid a war with Britain at the same time, Polk compromised on his previous insistence that the Oregon border be at 54° 40' and established the Oregon boundary at the 49th parallel.

Walker Tariff lowers duties on imported goods
The rise of free trade encouraged Americans to lower tariffs, thus ending the Whig reliance on this issue to gain political support.

Wilmot Proviso proposes prohibiting slavery in territories acquired from Mexico
David Wilmot, a democratic representative from Pennsylvania expressing northern concerns about the impact of adding new territory to the United States, added a proposal to the military appropriations bill that slavery be prohibited in the new territories that might be acquired from Mexico. The Proviso became the first antislavery proposal to win popular support.

1847 — **Winfield Scott captures Mexico City**
After a series of battles in New Mexico and northern Mexico, American forces struck at the heart of Mexico in an invasion that followed the route Hernando Cortés had taken three centuries earlier. When forces led by Winfield Scott took Mexico City, the Mexicans were compelled to ask for peace.

1848 — **Gold discovered in California**
Treaty of Guadalupe Hidalgo gives northernmost provinces of Mexico to the United States.
Free Soil Party organized
In the treaty of Guadalupe Hidalgo, Mexico ceded New Mexico and California to the United States. While the addition of these new territories to the country raised concerns about the spread of slavery, the discovery of gold in California triggered a large immigration that, within a year, enabled California to apply for statehood as a free state. California's application touched off major southern concerns about the future of slavery. Meanwhile, northerners opposed to the expansion of slavery coalesced within a one-issue party called the Free Soil Party organized to advocate the prohibition of slavery in the territories. Slavery was becoming the issue that politically divided America.

1850 — **Compromise of 1850**
Henry Clay and Daniel Webster tried to defuse the rising tension over slavery through compromise. In a series of legislative acts, California was brought into the Union as a free state, the slave trade was abolished in Washington, D.C., the Fugitive Slave Act was passed, and the territories of New Mexico and Utah were established on the basis of the new concept of popular sovereignty, which would allow the people in the territory to decide the issue of whether the territory should be slave or free. Instead of defusing tensions, the compromise raised both sides' concerns about the future of slavery. Southerners became convinced that northerners wanted to abolish slavery, while northerners believed that the Fugitive Slave Act and "popular sovereignty" undermined the Missouri Compromise and would allow slavery to expand wherever it was not prohibited.

1851 — **American (Know-Nothing) Party formed**
In response to the immigration of Europeans into the United States, a nativist party, the American Party, evolved out of the political confusion of 1850. Many of its members had been involved in the anti-Catholic, anti-immigration passions of the 1830s and 1840s and sought to formally limit immigration, slow the process of naturalization, and disenfranchise recent immigrants. The party was nicknamed the "Know-Nothing" Party because party members were sworn to secrecy about the party's activities and some, when asked about the party, would reply "I know nothing."

1854 — **Kansas-Nebraska Act**
Republican Party formed
Illinois senator Stephen Douglas, desirous of establishing a transcontinental railroad that went west from Chicago, submitted a bill for the organization of a new territory of Nebraska. To placate southerners, he amended the bill to propose dividing the territory in two and allowing "popular sovereignty" to determine whether slavery would be permitted in the new territories. The Kansas-Nebraska Act polarized the debate over slavery and accelerated the development of the Republican Party, a northern party with a platform of prohibiting slavery in new territories.

1856 — **"Bleeding Kansas" undermines popular sovereignty**
When opposing sides in Kansas resorted to violence in an attempt to gain control over the issue of slavery, the claim that the population of a territory could peacefully decide whether to permit slavery, as Stephen Douglas suggested would happen according to his idea of "popular sovereignty," was dealt a serious blow.

1857 — ***Dred Scott v. Sandford* allows slavery in territories**
Since the Compromise of 1850, northerners had opposed the Fugitive Slave Act in word and deed. When former slave Dred Scott sued his master for freedom, claiming that residency with his master in a free territory freed him, the Supreme Court, led by Chief Justice Roger B. Taney, ruled that Scott, as a slave, could not sue in federal court. Taney also declared that not only was Scott still a slave but an individual's right of due process prohibited Congress from taking slaves, a form of property, from an owner and, therefore, from making any laws prohibiting slav-

ery in the territories. The decision invalidated all laws prohibiting slavery in the territories, going back to the Northwest Ordinance of 1787 and including the Missouri Compromise, and made the platform of the Republican Party unconstitutional. The *Dred Scott* decision convinced many northerners that the Republican fear of a conspiracy of "Slave Power" to allow slavery everywhere was, in fact, valid.

1858 **James Buchanan backs Lecompton constitution Lincoln-Douglas debates**
James Buchanan's support for Kansas's entrance into the Union as a slave state under a constitution written by proslavery forces at Lecompton did little to allay northern fears. In famous debates in Illinois, Abraham Lincoln pressed Stephen Douglas on his definition of *popular sovereignty* and how he could still maintain that settlers had the ability to decide on slavery after *Dred Scott*. When Douglas suggested that a territory or local government could exclude slavery by simply not passing any legislation to protect it, he antagonized both proslavery forces and abolitionists, further separating northern and southern Democrats.

1859 **John Brown's raid on Harpers Ferry**
To foment a slave rebellion, northern fanatic John Brown attacked the Federal Arsenal at Harpers Ferry, Virginia. Seen as a natural extension of Republican policy, a charge Republicans tried to disavow but that some evidence seemed to confirm, the raid increased northern support for the Republican cause. On the other side, it convinced southerners that a Republican victory in the presidential election would mean an attack on slavery.

1860 **Abraham Lincoln elected president**
Pursuing a moderate strategy against a divided Democratic Party, Lincoln was elected with a plurality of the popular vote, though a clear majority in the electoral college. What had been feared for many years had come to pass: A party with support in only one region had elected a president. Fearing that Lincoln would pursue a policy directed against the South to abolish slavery, many southerners wondered if they could remain within the Union.

GLOSSARY

sectionalism A political viewpoint based on one's perception of the interests of a region or section as opposed to national interests. In the nineteenth century, sectionalism in America became more intensely felt as people became more aware of the differing political and social objectives of the North, South, and West in trying to shape national politics in the 1840s and 1850s. (p. 407)

Manifest Destiny The geopolitical, cultural, and social belief that the American people were destined to move west and control the continent all the way to the Pacific. Many believed that European Americans, culturally and racially superior, had a divinely inspired mission to carry their institutions and values to the West. (p. 408)

mestizos From the beginning of the Spanish empire in America, Spanish men had intermarried with Indian women. Their children, of mixed Spanish and Indian parentage, were called mestizos. In the nineteenth century, many Mexican mestizos moved north along the coast of California to develop cattle ranching. They also intermarried with local Indians, creating a new local population of mestizos (see Ch. 1). (p. 412)

ranchos The economy of Mexican California was predominantly agricultural. A small population of landlords controlled vast estates, or *ranchos* (ranches), worked by mestizo tenants and laborers. (p. 412)

free trade Free trade is the open and untaxed exchange of goods and services among foreign trading partners. It is argued that free trade, by allowing open competition to occur, will compel producers in different countries to achieve greater efficiency in order to lower prices. Lower prices, in turn, will increase trade and trade revenues. In the 1840s, Britain repealed import duties on corn and wheat, and the United States followed by dramatically lowering tariffs in the Walker Tariff, thus adopting a policy of free trade in the Anglo-American trading region. (p. 418)

free soil In the 1840s, some opponents of slavery and its expansion into western territories shifted their emphasis from the moral evils of slavery to the impact of slavery on republican institutions and the yeomen farmers who sustained republican values. Free land or "free soil" owned by yeomen farmers was, they argued, the foundation of a republican system. Free-soilers opposed slavery because it threatened the republican system. (pp. 419–420)

squatter sovereignty An idea of Lewis Cass, a Democratic candidate for president in 1848, that the people who settled in a territory, including those who had no clear title to the land—squatters—would be given the power to determine whether that territory should be slave or free. (p. 420)

popular sovereignty Stephen Douglas employed Cass's idea, but, to emphasize its legitimate republican foundation, called it "popular" instead of "squatter" sovereignty. (p. 425)

nativism The political belief that a country should be run and occupied predominantly by those who are born there. In the United States, nativism regularly appeared as an effort to restrict immigration, delay the naturalization process, and limit the right of foreign-born citizens to vote. The Know-Nothing Party of the early 1850s was a nativist party. (p. 430)

due process Each individual possesses the inalienable rights of life, liberty, and property. In 1791, the Fifth Amendment to the Constitution confirmed an individual's property rights by assuring that no individual could be deprived of property without a clear, agreed-upon, non-arbitrary method by which the government limited one's right to or ownership of property. In *Dred Scott v. Sandford,* Chief Justice Roger B. Taney argued that the Fifth Amendment prohibited the taking of a citizen's property without due process and, therefore, Congress had no power to declare slaves free if their masters took them into free territory. This ruling signified that any law that had limited slavery in the territories, such as the Northwest Ordinance of 1787 or the Missouri Compromise of 1820, had always been unconstitutional. (p. 433)

IDENTIFICATION

Identify by filling in the blanks.

1. Among the Americans who were killed by the Mexicans at the Siege of the Alamo were the legendary frontiersmen folk heroes _____ and _____. (p. 409)

2. The president who single-mindedly pursued his ambition of acquiring Texas, New Mexico, and California for the United States even at the risk of war was _____. (p. 414)

3. In the election of 1844, Polk's desire to annex Texas was symbolically portrayed on an American flag on which, outside the regular field of stars, stood a _____ waiting to come into the Union, giving Texas the nickname it has today. (p. 415)

4. The captain who led a military excursion into Mexican California in 1846 and fomented a rebellion that resulted in the establishment of the Bear Flag republic and who became the Republican candidate for president in 1856 was _____. (pp. 414, 431)

5. General Winfield Scott led American forces in an invasion of Mexico in 1847 and captured the capital, _____. (p. 417)

6. A democratic congressman, concerned that the acquisition of Mexican territory in a successful war would expand slavery, sought to attach to a military appropriations bill the _____ prohibiting slavery in newly acquired territories. (p. 418)

7. The champion of "popular sovereignty," one of the major negotiators in the Compromise of 1850, and an opponent of Abraham Lincoln in their famous debates in 1858 and for president in 1860, was _____ of Illinois. (p. 419)

8. The linchpin of the Compromise of 1850, reinforcing a 1793 law to strenghten federal ability to pursue runaway slaves in the North and meant to placate southern opposition to the entrance of California to the Union, was the _____. (p. 425)

9. Harriet Beecher Stowe played a major role in intensifying northern feeling against slavery when she published her bestselling novel about slavery, _____, in 1852. (p. 426)

10. _____, an ardent abolitionist and fanatic from New York and Ohio and a participant in the guerrilla war in "Bleeding Kansas," led the raid on the federal arsenal at Harpers Ferry, Virginia. (pp. 430–431)

11. The _____ was a short-lived party based on nativist opposition to immigration and naturalization that helped realign American politics. (p. 430)

12. In _____ *v. Sandford,* Chief Justice Roger B. Taney ruled that not only did a slave not have the right to sue his master but that for a slave to claim freedom from a master just because he had moved to a free state constituted a violation against the master's property rights. (p. 433)

13. Abraham Lincoln was born in _____ but lived in Springfield, Illinois, where he became, by profession, a _____. (pp. 434–435).

14. Lincoln had been a member of the Whig Party but in 1854 became one of the leaders of the new _____ Party in Illinois. (pp. 435–436)

15. In the presidential election of 1860, Lincoln acquired the advantage when the Democrats split and backed two candidates, northern Democrat Stephen Douglas and southern Democrat _____. (p. 437)

FEATURES EXERCISES

Voices from Abroad

Colonel José Enrique de la Peña, A Mexican View of the Battle of the Alamo (p. 411)

War is often portrayed as a noble struggle between brave men fighting against one another to prevail in a cause. Soldiers are depicted as fighting with courage and resolution, according to a code of rules. As you read this account by a Mexican colonel in the Battle of the Alamo, ask yourself the following questions:

1. How does de la Peña think Antonio Lopez Santa Anna violates various aspects of military conduct?
2. According to de la Peña, why were the men fighting? Why did the battle become so bloody?
3. Why did many of the officers object to Santa Anna's order to execute Davy Crockett?
4. How would Santa Anna have responded to this officer's criticism?

American Lives

Frederick Douglass: Development of an Abolitionist (pp. 422–423)

Frederick Douglass, born into slavery as Frederick Bailey in 1818, was one of many slaves who resisted the system and eventually ran away to freedom in the North. His remarkable energy, intellect, speaking skills, and political understanding set him apart and put him on the path to fame as a prominent American abolitionist and a spokesman for racial policy and issues. As you read this description of his development as an abolitionist, ask yourself the following questions:

1. How might Douglass's position as the son of his master have affected his status?
2. How did city life in the South open new opportunities for Douglass?
3. How did his choice of a residence in the North reflect his political instincts?
4. How did his series of political decisions and moves in the 1850s reflect his view of how he believed slavery would be abolished?
5. Why, in spite of the work he had done, do you think the Republican Party was so slow to reward Douglass?

American Voices

Mary Boykin Chesnut, A Slaveholder's Diary (p. 427)

Mary Boykin Chesnut and other wives of southern slaveholders understood that their lives were tied to slavery. Yet they also understood that slavery oppressed both black women and white women who believed they were benevolent and superior, and corrupted all who were involved in the system. Though she could never criticize the institution publicly, Mary Boykin Chesnut did so privately in the pages of her diary. As you read "A Slaveholder's Diary," ask yourself the followng questions:

1. What was the primary abuse that Chesnut believed corrupted all social relationships within the slave system?
2. How were women compelled to respond to this behavior?
3. Why were benevolent women adversely affected by slavery?
4. In Chesnut's words, how did slavery make the masters and their wives "martyrs"?

Axalla John Hoole, "Bleeding Kansas": A Southern View (p. 432)

As a result of the Kansas-Nebraska Act and the decision to let popular sovereignty decide whether new states would become free or slave, individual settlers became directly involved in politics. When discussion seemed futile, many men turned to violence to force settlers from the opposing side out of the state. As you read this account of "Bleeding Kansas," ask yourself the following questions:

1. How did Hoole become politicized between his first and second letters? What actions had he taken to become involved in the fight?
2. What were his goals in fighting? What did he think could happen if he became more aggressive?
3. Why did Hoole think that in spite of his actions the tide was turning toward Kansas's being a free state? What evidence does he offer or imply?

4. In what way did Hoole feel that the shift in power reflected the regional policies of the North and South? How did this account agree with more general perceptions about the goals and intentions of the North or the South?

SELF-TEST

Multiple Choice

1. Martin Van Buren rejected the new Republic of Texas's request for annexation to the United States because:
   a. he feared that it would upset the compromise between the North and the South.
   b. he did not like Texans.
   c. he did not want to insult the leadership of Mexico.
   d. he felt that Texas would strengthen the Whig Party.

2. Southern expansionists continued to argue for the annexation of Texas in 1844 because:
   a. they owned property there and wanted to make a profit by selling land to new settlers.
   b. they saw it as the first step in taking all of Mexico and enlarging the American empire.
   c. they wanted to thwart alleged British plans to block American expansion in the West and limit slavery.
   d. they saw it as a popular issue on which they could crush the Whig Party.

3. James K. Polk pursued *all* of the following plans to acquire Texas and California *except*:
   a. fomenting rebellions by American settlers in each province.
   b. declaring war on the basis of national defense.
   c. having American troops invade central Mexico and seize Mexico City.
   d. negotiating with the Mexicans about his territorial ambitions in the Southwest.

4. Though the Whig Party officially supported the Mexican War, many Whigs opposed it because:
   a. they were pacifists.
   b. they believed it was part of an immoral conspiracy by southerners to expand the institution of slavery.
   c. they believed the war was an immoral war of conquest against a weak country.
   d. they believed Polk was fighting the war to hide his incompetence at home.

5. The Compromise of 1850, hammered out by Henry Clay, Daniel Webster, and Stephen Douglas, included *all* of the following *except*:
   a. the Fugitive Slave Act
   b. admission of California to the Union as a free state.
   c. the abolition of the slave trade in Washington, D.C.
   d. the granting to Texas of all the land west of Texas as far as the Rio Grande.

6. Northerners resisted the Fugitive Slave Act by *all* of the following means *except*:
   a. legal action.
   b. noncompliance with laws.
   c. invading the South to foment rebellion of the slaves.
   d. propaganda against slavery.

7. The Whig Party fell apart primarily because:
   a. Daniel Webster and Henry Clay died.
   b. increasingly divided between southern Whigs and "conscience Whigs," it offered weak compromise candidates for presidential elections.
   c. the Democrats introduced the flexible idea of popular sovereignty to work out compromises within the party between northern and southern supporters.
   d. the Kansas-Nebraska Act drove both southern and northern Whigs out of the party in search of new party affiliations.

8. The Republican Party drew the least support from which of the following groups:
   a. antislavery northern "conscience Whigs."
   b. Know-Nothing Party members.
   c. anti-Nebraska Democrats.
   d. free-soilers.

9. The Kansas-Nebraska Act and the outbreak of civil strife in "Bleeding Kansas" over the issue of slavery had *all* of the following effects *except*:
   a. they convinced Americans of the evils of violence and increased the tendency toward compromise on the issue of slavery.
   b. they broke up the Know-Nothing and Whig parties.
   c. they empowered the Republican Party.
   d. they helped realign the American party system and the dynamics of politics.

10. In *Dred Scott v. Sandford* in 1857, Chief Justice Roger B. Taney argued *all* of the following *except* that:
    a. slaves were not citizens and did not have the right to sue for their rights in the court system.
    b. southern masters' property in slaves was protected by the Fifth Amendment and thus a slave did not become free by running away.

c. any laws passed by Congress to control the ownership of slaves in the territories were unconstitutional because Congress could not give to territorial governments powers that it did not possess.
   d. the platform of the Republican Party was unconstitutional.

11. Politically, Abraham Lincoln was, in 1854:
    a. a "conscience Whig" who supported abolitionism.
    b. a free-soiler drifting into the Republican Party.
    c. a Republican, formerly a Henry Clay Whig, who did not want to pursue a political career with a dying party and who supported a moderate gradualist view on abolition.
    d. a Republican, formerly an anti-Nebraska northern Democrat.

12. When Abraham Lincoln became the Republican candidate for president in 1860, his credentials consisted of:
    a. one term as a congressman and one term as a senator from Illinois.
    b. four terms in the state legislature of Illinois, one term as a congressman, and a defeat for the Senate seat from Illinois.
    c. aggressive party leadership and the former governorship of the state of Illinois.
    d. three terms in the Illinois state legislature and a successful law practice in Springfield, Illinois.

13. In 1860, Abraham Lincoln, Republican candidate for president, was characterized as:
    a. a failed politician who gained the nod for a presidential run through intense regional infighting.
    b. a moderately successful politician, a minor figure in the Illinois Republican Party, and a man of the people.
    c. a great debater and public speaker who acquired a large, enthusiastic national following.
    d. a somewhat successful politician, successful lawyer, party leader in Illinois, famed debater, and a Republican with the moderate views and western allegiance that fit party strategy against the Democrats.

14. The event that proved to be the last nail in the coffin of the Second Party System and contributed directly to the emergence of the Republican Party was:
    a. the Mexican War.
    b. the Wilmot Proviso.
    c. the Kansas-Nebraska Act.
    d. *Dred Scott v. Sandford*.

15. The person who helped the Republican Party gain members by alleging that there was a "Slave Power" conspiracy to extend slavery into the territories was:
    a. James K. Polk.
    b. Abraham Lincoln.
    c. Stephen Douglas.
    d. Roger B. Taney.

Short Essays

Answer the following questions in a brief paragraph.

1. How did the development of the Republic of Texas affect American politics? (pp. 408–410)
2. Why was the election of 1844 fateful for American politics? (pp. 413–414)
3. Why was James K. Polk so determined to expand the size of the nation? (pp. 414–417)
4. How did the Mexican War affect Polk's resolution to claim all of Oregon for the United States? (pp. 417–420)
5. Why did the United States win the Mexican War? (pp. 416–418)
6. Why did political parties in the United States become so unstable following the Compromise of 1850? (pp. 425–429)
7. How and why did the Kansas-Nebraska Act accelerate the dissolution of compromise and the political process to address the question of slavery? (pp. 429–432)
8. What constitutional issues were raised by the Compromise of 1850 and resolved by the *Dred Scott v. Sandford* decision? (pp. 433–434)
9. How did Lincoln contribute to the breakup of the Union? (pp. 435–437)

ANSWERS

Identification

1. Jim Bowie; Davy Crockett
2. James K. Polk
3. "lone star"
4. John C. Frémont
5. Mexico City

6. Wilmot Proviso
7. Stephen Douglas
8. Fugitive Slave Act
9. *Uncle Tom's Cabin*
10. John Brown
11. Know-Nothing Party
12. *Dred Scott*
13. Kentucky; lawyer
14. Republican
15. John C. Breckinridge

Self-Test

Multiple Choice

1. a.
2. c.
3. d.
4. b.
5. d.
6. c.
7. d.
8. b.
9. a.
10. d.
11. c.
12. b.
13. d.
14. c.
15. b.

Short Essays

1. In the 1820s, American settlers and their slaves moved into the Mexican province of Texas. By the early 1830s, the Americans in Texas sought independence for Texas and annexation to the United States. After a bloody rebellion, Texas became an independent republic in which slavery existed and immediately requested annexation to the United States. Because Texas lay outside the area covered by the Missouri Compromise, this request raised immediate questions about the extension of slavery into the new territories to the west of Texas. Texas's annexation threatened to unravel the Missouri Compromise and interject the issue of slavery into national politics.

2. By nominating Polk, the Democrats assured an expansionist platform that would bring Texas into the Union. That development would emphasize the issue of slavery in national politics and set in motion a process of sectionalization that, fifteen years later, resulted in two sectional parties. When Polk was elected, he pursued his expansionist policy with the results many feared: The issue of the expansion of slavery into the new territories acquired from Mexico dramatically polarized American politics.

3. Polk believed that expansion would unify the nation behind his presidential leadership. He also believed that more space would provide greater opportunities for American development and thus prevent rather than cause sectional discord.

4. Polk was concerned that northerners believed that the goal of expanding slavery lurked behind his Mexican strategy. Therefore, in order to gain support for his expansionist policy in regard to Mexico, Polk felt compelled to respond to growing American designs on Oregon. To avoid a simultaneous war with Britain, he accepted a compromise boundary at the 49th parallel, securing Oregon for settlers from the North.

5. The United States had settlers in both New Mexico and California foment rebellion. Mexican forces and resources were limited compared with the American military forces. The United States had talented military leaders who carried out an effective military strategy.

6. By allowing California to enter the Union as a free state and including the passage of the Fugitive Slave Act, the Compromise of 1850 undermined the careful balance that had prevailed for thirty years. Both southerners and northerners were passionately opposed to specific parts of the compromise, furthering the impression of people on each side that the other side was more interested in gaining advantage than in truly compromising. Instead of generating trust and good will, the compromise caused fear, anger, and suspicion to increase. As a result, people became less willing to compromise and were increasingly only able to join politically those who shared their views on specific issues. This led to the development of the Know-Nothing and the Free Soil parties, which created much political instability.

7. The Kansas-Nebraska Act convinced many northerners and southerners that their fears that one section would try to control another over the issue of slavery were, indeed, true. People started moving to regional factions of parties in which their views on the expansion of slavery and popular sovereignty were more narrowly defined as well as more uncompromising.

8. By allowing passage of the Fugitive Slave Act, the Compromise of 1850 raised the issue of the status of slaves as citizens, including whether slaves were free when they ran away to the North. Personal-liberty laws in the North not only made the act a dead letter, because no one would enforce it, but also directly challenged the right of federal law to contest state laws that forbade the taking of

alleged runaway slaves. In *Dred Scott v. Sandford*, Chief Justice Roger B. Taney affirmed federal power over state power by asserting owners' rights to their slaves based on the Fifth Amendment protection of property rights. He also denied blacks the rights of citizenship and declared that a slave remained a slave no matter where he or she went. Taney further denied Congress the right to pass laws that gave territories powers it did not itself have, such as the right to take away property, as reflected in laws prohibiting slavery.

9. Lincoln's cry against the conspiracy of "Slave Power" and his moderate abolitionist view of slavery were uncompromising views that few southerners could accept. By running as a candidate at the head of a sectional party, Lincoln excluded southerners from national political debate and contributed to the election of a president whose support came from only one section. A situation in which one section felt that it had no say in the policies of a federal government that threatened it could only imperil the Union.

Chapter 14

Two Societies at War, 1861–1865

LEARNING OBJECTIVES

1. At what point in the political stalemate of 1860–1861 did the chance for a peaceful settlement end and the use of military force to achieve political goals become necessary?

2. In what ways did both northern and southern politicians contribute to the outbreak of the Civil War?

3. What factors contributed to expanding the scale of the Civil War and extending the time frame in which either side might achieve military victory?

4. How and why did the Civil War become a total war?

5. How were the political and social goals of the war as initially understood by both sides transformed during the course of the war itself?

6. What were the primary reasons most northerners and southerners fought the Civil War?

CHAPTER SUMMARY

In spite of political leaders' last-minute efforts to find a compromise over slavery that would preserve the Union, the election of Lincoln, followed by the secession of six southern states, pushed the country into war. The North had twice the resources of the South, and the ability to create an activist centralized government to tap these resources to wage a total war. The South, however, needed only to fight a defensive war and hope for a military stalemate to achieve its goals. As a result, initial fighting quickly escalated into a series of major battles, and then a total war involving a full-scale invasion of the South in both the East and the West. As Lincoln expanded the Union's military strategy to achieve victory, he broadened the goals of the war to include emancipation and the end of slavery. Through war and policy, the northerners relentlessly pursued a revolution of southern society. How far they would be willing to go to reconstruct the South after achieving military victory was a major question.

Secession and Military Stalemate, 1861–1862 (pp. 442–449)

Before Lincoln was inaugurated president in March 1861, six southern states seceded from the Union and formed the Confederate States of America. In his inaugural address, Lincoln gave the seceded states—whose actions he declared illegal—a clear choice: Return to the Union or face war. War resulted when the Confederate government took Fort Sumter by force in April 1861. While Lincoln worked politically and militarily to keep border states in the Union, five other southern states joined the Confederacy. Meanwhile, the escalation of military activity, from an initial demoralizing failure at Bull Run to a failed effort to launch a campaign against Richmond and inconclusive carnage at Antietam, convinced Lincoln that to achieve his goal of a decisive military victory he would have to mobilize all the resources of the economy and society to wage a total war against the South.

Choosing Sides

While Lincoln mobilized forces, he moved aggressively to keep Maryland, Delaware, and western Virginia in the Union, and cautiously worked to do the same in Kentucky and Missouri. Meanwhile, the decision by Virginia, North Carolina, Tennessee, and Arkansas to join the Confederacy made it clear that the Confederacy was now a formidable opponent.

Setting War Aims and Devising Military Strategies

Initial encounters convinced both sides that a sustained military effort would be required to achieve their respective goals. Southerners were aware that all they needed to do was fight a defensive war, while Lincoln concluded that the North needed a decisive military victory to crush the rebellion. As Union forces pursued a campaign to take Richmond in 1861, which soon became bogged down, Confederate forces moved north through Virginia to invade Maryland in 1862. In the West, Union forces invaded Kentucky and Tennessee, where they faced less resistance. In each campaign, the fighting escalated into ever larger battles with higher casualties. While the North had put the Confederacy on the defensive in the West by the spring of 1863, both sides were locked in a stalemate in the East that seemed to assure a long and costly war.

Toward Total War (pp. 450-457)

The increased scale of fighting by 1863 transformed the Civil War into a total war. A total war drew on all the resources of opposing societies and economies in a struggle that often resulted in warfare against civilians. In the North, Lincoln's leadership of a strong party enabled him to create a strong central government that could mobilize the vast resources of the northern economy and society and wage total war. Southern leaders, lacking a strong party or a central government, and facing a confederacy of agrarian states suspicious of central government, would be less successful in waging total war.

Mobilizing Armies and Civilians

As the conflict developed into a total war, Lincoln transformed the federal government into an activist force in American life. He instituted a draft and suspended civil rights to control opposition to the war. Meanwhile, civilians backed government efforts with a campaign to provide medical aid to soldiers and develop hospitals. Women, in particular, entered the government and other private spheres to do the necessary work left undone by men at war.

Mobilizing Resources and Money

The Republican government, following the principles of Henry Clay's American System, made full use of the superior resources of the North to support the war effort. The government instituted higher tariffs, centralized the banking industry, took control of industrial production, and supported the construction of railroads. It also raised taxes, issued bonds, and printed currency that, because it accounted for only 15 percent of the costs of the war, maintained its value to pay for the war. In contrast, southern leaders struggled to impose a centralized government on states that were opposed to such a government. Unable to tax the citizenry fairly or to borrow money, the Confederacy was forced to issue currency that deflated in value, and, finally, to seize property outright, to pay for the war.

The Turning Point: 1863 (pp. 457-463)

As the federal government created a complex war machine and mobilized northern society, the tide of the war shifted in favor of the North. Lincoln and some Republican leaders moved toward giving the war a deeper moral dimension by turning it into a struggle against slavery. Though northerners remained mixed about emancipation, Lincoln transformed emancipation into the central goal of Union policy through the Emancipation Proclamation. As Union armies emerged as agents of revolution against the southern society, the northern war machine advanced to significant victories at Vicksburg and Gettysburg in the summer of 1863. Though encouraged by diplomatic successes, which secured the neutrality of Britain and France, the North now faced the daunting task of winning a quick victory before even northerners lost nerve or faith as they faced the prospect of a long-drawn-out invasion of the South.

Emancipation

Following the admonitions of abolitionists, and responding to the actions of slaves who freed themselves by fleeing across Union lines, the federal government confronted the issue of slavery. In quick progression, Congress declared slaves who escaped behind Union line "contraband" of war, freed slaves in the District of Columbia, and prohibited slavery in the territories. Buoyed by these actions and a growing popular support for punishing masters by taking away their slaves, Lincoln proclaimed the slaves in the South free in the Emancipation Proclamation of 1863. In doing so, he made emancipation an instrument of a broader Union policy to destroy slavery and restructure southern society.

Vicksburg and Gettysburg

The impact of the proclamation depended, of course, on the North's military success. Through early 1863, the outlook remained discouraging. As support for the war weakened, General Ulysses S. Grant led a western campaign to seize control of the Mississippi River, culminating in the successful siege and capture of Vicksburg on July 4. Simultaneously in the East, Union forces under the leadership of George G. Meade repulsed the invading forces of Robert E. Lee in an unplanned battle at Gettysburg, Pennsylvania. The victory at Gettysburg turned the tide of the war by strengthening the Union's diplomatic position while ending the Confederacy's chance of getting help from foreign powers.

The Union Victorious, 1864–1865
(pp. 463–473)

Although the Union victories in 1863 made it clear that the South could not win in outright battle, the North was tired and war-weary. Lincoln and his generals needed to achieve a military victory before too many northerners deserted the Republican Party and joined the Democratic challenge to Lincoln in the election of 1864. Once Lincoln survived this serious political challenge, the North was free to pursue the final military push to end the war. Union forces under Sherman launched a massive invasion of the South and, aided with troops that had been pushing toward Richmond for almost a year, surrounded the depleted main force of the Confederate army at Appomattox in April 1865, thus ending the war.

Soldiers and Strategy

The enlistment of nearly 200,000 African Americans significantly reinforced northern forces. Though black troops faced discrimination and prejudice, they constituted about 10 percent of Union forces and fulfilled secessionists' worst fears of a war against slavery. Yet, despite exhaustion and a depletion of resources, the South fought on, defending its territory against a full-scale invasion by Union troops for another two years. Lincoln's new commander, Ulysses S. Grant, understood that to succeed in a modern war of invasion one had to use new technologies, overpower the enemy by accepting higher casualties, and wage war against civilians.

Grant's Virginia Campaign

To make the final push, Lincoln appointed Ulysses S. Grant commander of the Army of the Potomac. In May 1864, Grant set out to destroy Robert E. Lee's army, while forces under William T. Sherman invaded the South and moved toward Atlanta. Grant soon found himself in another stalemate, laying siege to Petersburg using trench-warfare tactics while fending off Confederate offensive forays against Washington, D.C.

The Election of 1864 and Sherman's March

Lincoln faced political challenges both from within his party and from "Peace Democrats" in the campaign for the election of 1864, but Sherman's taking of Atlanta secured a clear-cut victory. Buoyed by his reelection, Lincoln legally ended slavery in the United States by passing the Thirteenth Amendment in January 1865. Meanwhile, Sherman's troops cut a path of destruction across the South, and Grant's forces encircled Lee in central Virginia. The South, faced with rising class resentment, resistance to conscription, and widespread shortages of materials, was beaten. Lee surrendered to Grant at Appomattox, Virginia, on April 9. At the cost of 360,000 men and enormous material expense, the Union had destroyed the South and slavery. The South had lost one in three of its soldiers, its economy was shattered, and many of its farms and cities lay in ruins. How the United States government would now reconstruct southern society, which had been both revolutionized by emancipation and devastated by war, became the main question of the postwar period.

EXPANDED TIMELINE

1861 **Confederate States of America formed (February 4)**
In response to Lincoln's election, six states in the Deep South followed South Carolina in seceding from the Union and, in February 1861, declared themselves a new nation—the Confederate States of America.

Abraham Lincoln inaugurated (March 4)
In his inaugural address Abraham Lincoln stated that secession was illegal, and that he would stand firm and use force, if necessary, to preserve the Union from the insurrection of the southern states. He left the choice to the southern states: End their insurrection or face war.

Confederates fire on Fort Sumter (April 12)
In response to a Union effort to supply Fort Sumter in Charleston, South Carolina, the Confederates opened fire and took the fort. Lincoln immediately called up troops to put down the insurrection. The Civil War had begun.

Virginia convention votes to secede (April 17)
As the Confederates hoped, the firing on Fort Sumter led Virginia to secede and accompany Texas in joining the Confederacy. North Carolina, Tennessee, and Arkansas also soon joined the Confederacy.

General Benjamin Butler declares runaway slaves "contraband of war" (May)
When three slaves reached his camp in eastern Virginia in May 1861, General Butler declared them "contraband of war," establishing a term for slaves who escaped across Union lines. As the number of slaves who fled to freedom grew, Union forces tried to define their status, raising questions about the North's war aims that would lead to the Emancipation Proclamation.

First Battle of Bull Run (July 21)
Rather than blockade the South, Lincoln chose to implement an aggressive military strategy. When a force he ordered South to move toward Richmond was rebuffed by the Confederates at Manassas in July, Lincoln recognized that the rebellion would not be easily put down. He began to enlarge the army, develop organization, and reformulate the central government for fighting a total war.

1862 **Congress passes Legal Tender Act**
Homestead Act and federal aid to transcontinental railroads
In response to the need to establish a strong federal government to wage total war, Republicans in Congress followed the ideas of Henry Clay's American System by creating a stronger national banking system, issuing national paper money, accelerating the transfer of public lands to homesteaders, and subsidizing a transcontinental railroad network.

Battle of Shiloh (April 6–7)
Confederacy introduces first draft
Battle of Antietam (September 17)
Drawing on the resources of the economy and society became increasingly necessary as the scale of the war expanded. Two great battles in 1862, one at Shiloh, where Union forces led by Ulysses S. Grant clashed with a large Confederate force, and the other at Antietam, Maryland, the bloodiest battle in American history, made it clear that the war would be long and costly and would require the total resources of both sides to achieve victory. In response to this need, the Confederacy was compelled to institute its first draft.

Preliminary Emancipation Proclamation (September 22)
Lincoln proceeded to institute military conscription, centralize the government's financial system, and respond to slaves who liberated themselves by crossing Union lines. He did this by making emancipation a central goal of Union policy. In a statement on September 22, he said he would free all slaves in states still in rebellion on January 1.

1863 **Lincoln issues Emancipation Proclamation (January 1)**
Enrollment Act begins draft in North; riots in New York City (July)
The Emancipation Proclamation made the end of slavery a central goal of the war and gave it a moral purpose. By mid-year, the Lincoln administration, still needing to mobilize all of northern society to provide the military with the manpower and the resources necessary to wage total war, passed its first draft law. The law met with considerable hostility from immigrants, most of whom were Democrats who opposed the war. Resistance boiled over into massive draft riots in New York City. The riots, in which a dozen African Americans were killed and massive amounts of property destroyed, were quelled only when Union troops marched into New York and killed more than a hundred rioters.

Battles of Gettysburg and Vicksburg (July)
Union forces pushed forward from the stalemate of late 1862 and in July 1863 achieved significant breakthroughs in the West and East. In the West, forces led by Ulysses S. Grant won the siege of Vicksburg and gained control of the Mississippi River. In the East, Union forces led by George Meade, beat back an invasion of the North by Robert E. Lee's forces at Gettysburg, Pennsylvania. Nevertheless, the Confederate armies remained intact and most of the South remained outside Union control. The war could continue indefinitely unless the North launched a full-scale invasion of the South.

1864 **Ulysses S. Grant advances on Richmond; siege of Petersburg**
Atlanta falls to William T. Sherman (September 2)
Lincoln reelected; Sherman marches through Georgia
To pursue total war, Union forces under the leadership of Ulysses S. Grant and William T. Sherman invaded the South. In his advance toward Richmond and Petersburg, Grant got bogged down in a bloody, slow campaign involving thousands of casualties. As the fighting intensified, his army lay siege to Richmond and Petersburg and constructed a vast system of trenches and emplacements around both cities. Meanwhile, Sherman's forces surged toward Atlanta, which they took in September 1864, then swept a path of destruction to the coast and back through the Carolinas, before heading toward Grant's position to corner Lee in south-central Virginia.

1865 **Robert E. Lee surrenders (April 9)**
In early 1865, Grant finally took Richmond and pursued Lee's depleted army into south-central Virginia. Lee surrendered at Appomattox Court House on April 9. Nine days later, Confederate troops surrendered to Sherman's forces in North Carolina.

Passage and ratification of the Thirteenth Amendment
Meanwhile, Congress had passed, and the states had

ratified, the Thirteenth Amendment to the Constitution, abolishing slavery in the United States. The two central goals of the war had been achieved: The defeat of the South preserved the Union, and slavery had been abolished. How and on what terms the devastated South would be brought back into the Union, and what the federal government would do to make sure the social revolution it started by abolishing slavery would transform southern society were now the central questions facing the victors.

GLOSSARY

demagogue A demagogue is a political leader who gains power by arousing the emotions and prejudices of the people to gain their support. Some non-slaveholders in the South thought the slaveholding elite were demagogues. (p. 442)

rule of law Order is established in democracies not by individual leaders imposing their own ideas, attitudes, and passions but by the citizenry's submitting to the laws of the land. Behaving according to the laws of the land is submitting to the rule of law. In July 1861, Lincoln articulated the Union's goal as a defense of Republican government and the rule of law. (p. 443)

total war A total war is a military struggle that employs all the economic and social resources of the competing sides. In a total war, the vast scale of the military conflict becomes directed not just at each side's military forces but at the civilian population of both sides. By the middle of 1862, the Civil War had evolved into a total war. (p. 450)

bounty A bounty is a cash payment given by the government in exchange for services rendered. Bounties are often paid for volunteering for military service and for apprehending and bringing in a criminal who's at large. During the Civil War, the Union paid bounties to those who enlisted or reenlisted. (p. 451)

conscription Conscription is the compulsory enlistment of individuals within a certain age range for military service to a nation. Both the Union and the Confederacy employed conscription to maintain the size of their armies. (p. 451)

habeas corpus A writ, or legal principle, requiring a person who has been arrested to be brought before a judge or a court and charged with a crime. This principle protects citizens from arbitrary detention. In the South, judges issued writs to order southerners who were held by the Confederate army but refused to serve to come before them, at which time the judge ordered their release. In the North, Lincoln suspended habeas corpus and imprisoned thousands of Confederate sympathizers without a trial. (p. 451)

commutation Commutation is the substitution of one thing for another. Sometimes judges commute a sentence by changing it to a different, usually lesser sentence. During the Civil War, individuals could get their conscription commuted for a cash payment. (p. 451)

greenbacks The nickname given to the new green banknotes issued by the federal Treasury as a result of the Legal Tender Act of 1862. These notes were backed by faith in the government rather than by specie. They are the precursors of American currency today. (p. 456)

contrabands Contraband is any item that has been imported or exported illegally. Such items are liable to be confiscated or impounded by authorities. When slaves transported themselves across Union lines during the Civil War, Union general Benjamin Butler declared them "contraband of war" and, having confiscated them, refused to return them to their owners. Within months, thousand of slaves had fled to freedom by crossing Union lines and were declared "contrabands." (p. 458)

IDENTIFICATION

Identify by filling in the blanks.

1. A last-ditch effort to forge a compromise between the North and the South, called the _____, sought to extend the line of the Missouri Compromise to the California border and to pass an amendment to protect slavery in the South. (pp. 442–443)

2. The Civil War began when Confederate forces under the command of General P. G. T. Beauregard bombarded the Union installation _____, located on an island in the harbor at Charleston, South Carolina. (pp. 443–444)

3. The first major battle of the Civil War, in which Union forces were driven back by Confederate forces, convincing Lincoln that the war would be long and costly, was fought at a railroad junction southwest of Washington, D.C., called Manassas Junction, or _____. (pp. 447–449)

4. The Union general who was appointed commander of the Army of the Potomac in 1862 and through organization and training turned it into a

modern army but whom Lincoln dismissed because he lacked the stomach to commit his forces to heavy casualties was General _____. (p. 447)

5. The bloodiest battle in American history was fought at _____, Maryland, on September 17, 1862. In spite of the carnage, the war remained a stalemate, even as it evolved into total war. (p. 448)

6. In July 1863, hostility to the draft, especially among Irish and German immigrants, erupted into five days of violent rioting and murder in _____. (p. 451)

7. American women played an important role in organizing the distribution of supplies and the staffing of field hospitals with nurses. One of these women, who later founded the American Red Cross, was _____. (p. 452)

8. Lincoln gave the war a moral and political purpose when, on January 1, 1863, he issued the _____ and freed the slaves in the rebellious states. (p. 459)

9. General _____ gradually emerged as a major figure in the Union army as commander of the western armies that successfully laid siege and took Vicksburg in July 1863. (p. 460)

10. On July 3, 1863, Robert E. Lee sent 14,000 men under the command of General _____ into a desperate frontal assault, or charge, into the Union lines along Cemetery Ridge on Gettysburg battlefield. (pp. 461–462)

11. In the wake of the Emancipation Proclamation in 1863, the War Department authorized the enlistment of free blacks and contrabands; by the spring of 1865, the number of African Americans in uniform had reached nearly _____, providing a significant boost to the Union war effort. (p. 464)

12. In 1864, the Union forces of Ulysses S. Grant laid siege by surrounding the town of _____, Virginia, with trenches, tunnels, and emplacements that looked much like those later employed in World War I. (p. 467)

13. Political opponents of Abraham Lincoln who campaigned in 1864 on the promise of ending hostilities and calling a special convention to restore peace and the Union were called _____, or referred to by the derisive nickname given to them by Republicans, _____. (pp. 467, 470–471)

14. The Union general who invaded the South, took and destroyed Atlanta, and carried out a scorched-earth policy in a march to the sea was _____. (pp. 471–472)

15. Robert E. Lee, commander of Confederate forces, was surrounded and depleted after being chased out of Richmond by Ulysses S. Grant in the spring of 1865. On April 9, he surrendered to Grant at the town of _____, Virginia. (p. 473)

FEATURES EXERCISES

Voices from Abroad

ERNEST DUVEYIER DE HAURANNE, "German Immigrants and the Civil War within Missouri" (p. 446)

In some of the border states, the political debate over the issue of slavery intertwined with ethnic identities and attitudes to escalate tensions that approached a localized civil war. The presence of Union troops only slightly defused these disputes and tensions. As you read "German Immigrants and the Civil War within Missouri," ask yourself the following questions:

1. Why did the two sides maintain the views they did?

2. How does this account contradict the notion that the fight over slavery was a conflict deeply rooted in past animosity between the two sides?

3. How did the fight over slavery simply bring to the fore old conflicts and hatreds between groups or classes?

4. Given this account, do you think the border states could have been kept in the Union without an occupying force?

American Voices

Jane Swisshelm, The Common Lemon: The Difference between Life and Death (p. 453)

Women's lives in both the North and the South were transformed by the Civil War. Drawing on their traditional role as caregivers and providers, women volunteered for service as nurses and social reformers. In doing so, they acted in more public roles than they had before, enhancing their self-esteem and elevating their social position. As you read "The Common Lemon: The Difference between Life and Death," ask yourself the following questions:

1. How did Swisshelm's connection to an organization allow her to have the impact she did?
2. How do you explain the difference between her reaction and the doctor's reaction to gangrene?
3. How does this account reflect the degree to which the home front was actively involved in supporting the war?

New Technology

The Rifle-Musket (p. 455)

The technology of war significantly affects the outcome. The technology of armaments tends to develop within a dynamic of offensive action and defensive response. As the killing power of offensive weaponry increases, ways to defend against it will be developed. When defensive responses make the offensive weaponry ineffective, new technology will be applied to increase the firepower of the weaponry. The number of casualties in any conflict depends on the balance between offensive firepower and defensive response. As you read "The Rifle-Musket," ask yourself the following questions:

1. What innovations did rifle makers develop to increase the offensive power of the musket?
2. What aspect of the older weapon did this new development make obsolete?
3. How did the new weaponry affect casualties?
4. How did the opposing side respond to the increased firepower?

American Voices

Elizabeth Mary Meade Ingraham, A Vicksburg Diary (p. 461)

As Union forces advanced across the South, slaves liberated themselves by fleeing across Union lines. Consequently, the Union army, without initially intending it, became a force for social revolution. Confederate Elizabeth Mary Meade Ingraham recorded her impression of the changing relationship between masters and slaves as a result of this social revolution. As you read "A Vicksburg Diary," ask yourself the following questions:

1. What was Ingraham's social status? What were her general attitudes toward slaves?
2. What impact did the presence of Union troops have on her slaves?
3. Was there any gender pattern in the departure of slaves?
4. How did some southerners try to keep the slave system intact?

American Lives

William Tecumseh Sherman: An Architect of Modern War (pp. 468–469)

William Tecumseh Sherman, like his colleague Ulysses S. Grant, was not particularly successful in civilian life. For a variety of reasons, however, the talents that did not serve him well in civilian life translated into military leadership skills that enabled him to rise in the ranks of the Union army and become the predominant architect of a new style of war. As you read "William Tecumseh Sherman: An Architect of Modern War," ask yourself the following questions:

1. Were there any clues in Sherman's civilian life before military service that might have indicated his later development as a military leader?
2. What ideas, characteristics, and beliefs distinguished Sherman's military leadership and help explain his success?
3. In what ways was Sherman's inclusion of the civilian population in what had traditionally been viewed only as a realm of military forces "modern"? How was his proposed version of war different from sieges, bombardments, or occupations of cities in the past? In arguing this view, what was Sherman saying about the nature of modern war?

4. Why, as a military man, did Sherman have little patience for politics?

SELF-TEST

Multiple Choice

1. In response to the secession of six states before he became president, Abraham Lincoln:
   a. joined John J. Crittenden in his effort to forge a compromise in early 1861.
   b. stood firm in his commitment to the Union and left little room for negotiation with the secessionists.
   c. was ambiguous and uncertain, thus contributing to fears that the secessionists would succeed.
   d. responded to President Buchanan's request to seek a compromise by doing nothing.

2. The Civil War technically began when:
   a. Abraham Lincoln sent a relief expedition to Fort Sumter.
   b. Major Robert Anderson, an officer at Fort Sumter, refused to comply with General P. T. Beauregard's call for him to surrender.
   c. Beauregard ordered the bombardment and surrender of Fort Sumter.
   d. Jefferson Davis ordered the military to take Fort Sumter.

3. *All* of the following states in the Upper South stayed in the Union *except*:
   a. Kentucky.
   b. Virginia.
   c. Maryland.
   d. Missouri.

4. In Abraham Lincoln's view, secession was:
   a. an invalid act that southern states claimed to have performed but that had no legal reality.
   b. an illegal act that constituted an insurrection against Republican government, the rule of law, and the Union that supported both.
   c. a bluff that would fizzle when it failed to have the effect the secessionists intended.
   d. a regrettable but legitimate act based on southerners' views of states' rights.

5. Lincoln and his advisors formulated a war strategy that called for them to:
   a. wage a defensive war.
   b. do nothing until they needed to.
   c. play it by ear and respond to Confederate military action as it occurred.
   d. launch an aggressive military campaign to take the war to the Confederacy and end it with a quick victory.

6. General George B. McClellan was relieved of his command of the Army of the Potomac by Lincoln in 1862 because:
   a. in Lincoln's view, McClellan lacked the stomach to commit his troops to achieve a major victory.
   b. he wanted to run for president as a Democratic candidate against Lincoln, who was outraged.
   c. he was ineffective in supplying, organizing, and training the army.
   d. he was a poor strategist.

7. To wage total war, the United States federal government did *all* of the following *except*:
   a. enact a military draft.
   b. pass an Alien and Sedition Act to arrest and imprison critics of the government.
   c. support the construction of railroads.
   d. tax businesses and citizens.

8. The Confederate government had trouble waging total war for *all* the following reasons *except*:
   a. many southerners opposed the draft.
   b. wealthy planters refused to pay taxes to the government.
   c. slaves refused to fight for the Confederacy.
   d. it was unable to borrow and thus had to resort to printing paper money.

9. Among the various reasons Abraham Lincoln issued the Emancipation Proclamation, the most important was:
   a. he wanted to fulfill the move toward free soil that he had promised in 1860.
   b. he felt the people needed a higher goal at the core of Union policy to motivate them to fight.
   c. he wanted to allow contrabands to fight for the Union.
   d. he agreed with Frederick Douglass that, for both moral and military reasons, the war was a struggle to end slavery.

10. Which best describes the actual change in status of slaves in January 1863 as a result of the Emancipation Proclamation?
    a. Because it freed only slaves in the states that were still in rebellion, it did not change the status of a single slave.
    b. It freed the slaves behind Union lines.
    c. It freed all the slaves both behind Union lines and within states occupied by northern troops.
    d. It freed all slaves everywhere in the United States and in the Confederate states.

11. The military turning point of the Civil War that tilted the advantage toward the Union was:

a. the battle at Antietam, because Confederate losses were too great for them to launch another effective offensive campaign.
b. Grant's victory at Vicksburg, because once the Mississippi was under Union control it was nearly impossible for the Confederacy to prevail.
c. the failure of George E. Pickett's charge into Meade's lines on Cemetery Ridge, because after Lee's defeat, his armies could never again launch an invasion of the North.
d. Sherman's taking of Atlanta, which completely demoralized the South.

12. As the Confederacy faced nearly certain defeat in the wake of Sherman's devastating march across the South, *all* of the following happened *except*:
    a. more and more southern men resisted conscription.
    b. thousands of southern soldiers deserted their units.
    c. Jefferson Davis offered freedom to any slave who would serve in the Confederate army.
    d. the remaining forces under Robert E. Lee launched a last-ditch invasion of the North.

13. The total number of military dead in the Civil War, including both the North and the South, was:
    a. 260,000.
    c. 900,000.
    b. 620,000.
    d. 360,000.

14. Which of the following was most important in turning the Civil War into a social war between two societies?
    a. the issuing of the Emancipation Proclamation and the ratification of the Thirteenth Amendment, because they ended slavery and assured a social transformation of the South.
    b. the military experience of thousands of men, which broadened support for the middle-class agendas of the Republican Party.
    c. the resistance to the draft in both the North and the South, which revived the immigrant and working-class challenge to mainstream middle-class society.
    d. the fact that northern women were drawn into service as nurses in the military hospitals and assumed new economic responsibilities and duties to fill in for men who were at war, enabling them to make considerable social progress.

15. The most important factor that contributed to the Union victory in the Civil War was:
    a. its troops were more dedicated to their cause.
    b. its generals had better strategic and tactical skills.
    c. the southern strategy of invasion to end the war was flawed.
    d. it had effective leadership that organized efficiently for a long and costly war, enabling it to launch a full-scale invasion of the South while depleting southern resources.

Short Essays

Answer the following questions in a brief paragraph.

1. Why did the southern states secede from the Union? (pp. 442–443)
2. Why was Lincoln unwilling to let the seceded states leave the Union? (pp. 443–445)
3. How did Lincoln keep several border states in the Union? (pp. 444–445)
4. Compare and contrast the military strategies of the North and the South. How were these strategies affected by the imbalance in manpower and resources? (pp. 445–457)
5. Which side was able to allay more effectively its full economic and social resources to fight a total war? Why? (pp. 450–457)
6. How were the societies of the North and the South affected by the war? (pp. 450–457)
7. Why was the Emancipation Proclamation passed when it was? Did it achieve the purpose Lincoln hoped it would? (pp. 457–460)
8. What impact did African American troops have on the Union cause? (pp. 463–465)
9. How significant was the Peace Democrats' challenge of Lincoln in 1864? (pp. 467, 470)

ANSWERS

Identification

1. Crittenden proposal
2. Fort Sumter
3. Bull Run
4. George B. McClellan
5. Antietam
6. New York City
7. Clara Barton
8. Emancipation Proclamation

9. Ulysses S. Grant
10. George E. Pickett
11. 200,000
12. Petersburg
13. Peace Democrats; Copperheads
14. William T. Sherman
15. Appomattox Court House

Self-Test

Multiple Choice

1. b.	6. a.	11. c.
2. c.	7. b.	12. d.
3. b.	8. c.	13. b.
4. b.	9. d.	14. a.
5. d.	10. a.	15. d.

Short Essays

1. Since the nullification crisis of 1828, South Carolina had argued that states' rights prevailed over federal power. The election of Lincoln convinced many southerners that a hostile federal government would seek to abolish slavery. "Fire-eater" secessionists argued that the only way to protect slavery was to leave the Union and protect it in their own states.

2. Lincoln believed secession was illegal. More important, he believed republican government was based on the rule of law within a union of states.

3. Lincoln used military force to quash secessionist movements in each state. He had Union troops occupy northwestern Virginia, Maryland, and Missouri. To hold Kentucky, Lincoln moved cautiously until Unionists had taken control of the state government. To assure their continued support of the war in 1863, Lincoln specifically left the status of slaves in these border states untouched by the Emancipation Proclamation.

4. The South wanted to be left alone. Early in the war, it developed a defensive strategy in which Confederate forces would seek to make forays into the North that in one major victory would demoralize the North and weaken its ability to launch an invasion of the South. In contrast, the North recognized early that to win the war it needed to launch an all-out invasion of the South and wage total war. Though the North had, in general, more than twice the resources, the need to launch an invasion of the South was a major disadvantage that required all these resources to prevail.

5. In the North the Whigs, followed by the Republicans, had long advocated an activist government to foster economic development through centralized financial policy, liberal land policy, and support of internal improvements. This political tradition gave the Republicans, in the midst of a war, full freedom to organize the economy, acquire manpower, distribute land, and fund the construction of transcontinental railroads. The states were not averse to the emergence of an activist central government. In contrast, the Confederate States of America were founded as a result of a secessionist movement that opposed powerful central government. Thus southern states resisted most efforts of the Confederate government to create a unified national policy. Lacking a strong national government, the Confederacy found it difficult to raise revenues or resources to fight the war.

6. In both the North and the South, differentiation between the wealthy and the yeomen farmers or the middle class increased. In the South, uneven tax burdens and a preferential draft system deepened class resentment and animosity. In the North, preferential treatment in regard to the draft sharpened class conflict between workers and immigrants and between the middle and upper-middle classes. Northern women took on greater economic responsibilities and filled in by performing work left undone by the men at the front, thus enhancing their social position.

7. In 1862, an increasing number of northerners advocated emancipation as the logical fulfillment of the republicans' free-soil policy. They also believed that by destroying the foundation of southern social order they could undermine the South's ability to wage war. Most important, Lincoln saw emancipation as a way to redefine the war and give it moral purpose. The Emancipation Proclamation achieved this goal by deepening northerners' commitment to see the war through.

8. By early 1865, there were nearly 200,000 African Americans in the Union army. Many saw action and performed effectively. Lincoln felt that black soldiers provided a critical boost to the Union war effort.

9. Lincoln believed he was in political trouble but refused to abandon his views on emancipation

and the unconditional surrender of the South. Support for the party continued to wane in 1864. The fall of Atlanta helped turn the tide by ending dissident Republican efforts to oust Lincoln and energizing the efforts of Lincoln's supporters to attack the Democratic opposition. With the strong support of Union soldiers, Lincoln gained a clear-cut victory in 1864.

Chapter 15

Reconstruction, 1865–1877

LEARNING OBJECTIVES

1. How was the Reconstruction of the political and social system of the South after the Civil War shaped by the struggle among different groups, each with their own goals and objectives?

2. In what ways did the quality of leadership, the use of force, the determination of participants, and the timing of a group or an individual's actions affect the course of Reconstruction?

3. How did the effort to implement a Reconstruction policy raise constitutional issues about the separation of powers in national government, the relationship between the federal government and the states, and the rights of all citizens?

4. What were some of the successes and failures of Reconstruction? Was Reconstruction, in the end, a success or a failure?

CHAPTER SUMMARY

With the passage of the Thirteenth Amendment and Lee's surrender at Appomattox, only three things about the postwar South were certain: the Confederate States of America was destroyed, the Union had been saved, and slavery was abolished. Within the scope of these three certainties, each group struggled to implement its policy for the postwar South based on the status it believed the South had held during the war, why it had fought the war, and what it had hoped to achieve.

Radical Republicans wanted to reconstruct, even regenerate, southern society by raising free blacks to a position of social equality with ex-Confederates. More moderate Republicans sought less, desiring only to adjust the social order and provide civil rights and social and political opportunities for former slaves. Democrats believed the South should be left to sort out its postwar reconstruction itself. They offered lenient terms for reentry into the Union, allowed former rebels back into politics, and would leave it to the states to settle the questions of civil rights for freedmen. In the South ex-Confederates wanted to return things as close as possible to antebellum social conditions. They wanted to "redeem" the South by restoring their political power. Meanwhile, yeomen farmers wanted more political power, and freedmen wanted land, civil rights, education, and the economic opportunity to establish themselves as yeomen farmers and craft workers.

The outcome of Reconstruction between 1867 and 1877 is a story of the struggle of each of these different groups to prevail in shaping the nature of life in the South after the war. In the end, neither Republican politicians establishing policy from the North, members of the Freedmen's Bureau in the South, nor freedmen in the South were able to sustain long-term changes in the face of the fundamental fact that the ex-Confederates regained or maintained control of the land. In a region economically devastated by war, ex-Confederates still exerted political power, determined social relationships, and controlled economic activity; and they would use whatever means—negotiation or resistance, terror or force—to achieve their goals. Living in the South, they were able to outlast Republican ideological fervor, which eventually waned, returning the South by 1877 to a racist political and social regime not unlike that which had prevailed before the war. Nevertheless, the Reconstruction programs of the Radicals had established three fundamental constitutional amendments, provided free blacks with freedom, and instilled in them the belief that they could help themselves. Reconstruction may have ended and even failed in the eyes of some, but it left a lasting legacy.

Presidential Reconstruction
(pp. 478–485)

Taking advantage of an accident of timing that delayed the convening of Congress until late 1865, the new president, Andrew Johnson, implemented his own Reconstruction policy. Rooted in his belief that the Confederate states had never surrendered their constitutional status, he argued that the president, acting alone, could restore southern states and their citizens to the Union. Johnson offered southerners widespread amnesty, allowed ex-Confederates to exercise political power and entitled them to recover their confiscated lands, thwarted the efforts of the Freedmen's Bureau to help free blacks, and attacked a civil rights bill proposed by the Republicans. Through his actions, Johnson enabled southern whites to gain the upper hand against the freedmen in shaping the postwar South, and energized the Republican Congress to launch a major effort to take over Reconstruction.

Johnson's Initiative

The assassination of Abraham Lincoln gave the presidency to Andrew Johnson, a man who had none of the wisdom or political skill of his predecessor. While Congress was on recess, Johnson launched his own Reconstruction plan. Initially, his requirement that southern states ratify the Thirteenth Amendment to be readmitted to the Union and that ex-Confederates pledge oaths of allegiance to the Union drew support from Republicans. But when Johnson vetoed the Freedmen's Bureau, and it became apparent that his leniency had allowed too many ex-Confederates to claim power and recover their lands, Republican opposition to his version of Reconstruction developed.

Acting on Freedom

Johnson's leniency also worked against former slaves. While freedmen sought to reconstitute their families, move around, form institutions and organizations, and engage in politics, they sought land above all else. Initially, Union forces had confiscated planters' land and given it to former slaves, but ex-Confederates, supported by Johnson and their own militia if necessary, now took back the confiscated land. Having to go back to work, many freedmen resisted gang labor or even wage labor as farm workers because both were a form of dependency not unlike slavery. In an agricultural society, to be one's own master meant to run one's own farm. Blacks negotiated for a system in which they could work as "freedmen" and become independent heads of their own households, with social and legal rights over their wives and control over their own affairs. In their tenacious struggle to negotiate a new kind of labor system, free blacks sought aid from the North.

Congress versus President

When Johnson vetoed the Freedmen's Bureau in February 1866, Radical Republicans were galvanized into action. They overrode the presidential veto—a first for Congress—and pushed for the Fourteenth Amendment, which guaranteed all citizens basic civil rights. Johnson established himself in opposition to the Fourteenth Amendment and suffered a crushing defeat before a Republican Party unified behind the Radical program.

Radical Reconstruction
(pp. 485–494)

By rejecting the Fourteenth Amendment, the states of the South brought radical Reconstruction upon themselves. A strong Republican Congress implemented radical Reconstruction legislation. Republican Party organizations, many members of which were black, gained control of southern state governments. These governments gained readmission to the Union according to the new requirements, funded public education, established better state institutions, and rebuilt railroads. Meanwhile, freedmen formed their own churches to strengthen their communities and established a system of sharecropping that, at least initially, seemed better than laboring for their former masters and offered the prospect of a better life.

Congress Takes Command

In the Reconstruction Act of 1867, the Radical Republicans placed the South under military rule, restrained the power of ex-Confederates, and required southern states to ratify the Fourteenth Amendment and grant freedmen the right to vote. Meanwhile, Congress waged a constitutional struggle against President Johnson by trying to force him to keep the only supporter of radical Reconstruction in his cabinet. The Tenure of Office Act required the president to gain Senate approval to remove from office any official whose appointment had required Senate approval. When Johnson dismissed his secretary of war, Congress impeached him and nearly removed him from office. By weakening the presidency, Congress reconstructed the office and ended a period of strong executive leadership. In the wake of a sweeping victory in 1868, resulting in the election of Ulysses S. Grant as president, the Republicans passed the Fifteenth Amendment, guaranteeing voting rights to all male citizens. By slighting women, the Fifteenth Amendment reinvigorated the feminist movement, which now focused its energy on gaining suffrage.

Republican Rule in the South

Protected by federal troops and supported by northern leaders and the Freedmen's Bureau, Republicans gained control of southern governments. Among those who acquired positions in the South were African Americans, some of whom were former slaves. These new governments implemented new constitutions and provided public support for schools, hospitals, institutions, roads, and public works. Though underfunded and corrupt, the governments made real progress in modernizing parts of the South. Within this framework, blacks established new institutions, particularly churches, which formed the bonds of new communities.

Sharecropping

Former slaves were also an active force in establishing the predominant production and labor system of the postwar South. Although the ex-Confederates had regained control of the land, they faced an intransigent class of freedmen who refused to work in gangs, for wages, or with any supervision over their private lives. Moreover, landlords lacked the money to pay wages, even when the freedmen did not resist. In response to the freedmen's desire to work independently and the landlords' need to pay workers in some form other than cash, the system of sharecropping developed. Sharecroppers would rent the land from the landlords and pay their rent with a share of the crop. Though the relationship remained unequal, and blacks who had no capital quickly fell into debt peonage, many black families did gain control over their lives and learned to work for themselves. Hence, for blacks, sharecropping, while it became a kind of trap and did contribute to the economic decline of the South, was also a framework in which they could live free lives.

The Undoing of Reconstruction (pp. 494–501)

Unwilling to accept radical Reconstruction, ex-Confederates launched a counterrevolution to regain control of southern politics. Though their resistance was formidable, they could have succeeded only if the North acquiesced to their agenda. The undoing of Reconstruction, then, resulted from a combination of southern counterrevolution and northern complicity.

Counterrevolution

As northern support for Reconstruction waned, the forces of reaction reasserted themselves. By 1870, racist whites in the Ku Klux Klan had launched a campaign of terror to destroy black institutions, deny blacks their voting rights, maintain blacks in debt peonage, and seize political power from the Republicans. Though Congress sought to counteract this counterrevolution, neither the military, the Justice Department, the Supreme Court, nor the Grant administration had the resources, the will, or the interest to sustain the effort and repulse the white backlash in the South.

The Acquiescent North

The continuing Republican commitment to the American System—an activist state that supported education, charities, health care, transportation, and public-works construction, as well as civil rights—seemed to bode well for Reconstruction. Economic boom enabled the federal government to continue to pay for Reconstruction policy. Yet discontent with investment returns in the South, corruption, political cynicism, and reemergent racism combined to undermine support. While the Grant administration became mired in corruption, dividing the Republican Party into supporters of Grant and liberal reformers, the country plunged into a recession in 1873. In the midst of growing anxiety about the corrupt new industrial state, concerns over Reconstruction waned.

The Political Crisis of 1877

When Republican outsider Rutherford B. Hayes and Democratic New York governor Samuel J. Tilden appeared tied in the electoral college in the 1876 election for president because of confusion over the submission of votes, an air of crisis gripped the nation. After a series of complex negotiations in Congress that may have included an inside deal, Hayes was inaugurated. Whether or not Hayes was involved in a deal, he quickly removed troops from South Carolina and Louisiana, the last Republican governments in the South, allowing those regimes to fall. Reconstruction was over. Democratic governments were back in power, ex-Confederates had pushed blacks out of offices, the Ku Klux Klan terrorized blacks to prevent them from voting, and more freedmen were falling into debt peonage as a result of sharecropping. Though it appeared to be a failure, Reconstruction did see three constitutional amendments passed and blacks emerge as a social force in the South.

EXPANDED TIMELINE

1863 **Lincoln announces his Ten Percent Plan**
Lincoln indicated his views on postwar policy by offering secessionist states a chance to return to the Union if 10 percent of the voters who accepted amnesty took an oath of allegiance. Many republicans thought the plan was too lenient.

1864 **Wade-Davis bill passed by Congress**
Lincoln gives Wade-Davis bill a "pocket" veto
When the radical wing of the Republican Party passed a strict plan outlining the conditions under which the southern states could return to the Union, Lincoln, wanting to steer a more flexible and moderate course, pocket-vetoed the measure. In so doing, he again demonstrated his strong political judgment in not committing himself to a plan of action until he felt it was necessary.

1865 **Freedmen's Bureau established**
As part of their radical program, Republicans established a government bureau that would provide emergency aid to former slaves during the transition to freedom. The Bureau offered freedmen food and clothing, legal assistance in acquiring land or signing labor contracts, and even some schooling and help in relocating family members.

Lincoln assassinated; Andrew Johnson succeeds as president
Soon after the creation of the Freedmen's Bureau, on April 14, Lincoln was shot and mortally wounded at Ford's Theater in Washington, D.C. He died the next morning, leaving the question of what he might have done to implement Reconstruction unanswered. Lincoln's vice-president, Andrew Johnson, a former Democrat and southerner with limited judgment, became president.

Johnson implements his restoration plan
While Congress was out of session for most of 1865, Johnson implemented a moderate program to allow southern states back into the Union. But support for the program among Republicans eroded when Johnson allowed too many ex-Confederates to regain power.

Joint Committee on Reconstruction formed
In late 1865, as Republicans became aware that Johnson's program was too lenient, they refused to allow southern delegations to take their seats in Congress and formed a committee to begin public hearings on conditions in the South. Republicans hoped that they could still cooperate with Johnson to formulate a strategy for readmittance of southern states.

1866 **Civil Rights Act passes over Johnson's veto**
When Johnson vetoed a new Freedmen's Bureau Act in early 1866, Radical Republicans put together the Civil Rights Act and passed it over his veto. This was the first time Congress had ever overridden a presidential veto. On the strength of their action, Radical Republicans passed and sent out for ratification the Fourteenth Amendment to the Constitution, guaranteeing all citizens civil rights and due process.

Memphis riots
The urgency to act to protect the rights and lives of southern blacks intensified as southern whites violently struck out to control freedmen. Massive riots in Memphis against blacks, resulting in forty-seven deaths, convinced Congress that it had to do more.

Johnson makes disastrous "swing around the circle"
Johnson defeated in congressional elections
Johnson, sensing the rising radical tide, opposed the Fourteenth Amendment and, by campaigning in the congressional elections on that issue, essentially stood as a Democrat against the Republicans. When he made the unprecedented move of actively campaigning on a railroad tour from Washington to Chicago and St. Louis, he was openly heckled and engaged in shouting matches with his listeners. Johnson was humiliated in the congressional elections of 1866, when the Republicans won a three-to-one majority in Congress, which enabled them to proceed with a more radical Reconstruction without him.

1867 **Reconstruction Acts**
Tenure of Office Act
Buoyed by a major Republican victory, the Radicals launched radical Reconstruction with the Reconstruction Act of 1867. The act divided the South into five military districts and established stricter requirements for readmission. The Radical Republicans also sought to control the president by limiting his ability to hire and fire officials in the cabinet, through the Tenure of Office Act.

1868 **Impeachment crisis**
When Johnson violated the new law (which was later declared unconstitutional), the Radical Republican Congress impeached him and the Senate trial came within a single vote of removing him from office in May 1868.

Fourteenth Amendment ratified
This amendment, which guarantees every citizen's civil rights and due process, would become the foundation for the civil rights movement in the mid-twentieth century.

Ulysses S. Grant elected president
On the strength of his opposition to Johnson and the rising tide of support for Reconstruction, Grant was elected by a strong margin and the Republicans maintained control of both houses of Congress. The Republicans now had a mandate to implement Reconstruction in the South.

1870 **Ku Klux Klan at peak of power**
Radical Reconstruction enabled Republicans, including many African Americans, to gain power in southern government. With support from the North, these new governments instituted significant political, economic, and social reform. In response, white racists in Tennessee formed a social club called the Ku Klux Klan, which spread across the South. The KKK was a paramilitary force whose members served the interests of the Democratic Party by launching a terrorist counterrevolution to push back gains made by blacks.

Fifteenth Amendment ratified
The Fifteenth Amendment, guaranteeing all male citizens the right to vote regardless of race, gained the required ratification of three-fourths of the states when the unreconstructed states of Virginia, Mississippi, Texas, and Georgia were required to ratify it before they were readmitted to the Union.

1871 **Ku Klux Klan Act passed by Congress**
Congress tried to halt the rising power and impact of the Ku Klux Klan, but there was decreasing support in the North for Reconstruction and the act was poorly enforced.

1872 **Grant's reelection as president**
In spite of a continuing activist government, cynicism, corruption, and growing interest in other issues weakened support for Reconstruction. The reform liberal wing of the Republican Party formed a separate faction and advocated civil-service reform, smaller government, and limited suffrage, and opposed, therefore, continuing radical Reconstruction. In response, Grant ran for reelection and won on promises of reconciliation with the South. For most Republicans, the terms of political debate had shifted away from Reconstruction.

1873 **Panic of 1873 ushers in depression of 1873–1877**
Support for Reconstruction was further undermined by economic depression, which deepened Americans' concerns about governmental corruption and increased tensions between the working class and the middle class and industrial leaders. The issue of Reconstruction was being pushed off center stage.

1874 **Democrats win majority in House of Representatives**
When Democrats took up the liberal Republican call for reform, limited government, and reconciliation with the South, the party shook off its treasonous connotations and reemerged as an active force in national politics. The Democrats essentially ended political debate about the South and the Republicans' ability to formulate any southern policy when they took a majority in Congress for the first time since the secession crisis.

1875 **Whiskey Ring scandal undermines Grant administration**
When Grant's secretary of the Treasury uncovered a tax-fraud scheme involving various government officials, scandal rocked the White House. Grant was left powerless and was soon abandoned by the Republican Party in the 1876 election.

1877 **Compromise of 1877**
By 1876, voters had lost interest in Reconstruction. When the presidential candidates tied in the electoral college, the election was thrown into Congress. A filibuster prevented any resolution from being reached in Congress, which appointed an electoral commission, resulting in a constitutional crisis that lasted for months.

Rutherford B. Hayes becomes president Reconstruction ends
Though it is unclear whether any deal was actually made, after meeting with Hayes, the Democrats ended their filibuster and allowed Hayes to be inaugurated. Soon after becoming president, Hayes ended Reconstruction by ordering federal troops in Louisiana and South Carolina to withdraw.

GLOSSARY

pocket veto Rather than actually veto an act, the president has the right simply not to act on it before the end of the congressional term, thus effectively vetoing the legislation. He puts it in his pocket, hence the "pocket veto." Lincoln exercised a pocket veto of the Wade-Davis bill, a moderate Republican act that established conditions for the readmission of southern states to the Union in 1864. (p. 478)

freedmen The name given to former slaves to distinguish them from blacks who had been free before or during the Civil War. (p. 479)

due process According to Enlightenment ideas, each individual possesses the inalienable rights of life, liberty, and property. In 1868, the Fourteenth Amendment reasserted that an individual could not be deprived of these rights without due process—a clear, agreed-upon, non-arbitrary method. In the twentieth century, the right to due process guaranteed by the Fourteenth Amendment would become the foundation for efforts to secure the rights and liberties of all Americans. (p. 484)

"waving the blood shirt" For a generation after the Civil War, Republicans, needing to make a point against the Democrats would remind voters of who was on which side during the Civil War. By implying that Republicans were the patriots who stood for their country and Democrats were traitors, they were "waving the bloody shirt." (p. 484)

scalawag A derisive term that ex-Confederates called southerners who joined the Republican Party to brand them as traitors. These southerners included many former Whigs and yeomen farmers who supported the economic development of the South with northern capital. (p. 489)

carpetbaggers A derisive name, referring to a cheap suitcase, that southerners gave northerners who came South to pursue their economic, political, and social goals. Among them were many veterans, reformers, and seekers of fortune. (p. 489)

sharecropping A system of farming in which a landlord rents a plot of land to a tenant farmer. That tenant has the freedom to plant his crop and organize his farm as he wishes. In return for the use of the land he pays rent, not in cash but with an agreed-upon share of the crop. (p. 492)

lien When one person is in debt to another, the creditor may demand collateral on the debt to assure himself of payment in case of default. By acquiring a claim to the property of the debtor, the creditor acquires a lien and thus effectively owns that share until the debtor repays the debt. (p. 493)

peonage When a debtor has fallen so deeply in debt that the debt becomes permanent, the creditor can require the debtor to work to pay off part of the debt. This is a kind of slavery called peonage. (p. 493)

cronyism Government in which a leader relies on, and provides benefits and appointments to, close old friends, or "cronies." Given the personalized nature of politics in the 1860s, the legacy of military experience, and a political culture of patronage in which friends were relied on and rewarded for their loyalty, cronyism was rampant during the Grant administration. (p. 499)

civil service An appointment to any office within the government is service to the higher public good, or civil service. Many felt that the system had been overcome by patronage and cronyism and objected that those who were appointed to government positions should have the skills necessary to carry out the jobs to which they had been appointed. (p. 499)

classical liberal In the 1870s, this was someone who believed in free trade, open competition in the marketplace, and limited government intervention in the economy. Classical liberals of the 1870s were the political descendants of Thomas Jefferson and Andrew Jackson, both of whom, in contrast to the Federalists and Whigs, respectively, believed in lower tariffs or even free trade and a limited government with a laissez-faire policy in regard to the economy. (p. 499)

IDENTIFICATION

Identify by filling in the blanks.

1. Abraham Lincoln was assassinated on April 14, 1865, by _____. (p. 478)

2. The Radical Republican government organization was established in 1865 and extended in 1866 to help freedmen with emergency relief during the period of transition to freedom was the _____. (p. 479)

3. The moderate Republican senator from Illinois who pursued the extension of the Freedmen's Bureau and submitted a proposal for a civil rights bill in 1866 was _____. (pp. 479–483)

4. Race riots that occurred in 1866 in _____ and _____ increased Republicans' determination to reform the South. (p. 484)

5. The _____ Amendment, which prohibited any state from abridging "the privileges or immunities" of any citizen, or depriving him of "life, liberty, or property without due process of law," was passed and ratified in 1866. (p. 484–485)

6. President Andrew Johnson was impeached by Congress when he violated the _____ Act by trying to remove Secretary of War Edwin M. Stanton from his cabinet post. (p. 486)

7. Disappointed that the Fifteenth Amendment did not extend the right to vote to women, leading suffragists such as Susan B. Anthony and Elizabeth Cady Stanton formed the _____. (p. 488)

8. During the period of radical Reconstruction _____ African Americans were elected to the U.S. House of Representatives from the South. (p. 490)

9. The federal government made a feeble attempt to provide freed slaves with land by passing the _____ of 1866. It was more symbolic than real, since much of the land offered was marginal. (p. 492)

10. The _____ was a paramilitary force that was founded in Tennessee and used violence against Republicans and blacks across the South. (p. 494)

11. The first leader of this paramilitary force was _____. (p. 494)

12. Republicans who opposed the politics of the Grant administration and wanted to return to policies of limited government and free trade called themselves _____. (p. 499)

13. The Grant administration was undermined by a system of fraud established between government officials and liquor distillers called the _____. (p. 499)

14. The Grant administration became so immersed in cronyism and corruption that critics began to call Grant's style of politics _____. (p. 500)

15. Rutherford B. Hayes's Democratic opponent, who essentially tied him in the electoral college due to a dispute about electoral votes from the southern states, was _____. (p. 500)

FEATURES EXERCISES

Voices from Abroad

DAVID MACRAE, The Devastated South (p. 480)

The Union waged total war against the South, leaving its military and civilian population exhausted, its cities and rural landscape devastated, and its economy depleted. Survivors of the war remained exhausted, maimed, impoverished, and embittered for years after the fighting had ended. When an outsider, a Scottish minister named David Macrae, traveled through the South in 1867 he encountered southerners' frustrations in response to northern efforts to reconstruct the region. As you read the "The Devastated South," ask yourself the following questions:

1. How did southerners' belief that they had fought long after victory was possible enhance their bitterness and resistance?

2. What impact did the war have on the economy?

3. What impact did emancipation have on the lives of the former planters? How might this have affected their views of freedmen after the war?

4. What point does Macrae want to make in this description of southern life?

American Voices

A Plea for Land (p. 483)

In 1865 President Andrew Johnson ordered the head of the Freedmen's Bureau to return land on the Sea Islands of South Carolina, which had been given to blacks, to their white former owners. Johnson based this order on his belief that the confiscation of property without due process exceeded the bounds of federal power. Blacks across the area resisted in pitched battles with former owners. In this letter, blacks with claim to the land petitioned the president to reverse his order. As you read "A Plea for Land," ask yourself the following questions:

1. How does this petition indicate the freedmen petitioners' knowledge of their legal rights?

2. What argument do they make against the property rights of white owners?

3. How does the freedmen's argument indicate an understanding of Republican government policy on land distribution?

American Lives

Nathan Bedford Forrest: Defender of Southern Honor (pp. 496–497)

Nathan Forrest's life was defined by a continual struggle to defend a way of life that was constantly under assault both from the outside and from within. Raised to use violence to defend himself against violence and possessing a violent temper, Forrest did whatever he had to do, legally or illegally, to achieve his goals. As you read, "Defender of Southern Honor," ask yourself the following questions:

1. How did Forrest define southern honor?

2. How did Forrest's involvement with slavery affect his determination to defend his honor?

3. What did Forrest's war experience teach him?

4. What were the most important principles for Forrest?

American Voices

HARRIET HERNANDES, The Intimidation of Black Voters (p. 498)

By 1871, the Ku Klux Klan, operating almost as a branch of the Democratic Party, had infiltrated no southern state more completely than South Carolina. The primary objective of Ku Klux Klan terror was to destroy Republican institutions and intimidate black voters from going to the polls. In this piece, a black resident of Spartanburg, South Carolina, gives testimony to a congressional committee's investigation of conditions in the South in 1871, in which the actions of the Ku Klux Klan are described. As you read "The Intimidation of Black Voters," ask yourself the following questions:

1. What evidence does Hernandes present to suggest that Klan activities were not random but regular occurrences?
2. How did the Klan try to achieve its goals?
3. How did blacks whom Hernandes knew respond to Klan violence?

SELF-TEST

Multiple Choice

1. Given Abraham Lincoln's political ideas and his leadership skills, what kind of Reconstruction policy would he most likely have implemented had he lived?
    a. He would have fostered party unity by agreeing with the radicals and followed their course.
    b. He would have understood that imposing a hard peace on the South would work to the disadvantage of freedmen and therefore would have been lenient and accommodating to the ex-Confederates.
    c. As a skilled political arbitrator, he would have pursued a policy that was fair and balanced for all sides.
    d. We don't know what he would have done, because he responded to practical political situations rather than insisting on clear ideals.

2. Johnson's lenient Reconstruction policy resulted in *all* of the following *except:*
    a. former confederates being sent as delegates to Congress in 1865.
    b. the easy reentrance into southern politics of former rebels.
    c. the dissolution of the Freedmen's Bureau in 1865.
    d. the southern government's passing Black Codes to essentially re-enslave freedmen.

3. Andrew Johnson was impeached as president on the charge that he:
    a. was a traitor to his party.
    b. had overstepped his powers when he instituted his own version of Reconstruction in 1865.
    c. had, by allowing ex-Confederates back into the government, condoned violations of the civil rights of blacks and thus violated his presidential oath to protect and defend the Constitution of the United States.
    d. had violated the Tenure of Office Act.

4. In the postwar struggle for land in the South between ex-Confederates and former slaves:
    a. about 14,000 black families in South Carolina acquired land, but otherwise ex-Confederates across the South had most confiscated lands restored to them.
    b. freedmen acquired about half the land across the South as sharecroppers.
    c. freedmen acquired extensive tracts of land through the Southern Homestead Act.
    d. ex-Confederates got all their land back.

5. Sharecropping developed as an agricultural system as a result of:
    a. a decree by the Freedmen's Bureau.
    b. an often difficult give-and-take negotiation between landlords (ex-Confederates) and freedmen based on what each had and needed.
    c. a take-it-or-leave-it demand by freedmen.
    d. the adoption by blacks of tenant farming as it has existed among whites in the North for many years.

6. The odds were stacked against freedmen sharecroppers primarily because:
    a. farms were too small to make a profit.
    b. the cost of capital was too high and the returns on cotton production too low to pay off debts.
    c. sharecroppers moved around frequently, thus adding to their costs.
    d. landlords and merchants illegally charged high interest rates and unethically increased prices.

7. Ex-Confederates and conservative whites across the South responded to Republican Reconstruction with *all* of the following *except*:
   a. riots in Memphis and New Orleans.
   b. Ku Klux Klan terrorist activity against blacks and Republicans.
   c. militia attacks to regain confiscated lands.
   d. support for Republican governments and the new South they promised to create.

8. The majority of African Americans who emerged as political leaders during the period of Republican rule in the South were:
   a. members of the free black southern elite.
   b. former field hands.
   c. escaped slaves returning to the South.
   d. free blacks from the North.

9. Which of the following goals of the Radical Republicans was *not* achieved?
   a. development of hospitals, asylums, and jails.
   b. establishment of schools.
   c. diversification of southern agriculture in order to move away from cotton production.
   d. financing of railroad construction.

10. Republican governments across the South fell one by one to Democrats in the mid-1870s primarily because:
    a. they were unable to diversify agricultural production and were voted out of office.
    b. ex-Confederate politicians, using demagoguery by day and the terror of the Ku Klux Klan by night, silenced the black and Republican vote.
    c. they lost the support of northern politicians.
    d. black politicians were unable to lead effectively.

11. Support for Reconstruction waned across the North for *all* of the following reasons *except*:
    a. northern Republicans were unable to afford the financial drain of defending Reconstruction.
    b. politicians became more concerned with labor issues than with Reconstruction.
    c. a wave of reform in support of smaller government swept through the Republican Party.
    d. both corruption and the depression of 1873–1877 drew people's political concerns in other directions.

12. As president, Ulysses S. Grant:
    a. acted effectively to continue the tradition of strong executive leadership.
    b. seemed unable to keep the cronies he appointed to his administration from corruption.
    c. was indecisive about which policies to support or implement.
    d. was in favor of increasing the amount of currency in circulation.

13. Scandals in the Grant administration involved *all* of the following *except*:
    a. illegal and unethical cronyism.
    b. abuses by financier Jay Cooke in using federal subsidies to run the Northern Pacific Railroad.
    c. a conspiracy by liquor merchants to defraud the government of excise taxes.
    d. Grant's acceptance of gifts and money from admirers and grateful countrymen.

14. In the case of a disputed count in the electoral college, the Constitution declared that the issue should be resolved:
    a. by Congress.
    b. by the electoral college.
    c. by the Supreme Court.
    d. The Constitution did not say.

15. The ultimate legacy of Reconstruction was:
    a. failure and bitterness that would simmer for generations.
    b. the solid foundations of a new South.
    c. passage of three constitutional amendments that would enable African Americans in later generations to fight for their rights.
    d. the rise of big activist government in reforming American society.

Short Essays

Answer the following questions in a brief paragraph.

1. How did the actions of Andrew Johnson and ex-Confederates in the South help spur the implementation of radical Reconstruction? (pp. 478–481)

2. How did African Americans' idea of freedom shape their actions during Reconstruction in the South? (pp. 481–484)

3. How were radical Reconstruction and Congress's struggle with President Johnson related? (pp. 485–489)

4. How effective was Republican rule in the South? (pp. 489–492)

5. How did sharecropping develop as a distinctive southern institution? (pp. 492–494)

6. Explain how a combination of southern resistance and northern loss of interest contributed to the end of Reconstruction. (pp. 494–501)

ANSWERS

Identification

1. John Wilkes Booth
2. Freedmen's Bureau
3. Lyman Trumbull
4. Memphis; New Orleans
5. Fourteenth
6. Tenure of Office
7. American Women Suffrage Association
8. sixteen
9. Southern Homestead Act
10. Ku Klux Klan
11. Nathan Bedford Forrest
12. Liberal Republicans
13. Whiskey Ring
14. Grantism
15. Samuel J. Tilden

Self-Test

Multiple Choice

1. d.
2. c.
3. d.
4. a.
5. b.
6. b.
7. d.
8. a.
9. c.
10. b.
11. a.
12. b.
13. c.
14. d.
15. c.

Short Essays

1. Johnson's leniency allowed ex-Confederates to regain their confiscated lands, establish Black Codes that sought to reestablish slavery, and even enter political office within a year of the war. White southerners also violently lashed out against free blacks in paramilitary attacks on landowners and riots against urban blacks. In their extreme response so quickly after the war, they aroused the moderate Republicans to agree with the radicals that more aggressive intervention in the South was necessary.

2. Freedmen defined *freedom* as being the head of a household, independent of the control of a boss or landlord and with control over one's family affairs. They did not want to engage in dependent wage labor because working for someone else seemed too much like slavery. Almost everything blacks did in the South—establish institutions and churches, engage in politics, and negotiate for the sharecropping system—focused on achieving a life as close to this goal as possible given the conditions.

3. Johnson's initial effort to proceed with Reconstruction without input from Congress and Congress's desire to act without interference from the president put the constitutional battle between Congress and the president at the center of emerging radical Reconstruction. In 1866, Congress overruled two presidential vetoes, the first time that had happened in the republic. Congress then sought to monitor the president's control of his staff by passing the Tenure of Office Act (an action the Supreme Court later declared unconstitutional). When Johnson dismissed his secretary of war in defiance of the act, Congress impeached him and nearly removed him from office. With Johnson nevertheless weakened by the impeachment, and a two-thirds majority in Congress, the Republicans could implement radical Reconstruction.

4. For a few years, Republican rule in the South achieved many of its goals. African Americans were brought into the political process and many were elected to local and state offices. Activist governments built schools, hospitals, and penitentiaries and asylums, supported railroad construction and public-works programs. They also implemented more egalitarian taxation codes. In general, Republican rule laid the institutional foundation for a new South.

5. Sharecropping was shaped by the negotiation between landlords and laborers with common goals as well as specific problems, needs, and expectations. Their common goal was to make a living from the production of cotton. The landlords had the land but no cash or labor. The freedman had the labor and the knowledge to cultivate cotton but no land. They also wanted to work independently as heads of their own households on their own farms and in control of their families' affairs. Landlords, confronting the stubborn resistance of blacks who were reluctant to work for wages, devised the sharecropping system, in which blacks rented a piece of land and a house in return for a share of the crop given to the landlord.

6. Both southern resistance and northern loss of interest had a significant effect on the end of Reconstruction. The wave of terror propagated by the Ku Klux Klan and the efforts of ex-Confederate Democrats worked together to destroy Republican institutions, drive Republicans from office, and prevent blacks from voting. The federal government lacked the will to continue to resist these guerrilla war tactics and eventually gave up trying to combat them. Though the North had both the activist government and the money to continue the effort, other issues—civil-service reform, labor, corruption, and limited government—concerned northern voters more by 1872. The financial panic of 1873 and the depression that followed accelerated this shift in political concerns.